Robert Southey, Caroline Bowles

Correspondence with Caroline Bowles

To Which are Added Correspondence With Shelley, and Southey's Dreams

Robert Southey, Caroline Bowles

Correspondence with Caroline Bowles
To Which are Added Correspondence With Shelley, and Southey's Dreams

ISBN/EAN: 9783337010676

Printed in Europe, USA, Canada, Australia, Japan

Cover: Foto ©ninafisch / pixelio.de

More available books at **www.hansebooks.com**

ROBERT SOUTHEY

AND

CAROLINE BOWLES.

WORKS BY EDWARD DOWDEN, LL.D.

STUDIES IN LITERATURE.
POEMS.
ROBERT SOUTHEY.
SHAKSPERE: HIS MIND AND ART.
SHAKSPERE PRIMER.

EDITED,
SHAKSPERE'S SONNETS.

DUBLIN UNIVERSITY PRESS SERIES.

THE CORRESPONDENCE

OF

ROBERT SOUTHEY

WITH

CAROLINE BOWLES.

TO WHICH ARE ADDED:

CORRESPONDENCE WITH SHELLEY, AND SOUTHEY'S DREAMS.

Edited, with an Introduction,

BY

EDWARD DOWDEN, LL.D.,

PROFESSOR OF ENGLISH LITERATURE IN THE UNIVERSITY OF DUBLIN.

DUBLIN: HODGES, FIGGIS, & CO., GRAFTON-STREET.
LONDON: LONGMANS, GREEN, & CO., PATERNOSTER-ROW.
1881.

BUT by the way (Madam) you may see how much I differ from the morosity of those Cynicks who would not admit your sex into the communities of a noble friendship. . . . I cannot say that Women are capable of all those excellencies by which Men can oblige the World; and therefore a female friend in some cases is not so good a counsellor as a wise man, and cannot so well defend my honour; nor dispose of reliefs and assistances if she be in the power of another: but a woman can love as passionately, and converse as pleasantly, and retain a secret as faithfully, and be useful in her proper ministries; and she can die for her friend as well as the bravest *Roman* Knight.

      JEREMY TAYLOR, in *A Letter to the most Ingenious
      and Excellent Mrs. Katherine Phillips.*

INTRODUCTION.

> It is not once an age two two hearts are set
> So well in unison that not a note
> Jars in their music; but a skilful hand
> Slurs lightly over the discordant tones,
> And wakens only the full power of those
> That sound in concord.
>   Happy, happy those
> Who thus perform the grand concerto—Life.
>
>   CAROLINE BOWLES, *The Birthday*, Part II.

IT was Southey's wish that his correspondence with Caroline Bowles, afterwards Caroline Southey, at a fitting time should see the light. "As for my letters," he wrote (December 18, 1829), "I will deposit them with yours (for I have preserved every line that I ever received from you). There is nothing in them which might not be seen by men and angels, and though written, as their utter carelessness and unreserve may show, without the slightest reference to any other eyes than those to which they were addressed, I shall not be unwilling to think that when time has consecrated both our memories (which it will do) this correspondence may see the light. Our earthly life, dear Caroline, lasts longer than in the hearts of those we love; it endures in the hearts of those whom we have never known, and who learn to love us after our work on earth is done. They who live on earth in their good works continue to make friends there as long as their works survive; and it may be one of the pleasures of another state to meet those friends when they seek us in heaven. I often feel that this will and must be so when, on reading a good old book, my heart yearns towards the author." And in a like spirit is the answer of Caroline Bowles—"I shall now keep those treasured letters while I live, with a clear conscience, and perhaps you may have created in my heart a feeling which before (as relating to myself) had no existence there—a degree of interest in something of me that shall survive on earth—I mean our correspondence. All my share in it will find indulgence for your sake." To the Rev. J. Wood Warter, Southey's son-in-law, Caroline Southey left these letters, with a well-founded confidence that in the hands of Mr. Warter and his family her memory would be strongly and safely guarded. Mr. Warter died before his purpose of publishing this correspondence was carried into effect. Shortly after the appearance of the volume "Robert Southey," in Mr. Morley's "English Men of Letters," I requested Miss Warter to allow me to examine the correspondence with Caroline Bowles, with a view to its possible publication in the "DUBLIN UNIVERSITY PRESS SERIES." She kindly granted my request: with her permission the present volume is published, and from her I have received in its preparation frequent and valuable aid.

On going through the material placed at my disposal, I perceived that a selection from the letters would appear with greater advantage than the entire correspondence. For two reasons:—first, as regards Southey—so considerable a body of his letters has already been put forth that Southey's life lies largely open, and many things told in letters already printed are told in almost the same words in some of his letters to Caroline Bowles. Secondly, as regards her—in consequence of her secluded life, in which incidents were rare, and of those shattering attacks of illness, often recurrent, which narrowed her world for the time being to her sick chamber, with its broken thoughts and memories and love, not a few of her letters lack the kind of interest which extends to strangers; yet especially in her days of pain and weakness Southey desired to be informed of her state, and it beguiled the time to converse on paper, when that was possible, with her absent friend. What is beautiful in these letters is her fine solicitude for the happiness of others; her aloofness from life, with an instinctive turning back towards life, as of a plant which loves the sun; those sudden beams and flashes which betray a spirit naturally bright; and as recovery advanced her pleasure in the delicate luxuries of convalescent senses—the light touch of a morning breeze, the brightness of a flower, a bird's passage or swift song.

Considerably less than half of the material placed in my hands now appears in print. As I went along I had my eye on "Southey's Life and Letters," and on the "Selection of Letters" edited by Mr. Warter, and I omitted many letters and passages of letters which repeat what is already known. But in some cases I have risked the danger of repetition: thus the letter to Caroline Bowles which tells of Southey's visit to the deathbed of Bell, the educational reformer, may with advantage displace that previously published, as being fuller of detail; and again, the letter describing his visit in 1836 to the scenes of his childhood says the same things which are said to Grosvenor Bedford; but it is in writing to Caroline Bowles that the outbreak like the sob of a strong man comes—"There have been times, and are, dear friend, when I feel like Eleëmon, as if the fountain of tears were dry; as if my eyes had been seared, and my heart had been so often and so long upon the anvil, that it had been rendered insensible. But to-day it was with great difficulty that I could so far command myself as not to let my emotions be seen." After making all omissions which seemed desirable, there is here a plentiful remainder to furnish forth an interesting chapter in Southey's life—one essential to its completeness—the chapter which tells of the most important friendship of his elder years.

In an Appendix will be found the register of fantastic dreams of which Southey speaks in a letter to Caroline Bowles, of October 2nd, 1826. It is to be regretted that Shelley hardly more than began his *Catalogue of the Phenomena of Dreams, as connecting sleeping and waking.* "Here," he says, "I was obliged to leave off, overcome by thrilling horror." But for this we might have possessed a second remarkable contribution towards the psychology of poets.* I do not know whether any such collection of a poet's dreams as this of Southey's exists elsewhere. What is extravagant in *Thalaba*, what is grotesque in the *Ballads*, is paralleled by the wild work which went on in their inventor's brain during sleep. The moral ardour which breathes through his poems, the passion of righteousness,† the fortitude of faith, must be recognised by every reader who knows Southey as the breath of his own higher life. The romantic incidents of his poetry were partly found by him as foreign materials, and were woven together by his constructive talent; but they were partly native to his imagination, and given by it. The caverns of the Domdaniel, the Afreet wardens, the Teraph and the Fire, the blue-eyed Sorceress, Khawla and Mohareb, were not ingeniously pieced together from Southey's notebook; they sprang wildly from his brain, and were subdued to a moral purpose by his dominant passion of righteousness. For vampires did not lodge in Greta Hall, and surely we cannot attribute Southey's elaborated horrors of phantasy to that one tumbler of currant rum, accompanied by the sedative of a sermon from some elder English divine, or a chapter of some foreign chronicler, which formed the last frugal meal for mind and body.

* "The poverty of my dreams mortifies me. There is Coleridge, at his will can conjure up icy domes, and pleasure-houses for Kubla Khan, and Abyssinian maids, and songs of Abora, and caverns, .

'Where Alph, the sacred river, runs,'

to solace his night solitudes—when I cannot muster a fiddle. . . . The degree of the soul's creativeness in sleep might furnish no whimsical criterion of the *quantum* of poetical faculty resident in the same soul waking. An old gentleman, a friend of mine, and a humorist, used to carry this notion so far, that when he saw any stripling of his acquaintance ambitious of becoming a poet, his first question would be: 'Young man, what sort of dreams have you?' "—CHARLES LAMB, *Witches and other Night Fears.*

† "Full of soft pity, like the wailings of a mother," says Carlyle, speaking of Southey's chief poems, and he rightly adds, "*yet with a clang of chivalrous valour finely audible too.*"

INTRODUCTION.

In the Appendix is also printed a short but remarkable correspondence, hitherto unpublished, of Southey with Shelley. The first letter—one of Shelley's, and unconnected with those which follow—accompanied a copy of *Alastor* presented to Southey. It serves as a link between the period of Shelley's personal intercourse with Southey at Keswick (1811-1812) and that of the renewed intercourse by letter, eight years later.* When setting forth to evangelize Ireland, Shelley beheld, through the luminous vapour of his boyish enthusiasm, a distorted image of Southey.† The real Southey, it now becomes apparent, re-emerged to view when time, experience, and disappointments had taught Shelley to estimate men more justly. The later letters—those of 1820—appear after the lapse of sixty years, in accordance with Southey's view as to what might be expected, and what was right to expect.‡ These letters set forth the characters and principles of two extraordinary men in a singularly vivid light. It is easy for the lover of Southey to be unjust to Shelley, and easy for the lover of Shelley to misinterpret Southey. There are perhaps some persons whose sympathy with man is wide enough to include types of character so diverse, and such persons—rejoicing in human goodness, piteous for human frailty—may be trusted to discover what virtue there is in the severe, yet sorrowful, arraignment by the one writer, and in the other's eager and solemn assertion of his innocence.§

---

* Peacock speaks of a meeting of Southey and Shelley in the autumn of 1814, of which Shelley gave him some account. I suspect that Peacock's memory misled him. In a letter to Bernard Barton (1822) Southey gives a brief survey of his connexion with Shelley, and neither in it, nor elsewhere, I believe, makes reference to any meeting later than 1812. "By-the-bye," Southey writes to Bernard Barton in this unpublished letter, "he [Shelley] was remarkably like Mr. Clarkson, though upon a small scale. His eyes were set in the same manner, and the resemblance between son and father could not be stronger."

† *See* M'Carthy's *Shelley's Early Life*, p. 136.

‡ *See* p. 76 of the present volume.

§ The central question at issue is this (and perhaps the answer to it is not hard to find): "How far did the *principles* held by Shelley open a way

INTRODUCTION.

Although many of Southey's letters have been printed, no correspondence has hitherto appeared having a unity of its own, and exhibiting his thoughts and feelings in their play and interchange with those of another mind. To none of his friends could he *give* so much as he gave to Caroline Bowles, and in friendship surely it must be more blessed to give than to receive. But he also received much. Not that elevating guidance into new realms of thought, that discovery of higher spheres of feeling which in some rare instances has been the gift of a woman to a man—

> "Alcun tempo il sostenni col mio volto ;
> Mostrando gli occhi giovinetti a lui,
> Meco il menava in dritta parte volto";

not that hardy comradeship founded upon equality, which is perhaps as rare. These it was not in the power of Southey's friend to bestow. But what she had she gave, and that was much—the answer of the spirit to every summons and challenge of his spirit, the assent and consent of a kindred mind, the quick perceptions of a bright and cultivated intelligence, the charm of graceful animation with that repose which the security of unvarying affection brings. She came to him as a friend in darkening days, after the death of his beloved son, and when he had begun to step downward from the heights of life. During the long insidious approaches of Mrs. Southey's malady there was sustenance for a heart often exhausted by anxiety in his friend's sympathy: among many difficult and perplexing things here was one thing without difficulties, and always sure. And when the true nature of his wife's malady declared itself, and the light of Southey's life was extinguished, in communion with a friend there was a refuge from calamity better than the des-

---

for conduct which led, directly or indirectly, to the ruin of one whom Shelley was bound to protect from others and from herself?" Southey certainly erred in supposing that Shelley's *character* had deteriorated since 1812; but knowing as much and as little as he did, Southey's error was inevitable. The first letter (March 7th, 1816) is printed from what I take to be the original in Shelley's handwriting; the rest from transcripts made by Caroline Bowles.

perate refuge of work, or the half shelter of uneasy slumbers. There have not been so many recorded friendships of man and woman, the source of mutual comfort, honourable, constant and untroubled through a course of many years, that we can afford to forget the friendship of Southey and Caroline Bowles.

In these quick and crowded days, it is perhaps unreasonable to expect that many persons will find interest in the days and hours of a quiet life spent a long time ago among flowers and birds and books. And yet there is pleasure in contemplating a modest precinct of order where a refined and cheerful existence grows from elements few and simple. As a writer, Caroline Bowles once held a place of some distinction, and she is still worthy of remembrance. Much that she wrote must drift away to give place to contemporary writings, equally good, if not better, and claiming the dues of novelty; but her best work, small in quantity, may rank with the best of its kind that English women have wrought in English verse.

Caroline Anne Bowles was born at Lymington, Hampshire, on December 6th, 1786 or 1787; in which of these two years she was herself uncertain. Her father's, an old Lincolnshire, family, is said to have been originally Norman.* Through her maternal grandmother, Mrs. George Burrard (born Durell), she was connected with the French-speaking aristocracy of Jersey, and there were traditions of their ancient manor in all its feudal greatness. In the home of Caroline's childhood might be seen representatives of four generations—stately old Madame Durell, her grandmother's mother; grandmother Burrard, now sixty years of age, with silver hair, apple cheek, unwrinkled forehead, and soft blue eye, gracious, gentle, and beloved†; Caroline's mother rich in old tales, and family legends

---

* The poet W. Lisle Bowles claimed Caroline as one of his kin, but the kinship was only one pleasantly fancied on the ground of the identity of names. In one letter, she speaks of Lord Herbert of Cherbury as her ancestor.

† In *The Birthday* Caroline Bowles describes her grandmother, as her nurse remembered, " among her maidens throned at the eternal tapestry." " Madame Burrard, as she grew old, used to be carried from the porch at

and traditionary lore; and the little fairy girl herself, the new-born future emerging from so long a past, bringing into the midst of so many twilight lives the breeze and gladness of a dawn. From this group the faithful *bonne* must not be excluded, more friend than servant, wearing still her "high Jersey cap, and large ear-rings and short jacket," who every 6th of December, in spite of frost or snow, must find a birthday nosegay for her child, and who, last of the elder race, died at a good old age in Caroline's arms.

Captain Bowles of the East India Company's service bought Buckland Cottage, "an old-fashioned, small house with great elms partly overshadowing its trim gardens and mossy lawns," while Caroline was still a little girl, and all her memories of joy and sorrow centred in that beloved home. An only child, and with no companionship but that of her elders, she was in some ways in advance of her years, while she remained at heart an unfledged thing. Her deft fingers, with skill inherited from old Madame Burrard, worked devices on the sampler, or fashioned raiment for her family of dolls; they drew what to complacent parental eyes seemed genuine landscapes; they cut in paper all Noah's menagerie from models in Goldsmith's *Animated Nature*, or the paladins and ladies of Ariosto—nay, on one occasion even Ulysses

"Locked in the shaggy fleeces of the ram."

Books were her playfellows, and before her father had gone far in her writing lessons, he was constrained—not needing strict compulsion—to become amanuensis to the small poetess

Buckland Cottage in a sedan chair to her pew in church. There, I am afraid, she bowed and curtsied to her friends before the service began; but I am sure that she stood up in her little high-heeled shoes of black velvet, with silver buckles, and that a diamond crescent sparkled just in front of her powdered hair, which was drawn up on a cushion under a lace cap and hood. The rest of her dress was invariably black; but she also wore the lace muffles, neck-kerchief and apron that had been in fashion when she was exactly like what her little grand-daughter afterwards became."— "Robert Southey's Second Wife," in the *Cornhill Magazine*, vol. xxx.

between his knees, who dictated such rhapsodies as those which a little later she would herself confide to the blank pages of drawing-books and receipt-books. Alone in her swing, when the pendulous motion had settled to stillness, she created in waking dream Eastern palaces, where Mesrour and Giaffer stepped behind the Commander of the Faithful with Zobeide at his side. All living creatures grew dear to her—all, except the parrot, whose diligence in learning had been odiously contrasted with *her* idleness; she fed with cream and sugar the Princess Hemjunah, a monstrous toad who lodged under the old gum-cistus; when Chloe's blind puppies needed an airing, her wheelbarrow became their barouche; in her hospital—a young Sister of Mercy—she nursed the maimed squirrel, the one-legged bullfinch, and that wounded leveret who grew up an ungrateful hare, and fled away. Dearest of all were her spaniel, and Juba her "little horse," who fed from the tiny hand of his mistress, a child half-tomboy and half-sprite. In a nook of the rambling garden her religion had its secret rites; there a mossy altar was erected (Gessner's *Death of Abel* lending inspiration), where with piety, a little haunted by self-doubt, she played the natural priest, and offered up bloodless sacrifice of flowers and fruits.

Captain Bowles, with a forefeeling of the nervous disease which left Caroline at an early age an orphan, was a sad and silent man; yet in his sadness ever gentle to the little daughter, who knew how to hold her peace, and only steal her hand into his, when the dark hour was on him. Angling was his patient pleasure; and on many a summer day, from early morning till late evening, Caroline was his companion along the banks of Royden stream. Under its rustic bridge, in a small cave her basket, stored with wholesome home-made viands, would lie; at noon came the delight of a sylvan feast; and when platter and flask and cup were safely packed, Caroline would draw from the fisher's pouch an old russet-covered book, her father's copy of Izaak Walton, and there in a ferny grotto, half circled by vast oak-roots, the river rippling below, the sunshine filtering from above, she would sit "like hare upgathered in her form," become the scholar of Piscator, con those scraps of divine Du Bartas, and Kit Marlowe, and holy Master Herbert, or listen well-pleased to the ballad sweetly sung by honest Maudlin.

Another spot where quietude and delight had meeting was Mr. Gilpin's study. His "Essay on Prints" and his studies of picturesque landscape in various parts of England keep that good man's memory alive. Rector of Boldre, on the borders of the New Forest, and now in benign old age, he united the characters (not always conjoined) of saint and artist. To be allowed the three-miles' walk which ended with the rose-clad rectory was Caroline's delight. There the white-haired hostess would give her greeting, would divest her of hat and tippet, cool her forehead with a sovereign wash of elder water, and prescribe sitting "quite still" until tea-time. But the wistful eyes which settled on the study door would betray the little visitor's impatience, and on leave given to ask admittance she would dart off, all weariness departed:

> "Blithe as a bird, thus freed, away I flew,
> And in three seconds at the well-known door
> Tapped gently; and a gentle voice within
> Asking "Who's there?" "It's *me*" I answered low,
> Grammatically clear. "Let *me* come in"
> The gentle voice rejoined; and in I stole,
> Bashfully silent, as the good man's smile
> And hand extended drew me to his chair."

When—bashfulness being lost in content while the old collector displayed some chosen treasures—the small tongue would trot, nimble in a critic's censure or delight, to which William Gilpin would respond with mild vindication or instructive word of sympathy.

The death of Caroline's great-grandmother, grandmother and father, left Mrs. Bowles alone with her little daughter and her faithful *bonne*. Caroline Bowles had early knowledge of death, but her spirits were those of youth, her disposition was naturally bright, and her girlhood had its fitting opportunities of mirth. At Lymington, during the war with France, there was at one time an encampment of French Royalists, at another an assemblage of English or foreign troops. Caroline Bowles, half French by her traditions, and connected with the army through her uncle, afterwards Lieutenant-General Sir Harry Burrard, had no lack of invitations, and was not proof against the charms of the Lymington military balls. We are assured that she had many admirers, and that her youth endured its joy and sorrow of the heart: "She did indeed return the attachment of one in every respect worthy of her; but it was at last decided by the family conclave that her engagement should be broken off. . . . She submitted her own judgment to that of her relations." *

Early youth went by, and Caroline Bowles continued to reside at Buckland, drawing closer, if that was possible, to her one inseparable companion, her mother. In 1816, death came once again, unexpectedly; and this time it left Caroline really desolate, "connected with the world by no filial or fraternal tie"; she was motherless and alone. Only her faithful nurse remained, and the beloved dwelling-place inhabited by so many memories. A year later, and the loss of her home seemed imminent, consequent upon the loss of her fortune through a guardian's unfaithful conduct. She clung to a place which affection made so dear, and now bethought her of the manuscript of a metrical tale which she had written, and for which a publisher might give a price. Herself in seclusion, away from the world of letters and of trade, she remembered how Southey had once found his pleasure in the generous exercise of power on behalf of Kirke White; and taking courage, she forwarded her manuscript, introducing it with the first letter of the present Correspondence. It will be seen how prompt and kind was Southey's response, and how the growing fears of her suspense turned into a glow of grateful happiness and wonder. Her poem, indeed, did not at once find a publisher; but she herself had found the friend of her life.

A return, with added interest, of her father's goodness, now

---

* "Robert Southey's Second Wife," in the *Cornhill Magazine*. To this article, written by one who was acquainted with Caroline Southey, I am indebted for a good deal of information. Its statements, however, are not all trustworthy.

b

made to his child, saved her from the threatening exile. "You may remember," she writes to Southey at a later time (Nov. 11, 1832), when again perplexities seemed gathering round her, "that when (in happy hour) I introduced myself to you, I was then in expectation of being compelled to give up my home, from pecuniary distress, the consequence of my guardian's fraudulent bankruptcy, from which only a little pittance was saved from the wreck. All on a sudden, as if from another world, started out to my assistance my father's adopted son, Mr. Bruce, then resident at Bushire, flourishing in splendid affluence. I think you know that in consequence of his vehement persuasions I remained on in this place, giving up those more prudent and then feasible plans which were already begun upon, and that to enable me to do so, he gave me an annuity of £150 a-year, a very small part of what he would have obliged me to accept had I wanted principle and delicacy so much as to accept more than was barely sufficient to enable me to live here with respectability." It was not only a part of his fortune which Captain Bruce desired to make over upon his sister by adoption; she tells Southey, with an amused smile at her Eastern friend's zeal on her behalf, of other treasures intended for her: "Think how I was like to have been mounted! You know I always told you I lived in fear of Captain Bruce's sending me over an elephant, or a dromedary, or a great adjutant, or some such gigantic beast or bird from his Eastern land. Well, some friends of his and mine are just come from Calcutta, and by them and in the same ship he had actually intended to send me a present of 'a splendid white ass of the desert breed, whose feet are as swift as the whirlwind, and whose bray may be heard three miles off'!! Think of his writing thus to me, all in sober seriousness, adding how disappointed he was that the captain could not take the freight. 'How you would have flown about the country upon him,' he adds; 'he was of the true breed ridden by the sons of the Prophet; my friend the Scheriff of Mecca sent him to me. But never mind! I have sent for a female out of Egypt, and then I shall have a breed and will send you the first foal.' Is not this friend of mine a comical person?

At one time he was going to consign a freight of fine young Persians to me; at another a frightful old colonel with half a liver, a daffodil face, and an emerald ring as big as half-a-crown on his little finger (I know the sort well). There is no calculating where his vagaries will end."

So, thanks to this brotherly friend, Buckland remained her home; there she passed her days among her books and drawings, and flowers, with visits (often as sick-nurse) to the houses of neighbours, and in particular to Calshot Castle, the old watch-tower of the Solent, of which Sir Harry Burrard was now governor. From the reputation of an authoress she shrank, until it could no longer be escaped; and her first poem, declined by Murray, but accepted by Longman, appeared anonymously. *Ellen Fitzarthur* is a metrical tale in the varying verse which Scott had made popular. It is no tale of adventure. Of extreme simplicity in its action, it depends, for awakening interest, on the truth and tenderness in its portrayal of the domestic affections and the pain of an injured heart. A youthful sailor is brought, hardly living, from the sea to the pastor's house; he wins the only daughter's love; compels her by a force which her heart cannot resist to leave her home; and when with her babe the poor deserted wife drags back her weary limbs, it is to find her father's house ominously dark and silent. She fears the worst, and to solve her doubts will search in the moonlight her mother's tombstone, and see if the space beneath her mother's name is vacant still. Under the blown lime-tree boughs the light is faint and wavering; for a moment she presses a trembling hand over her eyes,

"As if to gain,
'Twixt her and fate, a respite short and vain";

then gazes and discovers, while her cry of despair rings through the night, that another name is there.

During the first five years the interchange of letters between Caroline Bowles and Southey was irregular and infrequent. In June, 1820, they met in London face to face for the first time. All that Caroline Bowles meant and wished to say vanished clean out of her head in the Laureate's presence, and before she regained possession of her true self the much-desired interview was over. Her second volume of verse, *The Widow's Tale, and other Poems*, published in 1822, confirmed her in the place which she already occupied as a writer, in Southey's esteem. It exhibits a marked advance upon *Ellen Fitzarthur*. The principal piece is again a simple story, told in graceful verse, and rich only in the wealth of natural feeling which it attempts to interpret. A youth borne away by the press-gang from his bride returns, after many years, to find his wife dead, and his mother, a blind old woman, tenant of a mountain cottage, cared for by a little gold-haired damsel, who is his own daughter. Among the lesser poems is one, unduly prolonged, which, in its earlier part, catches the very spirit of a soft grey April day, when the clouds hang low, and the branches drip, and the earth is fragrant, and every bud is swelling; a day on which the sun, before setting, breaks out with amber radiance, and the blackbird sings in the delaying twilight. In *William and Jean*, a pathetic story of parting and love and death is preluded with a bright sketch of country folk returning from Sunday evening service, thoroughly English in character, and with touches of that humour which enlivens some of Caroline Bowles's prose writings. The volume contains also two dramatic sketches, one passionate and tragic, the other tender and plaintive; and it is much to say that neither of these wholly fails of its intention.

In the autumn of 1823, Caroline Bowles visited Keswick, and made acquaintance with Southey in his own home. It was a delightful time, and left a store of happy memories for the winter days at Buckland. After this visit, letters pass quickly to and fro; and a little later, Southey proposed that intellectual union of which a poem, written in common by R. S. and C. A. B., was to be the fruit. We can, I think, see how it came about. At Kirkby Lonsdale, one wet forenoon, while the ladies of his party are engaged with their knitting, Southey takes out the memoranda for his projected poem, *Robin Hood*, preparing at the same time to write to Caroline Bowles. He is journeying to Coleorton, the seat of Sir George Beaumont, a representative of the family of Beaumont the dramatist. Suddenly it occurs to him that he and his correspondent might unite their powers of imagination as Beaumont and Fletcher had done long since; and forthwith he writes off the letter numbered XXII. in the present selection.

What followed shall be told in the words of Caroline Bowles: "I read this letter with conflicting emotions. The proposal was most tempting, but a sense of incapacity withheld the free and full assent to it with which I should otherwise have responded.

"I dared not say *yes*, and I could not find in my heart to say *no*. So the memoranda arrived and the rough sketch followed, and in no long time came the writer. Full of his project, full of kindness, of energy, of hope, he did his utmost to encourage and inspirit me; and his hopeful spirit was at least contagious for the time being, if not altogether convincing.

"We talked over *Robin Hood* by my quiet fireside, suggesting, objecting, altering, disputing (it was pleasant to dispute); and when we came to the question of versification, the metre of *Thalaba* (for which, in an evil hour, I had declared my preference) was selected on that account, despite my plea that to admire and to achieve were two very different things, and that I was sure I should never succeed in it. My protest against having anything to do with 'battle scenes and such like' was more readily admitted, and 'the women, children and forest' were assigned to my management.

"So we parted, with a promise on my part to do my best."*

Two causes hindered the progress of the poem—Southey's incessant occupation with work, needful to supply bread to his household, and the real inability of his coadjutor to master the *Thalaba* verse. Gradually their first hopes faded, but the design was never wholly forgotten. Then came that sorrowful period when Southey's elasticity of mind was at length sub-

---

* Preface to *Robin Hood*, which see also for what follows.

dued, and the day's labour became a refuge from the day's distress. At last the cloud seemed to lift a little; at eventime there was light; old pleasurable projects revived; "*Robin Hood* was shortly to be taken in hand in good earnest." Alas, that night was gathering to which the only dawn was death. The fragment of *Robin Hood* was published by the survivor four years after her husband's release from earthly life. Offspring of such joyous energy, the poem is piteous, like an untimely birth that may not see the sun. Three lines of it live in my memory, as the undesigned record, brief yet sufficient, of Southey's sorrow for his beloved Herbert :—

> "He with a virile effort, self-controlled,
> Closed like a miser's treasure in his heart
> That grief of griefs."

Such force put upon oneself wears the heart, and makes ready the brain for coming calamity.

That visit to Buckland, with *Robin Hood* to plan and dispute over, was the first of several which Southey paid during his summer and autumn wanderings. In no other spot outside his own study could he carry on his literary work as he could in the quiet sitting-room of Buckland. His hostess was faithful, and would not exhibit him as her lion. Only once for an old and dear relative did she open the door while Southey was writing. "When you had shown my mane and my tail," exclaimed her guest, " you might as well have let me roar." As soon as the pages for the *Quarterly Review* or for Longman were finished, the Shetland pony would be brought to the door, and Southey, of stature fit to converse on equal terms with a little lady on a little steed, would stride along by Oberon's side. The shaggy pony had for companion a shaggy dog of about his own size. "Tell Cuthbert," his mistress writes, " my dog is quite big enough for him to ride; measures two yards and a-quarter from the tip of his nose to the end of his tail, and every now and then walks away by mistake with the tea-table upon his back. He is like a great white lion, curled all over, with black nose and ears."

INTRODUCTION. xxiii

These visits to Southey were to Caroline Bowles the heart and kernel of the year. Although naturally bright of temper, with some sprightly malice and no real unkindness of disposition, her frequent ill-health, attended by much suffering, caused her spirits to fluctuate, and in her solitude there was a danger that no glad chance would come to lift her out of the depths. It is impossible to estimate how much she gained of hope and vigour from Southey's personal presence and from his kind and constant communication by the pen. Without him her life would have narrowed and dwindled and grown grey. With him for her friend, the world always owned one thing which made life a valuable possession.

When, after change and grievous loss in his home, Southey set himself to apply the remains of life to worthy ends—for great works lay still before him—*The History of Portugal*, *The History of the Monastic Orders*, and *The History of English Literature*—when he dared to look forward to a quiet eventide of toil, he found that his friend of twenty years, whose age approached his own, and whose sympathy with his thoughts and strivings was constantly and instinctively right, would be the truest and most helpful companion for the close of life. Making no breach with the past, he might draw the bonds of their friendship tighter; he might perfect that friendship in the dearest way of all. When Caroline Bowles answered *yes* to Southey's request that she would become his wife, whether she anticipated declining years of peace, or (as some declare) saw the impending doom and gave herself up a willing sacrifice to love, she at least knew that Southey deemed her essential to his well-being. And, doubtless, if the anguish was great, the reward was great to be near him, and let him feel, however gropingly, that she was near in that dim antechamber to the tomb. We are told that while consciousness survived, her presence was a pleasure to him, and that his dulled eye would gleam with a moment's glad intelligence at her name. "Saint and martyr" are the titles which Walter Savage Landor assigns to Caroline Southey.

After her husband's death, in 1843, Mrs. Southey returned

to the home of her childhood. Life was over, as far as she was personally concerned. "Her old gaiety was gone, and she shrank from any new literary exertion."* In Southey's daughter, Edith May Warter, and her husband she found loyal friends of her old age. Of Caroline Southey, they always spoke "as one of the best and truest women that ever lived."† Through the exertions of her husband's brother, Dr. Southey, a pension of £200 a-year was granted to her by the Queen in 1852, but it came almost too late. Caroline Southey died on July 20th, 1854. Lymington churchyard is the place of her rest.

A writer in the *Cornhill Magazine*, who was acquainted with Mrs. Southey, describes her in a way which would have surprised some of her readers, yet which is certainly correct. The publishers insisted, as she complained, that she must appear in her books as "a Niobe, all tears," and stir the springs of pity, not of mirth. I am inclined to think the publishers were right; that when she bent her mind to strenuous work, her imagination could not choose but deal with the piteous facts of life; but on the surface of her mind were a gleam and ripple of bright womanly mirth. "Besides being agreeable herself," writes the *Cornhill* contributor, "she had the rare talent of making everyone she wished to please feel agreeable too; and rather surprised her visitors now and then, not with her own talents, but with those they appeared to be gifted with in her society. It is still only fair to add, that her strong sense of the ridiculous, and her utter absence of sentimentality, disappointed comparative strangers, who expected something pathetic from the writer of so many touching poems. . . . No one more readily caught a friend's idea; but it was quite a chance whether she would hold it up in a comical light, or with a variety of new shades added to it, that came from her own fancy."

The portrait of Caroline Bowles which appears in this volume is photographed from a crayon drawing by herself,

* "She paid at least one visit to London to see the beautiful recumbent statue of Southey" which lies in Crosthwaite Church.

† See a letter of the Rev. Edmund Tew in *Notes and Queries*, April 9, 1881.

made for Southey in 1833, and spoken of in the letters numbered CLVI. and CLVII. "It is a delightful picture," writes Southey, "as well as a very good likeness." This portrait occupied a place in the parlour of Greta Hall opposite to Southey's seat at the tea-table, where also he would sit, with a folio before him, for an hour after supper. The likeness in the upper part of the face to Southey himself, noticed by Henry Taylor, was also observed by Mr. Lough, the sculptor of Southey's recumbent figure in Crosthwaite Church.

By the publication of *The Widow's Tale*, in 1822, Caroline Bowles had acquired some popularity as a writer, and Blackwood encouraged her to put together a number of miscellaneous poems in prose and verse: Southey supplied a title for the little volume—*Solitary Hours*. It pleased her publisher, and pleased the public; two or three of its pieces of lyrical musing still survive, but it is inferior in value to the volume which went immediately before. *Solitary Hours*, however, proved that its author could write prose. *Blackwood's Magazine* and the Annuals, then coming into fashion, were open to her contributions, and in *Blackwood* first appeared her *Chapters on Churchyards*, afterwards (1829) published separately. The sketches of English rustic life in these *Chapters* are both bright and tender; and one tale, of conspicuously higher merit than the rest, *Andrew Cleaves*, exhibits genuine tragic power. Andrew is the hard-tempered, close-fisted, narrow-brained, respectable small farmer, who in prudent years weds a thrifty wife, and after a short time loses her, but keeps and cherishes little Joey, her only child. All the congealed humanity of the hard man's nature flows into a living well of love for little Joey; for his sake all toil is sweet, and every privation becomes a luxury. But Joey, as he grows in schoolboy wisdom, recognises in his father's affection only an instrument whereby to gratify his small greeds for pleasure. The petty vices and hard-heartedness of a child change into the deliberate profligacy of the man, and Joey's untimely end is on the gallows. With Andrew the fountains of the great deep are broken up; anguish restores him to his kind, yet with some of his native starkness still remaining. The shell containing his son's body is brought home upon Andrew's cart; with a strange gentleness he dismisses the neighbours, saying that he will now take rest; and when, through kindly curiosity, they come to look in through the dim-lighted window, there is the coffin laid straight upon the bed, and there is the desolate old man stretched beside it, in tranquil sleep, one arm flung over its side, and his head pressed against the deal. Andrew is of tough fibre, and endures; parting with his patrimony to clear off his son's ill accounts, he rubs along through life with the old mare, serving the country side for many a year as carrier. Andrew Cleaves is a distant kinsman, in our imagination, of that old man, so plain and real, yet almost visionary through the strength and solitude of grief, who left unbuilt the sheepfold

"Beside the boisterous brook of Green-head Ghyll."

The parsimony of means used to produce a pathetic impression by Wordsworth gives us in some degree a measure of his genius.

The actual miseries of English workmen and their children moved Caroline Bowles, in 1833, to write her little volume, *Tales of the Factories*—verses which indignation made. A notice of their origin will be found in Letters CXLIX. and CLI. Some of the gaunt misery of the factory life is powerfully expressed in the first of these poems. What is lurid and exaggerated in the remaining pieces is accounted for, if not justified, by the Minutes of Evidence taken before the Committee of the House of Commons. The dwarfed or distorted workmen testified to the horrors of the spinning-room and the card-room, and their testimony was accepted as true:— " What were the hours of labour at the giggs?—We began at five on Monday morning, and went on to Tuesday night at nine. You were perfectly straight-limbed before?—Yes. And a very strong youth?—Yes. Were the girls strapped, as well as the boys?—Yes. Were the girls so struck as to leave marks upon their skin?—Yes; they have had black marks many times." Through Caroline Bowles's poetry the cry of the

children had gone up, before a greater sister-poet made that
cry pierce deeper our forgetfulness of wrong.

The last volume, wholly her own, published by Caroline
Bowles, was that containing her autobiographical poem *The
Birthday* (1836), from which I have woven together my notice
of her childhood in this Introduction. It is this poem which
chiefly bears out Henry Nelson Coleridge's description of her
as " the Cowper of our modern poetesses." * " She has much
of that great writer's (Cowper's) humour, fondness for rural life,
melancholy pathos, and moral satire. She has also Cowper's
pre-eminently English manner in diction and thought. We do
not remember any recent author whose poetry is so unmixedly
native; and this English complexion constitutes one of its
characteristic charms." It is to be regretted that the poetical
Autobiography goes no farther than her childhood. The
reader who is unacquainted with the poetry of Caroline Bowles
will perhaps be pleased to have a specimen presented, and I
choose a descriptive rather than a humorous passage:—

"That was a lovely brook, by whose green marge,
We two (the patient angler and his child)
Loitered away so many summer days!
A shallow sparkling stream, it hurried now
Leaping and glancing among large round stones,
With everlasting friction chafing still
Their polished smoothness—on a gravelly bed,
Then softly slipt away with rippling sound,
Or all inaudible, where the green moss
Sloped down to meet the clear reflected wave,
That lipped its emerald bank with seeming show
Of gentle dalliance. In a dark, deep pool
Collected now, the peaceful waters slept
Embayed by rugged headlands; hollow roots
Of huge old pollard willows. Anchored there,
Rode safe from every gale, a silvan fleet
Of milk-white water-lilies; every bark
Worthy as those on his own sacred flood
To waft the Indian Cupid. Then the stream
Brawling again o'er pebbly shallows ran,
On—on, to where a rustic, rough-hewn bridge,
All bright with mosses and green ivy wreaths,

* *Quarterly Review*, September, 1840.

> Spanned the small channel with its single arch ;
> And underneath, the bank on either side
> Shelved down into the water darkly green
> With unsunned verdure ; or whereon the sun
> Looked only when his rays at eventide
> Obliquely glanced between the blackened piers
> With arrowy beams of orient emerald light
> Touching the river and its velvet marge."

Among the shorter poems of *The Birthday* volume are some of the best of Caroline Bowles's miscellaneous verses—*The Legend of Santarem*, telling in graceful stanzas the story (given to her in one of Southey's letters) of the Menino Jesus and his blessed fellow-children; *The Last Journey*, which moves as to the stepping of the Egyptian bearers of the dead; *Little Leonard's Good-night*, a poem that spoke touchingly to Southey's heart; and a dainty copy of verses, as our grandfathers would have called them, sent "*To My Little Cousin with her First Bonnet*," in which that most exquisite piece of human head-gear is commended to the care of elfin guardians.*

It is by a few of her shorter verses, *The Mariner's Hymn*, *The Pauper's Death-bed*, and one or two others, that Caroline Bowles is commonly represented, much as Southey must always appear as author of *The Battle of Blenheim*, or *Mary the Maid of the Inn*, and Mrs. Hemans of *Casabianca* and *The Homes of England*. There is some mysterious justice in the awards of fame with which one hardly dares to quarrel. But it seems to me that three or four pieces, each of considerable length, and each in the rhymed couplet, which appear in the *Robin Hood* volume (1847), stand upon an altogether different level from any other poems of their author, and give her a title to rank high among women who have had a part in English poetry. These are *The Young Grey Head*, *The Murder Glen*, *Walter and William*, and *The Evening Walk*. If her poetical autobiography brings her into comparison with Cowper, these narrative pieces suggest another comparison, and would justify us in describing her as the Crabbe among our modern poetesses—a Crabbe in

---

* The word printed *sonnet*, p. 159, l. 9, ought to be *bonnet*.

whom womanly tenderness replaces the hard veracity characteristic of that eminent poet.* I am glad to confirm my own opinion with the judgment of a cultivated critic, David Moir. "We doubt," he says, "if the English language contains anything more profoundly pathetic than Mrs. Southey's four tales," naming those mentioned above. This is, indeed, exaggerated praise; but it is the exaggeration which comes from high enjoyment. The difficult verse is managed for narrative purpose with an ease and strength which make one wonder how and where they were acquired. The poems do not well bear to be broken up, but a short passage may serve to show how the couplet is handled; it is from *The Young Grey Head*, where the farmer finds his two children at the swollen ford :—

> "' That's sure,' said Mark. ' So—let the lantern shine
> Down yonder. There's the dog, and, hark !'
> 'Oh dear!'
> And a low sob came faintly on the ear,
> Mock'd by the sobbing gust. Down, quick as thought,
> Into the stream leapt Ambrose, where he caught
> Fast hold of something—a dark huddled heap—
> Half in the water, where 'twas scarce knee-deep,
> For a tall man; and half above it, propp'd
> By some old ragged side-piles, that had stopt
> Endways the broken plank, when it gave way
> With the two little ones that luckless day!
> 'My babes! my lambkins!' was the father's cry;
> *One* little voice made answer—' Here am I!'
> 'Twas Lizzy's. There she crouch'd, with face as white,
> More ghastly, by the flickering lantern light,
> Than sheeted corpse. The pale blue lips, drawn tight,
> Wide parted, showing all the pearly teeth,
> And eyes on some dark object underneath,
> Washed by the turbid water, fixed like stone—
> One arm and hand stretched out and rigid grown,
> Grasping, as in the death-gripe—Jenny's frock.
> There lay she drowned. Could *he* sustain that shock,
> The doating father? Where's the unriven rock
> Can bide such blasting in its flintiest part
> As that soft, sentient thing—the human heart?

---

* The treatment of the rhymed couplet by Caroline Bowles is, however, very different from that of Crabbe.

In *The Murder Glen*, horror and pity are strangely and powerfully intertwined. The murderer's idiot child, whose only word is the half-articulate "Mam-mam," pleads, like one of Victor Hugo's piteous human grotesques, for all outcast, despised, downtrodden things.

In this Introduction I have chosen to speak of Caroline Bowles rather than of Southey, for Southey's character and life and work in literature are known. He appears in this Correspondence as he appears everywhere else—a man sound to the core, with affections, conscience, will, intellect, imagination working together towards worthy and honourable ends, and underlying all these a temperament almost as dangerously excitable as that of Shelley. Carlyle, in his *Reminiscences*, with some valorous blundering, and some quite reckless misstatements with reference to Caroline Bowles, has brought out vividly that union of passion with self-mastery and self-management which gave Southey his singularity among men of genius: "I said to myself, 'How has this man contrived, with such a nervous system, to keep alive for near sixty years? Now blushing under his grey hairs, rosy like a maiden of fifteen; now slaty almost like a rattle-snake or fiery serpent? How has he not been torn to pieces long since, under such furious pulling this way and that? He must have somewhere a great deal of methodic virtue in him; I suppose, too, his heart is thoroughly honest, which helps considerably.'" An Arab steed bearing the load of a pack-horse—this was Southey; and he bore his load steadily, gracefully, almost proudly; bore it long and well; then suddenly quivered, and fell beside the way.

Had I lived when Southey was a force in English politics, I do not doubt that I should have been of the opposite camp with respect to some great public questions—Catholic Emancipation, Parliamentary Reform, Free Trade, and perhaps others of deeper significance. It has been a lesson to me of no small value to learn why Southey and Wordsworth came to think on these and kindred subjects as they did; to learn how large was their portion of the underlying truth. And it has been no common happiness to know for a fact that love and veneration are not paled in by our poor penfolds of opinions, but follow freely the high constraint proceeding from a beautiful human spirit,

> "As the water follows the moon silently, with fluid steps, anywhere around the globe."

Praise, Southey would not have desired, and he does not need it, the life of a good man abiding as a part of the solid harvest —and also of the ever renewing seed-time—of our earth. But the judgment of his peers on Southey has been expressed in three monumental passages, and these have not yet been placed side by side. It is well to keep them on record, and here they shall stand :—

" Never in the course of my existence," wrote Walter Savage Landor, " have I known a man so excellent on so many points. What he was as a son is now remembered by few; what he was as a husband and father shows it more clearly than the best memory could represent it. The purity of his youth, the integrity of his manhood, the soundness of his judgment, and the tenderness of his heart, they alone who have been blest with the same qualities can appreciate. And who are they? Many with one, some with more than one, nobody with all of them in the like degree. So there are several who possess one quality of his poetry; none who possess the whole variety."

" There are men with whose characters it is the interest of their contemporaries, no less than that of posterity, to be made acquainted," writes S. T. Coleridge. "I know few men who so well deserve as Southey the character which an ancient attributes to Marcus Cato, namely, that he was likest virtue, inasmuch as he seemed to act aright, not in obedience to any law or outward motive, but by the necessity of a happy nature, which could not act otherwise. As son, brother, husband, father, master, friend, he moves with firm yet light steps, alike unostentatious and alike exemplary. . . . When future critics shall weigh out his guerdon of praise and censure, it will be Southey the poet alone that will supply them with the scanty materials for the latter.* They will likewise not fail to record,

---

* In an earlier passage Coleridge has spoken with an admiration of Southey's poems which would have satisfied even Landor.

that as no man was ever a more constant friend, never had poet more friends and honourers among the good of all parties; and that quacks in education, quacks in politics, and quacks in criticism were his only enemies."

"Of what he did accomplish," writes Henry Taylor, "a portion will not soon be forgotten. There were greater poets in his generation, and there were men of a deeper and more far-reaching philosophic faculty; but take him for all in all—his ardent and genial piety, his moral strength, the magnitude and variety of his powers, the field which he covered in literature, and the beauty of his life—it may be said of him justly and with no straining of the truth, that of all his contemporaries he was the greatest *Man*."

Thus it is that those who knew him best have spoken of Southey.

NOTE.—The proofs of the first two sheets reached me at a time when the originals of the letters were not within my reach, and I trusted to transcripts; hence the following errata:—p. 15, 4 lines from bottom, for *vale* read *wall*; p. 25, 10 lines from bottom, for *forward* read *favourite*; p. 29, 15 lines from bottom for *apprehensive* read *oppressive*.

CORRESPONDENCE.

I.

TO ROBERT SOUTHEY.

BUCKLAND, NEAR LYMINGTON, HANTS,
April 25*th,* 1818.

I AM startled at my own temerity, in venturing to approach Mr. Southey with a request which yet emanates from the very reverse of a presumptuous feeling—with a request that he will charitably devote some leisure hour to the perusal of the manuscript which accompanies this petition, the contents of which I scarcely venture to dignify with the title of poem. It must appear strange that, entertaining so humble an opinion of its merits, I should be solicitous to hazard them at the tribunal of Mr. Southey's judgment—the more so, as he is an entire stranger to the very name and existence of so insignificant a being as Caroline Bowles; and yet these considerations, far from deterring me from the measure, have decided me to adopt it: with regard to the first, it has even appeared to me that persons most eminently gifted are those who look with the greatest indulgence on the humble efforts of inferior minds; and, at all events, I would rather be " weighed in the balance, and found wanting," by one so competent to decide, than approved of and encouraged by partial or incompetent judges. That I am also personally a stranger to Mr. Southey emboldens me to prefer my present petition. His character is known to me, not only through the medium of common fame, but by the report of one who knew him well in former days. Concurring testimonies encourage me to address him, and I feel a cowardly confidence in doing so, which would not support me in approaching a personal acquaintance. This I am very conscious is a weak motive, but it originates in feelings of reserved fearfulness, which I cannot conquer, and (strange to say) I am sensible of less constraint in speaking on the subject to a stranger, whose eyes it will probably never be my lot to encounter, and who will soon lose the recollection of me, and my presumptuous folly, if such indeed it should appear to him. With this professed unwillingness to attract notice, it must be to you, sir, justly a matter of surprise I should ever have conceived the idea of intruding on the public. It is even to myself marvellous; but strong motives, and I hope blameless ones, have decided me.

A very sudden reverse of fortune, occasioned by the unfaithful conduct of a person who had acted as my guardian, threatens to deprive me of a house most dear to me from infancy. I am still struggling to retain it, and would, if possible, obtain from my own efforts some trifling pecuniary assistance, which, in its most limited extent, would be of temporary convenience to me, and might thus contribute to my grand desideratum, that of continuing to live where I have lived so happily. A stroke equally sudden, and far more tremendous than that which deprived me of fortune, took from me, a twelvemonth since, my only surviving parent—a most beloved mother, the only and inseparable companion of my life, whose age and constitution had afforded me reasonable hope that God would be pleased to spare to me till an advanced age the blessing of her society; He willed otherwise, and I am now so far desolate in the world as to be connected with it by no filial or fraternal tie. I remain the solitary tenant of this beloved little dwelling, where every object, and tree, and shrub, has more than local interest for me, and the extent of my unambitious desire is to spend the remainder of my days amongst them.

Forgive me, sir, for intruding on your time and patience the insignificant concerns of an obscure stranger; but I am tempted to believe Mr. Southey will not listen with a stranger's ear to the real, though common, affliction of a fellow-being, and I hope that this short detail will enable him to appreciate the motives of my conduct. I am too conscious that my attainments and abilities are not such as would authorize a hope that any production of mine can be entitled to more than indulgence; and indeed I sometimes fear, I almost suspect, that I have mistaken for natural taste a strong inclination for poetry, which has ruled me from childhood, possibly originating in the solitary reveries and pursuits incident to a very secluded life. I have never possessed the advantage of being acquainted with any person of literary habits; I have never even had access to a tolerable library; my reading has been too trifling and desultory to produce much good effect; and my life so stationary in this tame, though beautiful country, in a neighbourhood where the society, though large, is most uninteresting, that my imagination is probably coloured with these surrounding tints, and quite unable to aspire at any delineation beyond that of the home scenes familiar to me from infancy. I fear, too, I may have been an innocent plagiarist; for on looking over my manuscript many lines and expressions strike me as borrowed, which yet, when they were written, appeared to flow naturally from my pen; but I cannot positively detect the thefts, if such they are, not having the authors to refer to from whence they now strike me as proceeding.

And now what more can I say, but that I throw myself on your indulgence? Be as charitable as you conscientiously can, and I shall be gratefully satisfied with your decision. My pretensions are so humble, that I have little to apprehend on the score of mortified vanity; I should only have to shrink back into the obscurity from which I make a trembling effort to emerge. But I will tell you what most appals me: I shrink, like the sensitive plant, from the touch of a cold answer, by which I mean, not one which should gently and kindly tell me, "Be advised: you have mistaken your vocation: tempt not the public scorn," but one that should reply far more chillingly, "I cannot possibly, Madam, accede to your request; I should be inundated with such were I to attend to them; I beg leave to decline the office you assign to me." This is the repulse I should fear, were I addressing any other than Mr. Southey; and, I will confess, my nature is not cast in such heroic mould as to encounter unshrinkingly the rebuke of such an answer from a quarter to which I had anxiously looked with the ardent but fearful hope of gaining to myself a friend. I dare not ask myself why I should hope to inspire such an interest, without any claims but those of misfortune. To such a question, my reason might return too cold an answer, and I would willingly indulge in the novelty of hope till certainty confirms or destroys it.

At all events, I feel assured that Mr. Southey's humanity and gentleness of heart will not suffer him to repulse contemptuously what his candour and judgment may oblige him to condemn. I will intrude on him no longer than to subscribe myself Mr. Southey's

Most obedient Servant,

CAROLINE A. BOWLES.

II.

TO CAROLINE BOWLES.

KESWICK, May 28th, 1818.

This day, and not till this day, did I receive your manuscript and the very interesting letter by which it was introduced. You will have expected to hear from me ere this, and I think I know how you will have thought and felt; as a suspicion has arisen of something even less pardonable than the brutal sort of repulse which you have done me the justice not to anticipate. Parcels lie for me at Messrs. Longmans' till they have occasion to send to me; they then travel by wagon, which, owing to the change of carriers, is a business of eighteen days, or sometimes three weeks. Your packet has been fortunate in not having been longer in Paternoster-row.

I reply to your letter without the delay of a single post, and with sincere pleasure; for though what I have to say may in some degree discourage hope, in all other respects it will correspond entirely to your wishes. The success of a poem, indeed of any composition whatsoever, does not depend upon its merit—or less upon its merit than upon any other cause. Of the volumes of poetry which are published, not one in twenty—perhaps I might say in fifty—pays the expense of publication, though there is not one of the whole number which would not have excited attention and secured a remuneration to the author had it been published thirty years ago. No persons, therefore, should risk the publication of a poem on their own account unless the sacrifice of the money so expended were a matter of indifference. For the same reason booksellers will not purchase poetry, unless from some writer who is in vogue. But I must not leave you here, without trying what can be done. The " Caroline Bowles, to whose very name and existence I was a stranger" this morning, cannot now be to me an "insignificant" person, one whom I shall soon forget, or by whom I would willingly be forgotten.

Booksellers are not the most liberal, nor the most amiable of men. They are necessarily *tradesmen;* and a constant attention to profit and loss is neither wholesome for the heart nor the understanding. Of those with whom I have any dealings, Murray is the one who would be least unlikely to risk the publication of your poem, and the most likely to make the publication answer. He would perhaps take the risk upon himself, and give you half the eventual profits. Shall I write to him upon the subject? Poor as these terms may appear, they are the best that I have ever obtained for myself. My recommendation ought to have some weight with him.

I do not like such poems, because I am old enough to avoid all unnecessary pain. Real griefs do not lessen the susceptibility for fictitious ones, but they take away all desire for them. There is a great deal of beauty in it—a womanly fluency, a womanly sweetness, a womanly truth and tenderness of feeling, which I have enough of my mother in me perfectly to understand. It is provoking to think that if the same powers had been displayed in prose instead of verse, in a novel instead of a poem, there would have been little or no doubt of finding a publisher; for let the supply of novels be what it will, the demand is sure to outrun it.

Many years ago, I resided for a short time within ten miles of Lymington. I wish I were near enough now to see and converse with you. It is in planning a work that advice is useful; a single remark may then induce an author to avoid a fault which cannot afterwards be got rid of by any laborious correction. I do not mean to say that this poem has any such faults: a few verbal alterations are all I should suggest here, and a few omissions where they can be made without injury, chiefly for the sake of shortening it, because I foresee that its length will be a bookseller's objection. But to the point: if you think proper, I will write to Murray and ask him whether he will publish it; this I would wish you to consider as extremely doubtful; but if the application fails, it will not be for any want of warmth and sincerity in the recommendation. And if it should fail, you must not be discouraged, but turn your thoughts to something else, in prose or verse, in which, if I can assist you by any advice, or direct you to any subjects which carry with them some attraction, I shall be very happy to show that you have not honoured with your confidence one who is unfeeling, and therefore unworthy of it. For the present farewell, and believe me,

Yours, with sincere regard,
ROBERT SOUTHEY.

III.

TO ROBERT SOUTHEY.

BUCKLAND, *June 3rd*, 1818.

No, indeed, you have not guessed how I have "thought and felt" respecting the length of time which has elapsed since I had the boldness to address you. I was aware of the probability that it would be long before my packet reached you; and I felt assured that when you did receive it, you would honour me with a reply, and a gentle one. It will appear a little incomprehensible to you if I confess that, with a mind impressed by this conviction, I anticipated your answer with unconquerable and increasing dread; for, hardly had I sent off my manuscript, when I became panic-struck at my own daring, and after a very little time succeeded in convincing myself (greatly to the comfort of my feelings) that every line I had written was execrable, and that to obtrude such trash on your notice must appear to you the height of impertinence and folly. Under the influence of these pleasing after-thoughts, I endeavoured to console myself by reflecting, "Well! I shall never see Mr. Southey, and he will very soon forget me and my nonsense." With such anticipations, you may guess how tremblingly I broke the seal of your letter; but you cannot guess (for you have never felt as I have felt) with what sensations I read its contents; I almost fancied I could discern in them the kind interest of a friend who cared for me, rather than the good-will of a stranger, and I want words to express my grateful feelings. Your indulgence to my little poem exceeds my most sanguine hopes; but I assure you, in sincerity of heart, I am more gratified by the tone of interest and benevolence which characterizes your letter, than I should be by the public success of an attempt, the feebleness and imperfection of which I am so sensible of. How altered are my feelings since yesterday! I shall now deprecate the forgetfulness which I then assured myself would soon shut me out from

Mr. Southey's remembrance. He will live in mine till I become insensible to the charm of his writings, and (what is less possible) unmindful of the delicacy and feeling of his conduct towards me.

As my hope of success was never brighter than a twilight gleam, I shall feel little disappointment if it should be totally dispelled. I foresee from your representation, and from the kindness with which you prepare me for the circumstance, that Murray will probably reject it; and I am sensible its only chance of being accepted rests on your recommendation. And will you really condescend to recommend it? How willingly I accept your offer! How thankfully I shall avail myself of your directions to alter or curtail, and how eager should I be to claim your future advice and the guidance of your judgment, if I felt a hope of being able to profit by it; but I mistrust myself too entirely. Poor as are my powers of composition in verse, I should find it still more difficult to write in prose; and for a novel! I could as easily compose a treatise on chemistry. See on what a feeble and poorly-gifted mind you would bestow the honour of your encouragement. If Murray rejects the manuscript, do me the last kind office of committing it to the flames : it will only be spoiled paper.

I entirely agree with you: we need not create to ourselves fictitious griefs; life has too many real sorrows; but the mind recently afflicted colours everything with its own sadness. I wrote under such impressions, oppressed besides by the languor of a very trying nervous disorder. These circumstances may excuse me. Once, everything in life glowed with the brightness of my own feelings; but it was fit the painted vapour should be dispelled. Earth had too much of my affection, and when time has mellowed those shades of calamity, I may probably regain some feelings of tempered enjoyment. Your letter has imparted to me the most pleasurable I have known for many a day. Such a heart as yours will not be insensible to the assurance. In what spot near Lymington did you reside some years ago? How much I wish you were indeed near enough for me to see and converse with you. Such a neighbourhood would give a new interest to my existence; but I live in a desert, of which, however, my little house is still the green valley. If I indulge longer in such digressions, I shall forget how little I am authorized to weary your patience; forgive me for having intruded on it so long, and believe me,

Yours most gratefully,

CAROLINE A. BOWLES.

IV.

TO CAROLINE BOWLES.

KESWICK, *June* 17*th*, 1818.

I have just received Murray's reply, which is very much what might be expected. It is in these words: "I will have great pleasure in reading the lady's MS. poem, though unless it be very striking indeed it will not have the smallest chance of succeeding. I receive at least 500 poems every year, out of which I cannot venture to print six, and of these, not one half defray the expenses of publication."

Times are very much changed in this country with regard to literature—or perhaps I should rather say fashions are changed. A bookseller would formerly take the opinion of some man of letters, and be guided by his private and unbiassed judgment of the merits of the work. The trade are grown wiser now: they have discovered that the success of poetry does not depend upon its merit, but upon the humour of the season; and they have discovered also, what is not less true, that, living upon the spot, and being dealers in the commodity, they themselves are the best judges of what *will take*.

If it were possible, I would read this poem with you, and explain, as we went through it, wherein any expression is faulty, and why any part or passage requires alteration. Generally speaking, women write letters better than men, and they write novels better—I do not mean as to the construction of the story, or the conception of the characters; but their language is easier and happier; they express their feelings more readily, and therefore more naturally; and they write the real language of life when men would be thinking of fine composition, which has much the same effect upon a man's style as it would have upon his manners if he were always to be thinking of his clothes. But verse requires a precision both of thought and language (very rarely indeed attained—scarcely by two writers in a generation), to which women are less accustomed, and to which their education has not trained them.

You have the eye, the ear, and the heart of a poetess. What is wanting in you is that which I was twenty years in learning, and had hardly acquired when evening prospects and autumnal feelings unfitted me for what requires ardour, and an expenditure of spirits which I can no longer support with impunity. Competent criticism might most materially have abridged my course, but it was not my fortune to meet with it. Your poem deserves to be carefully corrected. I myself re-wrote two of my long poems, and a very considerable part of two others. The best passages of a poem are those which have been felicitously produced in the first glow of composition; but I have found in my own experience that those which have been inserted in place of something faulty have been next to them in merit.

It was at Burton, near Christ Church, that I lodged first for one summer, and afterwards took a cottage, which, however, owing to ill health, I did not occupy long. Once more—do not be discouraged. Tell me that you will correct your poem—valiantly, and if you will make up your mind by this resolution, I will go through it severely, book by book.

Farewell, and believe me,

Yours faithfully,
Robert Southey.

Miss Bowles, writing on July 16, 1818, from the Isle of Wight, whither she had gone to recover health, gratefully accepts Southey's offer to go over the poem with her, correcting its errors. Letters from Southey follow, containing a number of minute criticisms, of which letters the second concludes thus:—

These remarks are not worth much in themselves; but it is of some consequence to remove any grammatical inaccuracies, however slight, and it is of far more to impress upon a writer the necessity of adhering as strictly to sound sense in verse as in prose. For however brilliant a poem may be in parts, and however popular it may be because of that brilliancy, if the poet, either from a false system, or from the want of system, writes nonsense, his works will inevitably be forgotten, or only remembered to his dispraise. The *judgment*, therefore, must always be exercised in writing, and it is the last thing which a poet learns to exercise. The world may put up for a while with something that looks like sense, if it be flashy or striking; and thus it is that every age has had its favourites, whose reputation passes away like that of an actor or a beauty in high life, when anyone with equal pretensions comes forward.

When you have revised the poem, send it to Murray, and, if you do not like that he should know your name and address, say in a note that you send for his inspection the poem concerning which I had written to him, and desire him to make known his determination concerning it to me. And then, if he chooses to print it, I will refer him to you. Whether he will or no, or what the reception of the poem may be, if he should, I cannot pretend to augur. The last thirty years have produced a great change in these things. Even when I began to write, there was a fair field, and whoever appeared in it was sure to obtain notice. Now it is so crowded, that poems are entirely neglected which would then have been regarded with wonder and applause.

Tell me also what you have written (for you must have written other things), and what you think of writing, if you have anything planned. A happy subject may attract attention, and a word of advice respecting the plan may be worth fifty after it is executed. I wish you may be able also to tell me that your health is improved, and that with it your heart is recovering strength and genial feelings.

Believe me, sincerely yours,
R. SOUTHEY.

V.

TO ROBERT SOUTHEY.

BUCKLAND, *Sept.* 21*st*, 1818.

I thank you most gratefully for your two valuable letters; it will be my own fault, or rather my misfortune, if the criticisms they contain are not most useful to me, lenient as they are, for you cauterize with a gentle hand.

Yes—I have written lots of other things since five years old, I think, or rather composed, for at that mature period my father used to write them for his spoiled child; and I dare say my miscellaneous works would fill a decent volume, if they had been carefully rescued from the copy-books, drawing-books, and receipt-books, where I was wont to scribble them in all blank pages. Happily most of those sublime effusions have disappeared by degrees: out of the few remaining I venture to enclose one or two (I hardly know for what purpose, for they do not deserve your notice, and you did but ask me "if I had written other things"). I cannot resist my inclination to send you at the same time a little poem which fell into my hands a short time ago; it appears to me to wear the stamp of no ordinary genius.

I have nothing planned, and I have no courage to plan, for my stores of information are so scanty, and I have so little confidence in my own taste and judgment, that I can hardly hope to select any attractive subject. One of *your* suggesting might perhaps inspire me with more confidence (or rather hope) of success, and from your abundance of ideas you may venture to supply the destitute. See what a bold beggar you have made me.

I thank God my health is somewhat amended, and my feelings less dreary than they were. I am very grateful for your humane inquiry, and while I live I shall never forget your kindness to me, at a season when kindness and gentleness is most soothing to a wounded spirit.

I remain, most truly yours,

CAROLINE A. BOWLES.

Availing myself of your permission, I will desire Murray to acquaint you with his awful fiat.

VI.

TO CAROLINE BOWLES.

KESWICK, *March* 18*th*, 1819.

I wrote to Murray on the sixth of last month, to inquire the fate of your poem, and this day I have received an apology for not answering my letter till now, stating (which no doubt is the truth) that, not having answered it by return of post, it went out of his head.

I feared what his reply would be, and from this long silence you will have anticipated it. These are his words: "The MS. poem is such as to do its author very great credit. But the fact is that no poetry, except your own and that of some four or five others, has the least chance of sale at present, and I am obliged to refrain." There is but too much truth in this. Poets who would have obtained universal applause thirty years ago cannot now obtain a hearing, however great the promise their works may contain, and the vilest trash will be received from one who, by fair means or foul, has obtained a reputation. As for the incivility of Murray's long delay, you must remember that a great bookseller is a much greater man than the Prime Minister.

I am sorry for this, and perhaps more disappointed than you will be. A local poem, such as I suggested in my last letter,* would have a better chance than one of any other kind, because it carries with it a local interest. The New Forest is, both in its history and scenery, a rich subject; and with the help of prints a book might be made which would be bought by idlers at Lymington, Southampton, &c.; booksellers must look to the sale of what they publish, and this is a kind of sale on which they can in some degree calculate. The Isle of Wight is not so extensive a subject; but it would have the same advantage. The Forest, however, affords more scope, and would supply matter for a very interesting poem, especially to one who has so many feelings connected with it as you needs must have. Have you ever accustomed yourself to write blank verse? for that would be the most suitable metre. Think of this—of the convents and castles within its ancient precincts—of Winchester—of William the Conqueror and William Rufus—of its natural history, both as relating to vegetable and animal life—of what you have seen and what you have felt there. Think of these things, and tell me what you think of them, and believe me,

Yours faithfully,

ROBERT SOUTHEY.

* In a letter of January 8, 1819, Southey had suggested "The New Forest" as the subject of a poem.

From Clifton, Bristol, whither she had gone in search of health, Miss Bowles writes to Southey, on May 12, 1819, informing him that Murray's adverse decision was not unexpected; assigning reasons for her not attempting a poem on the New Forest, as proposed by Southey; and expressing her desire to submit to him an unfinished poem in blank verse, embodying recollections of her earlier years—the poem afterwards published under the title of *The Birthday.*

VII.

TO CAROLINE BOWLES.

KESWICK, *May 21st*, 1819.

I shall be in London, if no unforeseen circumstances occur to prevent me, in three or four weeks from this time; and if you direct your manuscript to me, at Dr. Southey's (my brother), 15, Queen Anne-street, Cavendish-square, I shall find it there, sooner than it would find its way to Keswick through the bookseller's hands. I dare say you wrote blank verse—your ear will lead you to the measure; but if you should have written under any erroneous notion of its structure, it will be very easy to show you where you are wrong, and what you have to correct.

Bristol is my native place, and the first imagery which I ever drew from nature was from the rocks and woods about Clifton. There was (and probably still is), not far from Cook's Folly, a horse-block upon the Down, close to the vale—a point from whence a stranger looks down upon the river and the opposite woods; immediately under that horse-block is a little cave, overhung with ivy, the access to which I should probably find difficult now; but, when I was between fifteen and eighteen, many and many are the verses which I wrote in that cave. One of my schoolfellows seemed at that time to have an inclination for poetry almost as decided as my own—we called ourselves Nisus and Euryalus, and the former of these names I cut in the rock, where I used to take my seat.

One thing before I conclude. An old friend of mine, for whom I have a great regard and affection, lives (I believe) within a few doors of your present abode. His name is King, he is by profession a surgeon, by birth a Swiss, and his wife, a sister of Miss Edgeworth. If you would like to have an acquaintance who would be desirous of rendering you any service in his power, let me know, and I will write to him that he may call upon you, and introduce himself as my friend. He is a man of great goodness and extraordinary talents.

Farewell, and believe me,
Yours faithfully,
Robert Southey.

VIII.

TO CAROLINE BOWLES.

Keswick, *November 20th*, 1819.

Yesterday evening a friend brought me your manuscript,* which had so long been lying in Queen Anne-street. I read it this morning, and will rather despatch a hasty letter than let a post elapse without telling you of its arrival, and exhorting you, by all means, to proceed with the poem. It is in a very sweet strain; go on with it, and you will produce something which may hold a permanent place in English literature. As you go

* The manuscript of Caroline Bowles's autobiographical poem "The Birthday."

on, you will feel what passages are feeble and require to be shortened or expunged—there is very little that stands in need of this. The flow of verse is natural, and the language unconstrained—both as they should be. Everybody will recognize the truth of the feeling which produces it, and there is a charm in the pictures, the imagery, and the expression, which cannot fail to be felt.

I made a long tour in Scotland, of several weeks. I saw a great deal that is fine, and a great deal that is in a high degree beautiful; but the general character of the Highlands is severe and mournful, and the impression upon me when I returned was, that these lakes gain as much by a comparison with the Scotch, as they lose when compared with the Swiss and Italian.

I intend to be in London as soon as my "Life of Wesley" is finished, which will be in the beginning of February. Shall I keep your poem till I can carry it so far on its way? I am too busy at present to say more; only understand these hurried lines as encouraging you in the strongest and most unequivocal manner to proceed.

Yours, very truly,

ROBERT SOUTHEY.

IX.

TO ROBERT SOUTHEY.

BUCKLAND, *January* 21*st*, 1820.

I have so often been guilty of replying to your letters with indiscreet haste, that in the present case I think myself rather entitled to commendation for leaving your last so long unanswered; but discretion has its limits, and shall restrain me no longer from thanking you for the kind approbation you were pleased to bestow on the MS. fragment I sent you last summer.

Encouraged thus by you, I cannot but proceed with it, and indeed the subject is such as I should be loath to leave, if only for the sake of the gratification I experience in giving something of durability to circumstances, scenes, and images long past, and now obliterated, except from my recollection. But the very interest which almost compels me to write, incapacitates me from judging fairly of what I write, for those passages on which I have dwelt with peculiar pleasure may, in fact, be tedious and feeble in the opinion of a cool observer. I wish, therefore, that when you read the MS. you had drawn your pen unsparingly through such parts as appeared to you most objectionable; but at all events I will endeavour to weed and prune it, when I transcribe that first copy, which I can wait for very patiently, till you take it to town, as you kindly offer to do, in February. There is a chance—just a chance—that I may be in London about that season, on my way (a very circuitous one) to Worcestershire. I look forward with apprehension to that possibility, for no pleasant business awaits me in the great city; but I should be in some measure reconciled to the painful cause which may draw me there, could I hope then to become personally acquainted with Mr. Southey.

I heard it said that the article in the *Quarterly Review* for August, relating to the Catacombs, was written by you. The brief account of Herbert Knowles particularly interested me; what an incorrect history of him was that I had obtained, and with which I favoured you so officiously! but I am perpetually finding out (when too late) that I have said or written something foolish or impertinent, a reflection which very naturally suggests to me that it is high time to conclude my letter.

I remain most truly yours,

CAROLINE A. BOWLES.

X.

TO ROBERT SOUTHEY.

CHELSEA, *June 7th*, 1820.

I should hardly presume to request Mr. Southey's acceptance of the insignificant little volume which accompanies this letter, had I any better means of testifying my grateful sense of his various kindnesses to me. As it is, I offer it with the thankful acknowledgment that, faulty as the poem still is, it would have been much more so but for Mr. Southey's advice and critical remarks. Last, but not least, let me thank you, my dear sir, more intelligibly at least than I could do *vivâ voce*, for your goodness in coming to see me at this place: to confess the truth, I derive more pleasure from the reflection that I am become personally acquainted with you than I did at the actual making of that acquaintance, for then I found that all I had meant and wished to say was clean vanished, and that I had only your charity (and penetration perhaps) to trust to for not setting me down as an unthankful and insensible idiot. It is not with me that "out of the abundance of the heart the mouth speaketh."

I leave town in a few days, and I shall give directions that this parcel may be sent to Keswick in a fortnight, by which time you also, I suppose, will have returned to your dear home.

I have not forgotten that Mr. Southey promised to write to me thence; I hope he has not forgotten it. You will see that Messrs. Longman have thought it expedient to christen my poem "Ellen Fitzarthur": they said the other name was too pastoral, and I cared little about the title, so Miss Fitz is their godchild.

Believe me,
My dear sir,
Most thankfully and truly yours,
CAROLINE A. BOWLES.

XI.

TO CAROLINE BOWLES.

KESWICK, *February* 13*th*, 1821.

I thank you for your book and your drawing. They arrived this evening. I have been intending and intending to write to you ever since my return home in July, and more especially since I got your poem in November, to have told you then how well I liked it in print, and how much it was admired by the reading part of my family. But you know what becomes of good intentions—the devil is said to pave his dominions with them, and, if it be so, I have furnished him with as many materials as most men. My excuse must be not so much the number of my own employments as the numerous interruptions to which I am liable, during part of the year, from unexpected visitors, and all the year long from persons at a distance who, with or without reason, write to me upon all imaginable and unimaginable subjects: one man, for instance, requests an acrostic for his mistress, and another consults me upon a scheme for paying off the national debt. My collection of such letters is not a little curious. The evil is, that in replying to them, either for the sake of getting rid of the application, or in mere courtesy, or in the kinder mood which those of a better kind excite, things which I ought and designed to do are left undone, time passes over, and the arrears become like a prodigal's debts, irksome to remember, because they are too heavy to be cleared off.

I wish I could have seen you again at Chelsea; but my very minutes were numbered while I was in and about London, nor did I ever feel anything like a sense of rest from the time I entered it till I got into the mail-coach on my return. I heard of you once from Dr. Thomas, who is an old friend of my family. I saw such an account of your poems as it was gratifying to see in the *New Monthly Magazine*, and I did what I could to recommend it for such notice as it deserved in another quarter, where the will must be taken for the deed.

Your stanzas upon the King's death are very good, both in thought, feeling, and expression. So are the lines upon the Proclamation. I do not see anything to censure. Go on with your blank-verse poem : if I am not deceived, the subject will secure for it a favourable acceptance, relating as it does to feelings which will find sympathy in every kind heart. I need not tell you that when you read contemporary poets the best thing you can learn from them is to avoid their peculiarities, and their mannerisms, and their affectations—in one word, their faults; but you are in no danger of catching them.

I am publishing an experimental poem,* which Longman will send you as soon as it comes forth—in the course of a fortnight probably. It is written in hexameters, the heroic measure of the ancients. Do not trouble yourself with the explanation of its principle in the preface, but read it as you would verse of any other kind, and you will soon feel and find the rhythm. The subject is the late King's death; considering that I might be expected, as a matter of duty, to write upon it, I chose to do it in this form.

You and I must be better acquainted personally ; you must become acquainted with my wife and daughter. Our spare room will be filled this summer; but next year we shall be very glad if you will let us show you this neighbourhood, if we may dare to look on so long !

Farewell, and believe me,

Yours very truly,

ROBERT SOUTHEY.

* " A Vision of Judgment."

XII.

TO CAROLINE BOWLES.

February 14*th*, 1821.

I forgot, when writing yesterday, to thank you for the drawing, and for the feeling which induced you to send it. I know the spot well, and the poplar tree; but among the nearest buildings are some high, tower-like chimneys, which look as if they belonged to a manufactory, and which, I think, have been erected since my time. For my recollections of Bristol are in the eighteenth year of their age—a large part of human life! Were I to visit that city now I should walk its streets like a stranger, and scarcely meet one person whom I remembered or who would remember me. When my poem reaches you, you will see that I do not think of Bristol without a natural feeling.

I please myself in thinking what pleasure you will have in sketching here, where, if you have never been fairly in a mountainous country, you will feel yourself almost in a new world. Farewell.

Yours very truly,
ROBERT SOUTHEY.

XIII.

TO ROBERT SOUTHEY.

BUCKLAND, *March* 16*th*, 1821.

The blank verse poem with which you encourage me to proceed has extended itself to twice the length of what you read; but the calm current of thought necessary to the continuance of such a subject has been violently broken in on with me this winter—first, by a very serious alarm (a fire which burst out after dark in my lonely little dwelling), and subsequently by a low fever, which unstrung my nerves and unfitted me for everything. During the last month I have amused myself by collecting and arranging various little tales and scraps composed within the last two years. These I am about to offer to Longman, and, if he will take them, shall be well satisfied with the transient interest and employment of thought the publication will afford me (a harmless interest, I hope, if not a wise one), without looking or hoping much further. Longman, however, may be of a very different opinion, and not choose to print solely with a view to my amusement.

You hold out to me a gilded bait—yet not so—a delightful hope I should call it—if I dared look on to next year, next summer. To visit you in your own world of lakes and mountains! to become really acquainted with you, with your family! How I should long for such pleasure, if I had not almost left off longing for anything, if I dared look forward beyond the springing up or flowering of the annuals I am now sowing in my little flower-garden. Sometimes, in a sunshiny mood of the mind, I say to myself, "Well, but who knows?—perhaps"—and then I stop, and the wide interval of time and distance spreads drearily before me, not impassably, however, and I *will* hope for once.

Is there any chance of your being in town this spring? I must be there *malgré, bon gré*, but have nothing agreeable in anticipation, except a sight of Haydon's picture. Surely you, who have half a hundred other works in the press, must have business in London.

Accept my grateful thanks, and believe me,

Very sincerely yours,

CAROLINE A. BOWLES.

XIV.

TO CAROLINE BOWLES.

KESWICK, *February 9th*, 1822.

Thank you for your little volume:* I received it yesterday evening. It was with pleasure that I saw it advertised, and with more pleasure that I saw it turn up among the contents of a heavy parcel. Have I perused it with pleasure? Both with as much pleasure and as much pain as you have wished to excite. And whether most to find fault with you for choosing such deeply tragic subjects, or to praise you for the manner in which you have treated them, I know not.

For the execution, it is not too much to say that you have become such a poetess as I believed and hoped from the first. You have the ear and the eye and the heart of poetry, and you have them in perfection. Had this volume appeared thirty years ago, England would have rung from side to side with its praises. And gay as the flower-market now is, take my word for it, it will flourish when all the annuals of the season have faded.

William and Jean would, to my judgment, have made two poems with advantage. The picture is like all your pictures— true and finely coloured by itself; but it is too cheerful, too happy, for the tale which follows. Your tragedy is always in the right tone, having with it the true and only balm. Yet it is too painful. I feel it to be so, and in this respect I may judge of others by myself. We are less able to bear these emotions as we advance in years. Youth courts them, because youth has happiness, as well as health and spirits, in excess. But at my time of life tranquillity is the treasure of the mind, and, if it must be broken, more willingly would I have it done

---

* "The Widow's Tale, and other Poems."

by comedy or farce, that makes the sides ache, than by anything which exacts a heartache for imaginary distress, especially with such possible and actual scenes as that of your Editha—perhaps the more painful to me because I have a daughter of that name.

Give us, I entreat you, a picture in summer and sunshine— a tale that in its progress and termination shall answer to the wishes of the reader. Make the creatures of your imagination as happy as you would make them if they were real beings, whose fortunes depended upon your will; your poem will then be read again and again with delight. You will please more readers, and please them more. It is a road to popular favour which has not been tried in this country, and it is a sure one. Goethe and Voss have found it so in Germany; and I speak sincerely when I express my belief that you can produce as fine a poem as the "Hermann and Dorothea," or the "Luise."

It is better for yourself, too, to dwell upon happier themes; you have no such exuberance of health and spirits that you can afford with impunity to shed so many tears as these poems must have cost you.

I must not forget to mention the "Sea of Life," which is throughout in a fine tone, both of feeling and versification. In p. 95, you should have written "*ignes fatui*"; but marsh-fires would be better, if the word marshes did not occur in the next line.

And now let me ask how you are? That you are in the sure way to reputation, and that of no mean degree or transitory kind, you must yourself know; and that feeling will encourage you in a forward pursuit. I think you are right in withholding your name. There is an advantage in exciting curiosity; and sometimes a comfort in privacy, which one is not sensible of till it is lost.

I shall send you my "Book of the Church" as soon as it is published. You will go with it in feeling, and find in it, I think, something that will interest you. But do not wait for it to let me hear from you, for it will not be ready in less than three or four months. I am fastened to my desk by many employments; but well both in myself and in my family (God be thanked), and no ways disturbed by such enemies as Lord Byron. God bless you.

Yours faithfully,
ROBERT SOUTHEY.

XV.

TO CAROLINE BOWLES.

KESWICK, July 7, 1822.

I have just received a letter from Bowles, in which he says: "You mention my namesake, Caroline. If you write, do make my warmest congratulations known to her. Have I read 'Ellen Fitzarthur'? There was only one copy in Bath; no one read a word of it; no one thought of buying it; no one spoke of it. I was the first in this neighbourhood to bring it into notice. I spoke to everyone with the utmost warmth of it, as deeply affecting in story, and beautiful in genuine language of poetry. I trumpeted it to Lord and Lady Lansdowne, Miss Fox, and all the *literati* of Bowood; and, without knowing the name, I flatter myself I contributed in some degeee to its more general notice among some distinguished ornaments of taste and literature. I should be happy to know Caroline, and more to think her a relation. I think a poem so remote from the golden-silvery-diamond-alabaster-Pontypool-style of the present Cockney race of dandy poetasters cannot be too much noticed; and I am rejoiced the real touches of nature and passion have awakened attention."

Thus far Bowles, and in a postscript he adds, "I think I shall write a note to Caroline, with my poem."

If authorship in its notoriety brings with it some evils, they are overpaid where there is desert by a large portion of good.

I owe to it not merely many pleasant acquaintances, but some valuable friends, and you will reap the same fruits. My question to Bowles was concerning your last volume, as well as "Ellen Fitzarthur"; if he has not seen it, he will look for it now, and he will find there all that he found in the former publication, and more. I have shown it to many persons, and in no one instance have I been disappointed of seeing it produce the effect which I expected.

I have a friend* with me now whom I have not seen since we parted at College, eight-and-twenty years ago, though our occasional communication by letter had never been interrupted. We parted just as we were commencing men, with the world before us; and we meet just at that time of life when age and decay are beginning to make themselves felt. You can better feel what the feelings of such a meeting are than I could express them. I should not have recognized him, so much is he changed: he says he should have known me anywhere. We have been comparing notes, and find our hearts and views just as much in unison as they were when we literally lived together at College; for we breakfasted together every morning, read together, and passed every evening together. In this respect I have been peculiarly fortunate, that most of my friendships have been formed for eternity, and grown stronger as they have grown older.

There is a very bad translation of "Hermann and Dorothea," by Holcroft, but it would show you the plan of the poem. The original, I am told, is a finished piece of versification; the translation is meant for blank verse, by a man who was no poet, and did not understand the common rules of metre.

You mention Shelley: I should like to show you some letters which passed between that wretched man and me about two years ago. He came to this place with his wife immediately after his marriage; I saw a good deal of him then, and

---

* Lightfoot.

hoped that he would outgrow the insane opinions which had their root, as I then thought, in mere ignorance, not in a corrupted heart and will. And I know a great deal of his accursed history since.

How are you? and what are you doing? I have been very much out of order. A cold, which comes regularly every year with the summer, and continues ten or twelve weeks, has this year attacked my chest; and, though materially better, I cannot yet say that it is fairly dislodged. I shall soon have a volume of the "Peninsular War" abroad; a noble story, which will set foul tongues railing, while it makes sound hearts throb with generous emotions. My "Book of the Church" will speedily follow it.

God bless you, sister-poetess. I have a right to call you so, though I cannot look for a relationship, like Bowles.

Yours truly,
ROBERT SOUTHEY.

XVI.

TO ROBERT SOUTHEY.

BUCKLAND, *July* 17*th*, 1822.

I was much gratified by the passage you were so good as to communicate to me from Mr. Bowles's letter. Could I fail to be so at such encomiums from one so gifted? But the kindness of heart which impelled you to impart so promptly what you knew would give pleasure, *that* I felt most sensibly, for in truth I need it most.

The volume you half announced to me arrived shortly after your letter. I write by to-day's post to thank the author for his valuable and valued gift; but I have charged him with the fact of rejecting me as a kinswoman in days of yore, when I—

an aspiring little damsel—was fain to claim relationship with the author of the "Sonnets."

Even as I wrote that jesting reproach, the thought came to my mind, "How different a creature I might have been, of how much better things I might have been capable, had my earlier path in life been gilded with that degree of encouragement which now falls upon me—now, when my days on earth seem so nearly numbered." Yes, I have been very ill, with repeated attacks in the head, each succeeding one increasing in seriousness and continuance, and yielding only to such violent remedies as shake almost to dissolution the fragile frame, at least, seemingly not built up for duration. This affection of the head is, I am told, more symptomatic of general debility, and consequent derangement of the nervous system, than in itself a primary complaint; but it is not on that account the less terrible to endure. I had almost said it is worse than pain; but that would be a thankless, a presumptuous assertion, when He who knoweth best what is best for me is pleased to exempt me from severe suffering. It is an almost total loss of memory, a confusion of ideas, a deprivation of all comprehensive power, with such a darkness of spirit as would, indeed, "turn my day into night," were it not for the one heavenly ray that pierceth all darkness. All this comes upon me, accompanied by an apprehensive weight and giddiness that, while it lasts, incapacitates me for all mental and bodily exertion, and the least attempt at the latter so accelerates the pulsation of the heart as to make every throb dreadfully distressing. So long an answer must I give to your simple question, "How are you?"

It is scarce necessary, in reply to your other question, to add, that I am about nothing. When the dark hour is on me, I can hardly see, hear, or understand; when it passes away, for a few days, a week, or fortnight, I enjoy the mere feeling of unopprest existence so exquisitely, that freely to breathe the blessed air, steadily to gaze on the fleet clouds and waving branches, to tread firmly on the earth, to comprehend what I read and hear, is enough for me, and I am too happy to be a very idler. And then I dare not look forward to better things, lest the anticipation of evil to come should follow in the train of thought, and cloud my little moment of sunshine. I have but too much reason for sad anticipation. My father I recollect to have been affected as I am. I recollect the dreadful intervals of gloom that came upon him, lasting for weeks, for months, and finally terminating in fits that wore away his mental power, and left only the bodily wreck to be dissolved by a paralytic seizure. I recollect, too, how often he used to look mournfully on me (always a little nervous, delicate creature), and say "My poor child, you resemble me too much in all things." When those words were spoken, I wondered at them; now they are but too intelligible to me. It is a pitiable weakness, I feel, to reveal to you so gloomy a picture; but in doing so I relieve a very heavy heart, and yours is not one that will turn away in contempt and weariness from the sorrow and infirmities of poor human nature. Now and then, during a sunny interval (and, thank God, the natural brightness of my spirit still shines out at such times), I compose a few scraps of verse or prose, most of which remain incomplete, and a few find their way to Blackwood—all idle nothings. If I should live and get better, ——; but God's will be done!

I wish (what signifies a hundred or two more miles when one sets about wishing) that there were a chance of your revisiting Hampshire. I should have a neat, quiet chamber at your service and Mrs. Southey's—a homely but most sincere welcome—and you are not a person to think scorn of such things. I do not like to think we shall meet no more in this world.

God bless you in your health, in your family, in your undertakings. Claim kindred with me as you will, I will gratefully admit the title.

Ever yours truly,
Caroline A. Bowles.

Do you know (how should you) that in a *soi disant* literary circle poor "Ellen Fitzarthur" has been claimed by a gentleman as "the work of his particular friend Mrs. Hayman"? He was "authorized to say so." Much good may it do them. I never saw this man, who writes, I believe, for some periodical work, and was joint editor of one; but I suspect I offended him once by declining the honour of his proffered acquaintance. He does me too much honour now. Shall you contribute to Joanna Baillie's projected miscellany? I popped upon you the other day unexpectedly in a volume of Hogg's works.

XVII.

TO ROBERT SOUTHEY.

BUCKLAND, *August* 6*th*, 1822.

I have just finished the first volume of a very mischievous book, which, however, as far as I can judge, carries its own antidote along with it. I allude to O'Meara's "Voice from St. Helena." Were I a worshipper of Buonaparte, bitterly should I accuse the rashness which has torn away the veil from that gigantic idol, and exposed the inherent weakness of its composition. Present and future generations must call Napoleon an extraordinary man; but will any rational creature, after reading O'Meara's book, affirm that he is a great one? The downfall of his huge fabric of ambition, the destruction of his armies, the loss of empire, all seem to have affected him but in a trifling degree, in comparison with the restraints and inconveniences incident to his captive state. He would have preferred, one could almost persuade oneself, one petty triumph over Sir Hudson Lowe to a victory over the Duke of Wellington and all the armies of Europe. But that Sir Hudson!—he was a true gaoler—something, in truth, of a "Sbirro Siciliano," harassed and teased to death, no doubt, by the humours and intrigues of the Longwood captive and his motley court; but still he had no command over his own temper, and seems, indeed, to have been wanting to himself as a gentleman and an officer. Buonaparte, in one of his conversations with O'Meara, endeavours to refute one of the stories which had gone abroad of him in his early youth— the seduction and poisoning of a young girl, while he was a student in his first *pension*. I am well acquainted with a French officer, a Baron de Gomer, who was a fellow-student of Napoleon's at the same college, and remembers every particular of that horrible affair, in which the young Corsican was as guilty as he is said to have been. First, before that flagitious act, he had committed one less glaringly atrocious, indeed, but equally indicative of a cold and callous nature. He had no friend at college but a dog, who shared his meals and his bed, and on whom all the human kindness of his nature seemed to expend itself. This dog stole one day a piece of cake which Napoleon had laid aside for a future regale. He caught the animal in the act, but did not even disturb his proceedings, nor further notice the step than by saying, *Ah ha, mon ami, tu me paiera cela*. Young De Gomer, with some others of his comrades, saw the transaction, and wondered at Napoleon's indifference, but were almost *transis d'horreur*, when, on passing through the courts the next morning, they found the poor dog tied up, still living, against a tree, and Napoleon very deliberately employed in flaying off his skin. On seeing their horror and astonishment, he only smilingly observed, *J'ai bien dit qu'il me le paierait*. The person who told me these anecdotes is a man of unimpeachable veracity.

Very truly yours,

Caroline A. Bowles.

XVIII.

TO ROBERT SOUTHEY.

BUCKLAND, *October* 18*th*, 1823.

The first feeling that with me, and with most persons, I should think, succeeds the painful one of parting from a friend is an impatient inclination to write to him, and if I had obeyed that impulse you would have heard from me from Ambleside. But sometimes (not always) sober afterthought restrains these foolish impulses of mine, and so you were deprived of the very interesting information that I was sitting all forlorn in a dull inn room, regretting Keswick with all my heart, and prevented by an incessant pouring rain from exploring, as I had hoped, some of the lovely scenery about Rydal and Grasmere. Nay, so pensive is my temper, every hour which diminished my chance of visiting Rydal Mount increased my inclination to deliver there the ticket with which you had provided me, though the evening before I had felt as if such daring would be utterly impossible. Just as we reached Rydal that evening, Mr. Wordsworth himself, and all his family I believe, came to meet the coach, and waited long beside it, while some parcel they were in expectation of was searched for, during all which time I very wisely shrunk back in my corner, instead of bowing to Mr. Wordsworth, as I ought to have done, having been introduced to him in your house. Hoping, hoping, hour after hour, that the sun might shine upon me for a brief interval, I stayed on at the inn till Saturday evening, and then, yielding to my fate, came on to Kendal. It was growing dusk when I left Ambleside, and just as I lost sight of its grey walls and roofs, when the black ridges of the mountains (the gates of your Eden) seemed closing upon me, very vivid flashes of lightning streamed up from behind them, succeeded by some loud thunder-claps. At Keswick you know I had been longing to hear the sound of thunder amongst the mountains;

but on leaving your happy valleys I almost fancied "Come no more" was audible to me in those solemn reverberations.

My homeward journey was safe, and as little disagreeable as possible, considering the circumstance of finding no coach ready to start for Leeds obliged me once more to traverse the country of the "Yahoos," and to rest in their unholy habitations. Tuesday night brought me safe to beautiful Oxford; and on Wednesday evening I stepped once more over the threshold of my quiet little home, and was welcomed by my dear old nurse, with such a welcome as those only can bestow to whom we are objects of exclusive affection.

Dog, cats, and poney, all in their several fashions, testified great joy at sight of me, and my old woman half insinuated that the very flowers—some of them—had put off blowing till my return. I got over the fatigue of the journey marvellously, considering that, from the time I left Keswick till last night, I never obtained one hour's quiet sleep, such a wakeful restless spirit sometimes possesses me. Till to-day I have been unable to reach the town and bank, consequently, to forward to you one half of the note for the loan of which I am indebted to your kind consideration. It did me good service, for part of my travelling exchequer was in old-fashioned guineas, and the people at the inns, &c., demurred about their weight and value, while your Bank of England was a *passe partout*. The note I expected at Keswick has not been forwarded thither, so, according to your direction, I forward the first payment of my debt, much rejoicing that your acknowledgement of it (which I am to await before I transmit the other half) will insure me the pleasure of soon hearing from you.

I have been amongst you to-day, enjoying with redoubled zest what I once thought nothing could increase my delight in—the introduction to your "Poet's Pilgrimage." How often I shall be in spirit in the midst of you, and revisiting with you some of those enchanting spots to which you were my conductor. To each and every member of your happy circle I send greeting warm and grateful; in particular, pray offer my best regards and thanks to Mrs. Southey. Tell Cuthbert my peerless Donna sends health to the magnificent Rumpel—"that terrible cat with the terrible name," far more unpronouncable than Tchitchigoff.

Pray convey a few more remembrances from me—to the Ladies of the Lakes, if they are still sojourning amongst you. Amongst a thousand things I should like to learn of you—alas! unteachable things—is the art of saying much in few words; but I suppose a woman's ink is like her volubility—

"A stream that murmuring flows, and flows for ever."

Hardly a drop of rain have I seen since I left Westmoreland. I had almost said "how provoking." Selfish creature that I am—not dissatisfied, however,—for I saw and enjoyed much, very much; and had I not done so, to have become acquainted with your family, and more thoroughly with yourself, would have made me ample amends; may I not say, to have acquired the privilege of calling you friend?

Most gratefully and truly yours,

CAROLINE A. BOWLES.

How much I am surprised and mortified at that intemperate and unfair letter addressed to you in *The London* by my old favourite Elia! I little suspected such gall and wormwood entered into the composition of one whose gentle nature seemed to me so greatly to assimilate with that of Izaac Walton. But his anger is intemperate, because it is causeless; and I can almost see that in his heart he is ashamed of the pair whose cause he espouses so warmly.

XIX.

TO CAROLINE BOWLES.

KESWICK, *October 22nd*, 1823.

Thank you for following my directions in halving the note; I shall gain by it another letter; and yet the advice was given in sober prudence, and not with that selfish purpose. I am heartily glad that you have reached home safely, and with so few disagreeables on the way, that the fear of such a journey will not stand in the way of your repeating it; for I will not believe that you have taken leave of these mountains for ever. You must not talk of sunset pleasures yet. Your evening is far distant; and many such pleasures as this country can afford (they are not light ones) are in store, I hope, both for you and for me. If you are half as desirous of partaking them again as I am that you should do so, the difficulties in the way will only be thought of with the view of overcoming them. Whatever we may think of dreams, you will allow that day-dreams may have some truth in them, and you have borne no small part in mine since your departure. These at least may bring about their accomplishment.

On the day you reached Oxford we effected our Watenlath excursion. Go whither I will among these lakes and mountains, I have more ghosts than Sir Thomas More to accompany me; there is scarcely a spot but brings with it some indelible recollection of those whom I have loved and lost. But the predominant feeling on this day was regret that you were not with us. Since then I have been close at work, preparing for my departure, and yet, after all, I must take with me work to finish at Streatham. We set out on Monday, November 3rd. Edith and I shall leave the Ladies of the Island at Derby, and go to Sir George Beaumont's, at Cole-Orton, near Ashby-de-la-Zouch, for two or three days: probably we shall reach London on the 15th. From thence you shall hear of my movements. I have a wide way to travel, and the sunniest spot in the prospect is the New Forest.

Lamb's letter I have not seen, and your account of it is the first intimation which I have received of its temper. It will not disturb mine. I am sorry that he should have acted thus rashly and unreasonably; but no infirmity of mind on his part shall make me act or feel unkindly towards one whose sterling goodness I respect as much as I admire his genius. If the matter of the letter requires answer or explanation from me, I shall probably give it at the end of the *Quarterly Review*, as the writer of the article. Anything personal, if I notice it at all, I shall notice privately by letter. You can hardly imagine how inirritable I am to any attacks through the press. When I have taken occasion to handle Jeffrey, or found it necessary to take up the pen against Lord Byron, it has been more with a feeling of strength than of anger, something like Rumpelstilzchen feels when he lays his paw upon a rat.

Cuthbert desires me to tell you that that worthy cat (who has recently been created a marquis) is very well, only that he has a little cough; and, moreover, that he has shown an improper liking for cream cheese. There is a rival of his, an interloper named Hurleburlebuss, who prowls about the house, and we are sometimes awakened by their nightly encounters.

I am charged also to send Rumpel's love to Donna, and Cuthbert's to you. There are remembrances, moreover, from each and all of my womankind, with all of whom you have left such an impression as you would desire to leave. For myself—but I must have done, for time presses, and the maid is waiting for my dispatches.

At present, therefore, I will say no more than,

Dear friend, farewell.

ROBERT SOUTHEY.

XX.

TO ROBERT SOUTHEY.

BUCKLAND, *October* 27*th*, 1823.

I have had a rude welcome home. The very night after I wrote to you my little lonely dwelling was beset by a complete gang of thieves, whose attack was, however, fortunately confined to the out-premises; there they made unsparing havoc, tearing down and taking away (in a cart brought for the purpose) everything at all portable—harness, tools, lead-work, &c., and what they could not carry off they broke or cut to pieces. So well aware were these depredators of the weakness of the garrison, that they by no means constrained themselves to do their work in silence; for, about 12 o'clock, I distinctly heard many voices of persons round the house. Like a fool, however, I lay still and went to sleep, instead of giving the alarm to my old German, the report of whose musket out of window might have scared away the robbers; but I am so accustomed to hear the nocturnal disturbances occasioned by smugglers and poachers, and have so often needlessly awakened the family, that this once the wolf came and robbed my fold in good earnest.

This is not to me the worst part of the disaster, though my loss so far is not inconsiderable; but the whole neighbourhood, having been lately kept in a state of alarm from the depredations of this gang, and just fears being entertained that as winter drew on they would not stop at out-door robbery, the police set to work in the present case with such prompt activity as to ferret out four of the ringleaders, one only of whom, however, they succeeded in securing, with just enough of my property in his possession to fix on me the necessity of prosecution, and that for a capital offence, they having broken open doors and windows. So one man is sent to Winchester, to take his trial at the assizes in March, and they hope to secure another.

I am obliged to submit to all this with what appetite I may, having no option allowed me in the case, and, if I had, could not, I suppose, on any warrantable grounds, decline prosecuting these public pests; but I heartily wish the duty had fallen on shoulders better fitted to the burthen. The expense, you may suppose, I do not much relish—neither have I any particular fancy for hanging people; but my scruples on that head are obviated by the assurance of the magistrates that the punishment in such a case as this is sure to be commuted for transportation for life, a penance I have no manner of objection to inflict.

I am kindly comforted on all hands with hints that I may expect divers malicious and revengeful acts from those of the gang still at liberty, and whom there is not proof sufficient to lay hold of. Maiming of cattle, house-breaking, house-firing—all these pleasant anticipations are tenderly murmured in my ear, but happily produce in me the very reverse effect to what might be expected; for, in the first place, I think myself in no manner of danger, and have not allowed myself to be frightened out of an hour's sleep; and, in the next, am spirited up to defend myself bravely, and, like a good general, have already put my fortress in proper state to withstand a siege.

First, by way of warning, I have stuck up a huge, frightful engine y-clept a man-trap (*not set at night*, but you are not to blab that secret); then I have bought a great fierce bull-dog; have provided my German with a blunderbuss, powder, and shot, and myself with a pair of pistols, with which I dare make a noise at least; for you know I told you my father had taught me to stand fire, and the report (soon spread) that one has such weapons, and dare use them, is almost as effective as an armed sentinel at one's door. Now dare you trust yourself in "my little lonely tower"? But you dare not draw back, indeed; you have too much chivalric spirit about you; and I will not let you off—no, nor part with you a day, nor an hour, nor a minute sooner than that you say must be the last.

I wish you would bring some of your work to do here as well as at Streatham; then you might afford to stay longer, and yet lose no time; and for quiet, you shall have a little study so still it might answer for the cell of silence; and for hours!—they shall be at your own disposal, as in your own home; so come and work here.

God speed you on your way, you and your companion, and protect those you leave behind you. Remember me to them all—all, not forgetting Cuthbert. I should think extract of mouse would be the best thing for Rumplestilzchen's cough, though perhaps instinct pointed out cream cheese as the most effectual remedy, a sort of *pâté de Guimauve*.

Farewell for a season, dear and kind friend of mine. I shall await your next letter impatiently.

CAROLINE A. BOWLES.

From a certain hint at the end of Lamb's letter, I half suspect that, in your schoolboy days, you were a party concerned in some outrage on Sir Cloudesly Shovel's nose in Westminster Abbey.

XXI.

TO CAROLINE BOWLES.

KESWICK, *November 2nd*, 1823.

I once declared in a poem that I never put out the eye of a Cyclops; and I now declare with equal sincerity that I never offered any outrage to the nose of Sir Cloudesly Shovel.

You have a good heart, and it stands you in good stead: would that some of my family had a portion of your courage! But the truth is, that your Job's comforters are as unwise in entertaining their fears as they are in communicating them. There is danger in acting against smugglers and poachers, because smugglers and poachers think they have natural justice on their side, and have some show of reason for thinking so;

they therefore think themselves aggrieved when they are prosecuted for their illicit practices, and feel as if they had a right to revenge themselves upon anyone who has taken part against them. But this is not the case with those who have committed a breach of the moral law; they are self-convicted of a known sin; and here in England not even a Bow-street officer has ever suffered the slightest injury from after-revenge, though sometimes very serious ones in the discharge of their duty. You may therefore sleep in peace.

Perhaps it would lessen in some little degree the unpleasantness of your appearance at Winchester if you had any acquaintance there; and I can very well introduce you to Mrs. Hill's sisters, who reside in that city. But I shall see you before that time; and persuade you, I hope, not only almost, but wholly, that there are yet hopes and enjoyments in store for you in this world.

This has remained unfinished till the last minute. It is now Sunday night, my table sadly disfurnished, everything packed, and my last despatches on the wing. God bless you.

Yours affectionately,

ROBERT SOUTHEY.

XXII.

TO CAROLINE BOWLES.

KIRKBY LONSDALE, *November 4th*, 1823.

We left home yesterday, and are now at Kirkby Lonsdale, waiting for weather that may allow us to see the Caves; for, from the time of our departure till this moment it has not ceased raining. The same ill fortune which persecuted you at Ambleside seems fated to attend us. The females, however, are company for each other; they have taken out their work;

and the opportunity is favourable for performing a part of mine, which is to ask you whether one of those day-dreams to which you have given birth (a very delightful one to me it is) shall come to pass?

I have put up among my papers the memoranda which were made many years ago for a poem upon Robin Hood. They are easily shaped into a regular plan, and, in my judgment, a promising one. Will you form an intellectual union with me that it may be executed? We will keep our own secret as well as Sir Walter Scott has done. Murray shall publish it, and not know the whole mystery that he may make the more of it, and the result will be means in abundance for a summer's abode at Keswick, and an additional motive for it that we may form other schemes of the same nature. Am I dreaming when I think that we may derive from this much high enjoyment, and that you may see in the prospect something which is worth living for? The secret itself would be delightful while we thought proper to keep it; still more so the spiritual union which death would not part.

Now on your side there must be no hesitation from diffidence. You can write as easily and as well as I can plan. You are as well acquainted with forest scenery, and with whatever is required for the landscape part, as I am with the manners of the time. You will comprehend the characters as distinctly as I have conceived them; when we meet we will sort the parts so as each to take the most suitable, and I will add to yours, and you to mine, whatever may improve it. Beaumont and Fletcher composed plays together with such harmony of style, thought, and feeling that no critic has ever been able to determine what parts were written by one and what by the other. Why should not R. S. and C. A. B. succeed as happily in the joint execution of a poem?

As there can be no just cause or impediment why these two persons should not be thus joined together, tell me that you consent to the union, and I will send you the rude outline of the story and of the characters. Direct to me at Sir G. Beaumont's, Bart., Cole-Orton Hall, Ashby-de-la-Zouch, where

I expect to arrive on Monday next, and to remain till the Friday.

Dear friend, God bless you,

ROBERT SOUTHEY.

XXIII.

TO ROBERT SOUTHEY.

BUCKLAND, *November 9th*, 1823.

How you have set me thinking! Thinking, wondering, wishing, debating, doubting, almost—yes, almost—despairing. What! I associated with you in any literary undertaking! I have dreamt often enough, and strangely enough, heaven knows, and have been (what I thought) daring in my dreams; but never in their very wildest flight glanced at such a possibility as you now point out to me. For a moment let me contemplate the possibility of such a scheme. That would be something worth living for, and rather would I be associated therein —yea, contribute thereto the very humblest, meanest portions, the very commas and semicolons, thereby cementing that undying intellectual union you speak of—than be the authoress, the sole authoress, of such a work as "Thalaba." I can find no language to express more warmly how, with heart and soul, I would say "Yes"—promptly and eagerly, "Yes"—to your tempting, tantalizing proposition, *if* only—that odious monosyllable! You know well enough all it implies. You must know, if you consider by the cold, clear light of reason alone, unmingled with the warm, illusive emanations from that kind heart of yours, which (in its zeal to make me in love with life) has conjured up all this beautiful fabric. But let it stand awhile; I have not the heart to demolish it with one resolute word. And "what if I were to try," whispers the longing spirit within me; "I could but fail at last, and there would be no harm done, and the friend who has conceived all this so delightfully would not withdraw his regard, nor think more meanly of me as a friend in the best sense of the word, because I fall on trial so immeasurably below him in the scale of intellectual worth." So whispers The Voice. Is it that of a friendly or foolish spirit? Answer my question by sending or not sending the outline you speak of. Nobody can detect the dovetailing of Beaumont and Fletcher's works: true; but their intellectual powers were matched as well as paired. Here the case is far otherwise. In *feeling*, I think, I believe (not surely in self-conceit) that I may go along with you; but when I would express those feelings, even in familiar conversation, I feel myself hemmed in like a salamander in his glowing circle—baffled, obstructed, repelled, in every quarter.

Moreover, you know I have told you I cannot write; I cannot sit down to compose; that would effectually *dis*compose my scanty stock of ideas. How am I ever, then, to coalesce in any regular consistent work of composition? Can you solve this difficulty? I know you can work wonders, and are more than half a magician; so speak over me (if within the compass of your art) words of such power as may make me what you say I can be. In short, your "day-dreams" are so enchanting, I must try to share in them a little while, at the risk, the almost certainty, of awaking at last to a blank and mortifying reality. When you are here (good angels speed you hither!) you will perceive my residence is far removed from real forest scenery, and, consequently, I am by no means so familiar with its local characteristics, as you suppose me to be; and then I believe our forest differs greatly, in almost every feature, from that of "Merry Sherwood." But I should never have done were I to go on enumerating the obstacles I perceive in my way. Would that genius and power were contagious qualities, I should have returned from Keswick rich in both!

Farewell, and God bless you, dear friend,

CAROLINE A. BOWLES.

XXIV.

TO CAROLINE BOWLES.

STREATHAM, *November* 19*th*, 1823.

I should feel more uneasy than I have done under the impossibility of replying sooner to your last most welcome letter, if I had not commissioned Dame Elizabeth (so named when we lay side by side in the boat of the Peak Cavern, like two figures on an old monument) to tell you I would write on the first possible opportunity. The endless round of occupations and engagements in which I am involved in London you can hardly conceive; they are such as literally not to leave me an interval of rest. Yesterday I got to this quiet Rectory, after a most fatiguing morning. To-day I have, as a matter not to be delayed, written a short letter to Charles Lamb, which can hardly fail of making him heartily sorry for what he has done; and if he can forgive himself as easily as I forgive him, we shall meet again upon our old terms. This done, I set out with you for the forest of merry Sherwood.

A tale of Robin Hood might without impropriety be as little regular in its structure as he was in his way of life. I think a striking introduction might be made by the funeral of his mother (dying in child-bed of him), the immediate departure of the Earl, his father, to the Crusades, and the delivery of the infant to a kinsman, Sir Ranulph, as guardian, and the parental care of Father Hugh, the Earl's foster-brother. Twelve years may be allowed to elapse, during which the boy has grown wild, his guardian being always engaged in political turmoils, and the Priest an indulgent man. The Earl's heart is then brought home from the Holy Land, to be deposited in the same grave with his wife. And then an interval of seven or eight years more, when the proper story of the poem commences, with a service for the souls of the Earl and his wife. After the service Father Hugh takes the opportunity of mildly lecturing the young Earl Robert for his propensities to forest sports and inferior company, and his utter neglect of knightly accomplishments—it having previously been shown that this had arisen from his guardian's constant absence and entire neglect. It appears now that Ranulph's intention is to bring about a marriage between Robert and his only child, Aveline; but Aveline has already given her heart to Gilbert with the white hand, a squire of low degree, and Robin, as his comrades have from childhood called him, declares his determination never to marry anybody but Maid Marian, the miller's daughter. Marian is a skylark, and Aveline a turtle dove; Gilbert of a gentle, poetical disposition, and yet Robin and he are bosom friends.

Ranulph arrives to effect the marriage, and in his anger at a refusal which disappoints the plan of securing the estates for his own family, sends off Marian (as a villain's daughter) to be forcibly married, and commits Aveline to the custody of a severe lady abbess. Robin collects his comrades, rescues his own love first, then storms the nunnery, carries off Aveline for Gilbert, and away they go to the forest.

Then for a rich pastoral book, describing the life of the outlaws. Ranulph is now one of John's favourites, and on the watch to arrest and make away with King Richard on his return from captivity. The story is to be wound up by Robin Hood's delivering Cœur de Lion from this danger, being reinstated in his rank, &c., but resigning them all to Gilbert and Aveline, and choosing to pass his days always as the king of the forest. It will be easy enough to make out this part of the fable, which, indeed, will shape itself while the rest is in progress. How like you this, my friend and partner dear? Are there not rich capabilities to be dreamt of now—to be talked of soon—and then to be realized?

But I must conclude, not to lose the post; and for the same reason must do without a frank. You may direct to me, under cover, to John Rickman, Esq., New Palace Yard. Only one word more. I *hope* I have put your books in the way of being reviewed in the *Quarterly*.

God bless you,

Yours affectionately,

ROBERT SOUTHEY.

I cannot tell you when I can move westward yet. Tell you me what coaches pass near you from the westward.

XXV.

TO ROBERT SOUTHEY.

BUCKLAND, *January* 24, 1824.

Your parcel never reached me till last night, long after our post-hour. To-day is Saturday—no London post; but I *must write* to-day. I must thank you, scold you—say something of what my heart is very full of, and which it would be great penance for me to keep quite in another whole day. You have made me very rich, and very grateful, and very angry. Your Poetical Works given by you, an inestimable treasure to me, and so they would have been in their plain suit of boards; and you should not have lavished on me that elegant binding, which I am determined not to let you know I think beautiful. With a few strokes of your pen you have made one volume more valuable to me than the whole art of binding could have rendered it. But you have been very niggardly in that respect: you might verily have enriched each set, at least, with the same talisman. You will laugh when I say I never open a book so inscribed without looking at the writing: this is among many odd fancies of mine.

I seized eagerly on the Minor Poems. Strangely enough,

the volume I took up opened at a page where the first words that met my eye were—

> "I am no sworn friend
> Of half-an-hour, as apt to leave as love:
> Mine are no mushroom feelings, which spring up
> At once without a seed, and take no root."

That sounded pleasantly to me, though I have not (I wish I had) the claims of "Cousin Margaret."

I have been at work trying that metre of "Thalaba," and fine work I make of it! It is to me just like attempting to drive a tilbury in a tram-road. I keep quartering, or trying to quarter, for a yard or so, and then down goes the wheel into the old groove. I cannot keep out of blank verse. When I have written off a few lines, pretty fairly as to look, on reading them aloud, lo! they are neither more nor less than a scrap of blank verse, snipt into longs and shorts; and if I force myself out of this track, then do I invent such horrible discord that the sound stops me short, as a false note from the orchestra stops one in the middle of a dance. You would laugh to see me in the agony of composition.

The magistrates of Guernsey have given notice to our magistrates that they have secured the runaway ringleader of the gang that robbed me, and two constables are gone over to fetch the gentleman, and convoy him here and then to Winchester, all at my cost; but our senators leave me no option.

God bless you, dear friend, and keep you safe and patient in "Vanity Town," and send you safe out of it, in which wish you will join me heartily.

Be so good, the first time you write to me, as to tell me (for the information of a person who wishes to possess a bust of you) where those are to be bought, such as I saw at your house and at General Peachey's, and of what those are composed. I rather suspect they were only made to order, and that others are no longer to be purchased. Once more, farewell.

Yours gratefully and affectionately,
CAROLINE A. BOWLES.

XXVI.

TO CAROLINE BOWLES.

NORWICH, *January 27th*, 1824.

Till now I have not had five minutes during which I could quietly put pen to paper since we parted. I breakfasted in the Close at Winchester on the morning after, saw the cathedral and the college, found room in the coach at noon, and reached London at night. The next day I secured places in the Norwich mail for Friday evening, and dined among "strange women," at Lady Malet's—a situation something worse than Daniel in the lions' den. Your note on the travelling frank reached me before I left town, and after a parcel had been sent off, which I hope reached you without mishap, though with no better packing than my hands (awkward at such work) could give it. You have there all my poems which have as yet been printed in that form. How many more such volumes may be added to them depends as much upon you as on myself. Many I hope and trust, very many, to your benefit and mine, to our mutual delight, to our lasting remembrance.

We arrived here safely on Saturday morning; Sunday I heard Neville* officiate in a little village church of which he is curate. One of his brother's hymns was sung there, and I dined at his mother's, where her whole family were assembled, with the father and mother of Neville's wife. Ten years ago, when he had no prospect of marriage, I volunteered to be godfather to his first son; and very obligingly the son made his entrance a month ago, and is this day to be christened Henry Kirke.

I do not believe that any act of kindness was ever so largely overpaid as that has been which I rendered to the Whites. It has been of far greater consequence to them than I could possibly have dreamt of; but their gratitude has more than

---

* Neville White, brother of Henry Kirke White.

kept pace with the benefit which they have received. And when I think that to the publication of Henry's "Remains" I am indebted for my knowledge of you,* I certainly look upon it as one of the most fortunate events of my life, and perhaps one of the most influential. If as a poet I am to have a second spring (there is still sap enough in the trunk—enough life in the root), to this it must be owing.

But the christening guests are come, and I must hasten to say two things—first, that you may introduce a few songs with good effect; and secondly, that I have promised to ask you for a devotional poem, as an act of charity to a poor music master here, now four years a helpless paralytic, for whom poets are willing to write, and composers to set the strains, and to whom I have promised something from myself and something from you, from whom I might venture to promise.

One thing more—do not forget that I wish, earnestly wish, to pay what tribute I can to Paul Burrard's memory.† Send me such notice of him as you may have heart to give. I will do my best.

And now, dear friend, dear Caroline, farewell. Let me have a letter from you in Queen Ann Street, where I hope to arrive on Thursday the 5th. Edith's love.

God bless you.

ROBERT SOUTHEY.

---

* Encouraged by the knowledge of his kind reception of H. K. White's Poems, Miss Bowles had sent to Southey her MS.

† See Southey's Poetical Works: "Inscriptions," "To the Memory of Paul Burrard." Paul Burrard was cousin of Caroline Bowles, who furnished Southey with some memorials of the heroic young man.

XXVII.

TO CAROLINE BOWLES.

LONDON, *February* 13*th*, 1824.

A few hurried lines in the midst of all the joy, dirt and discomfort of packing, hammering, cording, &c.

Thank you for the purse, though it was a dangerous inclosure, and might have been (perhaps ought to have been) stabbed at the Post Office, as coming from a part of the coast noted for smuggling. Remember that Rickman's frank will not cover more than two ounces.

Thank you also for both your little poems: the sea one I think will suit the poor petitioner's purpose well. The other is one of the most striking and original I ever met with in any language, and so it has been felt to be by the few persons to whom I have shown it.* There is a single line which needs alteration—

"O'er him he loved—that livid clay."

I wish I could see how to alter it. But I will examine the whole, and see whether in any word it can be improved, for be assured that little piece will take its place with Gray's " Elegy " and Herbert Knowles's.

So little rest have I had since I left you that my portfolio goes home full of unanswered letters. I will write with my first leisure to you about the irregular blank verse. You have only to unlearn the common tune, and then follow your ear, taking mere convenience for your guide, except where the subject brings with it, as it often will do, its own measure. Break yourself of the common tune by practising in six-syllable lines, and in eight-syllable ones.

Mary Wollstonecraft I had never seen when those lines to her were written. I saw her afterwards, twice or thrice,

---

* The poem spoken of is "It is not Death": *Solitary Hours*, pp. 57–59.

and dined once at her house: she was a delightful woman, and in better times, or in better hands would have been an excellent one. But her lot had fallen in evil days and the men to whom she attached herself were utterly unworthy of her. You shall see one of these days what I say of that tempestuous age; few persons but those who have lived in it can conceive or comprehend what the memory of the French Revolution was, nor what a visionary world seemed to open upon those who were just entering it. Old things seemed passing away, and nothing was dreamt of but the regeneration of the human race.

You asked about my bust. Smith in Upper Norton-street has the mould, and casts may always be had there.

I have no time for more. Sunday, thank God, I shall be at home, and, if I find all well, shall be truly happy. Yet I depart with a heavier feeling than I ever took from London before, for it is not likely that I shall ever see my uncle again. He is very infirm, more so than might have been expected at seventy-four. Last night I went to assist him into his carriage, and before he had driven off, or I had re-entered the door, some men passed between us bearing a coffin. Mere accident as it was, I wish it had not occurred, for it must have affected him as it did me. Edith's love.

God bless you, dear friend.
ROBERT SOUTHEY.

XXVIII.

TO CAROLINE BOWLES.

KESWICK, *February 24th*, 1824.

Since I returned I have been replying to the heap of letters, which as they followed me about were laid aside till a more convenient season. You will easily understand that such letters are meant as had no right to more ceremonious treatment.

I have been unpacking, arranging, and idling over the long

looked for box of books from Italy, and a parcel of some forty volumes which I dispatched from Norwich.

I have been enjoying an old coat, and old shoes; habits so regular that the clock might be regulated by them—my usual breakfast, my usual hours, my after-dinner sleep; the conciousness of being at rest—in a word, home after a long absence. All things are now resuming their old course. The children come to me regularly with their lessons, and I go down to supper with a folio under my arm, to be taken with the black currant rum, as a composer. Rumpelstilzchen arches his back to meet my salutation in the kitchen, and Hurlyburlybuss greets me with the like demonstration of good will in the garden. Proof-sheets are the only things wanting to my contentment, and I shall not be long without them.

I had been absent fifteen weeks wanting one day. To say nothing of the arrears of business which so long an interruption occasions, there were heavy arrears of sleep; and if on the former score I am debtor, here I am on the creditor side of the account. By a fair calculation, not less than three hundred and forty-five hours of good honest sleep were due to me when I reached home, at the rate of three hours lost in every twenty-four, besides six nights passed in stage coaches. Such arrears are like the national debt—too large to be paid off; and having taken out a small part, I am making a magnanimous resolution to cancel the remainder of the debt, and rise as early as I did in London. The produce of this time before breakfast will find its way to Buckland, and before you receive this letter I shall have made a beginning.

There can be no more difficulty in your writing the verse of Thalaba than there is in an expert dancer's acquiring a new step. The simple rule is to consult the ear alone, and when you use lines of less than ten syllables, let the pause generally be at the end of the line.

I sent your sea-poem to the poor musician at Norwich. The other and the finer of the two is not so appropriate to his purpose, and is, moreover, too good to be so bestowed. My admiration of it is nothing abated by frequent re-reading and re-considering it. The feeling and the movement are in beautiful accord, and the expression is everywhere excellent, except in the stanza respecting Lazarus. The poem, if it were set to music with a thousandth part of the feeling that it breathes, could not fail of doing good. What are Shield's merits as a composer? He is the only musician whom I know, but whether he has any merit or not in his profession is what others must tell me, for I am utterly ignorant upon that subject. If, however, you think well of him, he I know would think himself obliged to me if I sent him the poem.

I hope to do a great deal this year, and among other things to complete the series of "Inscriptions;" the sooner they are published the better, because every year lessens the number of those persons who would be gratified by seeing this tribute paid to their lost friends.

God bless you.

Robert Southey.

XXIX.

TO CAROLINE BOWLES.

Keswick, *Saturday, February 28th*, 1824.

I told you before you received my letter I should have returned to my old habit of writing verses before breakfast (at which time nine-tenths at least of "Thalaba," "Madoc," "Kehama," and "Roderick" were written). I began on Thursday, and in three mornings have produced—what you see. Five-and-twenty years ago I should have written three times as much in one. Without inquiring whether what is lost in measure is gained in weight, there is satisfaction enough in knowing that even at this rate a long poem may be completed in twelve months; and that if I hold on (as I *will* do, provided you bear your part), and you keep pace with me, half that time will complete our purpose, and we may publish at the close of the year.

I have not patience to proceed further with the first canto before I send you what is already written. You have here a beginning which, when I receive a copy of the book " from the author," I shall gravely pronounce to be a very good imitation of my own manner, and honestly add that it is quite as good as I could produce myself. The fragments shall be forwarded to you as I proceed, written all in the same form for convenience of arrangement. Now, dear Caroline, go you to work with the same mind and the same will, and we shall build something more durable, if not more beautiful, than the best castle that either of us has ever erected, great architects as we both have been in that line.

God bless you.

ROBERT SOUTHEY.

It is needless to say that the sample which you receive now needs polishing in some places. You will feel, as I do, when it fails to satisfy the ear or to express the thought felicitously.

XXX.

TO CAROLINE BOWLES.

KESWICK, *April 9th*, 1824.

Since your letter arrived I have been engaged at one time with the prevalent catarrh (not my annual visitor, or it would not have left me so easily or so soon); and afterwards with an unexpected guest. I send you now a few more stanzas; the next batch will probably conclude the canto. Send me some in return, and take up the story where you will; in the next canto if you like it, with the infancy and childhood of the orphan, and conclude it with the return of the few forlorn survivors who bring home their Lord's heart. I shall proceed with the better will when I am assured that you are at work.

Such resemblances in sound as that between *faith* and *fate* I gladly avail myself of, when they occur without the appearance of being sought for. The use of alliteration in our poetry is as old as that of rhyme, indeed it supplies the place of rhyme in one form of verse—that in which Pierce Ploughman's vision is written. Like every other artifice in versification it has been overdone, and thereby rendered disgusting. I was a great offender in this way in my boyhood, before I learnt to use my tools.

You asked me why Sara Coleridge did not rather begin with Joinville or De Guesclin than with Bayard. Because Bayard's is a popular name, and Joinville had been translated about fifteen years ago by Johnes of Hafod, villainously enough Heaven knows, never man having more liking for such works, with less taste.

A lady has translated "Roderick" into Dutch verse, and dedicates it to me in verse also. Her husband is the most eminent man of his age, as a poet and critic, Bilderdijk by name, and the translation appears to be very well done : that is, I can see it is true to the original, and the husband assures me of its merits in other respects. The dedication would please you, as it does me. She has lost a son at sea, I know not whether in battle or by course of nature, and she describes in these verses, how while she hoped for his return, she used to apply that part of the poem about Alphonso and his mother to her own heart.

God bless you, dear Caroline.

ROBERT SOUTHEY.

XXXI.

TO ROBERT SOUTHEY.

BUCKLAND, *April* 10*th*, 1824.

I send you what will, I think, be my first and last contribution to the grand coalition, for you cannot fail to perceive from this specimen—and you may be sure I have done my best—how utterly incapable I am of fulfilling your expectations. There is some heroism in sending you this stuff, which I desire you will give me credit for; but you must afford me a little compassion also, for it is mortifying to find myself excluded by my own incapacity from so delightful an association. It is said, "A bird that can sing, and won't sing, must be made to sing;" but I have tried to sing and cannot, so you must bear with me.

I tried to begin the second canto; but enough of this nonsense. Do not you relinquish the plan.

I have been very seriously ill almost ever since I last wrote; very ill in body, worse in mind, in my head; sometimes in that state, that if I had had a friend near me, I should have caught hold of him, imploring him to save me from—I know not what. I was getting a little better when your last letter arrived. The wind came to the south that day, and I was allowed to breathe it in the gravel walk before the house, when a bee came humming about me with its summer sound. Those three circumstances did me a world of good—your letter most, far most; and then, in a fit of grateful valour, I set about my task. I had put it off and off till then from a cowardly misgiving, and lo! you have the result. Pray do not love me the less because I have thus disappointed your expectations. Your acknowledged predilection for *Vrows* was a sort of presentiment of the compliment to be paid you by this Dutch lady. I envy her powers, and wish I could read her translation. You can burn this, you know, without saying anything about it, which will do as well as my writing upon a separate paper, for in truth there is not enough in this unhappy head of mine to manage the business cleverly now, and alas! for the secret.

Pray write to me, if only to scold. What would I give for only one poor half-hour of your society now and then! A letter from you is next in value. Tell me if "Paraguay" goes on, and "Oliver Newman." I had a great deal to say, but forget all now, except that I am

Your most affectionate friend,
CAROLINE A. BOWLES.

XXXII.

TO CAROLINE BOWLES.

KESWICK, *April 24th*, 1824.

If I were to wait some ten days or a fortnight, I should convince you in a very effectual manner that the grand alliance is not at an end, by sending you back the substance of your own lines in another form. You shall see them taken up and recast, when the first canto is finished; but I will not delay telling you that you must not be disheartened because you have failed to satisfy yourself with your first lesson in a new style of art. It is what would happen to you in music or in painting.

That it is difficult to fall into this mode of versification I believe, because you find it so, and because one other person who, though not like yourself, a poet in heart and soul, rhymes with sufficient ease and dexterity, made an attempt and failed in it. But that it is of all modes the easiest, when once acquired, I am perfectly certain, and so you will find it. But rather than break the alliance, we would turn it into rhyme. This will not be required.

You have only to learn what the simple principles are upon which these lines are constructed; perhaps they may be reduced to this simple and single one, that every line should in itself be a complete verse, a rule which, in the ordinary heroic cadence, would admit lines of four, six, eight, and ten syllables. That cadence (the iambic, that is to say, the short syllable followed by the long, for example—

> What *heart* so *firm*, what *nature* so *severe*)

should not be mixed with a different one (the trochaic, which is long and short, nor the galloping ones, with one accent in three syllables) in the same sentence, unless for the sake of producing a peculiar and designed effect. And then they must be blended, as you shade colours into each other in your landscapes. Look at some of my minor poems, and at parts of "Thalaba," and you will see what experiments I have made in this way. I wish I were with you. I should teach you as boys are taught to compose Latin verses, by making them write mere nonsense, till they learn the tune and the mechanism of the metre.

I write to tell you this, and put you in good humour with yourself and the alliance; otherwise I would have waited in the hope, and almost with the expectation, that tomorrow I might have sent you the inscription upon your noble cousin. After twice beginning, I am now in a fair way of finishing it, and it shall be sent you as soon as it is in a fit state for transcription, though it may probably receive many corrections before it goes abroad.

But I must break off, for I have letters of business to write. So, dear Caroline, farewell for the present. This weather I hope will bring health to you, as it does enjoyment to birds, brutes, and vegetables.

Once more farewell.

ROBERT SOUTHEY.

XXXIII.

TO ROBERT SOUTHEY.

BUCKLAND, *May 5th*, 1824.

I have received both your letters; the first, you will be surprised to hear, but one day earlier than the second, dated four days later. Of the second and its enclosure I must first speak, to tell you that the latter*—that most beautiful and touching tribute to the memory of one long lost, but dearly remembered—has imparted to my feelings such deep and soothing delight, such pure and sweet contentment, as I firmly believe no human agency save yours could have produced in me. Yours is a holy, a blessed power, and many are the hearts that will bear witness with mine that it is so, when that volume of records shall come forth. But I am commissioned with other thanks (and yet how imperfectly have I expressed my own grateful feelings!)—the mother of him whose memory you have saved from the oblivion into which it would have been consigned, when the hearts in which it now lives are cold. His mother was with me when I received your last letter, and you would have been perfectly, yet painfully, rewarded, had you seen the "joy of grief" with which she dwelt ever since on that precious record, and heard the tone in which she at last found strength to utter, "Such was my dear child!" and then she tried to frame such words of grateful acknowledgment as might convey to you, through me, a part of what she felt. They were very inarticulate thanks; but I will not profane the true language of the heart (which you will be at no loss to comprehend) by compressing it into the poverty of words. We both bless you.

Now for your first letter. You would fain encourage me, and comfort and help me, in despite of your conscience, and I am more gratified by your kindness to me than mortified by my own incapacity, for such it is, say what you will; and you cannot but see it too, not only as to the construction of the

---

* The Inscription, "To the Memory of Paul Burrard."

verse, but as to the substance of the thing, the poverty of ideas of language, of everything.

I do not think the metre would be difficult to any but the dullest of all creatures; and as for rhyme, it would be equally unattainable to me now, and ideas I have none, and fancy I have none, nor hope, nor courage: nothing but feeling, and that mute; and wishes, and they are futile; and regret, and that is unreasonable, for I ought to have known myself better. You will send me, though, the remainder of the first canto, will you not? The arrival of those fragments made such pleasant epochs in my life of nothingness.

I have had a comical enough adventure lately. A dashing Captain of Lancers, who has taken it into his head to turn author, took it into his head also to send *me* his precious MS. and to ask through a mutual friend my opinion of the same, intimating that he should have the honour to call on me and reclaim his papers. Lo! what should this sublime production turn out to be but a satirical poem mostly aimed at yourself—vile, execrable, miserable trash. So I sent it back to its author post haste, with a little courteous billet declining the honour of being acquainted with him, and recommending him, as he flattered me by asking my advice, to take his work to Hone, or Sherwood, or The Byron's Head, or some other treason and blasphemy shop, where it might possibly meet with a publisher. I have heard nothing more of the reptile.*

Farewell, dear friend.

CAROLINE A. BOWLES.

---

* In reply—May 10th—Southey writes:—" Your adventure with the Satirist is an amusing one. I remember writing in a printed satire of this kind many years ago these lines from a play of Sir William Davenant, for myself and the friends who were therein abused with me :—

> " ' Libels of such weak texture and composure
> That we do all esteem it greater wrong
> T' have our name extant in such paltry verse
> Than in the slanderous sense.'

I thank God that, as I have among my friends some of the best and wisest

XXXIV.

TO CAROLINE BOWLES.

KESWICK, *June* 7*th*, 1824.

I am under the visitation of my annual cold, which condemns me for a great part of every day to idleness. In the morning I do not rise before breakfast, because this visitor rises with me, and very soon afterwards I am fain to lie back on the sofa, and close my eyes, which have no complaint of their own, but are incapable of bearing the light, while the membrane which lines the nose and the throat are in a state of such extreme excitability. First I tried repose, and that almost long enough to disable me from exertion, by putting me, what is called out of condition; then I tried exercise, and am now again resigned to inaction and a darkened room, with an upper lip which no razor dare approach, and a proboscis half excoriated by the frequent visits of the pocket-handkerchief. In 1799, when I had the first of these inveterate catarrhs (which I never failed to have every year since, except when I was in Portugal), I wrote an ode upon it, being at that time Poet Laureate to the *Morning Post*, and it is worthy of being transferred from the rough copy in my desk to Edith's magnifico album. Behold a specimen of it !—

> Weave the warp and weave the woof,
> The pocket-handkerchief for me ;
> Give ample room and verge enough
> To hold the flowing sea.
> Heard ye the din of trumpets bray—
> Nose to napkin, nostril-force,
> Hot currents urge their way,
> And thro' the double fountain take their course.

---

of their age, so I have for my enemies the veriest wretches that disparage nature. This Lancer is only a poor coxcomb, but I have them in all degrees of ass-ishness, and in all degrees of baseness and villainy, from your officer up to Lord Juan the Giaour."

Mark the social hours of night
When the house-roof shall echo with affright,
The sneezes' sudden thunder!
The neighbours rise in wonder,
A room-quake follows: each upon his chair
Starts at the fearful sound and interjects a prayer.

Just half my life has elapsed since that ode was written, and among those parts of my character which remain unaffected by time, the love of nonsense, as you may perceive, is one.

Since you heard from me I have scarcely been able to write anything except a review of Hayley's "Memoirs" which I went through doggedly, making what I could of materials not very good in themselves, and miserably put together by their author. Having, however, some gratitude for Hayley for introducing me by his notes to the Spanish poets—a good deal of respect for his love of literature and the arts, and the country, for his total exemption from all envious feelings, his attachment to his friends—above all, for his devotion to that poor son—I have spoken of him in a style very different from the prevailing tone of Magazines and Reviews.

You asked me once about Mary Wollstonecraft: I had never seen her when that dedication was written. I saw her afterwards three or four times when she was Mrs. Godwin, and never saw a woman who would have been better fitted to do honour to her sex, if she had not fallen on evil times, and into evil hands. But it is hardly possible for anyone to conceive what those times were, who has not lived in them.

I wish Landor's book may fall in your way; still more do I wish that you could see Landor himself, who talks as that book is written, as if he spoke in thunder and lightning. Such of the sheets as frightened the publisher were sent to me, and I struck out what would either have given most offence here, or endangered his personal safety where he is. How it is received I know not, and indeed I know nothing of what is going on in the world of London, except that Edith is not yet ball-sick, and that poor Bertha, I believe, is homesick. The former goes into Devonshire at the end of this month with Lady Malet; the latter to the neighbourhood of Portsmouth with the Rickmans; and in case she should pass your way in any of their excursions—which is by no means unlikely—I shall tell her when she may hope to give you a passing call. We are parching here for want of rain. The History of the "West Indies" is my brother Tom's. I hear to-day that Bowles is out of health, and depressed by it. He is at present in London. How are you? and is your singing time come? for come it will. Love from all here. Cuthbert would be delighted to see you, and your Sultan also, being a great admirer of what he used to call oodleoos.*

Dear friend, God bless you.

ROBERT SOUTHEY.

XXXV.

TO ROBERT SOUTHEY.

CHELTENHAM, *June* 20*th*, 1824.

Were you to write about a broomstick, the essay would be sure to furnish forth something infinitely entertaining; therefore I expect to be entertained by your review of Hayley's "Memoirs," but the book itself is to me the most miserable, meagre, affected, ill-arranged string of common-places I ever yawned over. You are more tenderhearted and indulgent than I am. I cannot give Hayley credit for all the feeling he pretends to. Feeling does not thrust itself into notice so perpetually: feeling does not flow into verse, or even words, at the first moment of excitement, though I know that, when it subsides into calm melancholy, poetry is its natural language. Hayley wrote epitaphs upon his dearest friends before their eyes were well closed—a sort of poetical carrion crow! I never could have endured that man, with all his tender epitaphs. I dare-

* Query—Cocks, from cockadoodledoos?

say he helped to drive his poor wife mad—"his pitiably irritable Eliza." There is something very unsatisfactory even in his attention to the poor youth, his son. How strange that he should choose only to visit him in the day-time, making Felpham his own residence.

But all the particulars of Hayley's life did not bear telling.

Now, by so much as I am more splenetic, and more uncharitable than you, am I more fit for a critic.

God bless you, dear friend.

Ever affectionately yours,

CAROLINE A. BOWLES.

XXXVI.

TO CAROLINE BOWLES.

KESWICK, *July* 4*th*, 1824.

Hayley's book is as bad as you describe it, and there is truth enough in your view of his character to justify its severity. Yet he has his better points, and I verily believe the worst thing he ever did was writing those Memoirs; for, as they stand, they have the deadly sin of dulness, and as he left them they were much more sinful. By way of explaining his domestic history, he intended to publish details which ought not to have been whispered even in a confessional. Yet you will see that Mrs. H. must have made no secret of the matter to Miss Seward. Perhaps I am the more inclined to excuse him, because his wife has made a very disagreeable impression upon me by a silly, or worse than silly, essay called "The Triumph of Acquaintance over Friendship." I like him, not for his writings as you may well suppose, but for his love of literature. It is so rare a thing to find a man in Hayley's rank who prefers it to dogs, or horses, or guns, the common dissipations, or the common business of the world (which is not much better), that I could forgive him even if his epitaphs had been more numerous and worse than they are. You are right about the nature of his feeling; it was of a kind that easily worked itself off. As far as my observation extends, those persons recover soonest from their sorrow who let it take its full course at first.

Whether I have done as well with Hayley as you are pleased to say I should have done with a broomstick you will probably soon see. But for your sake I certainly will try what I can do with the latter subject; it does me as much good to indulge sometimes in nonsense as it did Hayley to draw off his sensibility in a sonnet.

Dear Caroline, God bless you.

R. SOUTHEY.

XXXVII.

TO CAROLINE BOWLES.

KESWICK, *August* 12*th*, 1824.

Dear friend, what is become of you? Day after day I have lived in hopes of hearing that you were laying in a new stock of health. There is a physical *regeneration* which sometimes takes place. You have a great deal to do, and I have a great deal to do which will not be done without you. If I have done nothing of late, it is because I have not risen early enough to write before breakfast since I commenced invalid. The attack has been an ugly one, and continued long. I am now tolerably recovered, though there are yet some remains of the cough; but I am regaining strength, and have taken my first long walk to-day.

This day completes my fiftieth year. Neither of my parents lived to complete their fifty-first.

August 21*st*.—A friend has just sent me from America the account of Philip's War, written by the son of the man who commanded when Philip was killed. It has been procured at last, after a search of seven years, and it contains portraits of Philip and of Captain Benjamin Church, the hero of the history.

Can anything be more incongruous with dignified poetry than the name of this latter person? Yes—his portrait is even more so. But I wish I could show you both, for you have a liking for odd things, and these I am sure would amuse you. I am bound, however, to pursue this long-delayed poem,* in justice to my Transatlantic acquaintances, who are looking so eagerly for it, and have been singularly obliging in providing me with everything they could find relating to those times. And I have a strong reason for wishing not to leave it like "the story of Cambuscan bold," which is, that if it were completed I could obtain a good sum for it.

Dear Caroline, God bless you.

ROBERT SOUTHEY.

XXXVIII.

TO ROBERT SOUTHEY.

BUCKLAND, *August 29th*, 1824.

You are almost the only living creature in whom I have never found myself mistaken or disappointed, and you do not shun me because I am in sorrow, as is the world's way, and as I have bitterly experienced in times past from some who had sought and caressed me in my happier days. Well, one friend of all weathers would compensate for the unkindness of fifty such worlds; and if I have found you late, it is not too late, for, as you say, we shall meet "surely and lastingly hereafter." God grant we may here, and I do not despair of it, because, though hopeless of the physical regeneration you speak of, mine is not a disease that very quickly accomplishes its work.

I hope you are now able to enjoy this lovely weather (if it is as lovely with you as with us), and to take the exercise so necessary to you. I often shut my eyes, and see myself standing with you on the point of Friar's Crag, the spot to

* "Oliver Newman."

which we walked so frequently. I see the fretwork pavement as plain as when I stood upon it; the crags and stones beneath; the red boles of the tall firs, through which we looked up towards the grand pass into Borrodale, and that conical mountain that stood like a sentinel at its entrance, always more darkly blue than its surrounding brethren. Such visions often fill me with a strange impatience that I cannot, like a glance of the mind, overleap time and space, and be corporeally where I am in spirit. My present state is a very restless one. I am suffering terribly, night and day, from past over-excitement and the dead calm which has succeeded to it.* I cannot fix to anything, and my strange fancy of the moment is that I should like to be out on the sea in some little boat that danced upon the waves, and over which the cool spray might dash upon me. As a proof of my consistency of character, be it known to you that I never willingly stepped into a boat in my life, being in truth a very coward on the water.

You have sent me a beautiful continuation of the work in which I have proved so miserable a defaulter. I hastened to unite it to the preceding part, and to read all over together, with an interest I scarce thought myself still susceptible of. I shall always have a peculiar interest in that poem, for you *will* complete it. And I am glad to hear your Transatlantic friends have, in a manner, bound you to the completion of *Oliver Newman*, and that you are likely to be remunerated by something more solid than barren admiration. You have not shown much genius for bargaining hitherto.

Here is the *Quarterly Review* just sent me, and where are you? No review of Hayley, as you promised me, and I sent for the *Review* on purpose. Is anything in it yours? As yet I have only looked over the list of contents.

My mind misgave me that "The Mariner's Hymn" would not chime easily into music. The other would have fallen into tune better; but if the first is too long, the second is still more inadmissible on that score, nor is it of the description of poem wanted. I have tried my hand again, but I fear very un-

* Following the illness and death of her aged nurse.

successfully, both as to subject and expression, and length too, for I could not get it into shorter compass, and I could not keep self out of it, as I would fain have done, nor strike a note but upon one chord. There was an ancient instrument called a "monochord," I think. My poetic harp is such a one, its diapason embracing but the single string responsive to the feeling of the moment, and I have no powers to vary the monotonous note.

God bless you, dear friend; bless and preserve you.

CAROLINE A. BOWLES.

P. S.—You wrote to me on your birthday. I shall not forget that day if I live till its next anniversary. If I live till the sixth of next December, I shall then complete my thirty-seventh or thirty-eighth year; I am not certain which. There is a cruel kindness in keeping (particularly marking) the birthdays of children and young people. I have felt it to be so, since one by one every voice has been silenced that was wont to hail the anniversary of mine. The next sixth of December will be doubly a wintry day to me, for it will be the first in my remembrance that will bring with it no tribute of affection. My dear *bonne*, according to the custom of her country, used always to bring me a nosegay on that morning; yes, flowers even on that wintry day; and I believe if we had dwelt on the Great St. Bernard she would have contrived to find some among its eternal snows. No voice, no kiss, no flowers now. It will be all winter.

XXXIX.

TO CAROLINE BOWLES.

KESWICK, *September* 10*th*, 1824.

Dear Caroline—Thank you for your verses, which I transcribed rather than [part with the original, and sent to the poor musician. I send you his Prospectus, and take it for granted that he will send you the work.

I am fairly rid of my annual disease, and in other respects materially better than when my last was written—so much so that I was on the summit of Helvellyn last week. Send me as good an account of your amendment, and we will look on to many meetings, some of them, I hope, here, in this lovely land.

Soon I shall have more verses to send you. You have *not* proved yourself a defaulter yet. And I have more schemes for you. I have plans for three or four plays which you could execute, for you will not pretend to deny or doubt that you can write dramatically.

To day we heard from Bertha and of Edith. Bertha is still near Portsmouth in high health and spirits. Of Edith I heard from Lightfoot, under whose roof she is at this time. If she is not contented there, it will not be for want of kindness on the part of the family, for if a dog were to scratch at Lightfoot's door with my name on his collar, he would be taken into the parlour, and made as much of as your poor old Ranger, whom I remember in a manner that proves the truth of the old saying.

This is a hasty letter, but I shall soon write again when I transmit a few more stanzas, and two half letters are better than one whole one.

God bless you.
ROBERT SOUTHEY.

XL.

TO CAROLINE BOWLES.

KESWICK, *November* 13th, 1824.

If procrastination is the thief of time, letter-writing is quite as great a one, and I find the two thieves very closely connected. Some unexpected epistle arrives which is neither wanted nor welcome, but which must be answered; or some other demand upon my hours is made, for which I am neither prepared nor willing, and then the intention which had been formed, of writing that evening to you, stands over for the morrow; and when the morrow comes, other interruptions of the same kind occur, and prevent me from passing an hour according to my wishes.

In reply to your letter, thank Mr. St. Barbe in what manner seems best to you, for Pope's letter, which I shall be very glad to have. Take for your own collection—as the first which has turned up—a note of Charles Lamb's, relating to a review of Wordsworth's *Excursion* written by him at my request for the *Quarterly*, and inserted there, but so mangled by Gifford as to be absolutely spoiled. It will go very well in the frank, and I will send you others as I meet with them.

Cuthbert is now in the very honeymoon of his happiness, having just been breeched; breeching, as I tell Sara, being to a boy what marrying is to a young lady, the great thing in life which is looked on to, and I ask her seriously which she thinks the greatest happiness. I wish you could see Cuthbert; during dinner he lifts up his pin-before to look at the buttons. It is pleasant to see him, and yet the change is not one which brings with it any cheerful thoughts, for it takes away the charm of childhood, and what charm is there in this world equal to it!

Landor has sent over another volume of *Conversations* to the press. Differing as I do from him in constitutional temper, and in some serious opinions, he is yet of all men living the one with whom I feel the most entire and cordial sympathy in heart and mind; were I a single man, I should think the pleasure of a week's abode with him cheaply purchased by a journey to Florence, though, pilgrim-like, the whole way were to be performed on foot. The title of his book reminds me of Lord Byron's *Conversations* as let off by his blunderbuss Captain Medwin. I have only seen some newspaper extracts. I fastened his name upon the gibbet (as I told him); his friends have now exposed him there in chains. I am told there is no mention of my correspondence with Shelley. Shelley probably kept it to himself. Miserable men that they were—both so gifted—and so guilty!

Since my last I have not composed any verses except a few stanzas of the *Paraguay*, which is the plague of my life, but I have been getting on with the *History* and the *Dialogues*. God bless you, my dear friend.

Yours faithfully,
ROBERT SOUTHEY.

XLI.

TO ROBERT SOUTHEY.

BUCKLAND, *November* 13*th*, 1824.

Pray give me some token that you are on this side Heaven, dear friend! I am rather disquieted at your long silence; the more so, as when you wrote last Cuthbert was only then recovering from a serious illness. Tell me you and all yours are well, and then I shall have no further uneasiness than the fear that you should think me a little importunate. But you must remember that I live out of myself and my solitary home, and so entirely in those I love and all that concerns them, that I am perhaps more excusable for taking alarm than those who are surrounded by friends and families; and all my social intercourse is epistolary.

I believe, however, I should have waited patiently a little longer but for a piece of literary intelligence which reached me yesterday, at which perhaps you will laugh only when you hear it, if, indeed (as is most probable), you are not already better informed than I am respecting it. Have you heard that there is preparing for publication, under the auspices and patronage, &c., of the Duke of Wellington, a History of the Peninsular War? The thing is certain. It is much talked of in the higher circles, from whence the report has travelled straight to me in my no circle at all. But it surprises and annoys me, as I cannot understand what can induce the Duke to promote a thing of the kind, knowing and approving of yours; and, moreover, I am not without apprehension that it may be disadvantageous to you in two ways—by interfering with the sale of yours, and by causing him to withhold from you such documents and information as may be essential to the continuation of your noble work. Murray advertises your second volume for this month I see. Pray set my heart at rest on this matter.

Farewell, and God bless you, dear friend.

CAROLINE A. BOWLES.

I have been staying for a few days at the Rose's lately, and read there a very curious and interesting collection of MS. letters, which is in their possession—the whole correspondence, in their own handwriting and very voluminous, of Sir Charles Hanbury Williams and Catherine of Russia while she was Grand Duchess, and before the death of Elizabeth. The greater part of the large subsidies England was then furnishing Catherine with, for the ostensible furtherance of political purposes, was lavished on Poniatowski through the very channel (Sir Charles) by which she obtained it from hence.

XLII.

TO CAROLINE BOWLES.

KESWICK, *November 17th*, 1824.

Your news is new to me; but it does not surprise, and can in no degree injure me. Indeed I do not think it will affect Murray's interest, who is the person interested; for the intended work will prove a military history exclusively. The Duke refused to communicate any paper to me, upon the ground that he reserved them for such a work. He said that I should do as everyone who wished to make a popular work would—

ascribe more to the Spaniards than was due to them. In this he is mistaken. But the truth is, he wants a whole-length portrait of himself, and not an historical picture, in which a great many other figures must be introduced. By good fortune I have had access to papers of his of a much more confidential nature than he himself (I am very sure) would entrust to anyone. And I have only to wish the work which he patronizes may come out as soon as possible, that I may make use of it. For my third volume, in all likelihood, it will come in time, and then it will save me some trouble, for I may rely upon its authority in mere military points. This must be the reason why Murray announces my second volume so prematurely, when only twenty-six sheets are printed out of a hundred. I shall neither hurry myself, nor be hurried. And you need not be told that I shall everywhere speak of the Duke exactly as I should have done if he had behaved towards me with more wisdom. Let who may write the military history, it is in my book that posterity will read of his campaigns. And if there had been nothing but a military interest in the story, the Duke might have written it for me.

Never, I pray you, suffer yourself to be annoyed by anything which concerns, or seems to concern me, as an author, for in that character nothing can annoy me. I go on, as I always have done, in my own way, endeavouring to do what seems best, according to my own judgment, with all diligence, and caring very little for any present opinion that may be passed upon my works. Like Landor, I am satisfied if I please ten persons who are competent to pronounce an opinion upon such subjects.

You will have received a letter before this time; but I write these hasty lines, to show you that I am not insensible to your solicitude for what you think concerns me. Would that you were within reach! and yet I cannot wish you here at this time, when for the last seven weeks we have had the worst weather that I can remember for two-and-twenty years.

I want to hear what the Monster* says to you. That

---

* Blackwood.

rascally passage concerning Sir Walter Scott which was cancelled in the *London Magazine,* beyond all doubt must have been written by Hazlitt.

Murray is in water as near the scalding point as flesh and blood can bear it about Lord Byron. This it is to have any dealings with a bad man.

God bless you, dear Caroline.

ROBERT SOUTHEY.

XLIII.

TO CAROLINE BOWLES.

KESWICK, November 26th, 1824.

The inclosure,* as you will have guessed, is for Mr. St. Barbe, to whom you will give it with as civil an expression of thanks on my part as his civility deserves. Pope's handwriting I, literally speaking, should not have known from that of my aunt, Miss Tyler.

I reply thus immediately to your letter, that I may thank you while the impression is fresh, for the extract from Captain Medwin, of which otherwise I might long have remained in ignorance. Undoubtedly I shall notice it, and most probably as I did his Lordship's former attack—by a letter in the newspapers, being the most summary method, and that also whereby the most extensive circulation may be obtained. Should you happen to have the book at hand, tell me if there be in it anything else which may seem to you to require any observation on my part. There will be plenty of time for this, for it is of no importance whether my letter appear a week hence, or a fortnight, or a month. It is not for the sake of repelling an accusation that I notice these impudent lies, but for the sake of showing that those who have advanced them are impudent

* An autograph of Southey, in exchange for one of Pope.

liars. To what an extent they are so you, who have seen my correspondence with Shelley, know. I am only sorry you have not a copy of it, which you shall have one of these days. It would not become me to publish it while there are any persons living who would be wounded by it: as for such *dead* as those to whom it refers, I know of no respect or tenderness to which they are entitled. A dead dog is entitled to no more than a living one. It will come to light in due season. You remember Latimer's saying: "Well! there is nothing hid but it shall be opened."

Have you heard that Hobhouse printed a pamphlet in contradiction of some of Medwin's statements, which he has been prevailed upon by his friends to suppress, because it would certainly bring on a duel.* It seems he had given Medwin the lie there in plain terms; but it is Lord Byron, and not his Blunderbuss, who is the liar. The Blunderbuss has only let off what it was charged with. And this I shall take care to say in my newspaper epistle.

"Sick and alone" are sad words in themselves, and more so when they are so coupled. If wishes would avail, you should be well and here.

God bless you.

Robert Southey.

XLIV.

TO CAROLINE BOWLES.

Keswick, *February 22nd*, 1825.

You have sent me one of the things in the world which I most wished to possess, and yet you say I shall not thank you

* Miss Bowles writes in reply: "Hobhouse's suppressed pamphlet is not destroyed nor unread, and if the heroes are sharp set they may get up a duel yet."

for it.* Likeness enough there is; I can perceive so much as to fancy it more. As to age, you are almost young enough to be my daughter, and for the other character which you give yourself, would to Heaven there were as little ground for calling yourself sick! No, you may be assured I will not send that drawing to Somerset House, not if they would give me the finest picture that ever was exhibited there in exchange for it.

I have read the poem with too much pleasure and too much pain to speak of it.† True it is as a picture and a most interesting one, but as a prophecy true only, I trust, in the general truth that death is never far from us. You are lonely, God knows; yet, if you could know how often I was with you in thought, you would feel that there is one person in the world who regards you as you ought to be regarded—as you would wish him to regard you. How difficult is it when we mean a great deal, not to say either too little or too much.

I am acquainted with Mr. Wilberforce, but have neither seen nor heard from him since the Book of the Church was published. The Bishop of London has written to me saying he hopes to see Mr. Butler's "flimsy structure of misrepresentation and sophistry" overthrown by my hand. Some progress is made in my reply, and more it would have been if I had not been more worthily employed upon the Tale of Paraguay. I hope and believe that another week will not elapse before that is completed. Indeed there can hardly be more that ten stanzas to write. When the last is written I will write off to you in pure joy to announce my deliverance, for a deliverance it will be.

In my last letter I ought to have said, that should you be

---

* In a letter of Feb. 17, accompanying a drawing which included her own figure, Miss Bowles writes—"The drawing of a little group very fine, very scientific as you will see, but two of the figures are faithful portraits, and for the third—one can't make such a little thing look sick, old and ugly—like, that is. Don't send it to Somerset House."

† A poem by Caroline Bowles which she describes as "a doleful ditty, but all true."

going anywhere for change of air or to drink the waters at the time of my movement, wherever that may be, I will take that place instead of Buckland in my course. So you are not to make any derangement in your plans on my account. See you I will, and the thought of seeing you, reconciles me more than anything else that I look on to in leaving home.

One word more. I have marked in my note-books from time to time such stories or hints for stories as in the course of my multifarious reading seemed fit for ballads or other tales in verse. If you will try your hand at them, you shall have as many as would make a capital collection for Azor.*

Dear Caroline, God bless you.
ROBERT SOUTHEY.

XLV.

TO CAROLINE BOWLES.

KESWICK, February 24th, 1825.

I promised you a gazette extraordinary, and here it is. This morning the *Tale of Paraguay* was finished. If I thought that any other poem would give me half the trouble that this has done, I should forswear verse rather than encounter it. Here have I sat, working at it doggedly, not following the natural course of thought and feeling, which always leads one the best way, and generally the shortest, but zig-zagging after the rhyme, selecting words not because they were the fittest, but because there were four of them which would chime together, and abusing my own fool's-head for getting with open eyes into such a scrape. For what the difficulty would be I very well knew from the first. Finished, however, it is, and never was man more glad of his deliverance.

If you were near enough I would call you in to "rejoice

---

* *i. e.* Blackwood.

with me"; but as that is not the case, you will be glad at a distance.

God bless you.
ROBERT SOUTHEY.

XLVI.

TO ROBERT SOUTHEY.

BUCKLAND, *February* 27*th*, 1825.

How delighted I am that you set so much value on that thing which (after it was gone) I would have recalled if possible. But I need not have so repented; you received it in the same spirit in which it was sent, and in that confidence it is I always write to you without taking thought, knowing I address one who can understand me, and will never mark unkindly what would be ridiculous or amiss to other people.

You are not to feel any *painful* interest in that little poem. The loneliness, I speak of there, is not, will not be desolate loneliness while you think of me as you say you do, and sometimes tell me so, as you have done. And for the prophecy, those are not my darkest moments when I anticipate its probable fulfilment. On the contrary, a feeling of security is mine at such times which I cannot always command—of security that I shall not outlive all that makes life still desirable. I seem to have stepped over a great gulf dividing me from my early years and from my early friends. My wish would have been, I think, *not* to overstep it, *not* to have gone further. But you met and took me by the hand on the brink of that dreary, unknown country; I found in you what I had never met with, even in my lost Eden, and while you hold me fast I shall not want courage to go on, nor inclination to tarry yet a little longer should it be God's pleasure.

At present I am disposed to be very much in love with

life, and very unwilling to leave it before May. I had no idea whatever of moving from home at that time, and I would not for the world receive your visit anywhere else, because your having been here (even for that visit *volant* you prepare me to expect) will leave a brightness over many succeeding months, and I, as well as you, converse with shadows. If it were good and pleasant for yourself to stay some length of time here how hard I would try to keep you! but what is best for yourself, that shall be best for me, so come without fear of persecution.

I have just got Butler's book. My motive for asking if you had heard from Mr. Wilberforce was, that I had just received a letter from a friend of his (who had been with him the day before) which says, speaking of your *Book of the Church :* "Mr. Wilberforce is delighted with it, but regrets Dr. Southey's not having given his authorities." Knock them down flat with authorities in your answer to Butler.

God bless you, best friend of mine.

Yours affectionately,
CAROLINE A. BOWLES.

XLVII.

TO CAROLINE BOWLES.

KESWICK, *March* 15*th*, 1825.

I spent the last week at Wordsworth's, mostly (for the ground was covered with snow two days, and then we had two days' rain to clear it away) in extracting from good, old, out-of-the-way books, pills for Mr. Butler, some of which will be bitter on the palate but very wholesome if he allow them to operate fairly. Your character of his book is drawn with perfect truth. My uncle says of him, "His contradicting you and saying that you misstated facts, may have the same answer as Warburton gave to one of his antagonists—*it may be so for all he knows of the matter.*" My reply is gone to the press, and in the course of a week I shall probably have the first proof-sheet. I am as civil as he is at the beginning; but as for the spider's web which he has spun, I demolish it without mercy.

It was my intention to have written to you from Rydal, but what with this employment, with consulting Wordsworth upon what I had written of this reply, and making some alterations in it, hearing some of his poems which he is about to insert in a new edition of his works, and with the interruption of company, the time was fully taken up.

I ought not to set mournful subjects before you, but here is one I took from the *Acta Sanctorum*, as the subject for a poem, three and twenty years ago.

In the wild times of Irish History, some four or five hundred years before the English conquest of that country, one of its petty kings was called Endeus, son of Counal, a youth pre-destined to be a monk and a saint. He had a kinswoman, Fanchea by name, who was an abbess, and was living in the odour of sanctity. Endeus returning one day from battle his men singing songs of victory, stopt at her convent, where she stood in the gateway and forbade him to approach nearer, because he was stained with blood. He justified himself for defending the kingdom which he had inherited from his father; but she told him his father was gone to hell, and he having inherited his sins, was in the way to follow him. Endeus took this very patiently, but desired her to bring out a certain maid of royal parentage whom she was educating, and give her to him to be his wife. Saint Fanchea told him to wait a little while and she would presently answer him. She went in, called for the maiden, and said to her—"You have now your choice; will you love Him whom I love, or will you have an earthly husband?" The virgin preferred a heavenly one. Saint Fanchea took her into her own chamber, and bade her lie down to rest. She did so, and immediately died, as if she had fallen asleep. The saint then covered her face, brought the young king into the chamber, and uncovering the corpse said to him—"Young man, behold the spouse whom thou desirest." Of course he entered a convent, and became a Saint.

I think you can make something of this, which, though very monkish and very papistical, is, nevertheless, well fitted for poetry.

I have another monkish story to the same tenor—that is, showing that death is the best thing—which is more singular, if it be not in some of its circumstances almost too puerile. Yet it impressed me very much. A Portuguese friar (a Dominican), Bernardo by name, taught children to read and write in his convent at Santarem. There were two who used always to come together, and bring their breakfast with them, and they were regularly left in one of the chapels while Bernardo performed his office of sacristan. There they used to spread their napkins on the steps of the altar, and take their meal. One day one of them asked the infant Jesus, who was in his mother's arms above the altar, to come down and breakfast with them. The invitation was accepted, and the visitor continued to do so every day, till at last the children told Bernardo, and complained that the *Menino Jesus* ate very heartily of their provisions, but never brought any himself. Delighted at this, the friar told them that when the *Menino* came to breakfast with them next, they should tell him he ought to invite them home to dinner in return, and their master with them. The *Menino* thought this reasonable, and fixed a day, but did not mention Bernardo. Bernardo, however, was not to be put off. He bade them tell the *Menino* (this is a term of endearment applied to a child) that, as they wore the habit, they were bound to observe the Rules of the Order. Obedience was one of those Rules, and their master would not let them go without him. The day came, Bernardo said mass, communicated with the children, then knelt between them before the altar, and there, with their hands raised in the attitude of prayer, and their eyes fixed towards the image, the three lifeless bodies were found. This is told as a true story in the history of the Dominican Order in Portugal by F. Luiz de Sousa, a most highly esteemed writer. And if you were here to read it with me in Portuguese, and see how beautifully he has told it, I think you would fall in love with the story, as I did some four or five and twenty years ago.*

I should tell you that this Convent at Santarem is the holiest of all holy ground, for the departed friars have been seen to go in procession round the cemetery, bearing tapers, at midnight (two kings have seen them), and when a grave is opened there a perfume comes out more delightful than art can imitate, or nature produce.

Dear Caroline, take these for the present. I will look out others in a different tone. If you like them I am quite certain that you can pitch them in the proper key, and make the most of them. Perhaps the latter is too puerile in some of its circumstances. Yet if it be told thoughtfully, and introduced as a legend which is fully believed in its own country, the objection may be removed. However, I will send you choice of subjects, and enough to make a volume.

Dear Caroline, farewell.
God bless you.
ROBERT SOUTHEY.

XLVIII.

TO CAROLINE BOWLES.

1, HARLEY STREET, July 27th, 1825.

I am arrived here well in body, but not so sound of limb as I had hoped. My foot, though nearly well to all outward appearance, requires rest, and is something the worse for the journey from Holland, and for two nights in the Ostend steam-packet, where it was impossible to take off my clothes and attend to it. Very, very unwillingly, therefore, my journey into Hampshire must be given up, and I must travel homeward by day stages. Night-travelling will not do for me till the

---

* The story is told in graceful verse by Caroline Bowles: "A Legend of Santarem," in *The Birthday*.

limb has recovered its wonted strength. This is a great disappointment, for, with all my eagerness to be once more at home, the prospect of seeing you was one of those things to which I looked on during my confinement with most pleasure. Next May I will leave Keswick before the cold comes on, and try whether a journey to London, with Hampshire for the farthest point of my travels, may not suffice to prevent it. This year's experiment has perfectly succeeded in that respect, and my general health is for a time completely re-established, which is not a little surprising, considering the length of time that I was confined to a sofa.

Something I told you of the Bilderdijks in my letter from Leyden. There are a great number of what may be called domestic poems among their works. Some of these I mean to translate for insertion in the *Quarterly Review;* and if I could get enough of them translated to form a small volume, it would gratify me quite as much as it would them. Perhaps you will help me in this design. I will translate the poems into prose as well as I can, and when I meet with difficult passages write over to Mrs. B. that she may send me the interpretation. They are poems (Mrs. B.'s) which always remind me of you, in the feelings which they express. I mean to say that, under like circumstances, they are such poems as you would have written. Your lot has not been a happy one, and yet you have not such sorrows to endure as have been her portion.

Bilderdijk has been twice married. By his first wife he had eight children, all of whom are dead. By his present, who is twenty-four years younger than himself, he has had seven, and one boy of thirteen is the only survivor—his life a very precarious one, his constitution being weak, and the place of his abode, and the want of exercise and playmates, unfavourable to it. The great disproportion of age can hardly be said to have alloyed their happiness, for never were two persons more attached to, or more worthy of each other. But the evil is felt now, when, at the age of forty-six, she sees her husband a man of three score and ten, and has the prospect of widowhood close before her. He found her in England when he came over to join the Stadtholder in his exile. She had lived here from three or four years old, had forgotten her own language, and was writing English verses, which I could not prevail upon her to show me. Upon becoming attached to him she resumed her own language, and the Dutch have thereby gained a poetess, who would else have taken her place with another friend of mine in English literature. Whether she was handsome in her youth I do not know; but infinitely pleasing she must have been, for even now her countenance sometimes assumes an expression which may be called beautiful. But you know it is always to countenance and expression that I look; mere features without the right expression are no more to me than waxwork.

Let me hear from you, dear Caroline, while I am in town. I shall leave it on Tuesday next. Before that time you will receive my poem. How much rather would I have been with you in person! And yet I believe there never was an author whose character, in all its bearings, was more clearly portrayed in his writings, and that you will feel this in the *Tale of Paraguay*. Will you not like Bilderdijk the better for having translated the *King of the Crocodiles*?

God bless you, my dear, dear friend.

ROBERT SOUTHEY.

XLIX.

TO CAROLINE BOWLES.

KESWICK, *August 30th*, 1825.

I cannot tell you what Mrs. Bilderdijk's maiden name was; it was never mentioned, and is not given in her title-pages, though it is usual to say *born so and so* after the name of a married woman. I therefore feared there might be some reason for this, and did not venture to ask what I wished to know. The portrait of Madame de Sévigné, in the edition of her letters published in 1820, is a most excellent likeness of Mrs. B. I cannot imagine anything more like what she must have been at five-and-twenty, both in features and expression. Her husband told me that she thought me very like what he had been twenty years ago; but as he had not been to the Promontory for a nose, there never can have been much resemblance. What there was must have been about the eyes and upper part of the face. I believe, however, few men could be found who resemble each other so much in disposition, pursuits, and opinions.

My books are not yet come, and I have not begun upon those volumes of his which I brought to England with me, and which reached Keswick on Thursday last. As soon as I can translate anything in verse you shall see it; and some you shall see in prose, sent in the hope that you may feel inclined to versify it. I have urged them to visit me next year, and am not without a hope that they may come. But they are far from rich. All his property he lost in the Revolution, for his attachment to the house of Orange. They have recompensed him with a paltry pension of 1800 florins, about £140. Something he gets by taking pupils during the terms of the University; by his writings very little, the profits of authorship being miserably little in so small a country, and in a language which has no circulation beyond it. But little as they are, they are of consequence to him. He, however, is contented and happy, and has the spirit of a prince, or rather which princes ought to have.

My foot prevented me from going to meet Canning at Storrs. To say the truth, I was not sorry that there was this reason for declining an invitation which it would have been some trouble and some expense to accept, and which I should have had little pleasure in accepting. Unexpectedly Sir Walter Scott made his appearance there, and came from thence to see me. We had not met for about twelve years, and I found him greatly changed—grown large, perfectly grey, and with the look of three-score, which is about five years older than he is. Lockhart was with him and his unmarried daughter.

I have seen also my ally the Bishop of Chester since my return. He wishes my book to appear in time for the next session. I am getting on with it, and wish you were at hand to see it as it proceeds. It would amuse you to see how I have treated Milner, and how well scorn can supply the place of anger.

Dear friend, God bless you.

ROBERT SOUTHEY.

L.

TO CAROLINE BOWLES.

KESWICK, *October* 14*th*, 1825.

You will see a Paper upon Sara Coleridge's *Bayard* in the next *Quarterly Review*, and know from whence it comes. The reviewal of *Paraguay* is by John Coleridge. He tells me a good story concerning Murray, who had heard the poem much ridiculed, and supposed it to be good for nothing. One day when Coleridge called on him he said: "I took up your review of the *Paraguay* yesterday evening, thinking to request that if you did not much care about it you would pass it by. God, Sir! I read on till I was quite affected. You have extracted some of the most beautiful things in the world. I was quite affected." And he proceeded to say "that Coleridge had begun too much in the way of apology." So it is, that as the wind blows the chaff flies. The tale is a good test for showing who those are who read a poem as they do a novel, not for the feeling or execution. It is almost like Wordsworth's Lucy—something which there are "none to praise," and "very few to love"; but then those few are worth all the rest of the world.

My books arrived a fortnight ago. A son of my old friend Lightfoot, who happened to be here, and assisted in unpacking them, told his father he had never seen any man look so happy as I did upon that occasion. And I was as happy as the arrival of eighty-nine folios, and about as many smaller fry, could make me. The honeymoon is not over yet. O, dear Caroline, what a blessing it is to have an insatiable appetite of this kind, which grows by what it feeds on, and for which food can never be wanting! With such pursuits nothing is wanting to my enjoyment; and the only thing I wish for is—now and then—the presence of some one who could fairly enter into my views and feelings, and partake the interest which I take in such researches. But of all my friends, the only one who does this is my uncle, and he is in the last stage of bodily infirmity from old age, but with his faculties perfect, and his love of these things unabated.

I am now writing doggedly for the *Quarterly Review*, that is to say, for the lucre of gain and the necessity of paying my half-yearly bills at Christmas. The subject is the Vaudois, which is interesting in itself, and not unconnected with my ecclesiastical pursuits. When this is done, which it will be by the end of the month, I must set tooth and nail upon the *Peninsular War*, and fairly finish the volume. It is just half printed—a proof is on the table now. The *Vindiciæ* go on well; the better for this importation from the Low Countries. I have just got through a sort of chapter upon the celibacy of the clergy, and the sort of morality (if I may use that word) which it has produced. When you read it you will be surprised to see what formidable creatures women are.

Cuthbert, among other accomplishments, is learning Dutch in my way of teaching all languages which I know anything of, except Latin and Greek, wholly disregarding the grammar, or rather picking it out by use. We read Mrs. Bilderdijk's poems for children and the dialogues in the Grammar, which are always worth reading in old Grammars. And thus ten minutes' amusement in the day (for amusement, and not task-work, it is) will familiarize him to the idiom of the language; and when we have done with Mrs. B. we shall enter upon Jacob Cats, the poet of all poets who has done most good to his country, and whose volume, in the good days of

Holland, lay upon the hall table with the Family Bible in every respectable house.

God bless you.

Robert Southey.

LI.

TO CAROLINE BOWLES.

Keswick, *November 20th*, 1825.

Two days ago I had a very pleasant surprise in unrolling the lithograph of our party on Honister Crag. It is a very pleasant memorial, and likely to be valued one of these days for your sake and for mine, when we shall be far off in our celestial journey, travelling, I hope, together. Will it not be delightful to visit the man in the moon, go from thence to the evening star with a wish, and make a trip to the sun as familiarly as we now might to the sea, and put ourselves upon a comet, instead of getting into a stage-coach!

Miss Fryer's likeness is very well preserved, and Dame Elizabeth also may be recognized by those who know her. John Calvert's back, too, is a good likeness, but the lithographer has uglified all the rest, and Kate and Bell dispute for which of them the ugliest of the two imps is intended. But it is happily caught and managed, and like everything that I see of yours, makes me wish more and more that we were near enough to set each other to work, and to work in unison.

So you wanted the monkey, the parrots, and the pigs in *Paraguay*. I had two reasons for not introducing them. The first was, that I was sick to the very heart of my task, and determined to put in nothing that should lengthen it. The other, that though these things might have been very pleasingly described in the second canto, they would have broken the simple, single interest of the poem in its better parts. What could have been done with them when Mooma was singing, with her arms and countenance raised as if she would fain have followed the voice which she had sent into the sky? I must tell you honestly that the real ground of that description is the pleasure I have myself in pouring forth "the voice which echo loves," and making a great noise indoors, out of doors, whenever I am at liberty. My woodnotes wild are as much beyond all other warblings as they are unlike them, and so you would acknowledge if you were once to hear a full display. Joseph Glover, the carpenter, who does our jobs and makes my book-shelves, says of himself: "I should be a capital singer, but the pity is, I have no voice!" Now, I have a voice, but the pity is that I do not know one note from another, and know no difference between in-tune and out-of-tune. But it is such a voice, that whereas other people stop at G H, I go on to X Y Z, &c.

Dear Caroline, you will perceive that this is not written in the worst spirits, and yet my spirits are not raised when I think of your loneliness, and the frequent accesses of illness, which seem to be the only things that vary it. Not a day passes that that thought does not come across me. Never was a creature more formed to be happy herself, and to make others happy, if Fortune had not in your case played strangely at cross purposes with Nature. At present it is only when I shut my eyes that I can see you; in this the absent are like the dead; but I shall see you, God willing, in good substantial earnest, when May comes, and I take flight from my summer visitant.

Do not be surprised at hearing that the lines upon Paul Burrard are published. I gave them to Alaric Watts for his *Souvenir*, having nothing else that I could so well give, and mended them a little before they went. My *Vindiciæ* will very soon be brought to a close, though I have got but half through Mr. Butler's book. I shall wind up at the end of the volume by bidding him good bye for the present, and resume the matter, or not, according to circumstances. You will often smile in the perusal, which the Roman Catholics will not, for it is long since the old woman of Babylon has had such a carting as I am giving her. My second volume of the *War* will just be completed in time for my start in May. Moreover, my

Dialogues are in the press. Judge how happy I am with proof-sheets.
God bless you.
ROBERT SOUTHEY.

LII.

TO ROBERT SOUTHEY.

BUCKLAND, *December 8th*, 1825.

For once (in return for your cheering, kind letter) I will treat you with a few notes less like a raven's than usual. I have been better lately, brightening up a little in health and hope, now and then feeling that there *is* enjoyment in life, and (since I last heard from you) now and then glancing forward, half fearfully, but still in hope, to another May which two months ago it made me sick at heart to think of.

Your confession about that beautiful passage in *Paraguay* is delightful; but you forget I *have* heard your " woodnotes wild " in perfection, I think, " The Bloody Gardiner," in the gloaming among the echoes of Borrodale, and at Waterend that pathetic ditty about " Tittymouse Bay." You never honoured me with a solo voluntary at Greta Hall.

Thank you for telling me you had given that beautiful inscription to the *Literary Souvenir*. I sent for the book directly for dear Paul's mother, who would have been painfully startled had she fallen upon it unawares. Coming from me it was a dear and precious gift. The additional concluding lines are beautiful, and perfect the poem; but I am disposed to quarrel with your alteration of one line—the last in the MS. copy you sent me.*

* " The original MS. referred to is now before me, and ended thus:
'But who would join with fervent piety
The prayer that saith, Peace in our time, O Lord.'
The inscription as printed is on p. 174 of the one-volume edition of the Poems." (*Note by Mr. Warter.*)

Do tell me, if you can, who wrote that first article in the last *Quarterly Review*, and is Lockhart to be editor of the *Review*, as currently reported. I hope not; let the "modern Athens" keep her Athenians.

Yes, I hope we shall travel together that journey after Time; but at present my spirit is far less aspiring than yours. It puts me quite out of breath to think of whisking about from star to star upon comets' tails. I have no great fancy for a trip to the moon (though I might find my wits there), and still less for a solar visit, though there is something sweet and alluring in the beam of the evening star. But, to confess the honest truth, my beatific visions are still fashioned very much after the manner of those of my childhood, when (about four or five years old) I acquired sublime conceptions of the joys of the blessed in heaven from the sight of a peep-show representing the Garden of Eden, all full of fruits and flowers, bright turf and crystal rills, beautiful birds and gentle creatures frisking around Adam and Eve in their bower of myrtle and roses. You may laugh as you please, but some such future paradise my fancy always represents to me, far better peopled indeed with those whose presence would make a desert Paradise.

I have a new favour to ask of you—you will think I am becoming an importunate beggar. Will you give me your *Devil's Walk*, that stolen feather in Professor Porson's wing? Perhaps, if you have no objection to let me have it, one of the *five* young ladies would copy it for me, or set it Cuthbert for a writing lesson. I am charmed to hear the *Dialogues* are forthcoming. Will you ever get to Sherwood again? You must make your way through that wood.

Farewell, dear friend: God bless you.

CAROLINE A. BOWLES.

LIII.

TO CAROLINE BOWLES.

KESWICK, *January 4th*, 1826.

As many new years to you, dear friend, as you can find comfort and enjoyment in life, and not an hour longer. But may those years be many.

You shall have *The Devil's Walk* whenever I can lay my hand upon the first rough draft, for I have no copy of it. It is probably in a great desk which is threatened every day with a new green cloth: in that case its contents must be turned out, and, amid the fearful accumulation of papers which will then be disturbed, I hope it will come to light. I will mark in it what stanzas are mine, and what Coleridge's.

The article upon Pope (which has been sorely injured by curtailment) was written by the father of my fellow-traveller, Henry Taylor, a most remarkable person for strength of character, as well as for intellectual powers—the sort of man with whom Cato might shake hands, for he has the better parts of an antique Roman about him. I am sorry for Bowles, and the more so because the criticism has been written in perfect sincerity, and with the fullest conviction that its severity was deserved.

The new number has a paper of mine upon the Vaudois. I am told it has been cut shorter to make room for papers which J. Coleridge might not else have been able to introduce; for his successor I understand pays no regard whatever to the arrangements which he had made. This I am sorry for, especially as there was special cause for delicacy. I am in correspondence with the new editor, but whether the studied deference which is now assumed toward me, and the overstrained commendations which usher it in, will open out anything like a frank and easy intercourse time must show. Frank on my part it will always be, for frank I am by nature, and it may be said by necessity also. Never was any man less able to dissemble either his likings or dislikings. Of what use would it be to carry a lying tongue with a countenance which always speaks the truth?

Your criticism is right, and I will restore the line till I can remove the fault without changing the expression, for I will do all I can to improve it before it is printed with my intended series of Inscriptions. The inclination for verse seems to be returning to me, if I were not so overdone with engagements that I cannot afford time for it. Think how many mouths I have to feed and all from an inkstand: if there were not a blessing upon it, as upon the cruise of oil, it must fail; but that blessing requires me to do my part. My hopes of ever getting the start of the world grow fainter as I grow older, for I am past the age at which it is truly said that those persons who are ever to enrich themselves are rich. But I go on cheerfully, in the full enjoyment of all that God has given me, and still finding as much pleasure in what is a business of necessity as if it were pursued for inclination alone.

God bless you, dear friend.

ROBERT SOUTHEY.

LIV.

TO ROBERT SOUTHEY.

BUCKLAND, *January 8th*, 1826.

Am I "quite forgotten, and clean out of mind"? Not with you I think, of all the world; but it is very long, unusually long, since you have given me any token of remembrance, and though my faith fails not, my patience does. You can hardly take such accurate note of time as I do. Sounds are unnoticed in the cheerful bustle of the day, that strike loudly upon one's ear in the deep stillness of night. So it is with your life and mine. Circumstances unmarked and unimportant in your crowded diary are events in my monotonous existence, and a letter from you makes sunshine in winter. Can you be very angry with me for dunning you?

I never cared much about the opening of Parliament till now that it will be heralded by your *Vindiciæ*. Will it not? Your article on the Vaudois is as interesting as I expected it to be. You never exercised your pen in a worthier cause, or more successfully.

The Monster is going to publish my bundle of scraps this month. Indifference and silence have fought my battle for me —brought him to terms—that is, to publish only what I stipulate for, instead of the thumping volume he wanted to make. There will be more than enough, but I can't furnish him with a title. All sorts of scraps have been hashed up in all sorts of ways, with all sorts of names. "There is nothing new under sun," that I can find out.

God bless you, dear friend. Don't call me a torment.

CAROLINE A. BOWLES.

LV.

TO CAROLINE BOWLES.

KESWICK, *January 20th*, 1826.

Your last letter did make me angry, but it was with myself for not having written sooner. However, I was pleased that you had *so* written, and that by the time yours reached me mine had found its way to Buckland. I was also glad to hear that you and the Monster were again on amiable terms. If I knew what sort of medley your book was, I could try to help you to a name, though my talent lies rather in naming cats than books. It is always desirable to have a peculiar title: the meaning is of less consequence, because any title very soon ceases to convey any meaning more than the name of that to which it is given. For example, when we talk of *As You Like It*, what do we think of but Rosalind and Jaques and the Forest of Arden? Upon this principle the *Book of the Church* was named; it puzzled some people, provoked others, set them criticising, which I did not care for, and talking about it, which I wished them to do; and now it is merely the designation of what could not well have been called anything else, and half a dozen works have been christened after it.

The *Vindication* is finished. I have put the last hand to it to-day, except that there are still about four proofs to correct. You will I hope receive it in about three weeks, and probably you will look through it with more satisfaction than Mr. Butler will feel in the perusal. He will say it is a dreadful book; for though there is as much personal civility as can be desired (and when I call to mind some parts of his attack I cannot but think more than is deserved), yet I have neither mealed my mouth nor minced my words.

The printer of my *Peninsular War* has contrived to lose a leaf of manuscript, and sends me a proof-sheet with a gap in it, and a query in the margin, as if I had neglected to send it. The hour's trouble which it would cost me to replace what is missing I will not take, till I have made him look after what could not have been missing without great negligence. It is by special good fortune that I can replace it without much difficulty, as it happens to be a part which required rather more than ordinary pains, and rather a rough draft of it was made, which by good luck has not been destroyed, and by further good luck is legible, which my rough drafts of later years have ceased to be, even to myself, when they have been written two or three days. This is a bad habit; and one which ought to be corrected, for it might prove very inconvenient, and there is no excuse for it.

Will you think me very much at leisure, or very idly laborious, when you hear that I have just finished the ten volumes of Madame Sévigné's letters? The book never fell in my way till I met with the last new edition at Bruges last year, and by reading in it for some half hour every day after dinner, by firelight, on the sofa before I take my *siesta*, I have gone through it, learning a few things which it is pleasant and may be useful to know, and having been much amused, and sometimes interested. It is some pleasure to see that in spite of all the profligacy of Louis XIV.'s court, aided by the Romish religion, and that irreligion which is its shadow, or its truly begotten imp, and constant attendant, there were yet in the very sphere and vortex of corruption so many persons who had original goodness enough to withstand these evil influences, and retain the natural integrity and affections with which God had blest them. One thinks the worse of the times and of the national manners, but perhaps the better of human nature; and certainly much the worse of the Romish religion, that is, a reader who did not know much about that religion would think the worse of it, when he finds such a woman as Madame Sévigné exulting in the revocation of the Edict of Nantes, and sees the cat put her head out of the bag every now and then, when the nunneries are talked of. I cannot feel any liking for Madame Grignan, who, whatever she may have been as a daughter, seems to have been a bad step-mother, and not remarkable for maternal affection. We might account for national differences if all men were made of clay, like Adam, for then the different sorts of clay might explain the matter. Flesh and blood are the same on both sides of the British Channel, but what a marvellous difference in the current of thoughts and feelings! The truth, however, is, that there are but two sorts of people everywhere—the good and the bad— and a great many varieties between them.

Dear friend, God bless you.
ROBERT SOUTHEY.

LVI.

TO ROBERT SOUTHEY.

BUCKLAND, *January* 28th, 1826.

It is very pleasant, truly, to meet kind looks where one had expected (and deserved) something like a frown; but then, perhaps, such lenient treatment encourages over-boldness, and here I am again, seizing upon a hint, and asking you for the title you say you might furnish me with, if you knew the contents of my volume. Why, it consists of such little poems as those I wrote in the two young ladies' scrap-books, in all moods and metres, and a few interspersed prose trifles, essays, stories (pitiful concerns, I think, but the Monster will have them in). Most of these miscellanies have such affected titles as make one sick, and I find it very difficult to separate the peculiar from the affected. I can compose ridiculous titles easily enough, but it would not quite answer the Monster's purpose or mine to stick a fool's cap upon one's own candidate.

I do not like Madame de Grignan better than you do, and what is more, I do not admire Madame de Sévigné's maternal tenderness half so much as it has always been the law to ad-admire it. *Elle l'affiche trop.* But her letters, her style, her amiable *enjouement, finesse,* and purity (for a Frenchwoman) are delightful. Madame de Sévigné was, I think, one of the most perfect fine ladies—I mean as to fine taste, fine breeding, tact, &c.—who ever adorned any court and country, and it is enchanting to find this high polish had neither destroyed nor deteriorated more valuable qualities. I have a French friend and correspondent, who would bear much comparison with her accomplished countrywoman—The Duchess de Damas Cruz. Pray, did Madame de Sévigné's letters please you better by fire-light than by any other light, that you have been taking such liberties with those precious organs given you for such useful and noble purposes, and to be treasured accordingly? You may as well blind one at once as use them by fire-light. See how sharp and dictatorial I can be.

Lockhart, I hear, is to have £1500 a-year for his editorship—is it so?—and, moreover, the lucrative sinecure office W. S. Rose has lately vacated. I sometimes wish you had succeeded Gifford.

Do you remember anything of a certain Monsieur Pichot, who—*selon la mode actuelle*—has been making a pilgrimage through the land of lakes and poets, and tells everything he could pick up while admitted to their domestic circles—a most laudable and honourable custom! I have a great mind to publish my visit to Keswick, not omitting the interlude of " Semid."

Fare you well, dear friend. If pain has chained my tongue (a loss to no one), it has not fettered my fingers, you see, or overcome my gossiping humour. But I will let you off with one " God bless you."

CAROLINE A. BOWLES.

I have been "idly laborious" of late, reading through lots of old French Mémoires, not the *very* old, but that series so historically interesting, extending from the reigns of Louis Treize to Louis Seize; of these, the eight volumes of Mademoiselle's (la grande Mademoiselle's) autobiography are to me infinitely curious and interesting, and Madame de Motteville's five form an admirable pendent for them.

Richelieu and De Retz, and others of those times, furnish out altogether a very complete history, not to forget Bentivoglio, though I bring him in *à la fin* instead of *au commencement*. How rich the French are in Mémoires!

LVII.

TO CAROLINE BOWLES.

KESWICK, *February 7th*, 1826.

Can I name your book? Will " Solitary Hours " do ? or " A Woman's Portfolio " ? or " Autumnal Flowers " ? I have been luckier in giving Murray's newspaper a name, or rather in shortening its appellation, and called it " The Rip." Huskisson sent him word the other day that, if there appeared in it such another article as that upon the trade question, the paper should have no assistance from him. Murray tells this to one of my friends, and says: "Fifteen years, Sir, I (he, John Murray) have supported the government, and there's a pretty message for a man to receive in this Land of Liberty!" It is long since I have heard anything so good as this—the said John declaring at the same time that, if he had taken the wrong side, it was the ministers' own fault, because they had not told him which was the right. Dear Caroline, never let me be told that there is nothing perfect in this world. Murray is perfect in his kind; and your Monster is a perfect monster; and a bookseller in general is perfect—perfect as a hybrid animal can be, which is between goose and cormorant.

This morning I took up *Oliver Newman* once more, and with a hope that when I get into the next book the interest of the tale will then lead me on. My *Tale of Paraguay* has not sold. It was not likely to find many admirers, and even some of those who admired parts have failed to perceive how completely the execution accords with the design—that the author has done nothing which he did not intend to do, and left nothing undone which he intended.

If I were at leisure, I verily believe I should produce a Spenserian poem about as long as "The Castle of Indolence," upon the notion of Sir Oleoso the Butler, coming forward as the champion of a lady's virtue, who is clothed in purple and scarlet. Some odd thoughts for such a satire, which might be at once grave and playful, have been running in my head all this day.

I have read none of those Memoirs which are amusing you, but almost all the earlier ones. You are in the more amusing series. Where is there more variety, and more development of individual character; less to admire, but also less to shudder at; and yet, perhaps, on the whole more to put one out of humour with the affairs of the world and with human nature?

My paper upon the Vaudois, which pleased you because it was mine, has been much hurt by mutilation. I hope the account of Sœur de la Nativité's Revelation in the next number will not be cut down in the same manner. It is such an exposure of impious imposture that it can hardly fail of producing some effect at this time.

God bless you, dear friend.

ROBERT SOUTHEY.

LVIII.

TO CAROLINE BOWLES.

KESWICK, *March 25th*, 1826.

What sort of an anatomist your physician may be I cannot pretend to say, but if there had been more reason for his opinion concerning your pain in the head than I think there can have been, it was not the part of a wise man to have alarmed his patient, as he did you. You must know that for six months of my life, and in the nineteenth year of my age, my thoughts were turned toward the medical profession; during which time I went through a course of anatomy at Oxford and read some medical books. I learnt just enough to have been a constant cause of disquietude and alarm when any of my children have been indisposed, and to apprehend the worst, oftentimes without cause, but sometimes with too much. And the only use my knowledge was of, was that it enabled me when writing *Joan of Arc* to kill men in battle in a scientific way, as the critics have lauded Homer for doing before me. I prided myself upon this (remember it was when I was just one-and-twenty.) One day walking in the streets at Bath, and telling my companion how I had killed the last man, and in what manner I meant to slaughter the next, I said, " I'll stab him in the back " : a man who happened to be passing heard the words, and looked at us with such an expression of astonishment in his face, that we both laughed honestly enough, I dare say, to convince him that no murder was intended.

Mrs. Opie (now Friend Amelia) talks and thinks of fixing herself somewhere in this neighbourhood. Borrodale she thought of, but the Grange will suit her better, if the scheme takes effect, which it will hardly do beyond a trial.

Milner, I am told, is dying, which I should have been sorry to have heard while my book was in hand. You give me credit for more management in that said book than was used in it. The truth is, that I had only looked through Mr. Butler's volume when I began to answer it; and being urged on all sides to be courteous in reply, and, moreover, really liking him for that sort of happy good nature which constant prosperity has fostered, I wished to separate him from his cause, and kept all my hard blows for Milner and Giant Pope. But as I went on, and discovered some fresh instances of unfairness in every page, I passed, not less imperceptibly than naturally, into the strain and temper which took from you all fidgetty feelings, whatever it might give to him. I have heard very little of my book, except from two or three persons who have read it, as you have done, with a personal interest. The composition, as you must have perceived, was matter of amusement. The perfect confidence which I felt made me in such good humour with the subject, that I could never be heartily angry with opponents, who were so completely at my mercy.

I am now half way through a paper upon the English Cathedrals for the *Quarterly Review*, being my ways and means for midsummer, a sort of miscellaneous essay, showing by the history of one Cathedral what sort of books concerning them might usefully and pleasantly be composed. My next paper will be upon the Jews: the Society for converting them will supply me with a text, unless I should find it impossible to treat the subject without bearing hard upon that not-very-wise Society; for in the chapter of accidents it has come to pass that they have laid me under some obligation, by affording a channel of communication with the Bilderdijks, in a way which I will explain when we meet in May. This I suspect is the greatest good that they effect at present with an annual expenditure of more than £20,000. If this subject be laid aside, I shall take the opportunity which is afforded by a new edition of Baxter's works to write his life.

Winter is returned to these mountains and they are covered with snow.

God bless you, dear friend.

ROBERT SOUTHEY.

LIX.

TO ROBERT SOUTHEY.

April 18*th*, 1820.

So Mr. Butler seems to have explained away one of your charges of unfairness, and you seem satisfied, and Murray is the scape-goat. By answering only half Butler's book at present, what a comfortable plea have you afforded him for waiting to take breath, and collect his astounded senses, and sort and unravel his tangled skeins of sophistry to strangle you with, when the time comes. And *en attendant*, just to sharpen his wits, there is Sœur Nativité!—an admirable Papist pendant for our Joanna Southcote. Sœur Nativité beats even Blanco White's heroines, though they were grand specimens.

I anticipate much pleasure from your paper on Cathedrals— a canvas which affords scope for the happiest creations of your brush, in outline and effect, and mellow colouring. But what can you make of the Jews?—" The Society" I mean. Nothing in its favour I am sure, if you tell truth, and that you cannot help. I am sick of the very sound of societies, committees, associations, and all the joint-stock companies on religious subjects, to such extravagances do they proceed, and so is "the world gone after them," particularly the female part of it, always well pleased to find itself of consequence, and certainly an indefatigable engine when set to work, and the wheels well oiled with flattery, which the saints of your sex supply very profusely and with good policy in the organization of their "female branch societies." One lady is President of this, another "Vice-" of that association—then, what with Secretaries, Treasurers,

Collectors, Tract-bearers, Expounders! Heaven have mercy on us! all womankind is whirling round in a vortex of religious dissipation—and their energies once set a-going pass my comprehension, their unwearied activity of body and mind, or rather of animal spirits. Go where one will the subject is forced upon one. One lady's drawing-room is full of little charity boxes, placed here and there amongst the ornamental litter; another keeps a stall of trumpery knick-knacks— "ladies' work"—to lay her visitors under contribution; another asks you to work for her (audacious!), and then a whole bevy of damsels sit congregated together, pasting and painting, and sewing and gilding, and what not, to get up a booth for the next religious fair. All this pious activity is going on round me, and no wonder if it bewilders my brain and offends my taste, and, I hope, right feeling; because when I see its ill effects on society, on domestic comfort, in the neglect of private duties, and the obtrusiveness of religious pretensions ("serious views" as the fashionable cant has it), I feel sure "something is rotten in the state of Denmark," something unsound in the foundation of these crazy castles. Lately people were employed to walk about Southampton with banners, begging for the Jews, and directing folks to the ladies' repository in aid of the funds for their conversion; and lately we had a fair here for something similar. Pray don't encourage this mania, or you will deserve that it should spread to Keswick.*

I have just been reading in *Cardinal de Retz* of a Spanish

---

* In his reply Southey writes—"Nothing can be livelier than your account of the Lady Presidents, &c., of the religious pick-pocket associations. In the Jewish concern the whole money thus received is merely wasted. The Bible Society must do some good, though immeasurably little in proportion to its pretensions. The various Missionary Societies are producing some immediate effect, and preparing the way for much more. With all these there is a great deal of fanaticism, a great deal of quackery, and not a little cant; but we must bear with the evil for the sake of the good, where they are so mixed as, in these cases, to be inseparable. But as to the effects of the proselytising spirit upon womankind in private life, you are perfectly right, and right as to the principle which the tarantula bite puts in action."

miracle which outdoes all you have brought to light—of a one-legged man of Saragossa, who being employed to clean and feed the lamps of one of the churches, rubbed the stump of the lost leg with the oil thereof, till a young limb sprouted out and grew to perfect size! I dare say you have met with this glorious legend somewhere.

Where is "the Grange" near you? I do not not recollect such a place. I should not think dear quiet Keswick would suit "friend Amelia" for a constant residence. She has been too long the centre of a little circle of Cockney blues to thrive in the shadow of your mountains. Sad work she has made of her last publication, *Illustrations of Lying*, an excellent subject, but requiring a finer touch than hers. She is radically vulgar in all her notions. And I am abominably spiteful, I perceive, and in a very gossiping mood this evening; but please to observe that I have allowed you a longer respite than usual, from my most punctual correspondence, for which you are indebted to a wearing pain in my side, which has made it distressing to me to write for some days past, and now makes my scrawl more scrawley than usual. But if I do not write, you will not, and that deprivation I cannot voluntarily incur.

The hawthorns in my garden are almost in bloom—the May—your welcome herald, and my prayer book is sure to fall open every morning first where that loveliest month of all the year is noted in the Calendar—you will acknowledge it to be so, if only for the sake of your Edith May.

I thought my little book (*Solitary Hours*) would have found its way to you before now; but it has not, nor, in the shape of advertisement, into any paper, which seems to me a very negative method of "promoting its success," with all that zeal and energy the Monster professes in its cause; and I rather wonder at it, as everything he publishes is generally advertised for months in all the periodicals and newspapers. It matters very little, however, in my case.

God bless you, dear friend. If I had "wings like a dove"—which verily I sometimes long for, that I might "flee away and be at rest"—they should bear me to-day to some of your haunts among the windings of Greta, or the mountain dells, where methinks there must be healing in the very air, and music, I am sure, in the voice of a friend.

CAROLINE A. BOWLES.

I wish Mrs. Lowell could see my anemones. Ask her if she would like me to save seed of them for her: she, I think, is the gardener amongst you.

LX.

TO ROBERT SOUTHEY.*

BUCKLAND, *May* 30*th*, 1826.

The author of *Oliver Newman* cannot find it in his heart to condemn me for obeying a first impulse, a blameless one, though none of the wisest perhaps, which irresistibly urges me to say to him before he leaves England—"God bless you for coming to see me." The words were in my heart, and on my lips when I parted with you, though they found no utterance, so my pen must convey them to you. I feel by what a sacrifice of time and convenience you have given me the highest gratification which can possibly fall to my lot, but I know at the same time you will never reckon as lost time the days you devoted to that charitable purpose,

So having relieved a very full and grateful heart in as few words as I can compress its feelings, I bid you farewell for the present, praying God to be your guide and protector by land and sea, and to restore you in health and safety to your beloved family.

Dear friend, farewell.

CAROLINE A. BOWLES.

* Written after a visit of Southey to Buckland, and before his departure for the Continent.

LXI.

TO CAROLINE BOWLES.

HARLEY-STREET, *June* 2nd, 1826.

Dear Caroline, God bless you. You have no reason to thank me for a visit, from which, short as it necessarily was, and therefore in part painful, I derived as much pleasure as it was possible that I could give. Be assured that whenever I come within the same reach of you, on my annual journeys, it shall not be a light cause which will prevent me from repeating it.

Something (among many other omitted things) I meant to have said about the Sherwood versification,* and the mode of practice by translating or reversifying into it. You will see its structure in Dr. Sayers' poems somewhat more plainly defined than in mine, though I think there is more force and freedom in my own. What you have to remember is, that the common blank verse is sparingly to be introduced, and that the basis of the metre is the six-syllable line. You will very easily accustom yourself to the structure, and then you will find that it may be written with more ease than any other measure, as much sweetness and equal strength.

God bless you, dear friend. I cannot promise to write before my return to England, for I have a Journal to keep which will require all the little leisure that travelling affords. About the 26th I hope again to reach England. Farewell, and God bless you.

Yours affecionately,

ROBERT SOUTHEY.

* The intended metre of *Robin Hood*, the unrhymed verse of *Thalaba*.

LXII.

TO CAROLINE BOWLES.

1, HARLEY STREET, *July 2nd*, 1826.

Dear Caroline, you will be glad to know that I am returned safely after a pleasant visit to my Leyden friends, and a pleasant journey; that my expected attack, though not prevented, has been fairly kept down and subdued; that I am in good health and spirits; and finally, that on Wednesday night next I set out for Cumberland, hoping to reach home on Friday morning.

Now for the next point which will interest you—my return for Parliament for the borough of Downton. Lord Radnor has done this without my consent or knowledge, solely on account of the *Book of the Church*. I never saw him, nor had any communication with him. The return is void, because I hold a pension of £200 a-year during pleasure. If this were not the case, I would not take the oath respecting the qualification. And if I were actually qualified, and no other impediment existed, my inclinations, habits, and plain straightforward sense would determine me to reject the seat without hesitation. Therefore I will not frank a letter. You, however, may direct to me as M.P. till Parliament meets, till which time the Post Office will duly honour those two letters. The affair is singular and amusing; and as it gratifies my friends, it gratifies me, now that I have done laughing at it.

I bought books enough to fill a huge chest, the arrival of which at Keswick will make me happy for a week, and the unpacking of which will be a great joy to all the juniors of the family. And as many volumes are full of prints representing the churches, chateaus, &c. in the Low Countries, even the elders will be reconciled to this importation, though I begin to have some qualms respecting the danger of carrying any greater weight up stairs in a house which was certainly not built with reference to such a library.

You will smile at hearing that I have found a Sister Providence, whom I must take the liberty of introducing to Mr. Butler in the *Quarterly Review*.

I dine to-day at the Bishop of London's, who is very kind to me at all times, and who urges me to go on with my *Vindiciæ*. To-morrow I pass at Streatham with my uncle, and under the apprehension that I shall hardly see him again—a feeling which I painfully experienced at parting from Bilderdijk. Life is so full of partings, that when one thinks of it there is a temptation to wish one's self at the journey's end.

But I am going home, to be at rest I trust, and get my after-dinner sleep and to be cool—and to be clean—and to write prose and also to write verse, and go on the lake and into the lake, and play with the cats, and talk nonsense with the children, and learn Dutch with Cuthbert, and receive proof-sheets, and rub through life as smoothly and pleasantly as I can.* If I could have you within sight I would not ask Fortune for much more.

God bless you, dear friend.

ROBERT SOUTHEY.

LXIII.

TO CAROLINE BOWLES.

KESWICK, *October* 2nd, 1826.

I am going this day, very much against the grain, to Lowther, where I go so seldom that I have a sense of discourtesy and ungraciousness in declining so many invitations. The distance, which is inconvenient for one who keeps neither carriage nor horse, and a great unwillingness ever to go from home and break up from employments, for which I have but little time at all times, occasion the apparent incivility on my part towards

---

* Southey's expectations were not fulfilled. On his return he found his daughter Isabel seriously ill, and on a Sunday evening in mid July she died.

a family who are very obliging in their attentions to me. Sir George Beaumont and Rogers are there. They spent nearly a fortnight in Keswick, and I saw more of the latter than I had ever done before. He has won the hearts of my daughters by his quiet, pleasant, playful manner, seasoned with a little maliciousness, which sharpens his sayings, and for which those who are wounded by it make him suffer in kind.

Some weeks ago, when I was fit for no other employment, I performed the melancholy one of arranging the correspondence of some five-and-twenty years. In so doing, among other buried papers, there came to light the original scrawl of "The Devil's Thoughts," for which you once asked me, and which at that time I looked for in vain. In some idle hour I will transcribe it for you. I found also a register of some fantastic dreams, noted down, as you may well suppose, not superstitiously, but for their strange combinations. The use of having kept such a register I felt when writing the *Vindiciæ*, and had very often regretted the loss of these few but curious pages.*

My papers, dear Caroline, will afford rare picking when I am gone. Henry Taylor, my companion on both my Dutch expeditions, will take the charge of putting them together according to the directions which I may leave. There is no one connected with me to whom the office could be entrusted, and he has, to recommend him for it, sufficient abilities, personal acquaintance, and goodwill.

I should like to show you a letter which I have received from an American poetess—a widow—telling me how she has been crossed in love.

I may perhaps bid farewell in rhyme to the letters M. P. Let me hear from you, and never be withheld from writing because I have not written. A letter from you is always wished for, and always welcome, if it did but bring better tidings of your own health.

Dear friend, God bless you.

ROBERT SOUTHEY.

* See Appendix to the present volume.

LXIV.

TO CAROLINE BOWLES.

KESWICK, *December* 11*th*, 1826.

The best thing I can do about the *Devil's Thoughts* (for that is the original title of the poem) will be to put in something about Porson himself, and the impudent story which makes him the author.* No sooner said than done, for the intention having arisen, as soon as I put pen to paper for the purpose of writing to you, with that same pen the following stanzas were rough-shaped. They will, I dare say, come into better form hereafter :—

> As he went along the Strand,
> Between three in the morning and four,
> He saw an odd-looking person,
> Who reel'd from Perry's door.
>
> And he thought that all the world over
> In vain for a man you might seek,
> Who could drink more like a Trojan,
> Or talk more like a Greek.
>
> But if anyone had told him
> It would one day be matter of talk,
> That this erudite bibber had written
> The story of this Walk,
>
> Why, that whosoever first said so
> Told a swinging lie
> Is what the Devil would have thought,
> And so say I.

---

* Miss Bowles had urged Southey to publish *The Devil's Walk* as his own, and so set at rest the question of its authorship. In a subsequent letter (December 21st, 1826) he sends a number of new stanzas, including that beginning

"A peeress drove by in her pride," &c.

It *is* a likeness, and so good a one that I should not like it to get abroad, for it would certainly be recognized." On December 31st he sends the lines describing Irving :—

"With gestures and throcs, and ahs! and ohs!
Far famed his flock for fright'ning,
And thundering with his voice, the while
His eyes zig-zag like lightning."

" Your favourite poem gets a little tinkering every now and then, so that

If Porson had been alive the verses should have carried a sting with them, for I have heard that he was inclined to take credit for this poem, though he had not the effrontery to claim it.

And now that I have begun with doggrel, you shall have some more. They are verses which are to be sung instead of said, composed upon occasion of some circulating letters soliciting subscriptions to all sorts of works by the writer, who happened to have a name which rendered him capable of the sort of immortality he deserved:—

>Mr. Frizzel, Mr. Frizzel,
>You may whistle, you may whistle,
> Long enough, long enough,
>Ere I answer your epistle.
>For want of asking, you
>Will lose nothing, it is true;
>And it plainly may be seen
>You succeed among the green;
>But however you may try it,
> Mr. Frizzel, Mr. Frizzel,
>You will get nothing by it
> From me, who am grizzle.
>Cunning shaver though you be,
>With your puff and flummery,
>You shall never frizzle me,
> Mr. Frizzel, Mr. Frizzel.

I know not when the Devil will fairly be laid. It now contains forty-nine stanzas, thirty of which have now been added, and four of the others [re-written?] since it was first written and printed. . . . The subject is not one which would suit Cruikshank; his grotesque ought always to be supernatural; there he has no equal; but when he deals with mere humanity his caricature becomes coarse. I have tales in store which he ought to embellish, if I had but time to write them." In a letter of January 30th, 1827, Southey writes: "Do not think that I overlook the lawyers; there is a stanza about them, alluding to Cain and Abel; but I have that to say of them, in sober prose and severe truth, which will make the whole profession, as far as its members are professional, hate me as heartily as the Whigs and Roman Catholics do—an *il*-liberal profession; and the first hopeful symptoms of an improved state of public feeling will be when it is regarded so, and when a counsellor, who for his fee will defend any cause, right or wrong, shall be looked on as out of the pale of honourable society. You know I gave the Court of Chancery the name of 'Eldon Hole.' "

You may praise and puff,
Or take it in snuff,
And set up your bristle
As sharp as a thistle,
If you will, if you will,
  Mr. Frizzel, Mr. Frizzel.
With my little money, I,
  Alack and well-a-day!
Have so many fish to fry,
  That whatever you may say,
I shall not be taken in
  To frizzle it away.
Mr. Frizzel, Mr. Frizzel,
I am grizzle, I am grizzle,
And therefore you may whistle
  Long enough, long enough,
Ere I answer your epistle.

The printer has delayed my second volume; it will be a week before his work is completed, and in another, I suppose, the book will be abroad.

              God bless you, dear friend.
                      ROBERT SOUTHEY.

LXV.

TO ROBERT SOUTHEY.

              BUCKLAND, *December 25th*, 1826.

I set you thinking of the Devil!*
  Fie, sir! fie!
  Pray, was it I
Gave you those curious particulars,
All so authentic and new,
About his red waistcoat and breeches blue,

---

* Southey had written on a slip of paper—
    "Who set me thinking of the Devil?
      You did, you,
      Caroline, Caroline;
        Yes, it is true.—R S."

And that elegant whisk of his tail,
Or, as Leigh Hunt would call it,
  "That jaunty swale?"
You must have been ——
  I won't say where,
To take such notes
  Of his dress and air;
And then to say it was I
  Set you thinking of the Devil!
    Fie, sir! fie!
The fact is 'twas little I knew
(Poor innocent I!) of the old Buggaboo,
Till that wonderful picture you drew,
  Which beats Mister Fuseli's out and out,
  That all the world made such a rout about
    (You know best where you stood,
      While taking the view);
But ever since I saw it,
  By all that's true!
I never think of the Devil
  Without thinking of you!

   Your affectionate friend,
        CAROLINE A. BOWLES.

LXVI.

TO CAROLINE BOWLES.

KESWICK, *February 21st*, 1827.

I am as busy in getting forward the third volume of the *Peninsular War* as any man need be, can be, or ought to be; and in the course of ten days I hope to have it in the press, with the full intention of completing it by Christmas. The materials which I have collected for it, and which have never seen the light, are very copious and good; but most of them were transcribed so long ago that I must have the trouble of again making myself master of their contents before they can be arranged. However, the whole work which lies before me here is easy and pleasant, and the first proof-sheet will put me in good spirits.

Captain Bruce wrote to me on the 10th from ship-board, off the Nore. I like him dearly, and the better because he writes earnestly and affectionately about you. He says that you brood over your affairs too much, that he is quite distressed at it, and that this is the only thing he regrets in leaving England. And he asks me to write to you and endeavour to combat this. Alas! I fear that uneasy affairs are like uneasy feelings, not to be got rid of, though the spirit should be willing. But that you do not give way to despondency, that you have a buoyant spirit, I believe. If the distance were not so fearful, for one who cannot take seat in a mail-coach, to be trundled along, day and night, like a coach parcel or a basket of game, to the journey's end, I would prescribe a summer and autumn here as the best remedy for ill spirits and ill health. Is it quite impracticable?

To-day's post has brought the news of Lord Liverpool's death-stroke, politically, if not naturally. It is a great public calamity, though if the life and talents of any individual are essential to the designs of Providence, Providence, we may be well assured, preserves him. A crisis, however, in the cabinet must, I think, be brought about by this unexpected shock. I heard some weeks ago more than was good of intrigues for forming a Catholic Administration. But Canning's own health is broken. At the time of Lord Londonderry's death, I know that his friends (Canning's) thought one harassing session of Parliament would destroy him, for he was then kept up by the regular use of opium and the warm bath. A session of fair weather saved him; but it is now squally again, and indeed he has been brewing storms for himself, which he will not find it either pleasant to ride in or easy to direct.

I too have had a loss, and one which cannot be supplied, in Sir George Beaumont, a most amiable and excellent man, with whom I had been acquainted more than twenty years, till that acquaintance had ripened into a cordial esteem and liking, which might almost be called friendship. If he were in London when I went to town, his house was one of the first to which I went after my arrival. This place he was very fond of, and enjoyed it never more than when he lodged here for several weeks last autumn. I parted from him at Lowther, and could have thought that, though twenty years my elder, his was the better life. Lady Beaumont has written to me since his death; she bears the bereavement with great fortitude at present, but it is an utter bereavement, for she has no object of affection left. This is her first sorrow, after a union of fifty years, and it will last till the end of her days, which, considering her excellent constitution, may yet be far distant.

So every year takes something from us! What will this take? I had better say what it will bring in the way of good, and I know nothing better than that it should bring you to Keswick.

God bless you, dear friend.

Robert Southey.

LXVII.

TO CAROLINE BOWLES.

Keswick, *April 5th*, 1827.

Do you remember saying something to me in a letter, some two years ago, about the share which the ladies took in the Joint-Stock Religious Societies of the day? It pleased me well at the time, and I fitted it the other day to a note for my *Dialogues*, putting only a —— where the word Southampton stood, that it might not be known in what part of England my lively correspondent lives.

That Paper which offends you by its attack on Smith (and which I have not yet seen) is written by a young man whom I introduced to the *Quarterly Review.* H—— is his name. He works as a law scrivener with his father in Carey-street, and has every possible disadvantage of education and circumstances; added to which his manners are far from pleasing, and he takes no pains to conceal an opinion of his own talents, which appears inordinate to all who are not willing to rate them as they really deserve to be rated, and which is more likely to give offence than to find sympathy or to excite pity. Lockhart was disgusted with it, but I suspect that he has taken him into favour upon the score of this very attack on Smith, for he has bespoken from him a continuation of the subject, with a retrospect to Scott's earlier novels.

My plans for the season of the hay-asthma are these:—I shall leave home the second week in May, for about a week's rambling with Wordsworth in a part of this country which I have never seen, which is Furness, with the vale of the Duddon and the lower part of the Esk. My whole family will join me then at Kendal, with Miss Hutchinson (Mrs. Wordsworth's sister), and perhaps Dora Wordsworth, and we go to Harrogate for a month, Cuthbert and all, in the expectation that it will be salutary for the girls, and a hope that the waters may also be useful to their mother. We shall visit the Caves and other things on the way, and return by way of Wensley Dale, thus including the finest objects in the West Riding. Had you been as much on this side London as you are beyond it, you might easily have met us there! We mean to go into a house, not to be at one of the hotels, and we shall also come away before what is called "the season" begins.

So much for my plans, which have at least this good, that they will not separate me from my family, and will give the younger part a great deal of pleasure. I shall feel the want of my books, and must be looked after, lest I should hang myself in a fit of despondency.

God bless you, dear Caroline.

ROBERT SOUTHEY.

LXVIII.

TO ROBERT SOUTHEY.

BUCKLAND, *April* 15*th*, 1827.

Are you not afraid of making me too vain by grafting any sentence of my writing into a work of yours? I shall be ready to sing when I see it. "Sure, says this little woman, this is none of I." Though I recollect writing something on the subject you speak of, I do not remember what.

There was another paper in the *Quarterly Review* which offended me as much, more, perhaps, than the dismemberment of poor Smith—the attack on Milman, of whose poetry I am by no means an enthusiastic admirer, and least of all of his "Ann Boleyn"; but I hate malice and unfairness, against whomsoever levelled, and I do think that critique a very malicious and unfair one. Shakespeare and Milman! about as fair a comparison as one would be between the full moon and an argand lamp; and yet the lamp is a pretty thing in its way, if looked at without the proximity of overpowering lustre. I hope you did not introduce the writer of that spiteful paper, too, to the *Quarterly Review*.

Half an hour ago I finished the last page of your second volume of the *Peninsular War* the most interesting book I have seen since I read the first volume. You have left off very cunningly at a point of the highest interest. I had no idea what a stupendous work was that of the Lines of Torres Vedras, though, parrot-like, I had spoken the words familiarly. I did not expect to have heard you speak as you do of Sir R. Wilson. Surely you can neither esteem nor place much confidence in the *man*, however you may justly commend his military conduct in the affairs you notice in this volume. Alas! alas! what do you say now of the Spanish and Portuguese character? Have not the people of both nations fallen grievously short of what was highly expected of them?

And what do you say to the chaotic state of *our* political

world? Mr. Canning has his hand on the helm, but how will he steer the vessel of the State through the straits into which he has impelled her? What a strange upset of old principles and old measures! Now we shall have the Age of Liberality, if not of Reason. I heard (from a quarter I can rely on) that the very first words Lord Liverpool articulated after his seizure were, "Where is Canning? Is he in the House of Commons?" *In my place*, I suppose, might have been the old statesman's first jealous feeling.

I am glad you are to move early in May, and can well understand the comfort it will be to you to have all your dear ones with you. But will you cheat the catarrh so well by remaining long stationary at Harrogate as if you continued moving about? I know your horror of locomotion, but truly I cannot fancy you a watering-place visitor, a pump-room lounger. I should as soon expect to meet an eagle sauntering up Bond-street. So surely as I cannot do what I like, I would if I could do what I like—betake myself this year to Harrogate, in the hope of being *noticed* by you and your family, and in despite of my horror of watering-places, and Harrogate water, which I smelt once, and that was enough! But *ifs* and *buts* are the thorns of life, or rather its thorn hedges, clipping one in everywhere. Just now, however, in spite of *ifs* and *buts*, I am in special good humour with life, having had a spell of better health for the last week, and not one lawyer's letter or other grievance—a rare halcyon season for me! and I hasten to write to you while it lasts. Sometimes I think with myself that what you so truly remarked of Alaric Watts might in some sense be apparently applicable to me. For if I am not often quarrelling, I seem to be always complaining; but you must not think me a willing complainer, though I acknowledge it is very weak ever to complain. But, indeed, I *am* weak, and the hand of God is heavy on me. Surely there are persons who seem set apart for almost continual suffering. I believe this; but then I believe also, that in the end the balance will be made even; and what will it matter then what weight has borne down the scale of misfortune? Now, I am sure you will not call this a desponding faith, though my kind Asiatic friend could not understand it.

The misery of a fretful spirit, which turns sweet to bitter, or mere scratches into wounds, is not mine, thank God! So, concluding with this modest panegyric on myself, I leave you to assent to it, if you will be so good-natured.

Your affectionate friend,
CAROLINE A. BOWLES.

LXIX.

TO CAROLINE BOWLES.

KESWICK, *April* 23rd, 1827.

The Paper upon Milman I have not read, caring too little for any such subject. But it is H——'s writing, and I am sorry to find him addicted to ill-natured criticism, which nothing that I had seen of him would have led me to suspect. I have seen him only twice, and with a strong disposition to like him; but there was something about him that rendered this impossible, though I never saw greater or more unequivocal proofs of ability in any young man's writings. I know Milman, who spent a summer here some years ago. He was then a little spoilt by Eton-ism, and has since been more so by admiration, fashionable society, and prosperity. None of his latter publications have fallen in my way, and I believe he has done nothing to equal the promise which his *Samor* afforded. Cumbrous as that poem is, and ill-pitched in its style, it was a very hopeful production—the more so for its faults, which were of the right kind.

Sir Robert Wilson has, I daresay, been as much surprised as you were to see himself so fairly and so fully spoken of by a man who, he must be conscious, thinks very ill of his character and general conduct. He must be still more surprised at the accuracy of the statement, for I had the whole of his letters to

Mr. Frere. The importance of occupying Ciudad Rodrigo at that time cannot be overrated; the merit of the individual in doing so is a different consideration. I fully understood it at the time, and when I talked over this part of the history with Frere, I found that he estimated it exactly as I had done. Wilson was a dirty, moody boy when we were in the same remove at Westminster.

The Spaniards and Portuguese are not fallen in my estimation, though I regard the condition of both peoples with commiseration and sorrow. Those countries require a very different kind of reform from what their reformers are attempting to bring about. They want an able Minister, who would employ arbitrary power in making the laws efficient, and preparing the people for a constitutional government. At present they are in the worst state for any experiments. In such struggles as Spain and Portugal have gone through, the best and noblest spirits are cut off; they sacrifice themselves in the first heat of the contest, and the actors who remain after such a series of events are left with blasted feelings, or, what is even worse, with hardened hearts.

Six months ago I heard that Canning was intriguing to oust those of his colleagues who have now withdrawn, and form an administration with the Whigs, placing himself at the head. The only quarter from which I have received any information upon the subject speaks of the seceders as ill-used by the king; in fact, as deceived by him till the very last. Living, as I do, in retirement, and having much less intercourse than I fomerly had with persons who are about the scene of action, it would be useless to speculate upon the course of intrigues which are now in progress. As for private concerns, I have nothing to expect or hope in any possible turn that affairs may take; and as for public concerns, my reliance upon Providence is such that I look with perfect composure upon a state of affairs which, were it not for that reliance, might make me tremble.

I go to Harrogate for the sake of the girls and their mother, all of whom, and especially the latter, need what I hope may be found there. It is a hideous place, but there are things within reach which will draw me out, so that I shall have change of air and exercise enough, and I reckon something upon the effect of the waters. I shall miss my books and the quiet uniformity in which my days pass here. But even a circulating library will supply something, and, moreover, old books may be found at Leeds, and probably I shall put myself some morning into the stage for that city, for the purpose of bringing back a cargo in the evening. I have no acquaintances in that part of the country, and whether we may pick up any remains to be seen; it is likely enough that there may be persons there who will be willing to pick up me.

If I had been in London I must have attended to receive a speech with the Gold Medal, looked like a fool, and made a fool's speech in return. The medal will please my wife and daughters, and serve as something which they may show their visitors. So, as it pleases them, it becomes me to be pleased; otherwise I could shake my head, and moralize upon the unprofitableness of such marks of honour.

God bless you.

ROBERT SOUTHEY.

LXX.

TO CAROLINE BOWLES.

KESWICK, *July* 10*th*, 1827.

Here we are, Edith and Bertha the better for the Harrogate waters, their mother only better inasmuch as the new circumstances there may sometimes serve to withdraw her from the melancholy and almost hopeless course of her habitual thoughts and feelings—a sore grief, of which I never before said as much as is now expressed here to any human being, but which presses upon me more heavily than my bodily infirmities.

Send to your circulating library for *Isaac Comnenus*. I

may whisper to you that it is the work of Henry Taylor, my fellow-traveller of the last and the preceding year, and was in part written while he was waiting for my recovery at Leyden. You will find in it originality, and feeling, and genius.

I have been letting Murray and his editor know that the incivility with which they have treated me during the last six months must be carried no further, and in consequence they are both my very humble servants. Still, however, it is uncertain whether I shall continue to bear any part in the *Quarterly Review*. Murray is, as you may suppose, in a woeful quandary, not knowing which course it is his interest to take, but beginning to apprehend that it is the safest way to keep the *Review* in its old course. During the perplexity Lockhart has been in no very comfortable state; the result I still consider doubtful, though Lockhart writes as if he thought otherwise. If the journal is to be guided by Croker's influence, and follow Mr. Canning's crooked path, of course I withdraw from it. If it keep to the better part, I have told the editor that my last paper, which he has so unceremoniously withheld, must be inserted, and that no future communication is to be postponed from one number to another, and that this is the *condition* on which those communications are to be continued, for writing in any periodical work as I do only for the purpose of helping out the means of a moderate expenditure, "I can neither afford to waste my labour nor to wait for its wages." Upon this plain statement he is now chewing the cud. Meantime I have enough to do with the *Colloquies*, which from their nature occupy much time in the composition, and with the *Peninsular War*.

Dear friend, God bless you.

ROBERT SOUTHEY.

LXXI.

TO ROBERT SOUTHEY.

BUCKLAND, *July* 3rd, 1827.

Well I know there are griefs far heavier to be borne than any bodily infirmity. If human sympathy could lighten yours, how greatly would the weight be lessened! But you have better comfort, more efficacious balm, and I pray God to bestow it unsparingly upon you. The perpetual sight of constitutional despondency in one nearly and dearly connected with us is an eating sorrow—one that began to prey upon me from my earliest recollection—and has no doubt cast its shadow over a temper naturally joyous.

I had a visit yesterday from Mr. Bowles of Bremhill—a very short one, for he had missed my habitation in the morning and driven past it to Milford and farther. He is looking remarkably well, and appears to be in particularly good spirits: inquired much for you, and desired me to give you his kind regards. A strange story he told me, which, though he gave it very circumstantially, I can hardly give credit to—that Lady Beaumont hearing (heaven knows how or where) that I "adored Mr. Wordsworth," felt assured that she and I were "kindred spirits," and had decided to write to me, and propose that I should take up my abode with her; "which," said Mr. Bowles, "I strongly dissuaded her from doing, assuring her you were not likely to accept the proposition." No indeed I am not likely to do so, nor should I have felt much flattered by the motive of Lady B.'s invitation. Admire and delight in Mr. Wordsworth's noble poetry I certainly do. "Adore Mr. Wordsworth" I certainly do not; and though I fear mine may be an enthusiastic and rather romantic nature, I never did or could feel that sort of enthusiasm which seems now and then to make women forget they are women, and have some little feminine dignity and propriety to maintain, and have no business to run about the world "adoring" poets or any such golden calves.

You know *you* could hardly send me to see Mr. Wordsworth even with your passport; and yet as far as respecting high intellect goes, I will yield to no one consistently with self respect. This effusion of dignified indignation will amuse you, I think; but perhaps you are not [surprised?] to learn that I can be a little bit of a virago.

God bless you.

CAROLINE A. BOWLES.

LXXII.

TO CAROLINE BOWLES.

KESWICK, *August* 17*th*, 1827.

Your story of Lady Beaumont surprises me, not so much at her having formed the intention, as that she should not have given me some intimation of it, and felt her way through that channel. She is an excellent woman, with a warm heart and a warmth of manners which even high life has hardly subdued; very much of an adorer herself, but the more she is known the more she is to be esteemed for her sterling worth. I wish you knew her, and should be very glad if she invited you to visit her, and carried you from London to Coleorton. You would then be within reasonable reach of Keswick, and I would call for you there on my next return from the south.

In half an hour I set off to meet Wordsworth and his family, Quillinan, and I know not who besides, at a lakeside pic-nic on Leatheswater, the half-way rendezvous between us. The weather is dark and cold, not, however, likely to end in rain. My cattle are now mounting the cart; I follow by a swifter conveyance, and have thus a scrap of time sufficient for making some [progress] in a letter. You will be pleased to hear that Murray has placed himself upon better terms with me than he ever had any pretensions to hold before. He took my advice concerning the *Quarterly Review* wisely, and accordingly there is an end of all vacillation there, and Sister Providence will exhibit in the next number, leading the way.

August 18*th*.—A party of strangers interrupted me yesterday, so little at this season can I reckon even upon half an hour early in the mornng.

Garrick's letters I hear nothing of, and am very well contented not to hear of them. But it is settled that I am to edit General Wolfe's and prefix his life. In the way of editing there is nothing to do except adding a few notes, where there are any pegs to hang them on. The letters will be thought very worthless. The life can be little more than the story of two short campaigns—that in which Louisbourg was taken, and that of the ensuing year in which he fell. With both, however, I can do something, especially as a sketch of Canadian affairs ought to be introduced. So if you know anything concerning Wolfe, help me to it. He was a man of heroic character, and in that respect has not been praised beyond his deserts. And he had the merit of being a disciplinarian at a time when the army was in its very worst state.

Our yesterday's party went off well. We met, to the number of twenty-eight, in a beautiful situation, and the weather could not have been more favourable for lighting up the mountains, while it was cool enough to make us enjoy a good fire on the shore. "There comes *Burn'em wood*," said Mr. Barber as Willy Wordsworth was bringing a huge load of sticks for the fire; upon which Mr. Quillinan rejoined—"You shall not be called *dunce inane* for saying that." These parties always dispose me to melancholy, and that produces an effort for mirth. Too many of our enjoyments in this life are but bitter-sweets at the best; it is a comfort to think and feel that the bitters are wholesome.

Dear friend, God bless you.

ROBERT SOUTHEY.

LXXIII.

TO ROBERT SOUTHEY.

BUCKLAND, *September 3rd,* 1827.

I like the thought of your editing Wolfe's letters and writing his life better than your undertaking the same office for Garrick's. Part of Wolfe's family has dwelt in this neighbourhood, for every Sunday, in my way to church, my eye glances on a tombstone, whereon it is recorded, that underneath lie the remains of Mr. William Burcher, "first cousin to the late General Wolfe;" and I recollect an old lady whose maiden name was Burcher, one of the same family, the remnant of which is now, I am told, settled in or about a place called Saint Cross, near Winchester. I daresay I could glean some information in that quarter if you thought it worth trying for. Moreover, in a country-seat in this neighbourhood belonging to friends of mine there hangs a very fine oil portrait of General Wolfe. The owners of the place have let it, and have been long absent, but I know where to find them, and would ask any question about the picture if you choose I should. I have a faint recollection of being told by some of the family, many, many years ago, that General Wolfe was their relation, and the circumstance of his picture being in their possession corroborates with that impression. I should not expect much from his letters, but very much from your relation of his brief and glorious career.

I suppose, among all your multifarious avocations, poor *Oliver Newman* never gets a line now; much less *Robin Hood*, and other things that I could name; but the wonder is, how you get through even half your labours—even the mere mechanical part of them. I have sometimes suspected you must have a familiar—not Mephistopheles—yours is a good angel. I never could form to myself any idea of heaven, except that, being a place where sin and sorrow cannot enter, it must be one of blessedness; but as a child I used to long to go to Paradise, my conception of which I had formed from a puppet-show,

where Adam and Eve were sitting in a bower of fruit and
flowers, surrounded with lambs and turtle-doves. And in after
visions, later on than becomes one whose mind should dwell
more upon serious truth, I have dreamt how well worth dying
for it would be, to be appointed the invisible minister of good
to some one we have on earth cared dearly for. I suppose
it is hardly possible to live as I do, so much out of the tangible
world, without creating for oneself a world of shadows. So
now you have a letter from the shades partly, and must excuse
the lack of sense and reason.

God bless you, my dear friend.

CAROLINE A. BOWLES.

LXXIV.

TO CAROLINE BOWLES.

[KESWICK, *October*, 1827.]

You are a good and faithful friend, dear Caroline, ready
for any service, and never sparing trouble where service may
be rendered. Thank you for both your letters and their
inclosures. The letter of General Wolfe which was inclosed
has been printed in *The Gentleman's Magazine:* it is valuable
for little else than for containing his opinion of Scanderbeg, of
whom he had probably read in Knolles's *History of the Otto-
man Empire*, a book which Johnson has praised highly (indeed,
above its deserts), and which, on that recommendation, I purchased and read when I was a youth at Oxford.

To-day I returned the proofs of the severest criticism which
I have ever written. It is upon Hallam's *Constitutional History*, a book composed in the worst temper, and upon the worst
principles. It contains even a formal justification of the murder of Lord Strafford. I am acquainted with the author, and
should therefore have abstained from this act of justice upon

him, if he had not called it forth by some remarks in his notes upon *The Book of the Church*, which take from him all right of complaint. You will see that I can be angry, not on my own score, because every attack upon that Book only serves to prove its strength; but where there is a spirit of detraction and malevolence manifested towards those who are entitled to respect, and gratitude, and veneration, my blood stirs when I see them traduced, and the same feeling which brings tears into my eyes when I think of them at other times passes on such an occasion into an anger which I do not account among the emotions to be repented of.

One of the first movements which I shall undertake after reaching London in May (if we both live so long) will be to embark in one of the steam-coaches, which are soon to travel upon your road, and be whisked to Southampton. But I will make it my last movement if you will muster heart and hope to travel northwards, under my care, and pass the remainder of the summer and autumn with us. Can you? Will you? Nothing is more likely to do you good than this mountain air.

The verses which you sent Alaric Watts have been printed in the *Standard*, with a note (I suppose of his) saying upon what occasion they were written.* I put them into my wife's

* The verses are those "To the Memory of Isabel Southey" ("The Birthday," pp. 187–189). Caroline Bowles writes (November 21st, 1827): " Your letter was surely intended to convey none but pleasurable feelings, and yet it has caused me very acute pain. I have not heard of Alaric Watts and his *Souvenir* since last spring, when, on his application, I sent him those unlucky verses, which had surely not been composed for his book, or any other. Having them by me, however, I gave them to him, entitled ' On the Death of a Young Lady,' under which vague designation I felt they could not suddenly shock you or any of your family, though I thought *you* would, as you read, adapt them to the occasion which had called them forth, and not be painfully affected by them. So far, I think, I was not blameable; but I now feel that I was extremely indiscreet in mentioning to Mr. Watts, in the letter which inclosed them, on what occasion they were written." Southey writes in reply (November 26th, 1827): "I must reproach myself, dear Caroline, for having led you, as I perceive I have done, into a mistake. The verses bore only the general title which you had given them, and the designation which belonged to them was given in a note with

K

hand, and she expressed that sort of pleasure which deep grief is capable of feeling. The pain would have been there in any case: the gratification was so much gain. Thank you, dear friend—thank you, thank you, and God bless you.

ROBERT SOUTHEY.

LXXV.

TO ROBERT SOUTHEY.

BUCKLAND, November 15th, 1827.

Never since you called me "friend" has your silence been of such long duration, and I am growing too anxious to wait its voluntary termination. If I find only want of time and leisure have prevented you from writing, I shall be heartily ashamed of this importunity, and will promise to scold myself; but do not you be angry with me, for indeed I am anxious. My last to you was a strange scrawl, but I had just been half choked with salt water, and quite killed with fright, in my passage across from Southampton to Hythe. I was thinking all the way over, when the waves gave me breathing time, "Now if this were to fetch Mr. Southey from Southampton (you know I took you there), it would be worth encountering."

I will have nothing more to do with any Sister Providences you may please to bring out in future; I was worse than sea-sick with the last, and could not even laugh, for shame at the degradation of human nature.

a 'we believe.' There is nothing for which to blame yourself, and Alaric Watts might very well be excused even if any shock had been given: no doubt he expected to gratify me, and had no apprehension of displeasing you. And, in fact, a gratification it has proved, in a quarter where I should never have had heart to have pointed out the application, even if I had made it. So all is well, and will be better if you will be thoroughly assured that *I know* you never would, never will, never *can*, act otherwise than wisely, and with perfect feeling, wherever feeling is concerned."

God bless you, my dear friend. If you are too much engrossed to write to me, just say so in one line (no bull that!), and that you are well, and that will content me, for I am not very, very, very unreasonable.

CAROLINE A. BOWLES.

LXXVI.

TO CAROLINE BOWLES.

KESWICK, December 27th, 1827.

Thank you for the extracts, both which I shall be glad to use. Wolfe's correspondence during his last campaign with Monckton, who succeeded him in the command, has been offered me in a roundabout way by the daughter of the latter; and another stranger has enabled me, by the testimony of one of the last survivors of his companions, to ascertain that Wolfe was not dying of consumption when he was killed, which I had been led to believe.

The poems in Wordsworth's volume concerning which you inquire are written by his sister—a most excellent person in all respects. Indeed, no man was ever more fortunate in wife, sister, or sister-in-law, than he has been. There is no woman out of my own house (except one whom I shall not name to you) with whom I am so intimate as Miss Hutchinson, or whom I love altogether so well. One likes to see hereditary intimacies, and, therefore, I am glad that Edith May has taken to Dora Wordsworth much more than to any other of her contemporary friends.

I did not see the lying account of Bilderdijk in the *Morning Herald*. He was no flatterer of Buonaparte. It was his business once, as President of the Royal Institute, to receive him, and Buonaparte on that occasion put this curious question to a person holding that rank : *Êtes-vous connu dans la république des lettres?* Bilderdijk looked at him, as he could look in those days, and replied, *Au moins j'ai fait ce que j'ai dû pour l'être.* And these, I believe, were the only words that he ever addressed to him in any shape. Louis Buonaparte he was attached to, as all the Dutch were; and he speaks of him with great affection, as a man of excellent disposition and the best intentions. But for Napoleon, he ever considered him as what he was—an unfeeling and short-sighted tyrant.

God bless you.
ROBERT SOUTHEY.

LXXVII.

TO CAROLINE BOWLES.

KESWICK, *February* 2*nd*, 1828.

A little man, who is travelling about the country with some black paper and a pair of scissors as his stock-in-trade, took the profile of which you have a copy by Edith May. The artist, having completed his education as a surgeon and apothecary, found out accidentally that he could thus take likenesses by the eye, and wisely enough resolved to try whether he could not by this means raise the money which he wanted for starting in his own profession. When he called at this door the girls, luckily for him, would have him try his skill, and this introduced him into considerable employment here and at Ambleside; charging one-and-sixpence for a single profile, a shilling when several were taken, he took whole families everywhere, and very often duplicates and triplicates for sending to a distance. I believe he sells me for sixpence among my neighbours, and found mine a very profitable face even at that price. When Edith returns she means to fill a little book with the profiles of this family and of the Rydal one.

Lord Radnor's death makes me feel the sin of procrastination, not, indeed, in any painful degree, nor with much cause for self-reproach, but yet with a twitch of that kind. I intended in the shortest and simplest manner to have dedicated my *Colloquies* to him *gratefully*. That word would have expressed all that was intended, and I am sorry the opportunity has been lost of manifesting thus publicly my sense of what was meant to be a great benefit. As regards myself, the object may be equally attained by inscribing the book to his Memory, but in such things the pleasure that is given is the main motive.

Murray has been printing my *History of the War* in octavo, without giving me any notice of his intentions, so that I knew nothing of it till the other day, when I saw it advertised. It is of no other consequence than that I should have been glad to have corrected a few slips of the pen or of the press. The third volume, like everything which I have in hand, moves slowly. Shame to say, but so it is, the older I grow, and the more clearly I see and pressingly feel the necessity of working that I may get through what is to be done while the day lasts, the more tardily I proceed, and the more I am disposed to pause and linger and dream over what I am about. And then to make ill worse, when I have brought myself into the right train of thought, comes the time round for periodical journey-work, and then matter of more pith and moment—prose and poetry alike—must be laid aside for what, in the worldly meaning of the words, is " the one thing needful." A true and sorrowful confession!

That I have done much is certain, and have the credit of doing much, but it is not less certain that with half the industry which is exercised by any lawyer or clerk in an office I could have done seven times as much.

I am now writing upon the Emigration Report for the *Quarterly Review*, and stealing whiles of time for the *Colloquies*, which are approaching to their close. The first part of the intended reprint of my *Essays Moral and Political* reaches London this day, and I shall look in about a week's time for the first proof—proof-sheets being among the pleasures of my life. Now I must make up my despatches, put on my walking shoes, and set out for exercise.

God bless you, dear Caroline.

ROBERT SOUTHEY.

LXXVIII.

TO ROBERT SOUTHEY.

BUCKLAND, *February* 26, 1828.

I only received your letter yesterday, but rest for me there will be none, I find, till I have said as well as thought, "God bless you for striking out that sentence in the new edition of the *Peninsular War*." * I say no more, for those three words will make you understand all I feel. If this were a world of requital as well as trial you ought to be very happy, delighting as you do in making others happy. Indeed I heartily agree that there are many good people in this world, and it is my fortunate lot to number many among my own friends and acquaintances. These have mostly fallen to me of late years. It is sad to tell that almost all the best years of my youth were (from strange circumstances) passed among those who had little fear of God before their eyes, and it was God's special mercy that I never lost sight of that, though compelled to associate with those unprincipled people, too many of them talented and clever and most agreeable, and by that means utterly duping my dear mother, who never *would* think evil of any—till too late. A strange whirl of dissipation and danger of all sorts I lived in, too often drawn for a time into the vortex, but always, thank God, with a sense of danger—a something within me that was not of the world I lived in; and it is impossible to express my happiness during about three months in the year, when with my dear uncle at Calshot or in London. I recollect feeling when I first got close to him as if I might then throw off all guard over myself, and be as young as my years, and as confiding and thoughtless as my nature. It was like stepping from a creaking plank across a chasm upon hard, firm ground. So I have been an arch deceiver, and played two very different characters. Among one set of people—the light, the wild, the

---

* A sentence concerning Caroline Bowles's relative, Sir Harry Burrard, in the account of the battle of Vimeiro.

unprincipled votaries of pleasure—I was comparatively cold, proud, and reserved, and older than my elders, and thought a pattern of prudence; and when with those whose opinion I really valued, I was the gayest and giddiest of the gay and giddy, the promoter of all mischief, and the deepest in all scrapes. My autobiography would not be unentertaining, but I will take special care not to favour the public with it.

I have worked hard—for me—for Blackwood this winter, urged on far more pressingly than I liked or bargained for. As for the Annuals, they must eventually run down each other. Alaric Watts wrote me last week he had sold 11,000 of the *Souvenir*.

God bless you, dear friend.

CAROLINE A. BOWLES.

LXXIX.

TO CAROLINE BOWLES.

KESWICK, *March* 18*th*, 1828.

I have been kept from writing to you by a perpetual interruption of letters upon matters of all kinds, whether they concern me or not, this being one of the evil things that publicity draws after it. To me it has brought a great deal more good than evil, and therefore I submit to the drawbacks with a good will. It would have done this, if it had done nothing more than bringing me acquainted with you.

Do not *give* anything to any of those people who make money by raising Annuals. I ought to have given you this advice before. They prize most what they pay for, and I will never give them anything again. I will be as mercenary with them as if I were a Jew; my winged steed shall not be led out, unless there be money to make her go. I will even call her Pegasa, and swear that she is of the feminine gender, that the proverb may be fulfilled.

Let your circulating bookseller send you Horace Hayman Wilson's *Select Specimens of the Theatre of the Hindus*, three volumes printed at Calcutta, but now on sale in London. The translator, of whom I know nothing, not even how to thank him, has sent me the book. I have as yet read only two of the seven dramas that it contains; they seem to be very well translated, and the state of manners and feelings which they describe is so unlike anything to which we are accustomed, that I am sure you will be interested by them. It is pleasant also to find that there is a sort of poetry which belongs not to time or place, but to human nature.

Let him send you also the first number of the *Foreign Review*, not for my paper upon the Dukes of Burgundy (though you will read it and like it), but for a very interesting account* of a crazy German poet, Werner by name. Our wildest geniuses would be tame in Germany. Shelley should have been a German—happy if he had been so! He would have been whirled about there in the vortex of speculations till he was giddy and exhausted. Actions which in this country put a man into Bedlam, or out of society, seem to be there in the ordinary course of things. The mere appearance of the students whom I saw at Heidelberg (I mean merely *seeing*, in the streets and gardens) makes me understand this. I can believe anything of a people whose youth are so trained up, and should wonder at nothing that might happen among them.

A plague on this review for keeping me at this time from worthier employments! I am writing a paper upon Columbus's voyages, parts of his own Journal and other of his papers having come to light. Heavy work am I making of it thus far, but there is something better in prospect when I get rid of the book and look at the subject in its wider bearings.

God bless you, dear Caroline; I am beginning to grow uncomfortable at the prospect of leaving home, and should be utterly out of humour with the journey, if it were not for

* By Thomas Carlyle.

the little time that can be taken out of it for Hampshire.
Once more,
                    God bless you.
                            ROBERT SOUTHEY.

LXXX.

TO ROBERT SOUTHEY.

BUCKLAND, *April* 3, 1828.

Thank you kindly for your noble charge against giving to the Annual beggars. But truly there is no fear lest I should be too liberal in that way; for you know, nobody knows *me*, and that by-the-bye I might have observed to you when you bespoke my good will for Allan Cunningham if he should apply.

Alaric Watts was handed over to me by Mr. Bowles, and the said Goth has hitherto paid me in sweet words *quantum suff.* and with sundry books, and with his last petition came certain allusions to "worthier remuneration in a pecuniary sense." But really if I only give him some four or five stanzas, what *can* the man pay for them, or I accept conscientiously, for you know my poetic steed is no "Pegasa," only a Peggy?

I have been rather hasty in promising something to his wife also, but her letter pleased me, and so did her plan (for children, just suiting my capacity), so I promised without thought or calculation, to which I am not over prone. I should have liked well enough to have given something to the *Keepsake*, as a retainer for the very pretty book, but now the Editor has secured all you magnates, he would hardly give even the volume for an inferior contribution, and I am not going to volunteer. This Annual mania cannot last; the market must soon be glutted. I think the *Quarterly Review* (not this last) might have spared the poor ephemerals; the letter-press (though not the engravings) of Alaric Watts are decidedly the best, and they crushed it with one *coup de grâce*. I felt peculiarly flattered by their condescending intimation that they were, however, "half tempted to exclude from this sweeping condemnation the lines on the death of a child at such a page," meaning mine. These trifles seem to me beneath the notice of the *Quarterly Review*, but when the *Keepsake* comes forth in its strength, with long poems of yours and Sir Walter's, it may be worth dissecting.

You were unkind to grow "uncomfortable at the prospect of leaving home"—a home that has you, and will have you, almost always and altogether, and which you leave but for a very little while, of which little my share will be the least fraction, and yet comprising the all of pleasure I anticipate till—but I look no farther. However, I will allow you to grumble at the trouble of moving, for I hate it too mortally. I send you some verses composed while I sat before the glass brushing my hair the other day. It is very hard one cannot be permitted to grow old and ugly without one's very identity being called in question, which mine has been, all owing to the subject of my verses; and I never meet with any person who has not seen me for years, without being questioned (after a few oblique glances) as to what I have done with my hair. The other day a very pretty young friend of mine ventured to ask if such and such reports of what it had been could possibly be true, and I promised to get her a certificate signed by a few surviving witnesses of its "long-faded glories," as Mr. Moore would say, which only set the saucy damsel laughing very incredulously, and me composing rhymes in revenge. Do not you also laugh when you read them.

God bless you, dear friend,

CAROLINE A. BOWLES.

LXXXI.

TO CAROLINE BOWLES.

KESWICK, *May* 6*th*, 1828.

Here, then, is the month of May, and it has entered as merrily as in the years of old. I heard the cuckoo on Saturday. The leaves are opening, the fruit trees in blossom, the birds in full song, and I looking on in discomfort to my departure from this country, just at the very season in which I advise all travellers to visit it. The day which, in my own mind, is fixed for my setting off is Monday the 19th. By that time I trust I shall be ready with work which cannot be postponed; that which can, I must, however inconvenient, take with me to Streatham. It will be about the middle of June before I can get to you. Three weeks between Streatham and London, mostly at the former place. A melancholy visit it will be, for in the course of nature there is scarcely a possibility that I should ever see my uncle again, and that possibility is not to be wished. I shall then come to you, halting twenty-four hours on the way with Chauncey Townshend, near Guildford.

I will bring with me the provoking poem out of which I have fooled myself for the *Keepsake*, bargaining for something which might run from three to five hundred lines, and producing what has extended very nearly to fifteen. It would have pleased you could you have witnessed the extreme interest which Bertha and Kate and Cuthbert have taken in the progress of this story. If the latter heard me at any time mouthing out a stanza in the room over his head, up he was in an instant, to ask how I was going on, and if he might hear it. "*All for Love, or a Sinner well Saved*," is the title, and the devil bears a great part in the business. It is a legend from the life of St. Basil, which only required purifying to be excellently adapted for this sort of ballad poem. Nothing could be more gross than its original character. This I easily got rid of, and have produced something which I daresay you will like. And as very likely it might have always remained unfinished if I had not bargained for it with Mr. Keepsaker, I am by no means disposed to be out of humour because of the improvidence of the bargain, especially as I reserve the right of printing it hereafter.

D'Israeli has this day sent me a new edition of his book on the Literary Character, which he has dedicated somewhat at length to me. I learn from it two things respecting Lord Byron—that he had thought of turning Turk, and regretted that he had not done so; and that he had written and printed a pamphlet against me. More of this we may perhaps hear when Moore's life of this worthy makes its appearance. Moore will have a ticklish task to perform all through, and if he brings me in, which he can hardly help doing, I may, perhaps, make him cry O, if he does not take care of his *p's* and *q's*.

God bless you, dear friend, and farewell till you hear of me from London.

Robert Southey.

LXXXII.

TO CAROLINE BOWLES.

Keswick, *July* 27*th*, 1828.

Here then I am, thank Heaven, dear Caroline, once more at home and at rest. Our journey was performed under the most favourable circumstances of weather, there being neither heat, nor cold, nor rain, nor dust to incommode us. I was very much the better for the air and bathing, and for the perfect quiet which I enjoyed at Buckland during the only days of my whole absence on which I can look back with unmingled satisfaction. The week which ensued was one of great fatigue, but I began to rest when I got into the mail for Manchester, and to-morrow I shall fairly have fallen again into my old habits and occupations, having at once recovered here, as at Buckland, the most useful of all habits, that of sleeping well.

That sweet tale of the friar and the children would turn to good account in your hands. Perhaps I may have fallen into the error (a very easy one for an omnivorous reader like myself) of attributing too much importance to a full knowledge of circumstantial particulars concerning any subject on which I am writing. Certainly I consume a very great deal of time in acquiring more information upon every subject before me than it is possible to bring to bear upon it. Do not you then be deterred by an apprehension that you have not the means of information at hand; the want of them will not be perceived if you keep to the essentials of the story; and perhaps I may have been seduced into overcharging my verses sometimes with allusions and indications of knowledge which not half-a-dozen readers in a generation will ever wholly understand, and not half of these would value when they understood it. In these cases knowledge may sometimes be a hindrance, as well as a help.

Murray talks of a "Country Magazine," to be kept free from personalities and politics, and all matter that might be either offensive or injurious. If he bring it to bear I may write, perhaps, more tales in verse and more scraps in prose; and shall tell him and his editor, moreover, where they may apply for aid to one who wants no other requisite than that of confidence in herself.

Cuthbert is delighted to hear of Mufti, and thanks you with great pleasure for *John Gilpin*.

Dear friend, God bless you.

ROBERT SOUTHEY.

LXXXIII.

TO ROBERT SOUTHEY.

BUCKLAND, *August* 11*th*, 1828.

I was more pleased than you can well conceive—and more surprised, too, at your favourable opinion of my legend. I assure you I feared it was a very meagre jejune performance.

What do you think of the conscience of Mr. and Mrs. Watts (Alaric and Zillah Madonna) writing to me for a second cargo of prose and verse for each of their books? A proof, I think, that they are very hard run. He proposes payment, but in such a round-about way, that I cannot tell what to answer, for I cannot value my goods. I answered him, however, that I should be very well satisfied to receive whatever remuneration other scribblers of my calibre receive for contributions to his Annual. Was that right? I wish there were literary agents to sell for one upon commission. I shall never manage these affairs well, however important to my finances. I returned home from a few days' visit to Southampton the day your letter arrived here; and how do you think I treated that letter, expected and wished for as it was? It lay among half-a-dozen others on my table; I caught up the whole handful, shuffled them over in search of one from you—no writing of yours on either; no franking hand known to me; "Horace Twiss" on the last—"some begging Annual-mongers again," and away I whisked the poor letter farther than the end of the table, just as some three or four-and-thirty years ago I whisked away a hideous doll that my father brought me from London, instead of a pretty one which I expected. Luckily there was no one to see how like a fool I looked, between laughing and crying, when, on condescending to pick up and open the poor letter half-an-hour after, I found what it contained. If I were to live to the age of Methuselah, I should always be a child, I fear, and a spoiled child too, in some things; and it is too late now to promise to "be good, and never do so any more."

I do not mean you to like me a bit the worse for my confession, remember, or because I cannot promise now even to be wise.

To-day I am expecting an uncle of mine who has been couched with success after being blind for seven years, during which time I have not seen him. He will stay some ten days or a fortnight with me, and I should greatly enjoy the visit, but—" The Thane of Fife hath a wife"—and she comes too.

God bless you, my dear friend.

CAROLINE A. BOWLES.

LXXXIV.

TO CAROLINE BOWLES.

KESWICK, *September* 23rd, 1828.

Your *Santarem* poem has pleased every person to whom I have shown it as much as it pleases me. You have hit the right key, and have told the story better than I could have done, for you have had a singleness of purport and of feeling; and I should have lost that charm by an intermixture or an introduction of reasoning, which, with whatever care it might have been managed, would have disturbed the reader's enjoyment. This I am made sensible of by perceiving how deeply it is enjoyed by these girls.

You will think it, as I do, an ill symptom of public opinion that Allan Cunningham's publisher objected to my *Cock and Hen*,* upon the ground that it would injure the sale of the book among the Roman Catholics. Whether to print it with Eleëmon or not I have not determined, and may perhaps be guided by Murray's opinion. It is very much improved since you saw it; I like it the better for having finished it at Buckland. In

* " The Pilgrim to Compostella."

its stead Allan has an epistle addressed to himself, in which occasion is taken from Chantrey's bust to introduce the Gallery of my Portraits.* I would have this transcribed for you if I did not know that you will have the volume as soon as it is published. It goes through about half the collection of my unlikenesses in a way which will please you, and being long enough for the subject and the place (filling up, in fact, all the space that Allan Cunningham had left for it), I broke it off just where it was convenient for him and for myself that I should stop. Matter enough remains for a second epistle if there be occasion to write one, and then I would pursue a picture of myself, beginning thus, and left unfinished because the poem broke off before I had reached the place where it should be introduced :—

> " An open forehead, a strong brow,
> A proditorious eye, for no dislike
> Can lurk dissembled there; a nose, withal,
> Which, tho' it passed the Rhine at Strasburg Bridge
> Unnoticed, is (as, Allan, I am free
> In parliamentary language to admit)
> A noticeable nose." †

And so I may perhaps go on, when the humour takes me, in this sort of strain, giving the inner, as well as the outer, likeness.

I borrowed the conception of this poem from one of Bilderdijk's. I have, therefore, inwoven a translation of so much of his as could well be introduced, and gladly took the opportunity of expressing my affection and admiration for him.

Dear Caroline, God bless you.

ROBERT SOUTHEY.

* *See* Southey's "Poetical Works," 1845, pp. 209-212.
† These lines do not appear in the "Epistle to Allan Cunningham," as printed.

LXXXV.

TO ROBERT SOUTHEY.

BUCKLAND, *October 21st,* 1828.

Last night I had written the accompanying letter. This morning's post has brought me your kind note. Pray do not grudge it me (though you would have heard from me without), for it is a better cordial to me than any in the Materia Medica, and just now I am in special want of one.

The owners of General Wolfe's picture have just been in this neighbourhood to let their estate for seven years, and remove the furniture, along with which the General is gone, or going, to Penzance, in Cornwall; so if Murray thinks proper to affix him to your book he will have to send far for a copy. I should think a good copy of this picture would be really valuable, for I find from Mr. Armstrong that the General never sat for any other, and after his death his mother begged and obtained a copy. Mrs. Armstrong's grandmother (the wife of General Wolfe's tutor) destroyed unread more than 500 letters of the General to her husband after the death of the latter. I wish they were still extant and come-at-able.

I saw in some country papers of late a notice of your forthcoming poem "Eleëmon," that diverted me not a little, and will, undoubtedly, if friend Amelia* sees it, excite all her curiosity. It set forth that you had chosen rather a singular subject for your poem, the *dramatis personæ* of which were composed of the persons "called friends." No doubt the sapient advertiser had heard something about fiends, and in his miscomprehension inserted the *r*, which makes such a considerable distance.

I have just looked over friend Amelia's book about "detraction," and rose from the sermon with the most backbiting inclination I ever felt in my life. She has certainly lived in the most vulgar and wicked circles of society, for nowhere else could she have found such examples as she treats her hearers

* Amelia Opie.

with. But you will never read the book, so I am wasting my valuable commentary.

I wish, I wish, I wish you would write something to write down ladies' bazaars, repositories, fairs, charitable female congregations of all sorts, for you cannot think the mischief they are doing (to say nothing of their detestable exhibiting character) among the class of little toy shopkeepers and poor women, who really get their bread by these knick-knacks, the sale of which is now monopolized by the ladies. A friend of mine went into a shop in Burlington Arcade lately, to purchase some trifle, and on her remarking how little choice there was, the shopkeeper said all those of his class were half ruined by "the charitable ladies," who came and bought the first of every pretty new invented toy, set to work themselves, and so effectually ruined the tradesman's market. One fair young girl of rank said to another acquaintance of mine, pointing to a young moustachioed lancer who had just turned from the booth, where she was selling her fancy wares: "There," said she; "I have just made him pay me fifteen shillings for a pair of garters."!!! How should you like to see Edith acting charity in that style?

God bless you, dear friend. You have drawn this second edition on yourself, but do not regret it; your note raised the quicksilver of my spirits from near zero to a degree or so within fair. Thank your stars that with you the mental tube is not filled with so fluctuating an element.

CAROLINE A. BOWLES.

LXXXVI.

TO CAROLINE BOWLES.

KESWICK, November 14th, 1828.

The two *Souvenirs* of Alaric Watts and his wife arrived here to-day and my young ones have got possession of them, but not till I had read your " Death of the Flowers," and " The Inflexible." It is needless to say how much I like the first, and the second has satisfied me that in comedy as well as in tragedy you migh tbear away the bell from all your contemporaries. I never remember any dialogues more excellently managed. The Goth writes to me in a pitiable, querulous, sore state of mind, out of heart, as it appears, with his speculation in *Souvenirs*, and out of humour with everything and everybody. He wants some prose from me, and offers a fair price for it; but both inclination and time are wanting, and so I shall curtly decline his offer.

The *Keepsake* has kept back one of my three pieces: they are all good for little—so little, that I do not think they are worth sending to you: just as much task-work as a school exercise, and performed with no better liking for the occupation. The prints no doubt are better than the verses, but the book has not yet reached me, neither has Allan Cunningham's—*his* I shall like you to see, because my epistle will please you.

That odd person, Mrs. Whitbread, instead of being here, as you supposed, is on her way to Switzerland, called thither by the illness of her son, but I conclude only to nurse him during his recovery, for the letter which announces her departure is written gaily. She speaks of a report that King's College is to draw me from this place, and fix me in London; this I have heard of from no other quarter, and am very sure that no such thought has ever entered the head of any person concerned in projecting the said College; and that if it had, I should neither be inclined, nor qualified, to accept any office that might be offered me. Yet when her letter put the possibility into my head, I had waking dreams half through the night of how easy a distance it would be from London to Buckland; and were the matter ever seriously to be weighed, that consideration would be one of the weightiest in the scale. I would give a great deal to be near you.

November 27.—Thus much you will see was written a fortnight ago—why then has it lain unfinished till your note arrived this day? Why, but because it is one of my besetting sins to be always doing *something else*, instead of what I ought to do, and in good truth wish to be doing; something pressing, or something preparatory, or something which I take to be preparatory, is always elbowing some worthier, and better, and pleasanter occupation aside. But my own faults are not the sole cause, for I am disturbed with letters and with business, touching me more and less, and more or less urgent, but all troublesome and consuming time.

I have read Marivaux' book, very French, but very clever, and everywhere very agreeable except in the odious story of Lindamere, which is an abomination as well as an impossibility. One gets in such a book traits of national manners and feelings which are not to be got from any other books. I felt in reading this how much more I relished it from having been at Fontainebleau.

Neither *Keepsake* nor *Anniversary* have yet come to me. I have a capital story to put in verse for the latter when the humour takes me—of an Irishman whose head dropt off upon his taking a false oath before St. Kiaran, and the saint took him home with him and put his head on again. Something good may be made of this: think of him walking with his head in his hand (like a lanthorn) because he could not see his way without it!

My respects to Mufti. The Townshends have brought a dog with them as ridiculously little as his Muftiship is formidably large, and this ridiculous dog walks out with them, as Mufti does with you. I hope Rumpelstilzchen may not some day mistake him for something between a rat and a rabbit, and eat him accordingly.

Dear Caroline, God bless you.

ROBERT SOUTHEY.

LXXXVII.

TO ROBERT SOUTHEY.

BUCKLAND, *December 22nd*, 1828.

I had so forgotten "The Inflexible," and the attempt had been so unnoticed, except in the *Literary Gazette*, which said it was "too long" only, that really I did not for a minute recall my own sketch to mind, when your sentence about it struck my eyes; but when I did, your praise of it pleased me not a little. Such things are rather entertaining and mighty easy to compose, but somehow all the worthies I have ever written for think fit to discourage my comic vein. Whenever I treat the Monster* in that way he thanks me for "the admirable production," but hints that "in the pathetic I am super-admirable." I sent "Inflexibility" to the Goth, and he thanked me too—"It was very clever, but unfortunately he was overpowered with contributions of that description: would I write him something serious?" So you see they *will* have me "like Niobe, all tears."

Poor Goth! do you know he has lost another child. So the papers tell me, and that accounts too well for my not having heard from him. I wish, if you write for any of the Annuals (I would not in your place), you could have rummaged out something for him, for I fear the world goes ill with him, and if the poor, unhappy man will tread upon all its prickles and thorns, when he might avoid some by stepping aside, he is much to be pitied. I cannot help suspecting he has been running headlong into a ruinous speculation, and there seems a disposition to beat him down, which makes me long to hold him up.

I had almost forgotten to tell you that George Bowles, who came to see me last week, told me a gentleman, who pretended to speak from "excellent authority," asserted, at a dinner-table

* Blackwood.

of which my cousin formed one, that Mr. Southey had become an avowed Methodist, and that his sectarian principles would soon be made evident in a forthcoming poem called "The Sinner well Saved." "The title speaks what it is," said the man of good authority, "but I have seen it—I have had a peep at the publisher's. Such a rant!" Can you not fancy how demurely I kept my countenance while this story was telling, and my cousin very seriously asked "Is it possible?" and how demurely still I replied," "You shall judge ; I am afraid there is some truth in it." And then out came your proof-sheets, and I read, and very soon the reverend gentleman exclaimed, and I still read on till his wonder was lost in delight.

God bless you, dear friend! God bless you, and all yours, and make the coming year one of peace and content to you.

CAROLINE A. BOWLES.

LXXXVIII.

TO CAROLINE BOWLES.

CATS' EDEN, KESWICK, *January* 1*st*, 1829.

If there were sky-packets to the other world, dear Caroline, as perhaps there would have been if Sin and Death had not entered into this, and may be hereafter when the victory over them shall be completed; if there were such packets, I would not wish you many happy returns of a new year, for I should rather take counsel with you about making a party, and setting off for one of those lovely stars which one can hardly look at without fancying that in some of them there will be a resting-place for us. But things being as they are, I pray God to give you better health, fewer vexations, more comforts, and life long enough to enjoy the fruits of the reputation you deserve, and cannot fail to obtain.

You have sent me a precious drawing and a pleasant letter. Your letters indeed are always pleasant except when they tell me that you have been suffering sickness, molestation, or such mishap* as this late one, which might have been so much more serious in its consequences. I have just been transcribing from one of your former letters a passage upon the Ladies' Bazaars as a note for my *Colloquies*. That book I trust will reach you in February, for I am now near the end. Do you know the portrait of Sir T.! More as engraved among Houbraken's heads? Houbraken was not (like Vertue) a faithful engraver, and in this instance I am right glad that he was not, for this print of his is a most excellent likeness of what my uncle was at my age. I have desired Murray to have it copied for a frontispiece, and, instead of any other dedication, have commenced a poem in relation to this accidental likeness. How the verses may turn out remains to be seen, but they will come from the right spring. You will like the intention I am sure.

To assist you in the collection of portraits,† I must tell you what are attainable and what not. The first was engraved in the *European Magazine*, and is from a picture by Edridge. The Landlord exists only as a miniature here by poor Miss Betham. The Evangelical is in the *New Monthly Magazine*, and the French and German copies are of course not attainable in this country. Sir Smug is poor Nash's miniature. Sir Smouch belongs to the *Percy Anecdotes*. Smouch the coiner is published for one shilling by a fellow named Lombard, in the Strand. And the Minion is the mezzotinto from the villainous picture by Phillips. So you see there are six which are procurable—the two from the Magazines, the two Smouches, the Barber on the card, and the mezzotinto. We have an intention of making such an illustrated copy here.

The *Keepsake* is not yet arrived. As for my verses, you are very good-natured to like them. They are good enough for their place and their company, I suppose, and as good as could be expected from task-work, for it was just as much task-work as an exercise at school. There is a poem of Wordsworth's ‡

---

* The sinking of a wall of her house.   † *i.e.*, Portraits of Southey.
‡ "The Triad."

there which I have not seen, but which relates to his own daughter, Sara Coleridge, and Edith May, for the love of which poem the three aforesaid damsels are looking eagerly to the arrival of the volume.

Dear friend, God bless you.

ROBERT SOUTHEY.

LXXXIX.

TO ROBERT SOUTHEY.

BUCKLAND, *January 22nd*, 1829.

I cannot wait to write you a "pleasant letter"; you must make the best of one from a sick room, to which, though fast recovering, I am still confined from the effects of an ugly attack in the throat, a painful inflammation terminating in an abscess, which was so good as to break three days ago without quite choking me; and here I am now with only a hole in my throat, which is healing, and able to talk with my pen at least, if not with the living organ. The letter from "Cats' Eden" came before I was taken ill, and many times since I thought of the "sky packet," but if it please God we will have some terrestrial meetings yet, if but to settle our celestial travelling plan.

Of course you have received "The Book of Lords" * before this. I guessed at the originals of *The Triad* sketch, but compassionate my dulness, and tell me which is which. "Abominable stupidity," the young ladies will say, but you need not betray me to them. I guess, but do not feel sure, as I ought, doubtless. One (Miss Wordsworth) I am unacquainted with, but I should have fancied no two portraits could be more dissimilar in their different styles of beauty than those of Edith and her cousin. I am angry with myself for being at fault.

* i.e. *The Keepsake*, in which there were several noble authors.

I do not know that head of Houbraken's you speak of. It is a happy coincidence that it should be characterized by the resemblance you are going to turn to such good account. If I dared wish away time, I would wish for February and the Book.* In my happier days I was but too prone to long that the hands on the dial would move faster than my eager anticipations, but I was affectingly and awfully cured of the presumptuous folly, and never now, under any circumstances, dare I wish for the morrow. It was twelve years ago last week since a well-remembered night, that on parting with my mother before we went to rest, after spending the evening merrily with our large family, I said to her " Oh, Mother ! how I wish this day fortnight were come." "Do not wish that," she replied in a tone that startled and made me look round at her as I was leaving the room, and yet in my obstinate impatience I repeated, "but I *must* wish it, Mother dear, and I *will* wish it." " You have wished away your time," she said, " and a fortnight hence how you may repent your impatience—you may have no mother then." She looked as I had never seen her look before, and spoke as I had never heard her speak; but she was in excellent health, and afterwards, when she saw how I was struck and affected, laughed at my superstition, and said she did not know why she had spoken thus—"It was without thought or meaning," and she seemed to forget it. That day fortnight she was in her grave.

God bless you, dear friend.

CAROLINE A. BOWLES.

Southey's " Colloquies."

XC.

TO CAROLINE BOWLES.

KESWICK, *February* 15*th*, 1829.

I cannot express to you with what emotions I read your last letter, nor will I endeavour to do it. My heart also is full of recollections like yours—"last words, last looks"—for which there is no Lethe in this world. If there were, methinks I would go a long pilgrimage to drink of it, but not if it were to wash away more than I wished to part with.

My slow pen is approaching the end of the *Colloquies*, and my slow printer will soon have finished the little volume of verses.* Turn over and you will see the dedication. Forgive the verses for being no better; if they had been the best I ever wrote, you could not have been half so well pleased in reading as I should have been in writing them.

February 22.—These overleaf lines are the very bad reason why I have been silent so long; I hoped to make them better. Meantime the *Colloquies* are finished, and the last portion of MS. for them goes up under the cover in which [this] will be enclosed.

God bless you.

ROBERT SOUTHEY.

I have neither time nor heart to say anything of State affairs, but you will of course conclude that I do not turn with the wind.

TO CAROLINE BOWLES.

Could I look forward to a distant day
With hope of building some elaborate lay,
Then would I wait till worthier strains of mine
Might bear inscribed thy name, O Caroline;
For I would, while my voice is heard on earth,
Bear witness to thy genius and thy worth.

---

* *All for Love*, and *The Pilgrim to Compostella*.

But we have both been taught to feel with fear
How frail the tenure of existence here;
What unforeseen calamities prevent,
Alas how oft! the best resolved intent;
And therefore this poor volume I address
To thee, dear friend, and sister Poetess.

XCI.

TO ROBERT SOUTHEY.

BUCKLAND, *February 20th*, 1829.

Twenty years ago, if such a letter and such verses had been received by Caroline Bowles as those which reached her yesterday, some taint of youthful vanity might have been mingled with her affectionate gratitude. Far other feelings overpowered her yesterday. A moment's surprise—but a moment's—for, I was not to learn that you delight not to honour those whom the world honours; then a sense of deep unworthiness, a gush of tears, and an inward prayer to become more worthy of such friendship as yours—such distinction as you have conferred upon me. I commission your own heart to reward you, and tell you what mine feels, but cannot find words to express.*

I tried to write yesterday, but could not recover myself sufficiently. A long illness which was but coming when I last wrote to you, and thought it going, scarcely allows me yet to leave my bed, and that must account for this strange scrawl. But they tell me I am much better, and shall soon be tolerably well again, and I feel I do not care to die while you remain to me, though I should like just to take precedence.

* In his next letter (March 1st, 1829) Southey writes:—"You have taken those verses more to heart than they deserved, or could have deserved, had the execution been as good as the intention. They tell you nothing but what you knew before; but they may tell many persons what they did not know before—that there is a certain Caroline Bowles whose poems they ought to send for; and if they have this effect they will be good verses, according to the old saying, that 'handsome is that handsome does.'"

Pray, when you write next, tell me in so many words how you are. I have had ugly fancies about you while you were silent, and because you have never answered me lately how you were. I shall get well much faster for knowing you are well.

I want to say a good deal, but cannot a word more now, for my dizzy eyes can hardly bear even this effort. God bless you, dear friend. I long for the books.

CAROLINE A. BOWLES.

XCII.

TO CAROLINE BOWLES.

KESWICK, *April 9th*, 1829.

Whether my books reached you, or whether they are published, or when the greatest of Murrays means to publish them, I know not, the greatest of Murrays, who is also the greatest of Men, not having condescended for many months to favour me with any communications. In the *Literary Gazette* (which we call here the "Tom Noddy," to distinguish it from the *John Bull*) is an account of it as "not yet published," and a very Tom-Noddy-like account it is, giving *as a specimen* an extract altogether unlike any other part of the book, and explaining Montesinos to mean a stranger from a distant country! And these are the critics upon whose good or ill report the sale of a book among book societies mainly depends!

I must tell you of an odd incident in one of our walks. In a field near Ormathwaite there is a row of old cherry trees of great size, and at the foot of one of these we found about a pint-basin-full of cherry stones, which had been laid in by some kind of mouse, I suppose, for his winter store, in a hole under the root. Every stone was perforated with so small a hole, that I hardly know how the kernel could have been got out, but having been thus hollowed, they were cast out from the nest. We brought home some of these as curiosities.

My house is in discomfort; the painters are coming to my bookcases in the study, and every book must be taken out. I have, however, very comfortable quarters in a book-room on the ground floor, fitted up since you were here, and well stored. Yesterday I sent to the press a portion of the *Peninsular War*, which I long to rid my hands of. I am also getting on well with the Introduction to "John Jones's Rhymes," and have this evening to begin a paper on Portugal. Thus I go working on, and find days, weeks, and months passing faster than, considering what there is for me to do, I could afford to let them pass if my speed were to be regulated by my conscience. Some progress, however, is always made in one thing or another, and though I have neither the ardour, nor the activity, nor, perhaps, the industry which were mine thirty years ago, I have no cause for any serious quarrel with myself.

The eldest Miss Charter, after a long decay, which was not supposed to be dangerous till a short time before its termination, has lately been removed to a better world. She was an excellent woman, and Elizabeth will feel the loss sorely, affection for that sister having, I believe, occasioned her to decline more than one offer of marriage. Dear Caroline, these are the things, these virtues which are neither seen nor heard of men, upon which we may better rely for deliverance from the evils which threaten the nation, and which the public (so-called) thoroughly deserves, than upon any human wisdom or human probabilities.

Dear friend, God bless you.

ROBERT SOUTHEY.

XCIII.

TO ROBERT SOUTHEY.

BUCKLAND, *April* 28*th*, 1829.

I will tell you that I think your cherry-stone hoarder—your mouse, is a bird. Listen, why I think so. You may remember, or you may not, that I have a filbert walk in this garden. Last year the trees were very productive, and I and some cousins who were with me watched them, anticipating the winter store. But we were forestalled. Day after day, before quite fit for picking, the filberts disappeared, and one morning I found two separate piles—one in the fork of a hazel, another in that of a walnut—of filbert shells, not much broken, but hollow, the kernel extracted mostly through a small hole; some of them were cracked, but each heap was piled with the hole downward into a little pyramid, exactly as if a housekeeper had piled them for dessert. "Children have been in the garden" was the cry at first. "Little rascals!" said the gardener: he would watch them. And so he did; and the next day I was summoned in all haste to see the thief at work, and saw and heard him too—a thick-made, clumsy, greenish finch—not a green linnet—who carried the nuts one by one in his claw to an old oak-post, into a convenient hole of which he stuck them fast, and then struck them with his short, strong bill, as with a hammer, so loud, till he had perforated the shell, and could extract the kernel at his ease. So far his motives were plain enough; but I wish any ornithologist would explain to me why, after his meal was ended, he was at the farther trouble of carrying the empty shells, and piling them, as I have described, so symmetrically in the fork of trees at a considerable distance. "There are more things in heaven and earth than are dreamt of in our philosophy." Afterwards I found many more such hoards. When a mouse has been the consumer, one can always distinguish the marks of his nibbling teeth.

I have just read a little book that charms me, that "babbles of green fields" to me even in this dull room—*The Journal of a Naturalist.* I have seen no book of that sort so pleasant since White's *Selborne.*

Good night, dear friend, for I am writing to you at night, my hour of life.

29*th.*—I expect, if I should live, and ever be a creature of this world again, and there is a royal nursery in my time, to be made laureate to that same. Some time before my illness, in an evil hour, I sent a sonnet to a baby cousin of mine (Sir Charles Burrard's first-born), and ever since not a brat can be born, or die, or change its long petticoats, but the mammas send to me for verses on the occasion. This is worse than the album conscription. I copied the rashly-written lines, that you may keep them for your first grand-daughter, and now I will put them in this frank. It snows!

God bless you, dear friend.

CAROLINE A. BOWLES.

XCIV.

TO ROBERT SOUTHEY.

BUCKLAND, *May 2nd*, 1829.

Yesterday and to-day, almost our first spring days, have revived me so far as to enable me to get down into the lower flower garden, lured thither also by the attraction of a new plaything which was sent me two days ago—would Cuthbert could see it!—a little horse, just three feet high, a perfect little creature, mouse-coloured, with black mane, tail, and feet, and following me like a dog about the garden and into the house, where the first interview between him and Mufti was delightful, both eating bread together at the same time out of my hand, with their noses touching. When you were last in Fairyland did you hear the name of Titania's palfrey? If you did, pray let me know it, that mine may be so christened, and then he shall have green housings with silver bells. Oh! if he were of the true elfin breed how soon he should set me down at the door of Greta Hall.

My little Persian charge, now in his sixteenth year, though not looking eleven, is going out the end of this month in the "Roxburgh Castle," and I send him up to London in about ten days to be fitted out. He has turned out most happily; but I am fearful the poor fellow is now taken away very prematurely from his school, to be placed in a mercantile house at Calcutta.

Fare you well, dear friend. I leave you for your *Colloquies*. I think my name looks beautifully in print. I never liked it so well before.

CAROLINE A. BOWLES.

XCV.

TO CAROLINE BOWLES.

KESWICK, *May 9th*, 1829.

You are right: the paper upon Dr. Parr is not mine (if it had been, you may be sure there would have been some allusion, which you would perfectly have understood, to his portrait); the paper upon Surtees's *History of Durham* is. In the preceding number I have a paper upon school education, much the worse for the clipping which the editor bestowed upon it, what he cut out being curious historical matter, only to be met with in the course of such out-of-the-way reading as mine.

You are a good nursery laureate, and I might promise and vow for my grand-children, if any there should be, that they would very dutifully be pleased with your performances.

Is not your bird the Nuthatch? So called from the very practice of carrying nuts to a tree or post, and fixing them where he can hammer, or *hack*, at them with his bill. My cherry stones were thrown out from a hole at the root of the cherry tree, certainly not the abode of a bird, and I think the marks of teeth may be perceived on them. Your hoards are quite inexplicable upon any supposition of use in them; but why may they not be the bird's trophies, which he may take pleasure or pride in erecting, as if to show us that there are others of God's creatures as well as ourselves who spend their time in vanities? Murray sent me *The Naturalist's Journal*, and a delightful book it is. White's *Selborne* was wickedly reprinted, in the edition which I possess, in a garbled state, omitting everything which did not relate to natural history. Now, one charm of the book was that this good man took an interest in antiquities, and his book is the most delightful specimen of the interest and enjoyment which a good man can find anywhere in the country, if he will but look for them.

Lockhart will not so easily hang out the Liberal flag as Sir Walter has done. Sir Walter had cautiously kept clear of what is called committing himself. Lockhart has taken a decided part, from a clear view, I believe, of what was politically right, though perhaps without any other feeling on the subject. I should be sorry to find him going wrong, because, in spite of strong prepossessions, I am inclined to think well of his nature, and to like the little I have seen much better than all I had heard or otherwise known had led me to expect.

The change in *The Anniversary* you probably know from Allan Cunningham, as I have done. There is a ballad ready for his first number, if he chooses to have it, called *Roprecht the Robber*, a good story, with which Cuthbert and his sister are much amused. I have just taken up another to finish it, begun before Edith was born! And indeed I want only leisure to become as prolific a ballad-writer as I was thirty years ago. The one in hand is called *The Young Dragon*, so called to distinguish the said Dragon from his father, the Old one. I like better to play with grotesque subjects than to take up any which excite a serious abiding feeling in their progress; and sometimes I am tempted to lay aside graver things for such as these by the interest which Cuthbert and the girls take in them. "Papa, have you hatched him yet?" is the question with which I am now assailed concerning *The Young Dragon*, and perhaps when you have read all that is yet written you will not wonder that I hear the question eagerly repeated. [Four stanzas are here given.] Farther Robert the Rhymer hath not proceeded. You will smile at this, and hope that the egg will neither be addled nor over-roasted in hatching.

Dear friend, God bless you.
ROBERT SOUTHEY.

XCVI.

TO ROBERT SOUTHEY.

BUCKLAND, May 10th, 1829.

I have a letter from a 'womankind' that rather troubles me, a friend of Mr. Wordsworth's; I think you know something of her, Miss Jewsbury. Said Miss Jewsbury has been so good as to take a fancy to "A Brook and a little Star" of my writing, and "A Story of a Broken Heart," and thereupon she sends me two books of hers—"Lays of Leisure Hours," and "Letters to the Young," and writes me sweet things and fine things—so fine I do not know how to answer her, about life and a wilderness, two Ravens, and a brook Cherith! But I have read clever things of hers, and being a friend of Mr. Wordsworth she must be good for something, and I am obliged to her.

Do you know anything of Le Bas's theological writings? His Sermons are among the very few modern ones I can read without going to sleep—graceless confession! smacking too much of the original sin which made me, when I was a wee thing, answer my father in a manner which I well remember shocked him vastly. He gave me some fables (I forget what), charging me to read the morals; "But Papa," said I, "I hate morality."

Certainly my bird is the Nuthatch; stupid I was not to think of that ingenious creature. Strange doings are going on in my feathered world. Two pairs of blackbirds have lived for the last two years among the shrubs in front of this house, and till lately held the little territory very amicably in common. About a month ago one of the cock birds disappeared, and forthwith, instead of going into mourning and retirement, as any decent widow would have done, the widow blackbird intruded herself into the other establishment, fell upon the legitimate wife, half picked her eyes out, and I am afraid succeeded in her unprincipled attack upon the surviving cock's fidelity, for certain it is there are two nests, containing two families, upon two neighbouring bushes, and his conjugal and paternal cares seem equally divided between the rival zenanas, though he has by no means reconciled the rival sultanas, who regularly come to a pitched battle every time they meet, which the black sultan seems to contemplate for a time with strict neutrality, but if it holds out longer than his patience, he comes down from his lime-tree perch, beats both ladies with most impartial execution, and having sent each back to her business at home, celebrates the triumph of his domestic rule with such a burst of song as rings through my very bedroom, from whence I have taken notice of these incongruous proceedings. I am idle enough you see, but you cannot say I tell you a story of a cock and a bull. Now I must go and write to my friend of the Brook Cherith, and I must try to write well (oh dear, oh dear!), which I never do to you.

God bless you, dear friend.

CAROLINE A. BOWLES.

XCVII.

TO CAROLINE BOWLES.

KESWICK, *May 19th*, 1829.

Your *Chapters** came not from London, but from Edinburgh. What a cruel woman you are to write such chapters as some of

* " Chapters upon Churchyards."

them are! To sit down deliberately with pen and ink for the purpose of making other people as unhappy as the contemplation of ideal suffering can make them! And yet in this same book to show them that when you please you can be the playfullest and pleasantest of writers. Time was when such a book would have made the fame and the fortune of its authoress.

Your new correspondent is the daughter of a person in the iron trade, at Manchester I believe. Her mother died when she was young, and the care of bringing up younger brothers and sisters devolved upon her. A long illness broke the cheerfulness of her disposition, and has, I understand, thrown her into a gloomy sort of religious feeling, which makes her *repent* of her former publications. The Wordsworths know her and like her; indeed she is to visit them about this time. I never saw her. She was bred up, I suspect, among persons who hold me in no good liking, from political or sectarian prejudices, and, like many young writers, upon commencing her career she thought me a very proper object of attack. The Wordsworths were unlucky enough to bring this to my knowledge, for otherwise I should never have heard of it. They sent over the book in which this little piece of indiscretion was contained for my inspection, in the hope that I would say something civil of it in the *Quarterly Review*. I wrote back word that the only kindness I could show to a young lady who in what she had said of me had shown as little sense of modesty as of truth, would be to say nothing of her. There of course ended my resentment, which was quite as much as the offence deserved. What I said would not be repeated to her, and I daresay she finds it now much more difficult to excuse herself than I do to excuse her. Do you know my ballad of "Old Christoval's Advice, and the reason why he gave it"? Perhaps not, as it is not among my poems, but in the two-volume edition of my "Letters from Spain and Portugal." 'Tis a good wholesome story, the application of which I often make to myself.

Wednesday, 2 o'clock.*—All in confusion and discomfort; trunks open, linen in one place, coats, waistcoats, and innomi-

---

* Before starting for the Isle of Man by way of Whitehaven.

nables in another, shoes, boots, caps, gowns, bonnets, books, and all the etceteras of preparation for such a family movement; my Governess miserably unwell, and the worse for the bustle and the intended expedition, which is mainly intended for her good; Bertha with a bad cold, and a stomach which is never well; Edith white as a lily; Kate quite contented, and now, thank God, in comfortable health. Cuthbert happy as he can be, and I myself in a state of resignation to the discomforts before me, consisting of separation from my books, my business, and my old shoes. Just finished a paper for the *Quarterly Review*, and made up the packet which is to convey the latter half and the proofs of the first half to Lockhart. To-morrow at eleven we start, and my next, I trust, will be from the Isle of Man.

God bless you.

ROBERT SOUTHEY.

XCVIII.

TO ROBERT SOUTHEY.

BUCKLAND, *June 8th*, 1829.

That dedication of yours (it must be *that*) has opened to my merits, genius, and so-forth, eyes many that would never otherwise have honoured me with a glance; and I have been particularly charmed with the originality of one kind unknown friend, who writing of me as the authoress of *Chapters on Churchyards*, in a paper called *The Spectator*, after calling me an ornament to my sex, and so on, finishes by remarking, with infinite naivete, "Why have we never read Ellen Fitzarthur, The Widow's Tale, &c., &c.?" Is not that good? I have had one letter that charms me, however, from the real kindliness of spirit and good-will towards me that characterises its otherwise beautiful style. Moreover, it is from a person who I am ready to believe is sincere in her praise of what she has read of mine, because I believe in sympathy, and for some years I have always looked out with more than common interest for the beautiful little poems of Mary Howitt (of William and Mary). Probably you [may know something of these Quaker Poets; I take to them mightily. Not so to Bernard ¦Barton, and yet I can hardly tell why I cannot take to him: I have dreamt, I believe, that he is a sort of priggish Quaker, and I hate his straight-haired effigy—a reasonable reason!

If it were not for bringing a scandal upon my habitation, I could tell tales of my favourite pigeons, evincing as profligate disregard of propriety as the blackbirds have shown, and utterly confuting the old comparative saying "As constant as a Turtle." I have a pigeon called "Blue Tom," who, with Grizzle his wife, was for some time sole occupant of my little dove-cot, of which, though two other pairs have since been added to the inhabitants, he has always kept mastery. But for more than a twelvemonth he and Grizzle dwelt alone there, patterns of connubial happiness and decorum, so long as the lady could take her pastime abroad with her lord and master and make herself agreeable. But the cares of a family came on; she very properly stuck close to her eggs, and when she came out to shake herself Blue Tom occasionally took his turn of sitting. But then I suppose he considered his duty ended, and on the second morning of Grizzle's seclusion he flew away to Lymington, his first flight there; seduced a dirty yellow hen pigeon from perhaps a disconsolate mate, and brought her home in triumph, assigning her no better lodging here, however, than the eaves of the house, and never taking any notice of her when his old wife came out of doors, though at other times he brought her to feed at the window where I throw food to them, and flew about the garden and fields with her on the most social terms. The most wicked part of the business was to follow; when the young pigeons were hatched and thriving, and their mamma able to leave her nursery, Blue Tom half murdered the yellow unfortunate, and he and Grizzle united forces to drive her fairly off the premises; no easy matter, as I suppose she was outlawed at home, and could hardly hope for even a separate maintenance. So much for Turtle-dove constancy! But what a strange anomaly! was it not? I am afraid there must be something morally deteriorating in the air of this place. At last I settled two more pairs in the dove-cot, and ever since Blue Tom has passed his widowed hours very contentedly in their society without fetching home an extra partner. I think I shall send this anecdote to Colburn for his new journal of scandal.*

I thought I had not a word to say when I took up my pen (lifted it up, as a correspondent of mine used to express herself), but I find nonsense flows in naturally, and the only difficulty is to stop the torrent. Tell me how your hay fever goes on, or goes off I hope. I have never heard anything of Allan Cunningham since he sent me his *Anniversary*—and so much the better: at present I am incapable of writing anything, and have refused the Halls and some other people. The slightest mental excitement brings on the terrible beating of that vile heart of mine, which is never quite still now, and once set a-going seems running a race against time; and its pace is audible to other ears than those of my nervous fancy.

* A passage from another letter pleasantly illustrates the interest which Caroline Bowles took in our foster brothers

"Of that folk in fur or feather
Who with men together
Breast the wind and weather."

"The other day my attention was attracted for some time to a curious scene of dumb show performance, the actors of which were a Robin redbreast and a mole. The miner was invisible, but his operations were stupendous and their effect marvellously rapid and obvious in the soft earth-bank he was excavating; beside which stood the Robin in profound contemplation, just hopping on a step or two as the ridge of black mould heaved and lengthened, now and then swelling into hillocks in its progress. Robin I suppose was watching for worms, but the engineer below did not throw up any, and the bird's attention seemed so philosophically profound that I made no doubt he was taking notes of the mimic earthquake, and would go home and write just such a letter about it as Pliny's the younger. You shall see it if it is addressed to me: and I am a very popular person among dumb creatures of all sorts, so Rob may honour me with his confidence."

God bless you, dear friend; the mechanism of the heart will run down at last and be still enough, but that of the mind will not, so I shall never bid you farewell.

CAROLINE BOWLES.

XCIX.

TO ROBERT SOUTHEY.

BUCKLAND, *July* 12*th*, 1829.

I have for a considerable time been totally incapable of writing anything, except now and then an idle verse or two. Very possibly I may never be able to do more, and no matter; but if I should, perhaps I might ask you to indulge me by the accomplishment of a wish you first suggested to me. Assuredly I should never else have had the boldness to conceive it. You commended my versification of the Santarem legend. If ever I could succeed as much to your satisfaction in one or two other little poems, would you of your abundance contribute two or three, and so make up a little volume with me? I ask without further circumlocution, because I feel—I think, at least—you can appreciate my motive—no vain or worldly one, God knows. Your plan was a far more tempting one, inasmuch as I would much rather have worked upon the same structure with you, though only on its most insignificant parts; but then I tried, and was found wanting, which proof of my incapacity pained me only so far as it dispelled the pleasant vision you had conjured up, and I took that dispersion more to heart than you, who have so many objects of dear interest, can well conceive. Lately this less ambitious vision has haunted me: you have only to wave your hand, and it is gone.

God bless you, dear friend. If my proposal appears to you an indiscreet or presumptuous one, try to forget it; it is but a dream, like my life. But do not forget me.

CAROLINE A. BOWLES.

In a letter of July 16th, 1829, Southey writes:—" I will rather send a few lines, dear Caroline, than let a post go by without telling you that the wish which you have expressed has been more than once at the top of my pen, and would very soon have found its way to paper. I shall dearly like it in effect. So go you to work. Moreover, please you not to consider the original scheme* as abandoned, but only as in abeyance, till you will let me bring you to pass a summer and autumn here."

C.

TO ROBERT SOUTHEY.

BUCKLAND, *July* 30*th*, 1829.

It is not in your nature to give pleasure by halves. You might have granted my request, and yet have left me unsatisfied (dissatisfied with myself, that is); but you persuade me you have pleasure in granting it, so the ratified covenant is delightful to me, visionary as its fulfilment may long remain.

"Queen Mary's Christening" is, I suppose, the ballad you spoke of in your former letter, as one you had designed for Allan Cunningham's share of "The Three Chapters." The title sounds well, and a title is everything, Mr. Colburn says. You might be sure I should like that half-sportive, half-serious prelude which brought the family group at Greta Hall so distinctly before me, and you know I can laugh with those that laugh, as well as weep with those that weep. Full sure am I it is wisdom's part, and religion's too, to make the most of every sunbeam that brightens this chequered valley of our life—more especially those that gild its decline—assurances of a more cloudless morrow ; and as to compromising the dignity of learning and graver years, I can only say you may venture to be

* " Robin Hood."

sportive, though dulness and mediocrity cannot afford it. So I will be your abettor in all trespasses on formal gravity, provided you treat me now and then with a strain such as my soul loves —serious, not sad, full of human feeling and heavenly hope.

Oh! for a little summer. I long for it as for life; so reviving is it to me to bask in the sun and live in the open air. For the first time in my life I have quarrelled with trees, green trees, for being shut in weeks together by the perpetual floods and storms, almost unable to employ myself all day, and with nothing to look at but trees, that you know surround the house, and now press close upon the front windows. The perpetual mopping and mowing of an old acacia, top heavy with rain, has so worried me by day, and haunted me by night, that I could fancy it my evil genius.

God bless you, dear friend.

CAROLINE A. BOWLES.

CI.

TO CAROLINE BOWLES.

KESWICK, *August* 17*th*, 1829.

I shall draw some tears from your eyes, dear Caroline, by the history of a young American poetess* which I am just finishing for the next *Quarterly Review*, and have, indeed, this moment broken off, that I may not longer delay writing to you. You are a *cruel* writer, for you imagine tales which I, with all my love for the writer, and with all my admiration for the passages that catch my eye, cannot bear to read, though thirty years ago I should have devoured them. In my future fiction I will make everybody happy as far as I can, for the sake of making myself so while I write, and will tell no sad stories, unless they are true ones, as this is. She was a beautiful creature, who died at the age of seventeen, the victim of over-excite-

* Lucretia Davidson.

ment, like Kirke White—a name which I think of with as much gratitude as his relations feel towards me, because, had it not been for him, you and I should, in all likelihood, never have known each other in this world.

You will soon hear a great deal of the Co-operation Societies. Gooch has written a paper upon them, which Lockhart (a little to Gooch's surprise and mine) has printed for the next *Quarterly*. Both Gooch and Rickman and I see in its full extent the great, palpable, and immediate benefit which these societies must confer upon those who engage in them. They are spreading marvellously fast: no experiment in society ever spread so fast; and none, I expect, will ever have gone so far. The difficulty will be, where to stop, for some of them already proclaim that they aim at a community in lands and goods. Now, I am more than willing to see small communities formed upon this principle; but I do not like to think of its being brought, like a steam-boiler, into the midst of our crowded society, and bursting there. The levelling principle, if carried to its full extent, must level everything. Now, I want to do away the circle of inequality and its iniquity, which consists in its excess, yet at the same time to preserve the gradations of society, and our institutions which are founded upon them.

I have begun in hexameters the story of a shipwreck for our volumes—thus:—

> Hear in Homeric verse the pitiful tale of a shipwreck
> Which, in the Mexican Gulf, the Licentiate lAonso Zuazo
> Suffered, long ago. I found the story in Spanish,
> Told in that noble tongue by old Oviedo of Valdez,
> Who from Zuazo himself received the faithful relation.*

This is the beginning. Some fifty more lines are written, which bring me to the shipwreck, and I suppose the whole will extend from 500 to 1000 lines.

Dear friend, God bless you.

R. SOUTHEY.

* The passage goes on to the fourteenth line of the fragment, as printed in *Robin Hood, &c.*

CII.

TO ROBERT SOUTHEY.

BUCKLAND, *September 8th*, 1829.

The Bishop of Chester, Bird Sumner, is a far more able man than Charles Sumner, our bishop. I believe, in my conscience, both are sincere men, however warped in some of their religious and political views. But both undoubtedly favour sectarian principles, though our bishop has just expressed himself strongly in his charge against the desertion of the Church for the Meeting-house. But thus that peculiar party in the Church to which the name of Evangelical is now so improperly applied as the designation of a sect, instead of that of the Church of Christ, does little less than convert the church into a meeting-house, whenever one of their ministers gets possession of a pulpit, and to this party both the Sumners have ever belonged, and are now, of course, its strenuous favourers, with immense influence, since their accession to so great ecclesiastical dignity. If I had not lived in a land of sectarians—if I had not, from family and other connexions among them, seen, and heard, and known so much of all they do, and all they aim at, so subversive of our present religious constitution, I should enter with untempered enthusiasm into the scheme of the Church Methodists; but now I find it hard to believe that such an establishment will not be made conducive to their own peculiar views by men as ingenious (and in some instances as unscrupulous) as the Jesuits in promoting them. The theory is admirable. Nobody could be more taken with it than I was; nobody can be more anxious that a safe and stable fabric may be built upon it, sustained by "zeal without innovation," without insidious views towards the subversion of our present Church establishment. But I hope with fear, and with regard to the Co-operation Societies, fear is uppermost in my mind. Do not "contempt" the weakness. I know that no great good will ever be attained by those who will risk no possible evil, and that some evil must intermingle with the most perfect human system. But in the times we live in, when everything seems unsound, undermined, tending portentously towards great and awful change, especially towards anarchical subversion of rank and order, and all old things (some, doubtless, may be well spared from among us), I tremble to think of what may be the still accelerating force of an engine, set off with so powerful an impetus, without a drag-chain to the wheels. You say they "already aim at a community of lands and goods"; they have little more to aim at. Remove those old landmarks, and all the enclosures and high places of society must be levelled and laid open to the equalizing rabble, and then God help us!

Ever since the publication of the *Colloquies* I have been looking out for some sign that your cunning lure had taken with Friend Amelia, and that her superabundant energies will for some time at least flow in the channel—and a very good channel too—to which you have directed them. But, dear friend of mine, having thus taken upon yourself in some sort, like St. Vincent de Paul, the directorship of female energies, for Heaven's sake hold the reins tight; keep a sharp curb upon them; suffer them not to strike out right and left; and, above all, exclude from your new order all candidates under forty at least. If our ladies will faithfully take pattern by the admirable Flemish and French institutions, such an establishment as may owe its existence to your delightful pen (which would infallibly have made me a Beguine, or a *Sœur de la Charité*, if I was not a most ungregarious animal) must and will be an inestimable benefit to this country. But 'ware missionary zeal in this case too!—the co-operation of "tract-trotting misses" and the precious ministers they "sit under." Of late years a Magdalen Hospital has been established by persons of the above denomination at Southampton, where ladies of all ages, but mostly young ones, some very young, act in concert with their spiritual directors, often accompanied by them as visitors, superintendents, confessors, to the unfortunate persons with whom it makes one shudder to think a youthful, uncontaminated creature should have a moment's contact; and some of these young confessors expatiate unblushingly on the "miracles of grace" it is their good fortune to witness among these regenerated proselytes. These lady-errants will be all ready to swarm into an hospital nun establishment; but keep them out for Heaven's sake. One cunning way of excluding the young ones would be to prescribe a very unbecoming uniform. It will still attract elderly women, for the sake of distinction, which so often succeeds that love of dress which made Johnson (was it not?) designate us as "animals delighting in finery," and he, the "cooking animal," was right enough.

For all your threat of drawing tears from me, I look eagerly for the next *Quarterly Review*, and your story of the young American; but truly I must take leave to observe that, by your own confession, you are as deliberately cruel as I am. Do you break one's heart less with melancholy truths than if you tried it with mournful fiction? And be it known to you, that (except in the story of Andrew Cleaves) I have only been guilty of working upon prepared canvas. Circumstances within my own knowledge, or recollection of my mother's inexhaustible traditionary store, supplied me with abundant materials. I wish you joy of your noble determination to make all your creatures happy. I find it much easier to kill them out of the way, and then I take special care, when my work is done, never to read a page of it.

"Our volumes! our volumes!" how pleasantly that sounds! and I like well the hexameter opening of the shipwreck; but when will the time come when I shall be able to send you some beginning of mine?

My wits are all bottled up in the moon, I believe, or rather they are crushed into stupor by the load of mortality that presses on them—no heavy burthen, it should seem, by specific weight of flesh and blood; but "the ills that flesh is heir to" are heavy makeweights; and yet I am at present something better than I have yet been since January. Do not you rejoice in these floods, and storms, and cruel cold, if it gives you a respite from company? It kills me. No heliotrope ever turned sunward so wistfully as I do, and I rejoiced doubly in the bright sunshine of the 4th, hoping it looked down on Crosthwaite Church and the wedding train it was to receive that day. Miss Coleridge's maiden home must have been a happy one. I heartily wish her wedded one may be not less so. Is she to reside henceforth in London?

Farewell, dear friend. I have written a great deal of senseless stuff, I suspect. Would you were near at hand to make me wiser; at all events, make me happier; for wisdom is not my vocation, and I suspect happiness might have been.

CAROLINE A. BOWLES.

CIII.

TO CAROLINE BOWLES.

KESWICK, September 14th, 1829.

You say nothing concerning the Beguines, the Church Methodists, and the Co-operatives but what is perfectly sensible and true. With regard to the two former, hypocrisy will intrude in all such things; and with it everything that is odious, but among Beguines it has little opportunity of doing mischief. In Methodism I see all the danger that you apprehend; but without assistance the Church Establishment must continue to lose ground. The number of the clergy is inadequate to that of the people: any proportionate increase is not even to be dreamt of while our rulers both in Church and State are what they are, and what they are likely to be. The clergyman acts everywhere alone; whereas every sectarian is as far as he can a coadjutor to his minister, a recruiting, or a drill sergeant for his sect. There is undoubtedly great danger in calling in such auxiliaries as I have proposed, but that danger is diminished by wise management; such persons if not with us would be against us; and without aid it is I think (looking at human causes) impossible that the Establishment should keep its ground. Indeed it is more than rumoured that there is an intention of selling the tithes upon Mr. Pitt's plan. The consequence of which would be that the right of the clergy to their revenue, which now rests upon the Constitution, would then rest upon an Act of Parliament, made in one session, and liable of course to be repealed in any other. Their incomes would then be to be paid from the funds, that is from the taxes; and the first great reduction which would be called for by the Radicals and willingly conceded by the Whigs would be that of getting rid of this charge. One proposal might be to pay the clergy of all denominations, but the end would surely be that of leaving our clergy, like those of the dissenters, to be supported by the free will of their respective congregations. And what the dissenting clergy have become in consequence of such dependence you know; what a sleek, sycophantic, supple race the thriving ones among them are; and in what wretched dependence the poorer ones are held.

I have been disappointed of meeting Sadler, who is too busy in preparing his book. But I shall propably go to Lowther in the course of a few days, and then to Ripon. From Sadler I have been looking daily to hear in reply to the inquiries which I have made of him concerning the Church Methodists. I suppose his Whitby speech has prevented him hitherto from answering me. That speech is too rhetorical for my taste, though not for its auditory. But in all his views I go with him, except in his opposition to emigration, which I am convinced must always be our safety-valve.

The Co-operatives will better their own condition, both morally and physically, so greatly, as in my opinion and in Rickman's also (whose opinion in all such matters is worth more than that of any other man whom I have ever known) to produce a great reform among the lower classes, by the example of thrift, industry, and comfort which they will set. They will make the value of good character conspicuously visible. Mischief will be intended by some who take up their cause, but in the papers which the Brighton Society publish there is nothing but what is temperate, wise, and cogent. And certainly I look upon the movement which has thus commenced as the most important that has ever yet occurred in civil society; the most important and the most hopeful.

Henry Taylor has been passing a week with me, and takes his departure to-day. The flight of summer birds are off also, or on the wing. This evening I shall have the rare enjoyment of a quiet evening's work, which will be an enjoyment, though I am never willing to part with Henry Taylor, he being, except yourself, the only *friend* whom I have made in later years. Our volumes will fare the better for the leisure which I now begin to promise myself. I am in the vein of verse—were there but time to work it; and rich mines there are to work in.

Mrs. Coleridge is on her way to her son Derwent, at the Land's-End. A very agreeable woman (Miss Trevennion), who is a very useful and good friend to Derwent, was here at the wedding, and takes Mrs. Coleridge with her in her carriage, which is a great God-send for so long a journey. The new married couple* are lodging in Keswick and taking their pleasure. All change is painful to me: this, however, was a desirable one; being (it is to be hoped) for the happiness of those who are gone; and to the convenience of those who are left. This change gives us room, which was beginning to be wanted: the next, whatever that may be, and whenever it may come, will make a void. Whether the next set-forth from the house be for a marriage, or a funeral, who can tell! Thank God, when I look forward, it is always to another world; overlooking the whole of the down-hill road before me.

God bless you, dear friend.

ROBERT SOUTHEY.

* Sara and Henry Nelson Coleridge. On November 18th, Southey tells Caroline Bowles how he had accompanied the new married pair as far as Ripon: "Sara was much affected at parting from me, and I could not suppress my own feelings as I am wont to do."

CIV.

TO ROBERT SOUTHEY.

BUCKLAND, *December 7th*, 1829.

Whatever tricks your memory may play you, by making you doubt sometimes whether you have written to me or not, mine, though in general a very treacherous ally, never leaves me a minute's doubt whether or not I have heard from you; and just as I received your last letter, she had been telling me your silence had lasted two whole months! and at last you put by the *Peninsular War* and the Suchet for me—unworthy me. Not so, however; a few moments spared from even important avocations to a friend, and an old friend (I claim the title now), is never time wasted. My old nurse used to tell me, when we deliberated about giving something that could not well be spared at the time, "You'll never miss it at last, my child." I apply her saying to the sacrifice of time you must so often make to me—" You will never miss it at last."

Now I must tell you that I waited the more patiently for a letter from you as I had gleaned tidings of you, and guessed from them that you were absent from home. A lady wrote to another lady, who wrote to a third, who told it to me, that she, viz., lady the first, was going to dine at Colonel Howard's at Levens, to meet the two Poets of the Lakes. Who could those be, but yourself and he of Rydal Mount ? So all is well, said I to myself, and waited with exemplary patience. I am to ask you, Was not the lady who "talked to you of the Levetts" at Levens a sort of Bridgettina Botherum ? She intends to be very azure, makes dead sets at poets, would go twenty miles any day to see his poetical shadow; talks him dead if she can, and certainly talks all her friends to death for six months afterwards, with describing his characteristics, personal, moral and intellectual; "his eyes in a fine phrensy rolling," his sublime abstraction, his half words, hums and has! whether he took water at dinner, or eat his fish with a fork (for she slips in at the table by the victim's elbow if she can); and if afterwards she can ensnare him to commit himself in her album, she would not exchange her good fortune, for the time being, with the best lady in the land, though privileged to write herself Mistress instead of Miss.

What a pity your fair and interesting new acquaintance at Swinton was not daughter instead of wife to the good and amiable old man you describe; but, especially as he is so rich, I cannot forgive her marrying him. Once in conversation with some ladies on a something similar circumstance, I said very seriously what brought upon me such a storm of outraged decorum, that I have never dared think aloud on such subjects again: I got my rebuke on that of Lord Fitzwilliam's marriage with Lady —— I forget her name, but she was past seventy and he near eighty; old friends, and nothing more natural or rational methought than that they should wish to spend the rest of their days together; "But why need they marry?" was my unlucky comment that scandalized the whole female coterie, which, by-the-bye, had not been sparing of satirical remarks on the poor old lord and lady.

Farewell, dear friend, and God bless you.

CAROLINE A. BOWLES.

CV.

TO CAROLINE BOWLES.

KESWICK, *December* 18*th*, 1829.

Dear friend, I must not let your letter remain a single post unanswered. If you go before me to that world in which I trust we shall meet, not to be separated, I will take charge of your papers, and make it my first business to publish in a fitting manner the whole of your writings, to be a lasting monument of your worth, and of my affection. As for my letters, I will deposit them with yours (for I have preserved every line that I ever received from you). There is nothing in them which might not be seen by men and angels, and though written, as their utter carelessness and unreserve may show, without the slightest reference to any other eyes than those to which they were addressed, I shall not be unwilling to think that when time has consecrated both our memories (which it will do) this correspondence may see the light. Our earthly life, dear Caroline, lasts longer than in the hearts of those we love; it endures in the hearts of those whom we have never known, and who learn to love us after our work on earth is done. They who live on earth, in their good works, continue to make friends there as long as their works survive; and it may be one of the pleasures of another state to meet those friends when they seek us in heaven. I often feel that this will and must be so, when on reading a good old book my heart yearns towards the author.

Henry Taylor undertakes the disposal of my papers if he survives me—which I sometimes fear he may not: not calculating, God knows, upon any likelihood of longevity in myself, nor desiring it, except for the sake of those who would feel my loss, but because he is the son of a consumptive mother, and was born but a little while before her death. Among those who are much my juniors he is the only man whom I have taken to my heart.

But now let us put away posthumous considerations, and think of what we may yet do for ourselves. I knew you would delight in Stewart's book, and so you will in Ellis's, and in his *Polynesian Researches*. They are all most interesting books, and you will find in them subjects which I hope will tempt you to produce something for our projected volumes. Or if you will think again of that Irish story, I will send you what I have thought as to the manner of treating it, and the matters of times, places, and circumstances, for dressing it up.

Longman has applied to me for a volume of our naval history, given in the form of biography, for which he offers the same price as he pays to Scott and Mackintosh, being £750 for the volume. The volume is small, but holds much; and the prescribed extent is from 350 to 400 pages. But this is large pay—about the rate of my *Quarterly Review* payment, and with the advantage of one straightforward subject; and as the task is neither difficult nor unpleasant, I have undertaken it, but not to make it my employment till midsummer next, if I am living and well. At present I am on a life of John Bunyan; on Maw's voyage down the Orellana, for the *Quarterly Review;* and on the *Peninsular War*—working tooth and nail. The more quietly and steadily I am employed, always the more cheerful I am: such exercise of the mind seems as necessary for my perfect health and spirits as exercise of body is for others. But I do not neglect the body; and as the sun shines just now, which he is little in the habit of doing, I shall make up my despatches (put my clogs to the fire meantime), and, in vulgar English, fetch a walk.

Now remember that I love your letters, and that it will be a great pleasure to hear that you continue to amend.

Dear Caroline, God bless you.

ROBERT SOUTHEY.

CVI.

TO ROBERT SOUTHEY.

BUCKLAND, *January 4th*, 1830.

Your letter came to gladden me on Christmas Day, dear friend—not till then, though dated the 16th. Kindly and freely you have always answered and granted every question and request of mine; kindest of all is your last answer—all, much more than all I asked. I shall now keep those treasured letters while I live, with a clear conscience, and perhaps you may have created in my heart a feeling which before (as relating to myself) had no existence there—a degree of interest in something of me that shall survive on earth—I mean our correspondence. All my share in it will find indulgence for your sake.

I hardly thought you would have preserved letters many of which, I feared, had tried your patience. As for any manuscript fragments I may leave behind me, I may tell you, for your comfort, the longer I live the fewer these will be, for I have ruthless fits of destructiveness. In the meantime, I mean to live, if I can, just as long as you do, though it would be pleasant to bid you the first welcome to our better country. Thank you, my dear friend; I will dwell no longer on a subject so satisfactorily settled—to me.

"The Keepsake" has been sent to me for a birthday offering. It pleases me well not to find you among that "mob of gentlemen who write with ease." Let them have that red book all to themselves; there is now a charming equality, a beautiful keeping throughout, nothing to distract one's attention from the pretty pictures. Poor Alaric the Goth keeps ahead in the Annual regatta. As to the poetical part of his volume, there are no great literary names in his catalogue, to be sure, but then there are no lords.

No, indeed, I will not think again of the Irish story, otherwise than that you are to work upon it. I am angry with myself that Stewart and Ellis's books, though I do delight in them, tempt me not (as you thought they would) to glean from them subjects for verse. I cannot identify my feelings, my nature, with those of your Polynesian friends, interesting as they are; and, therefore, I cannot make anything of them more than if they were seals or codfish.

I can the more entirely enter into your beautiful view of the possibility of making friends here, when we are gone, who shall claim acquaintance with us hereafter, because I feel that I know and love some who departed hence before my birth almost as well as if we had met in the body, and I have sometimes fallen into conversation with them as familiarly as you with Sir Thomas More.

One worthy of a past century I have just taken an inveterate dislike to, from that first volume of his Life and Correspondence (I have not yet reached the second). I mean that sanctified coxcomb, Philip Doddridge, that prig of holiness.

What did the women of that day see in the creature, or find in his fulsome flattery and general love-making, rendered so odious by the profane admixture of professedly pious with very earthly feelings, as to run after him as they seem to have done, swallowing with equal docility his inquisitorial impertinence and more impertinent adulation?

God bless you, dear friend.

CAROLINE A. BOWLES.

CVII.

TO CAROLINE BOWLES.

KESWICK, *February* 15*th*, 1830.

Concerning Horace Smith. He was here some two or three years ago with Baron Field (the person to whom Charles Lamb wrote that amusing letter to Botany Bay). Milman's *Fall of Jerusalem* was mentioned, and I said something of the want of judgment, as well as of feeling, in mixing up a love-story with so awful a subject, in which any mixture of fiction appeared almost sacrilegious, for it belonged to something more than mere human history. He sent me his *Zillah* some twelve months afterwards, with a letter, saying, that what he had heard me say had influenced him in timing his story so as to avoid all interference with sacred history. I thanked him, in reply, for his book, said something civil about it, praising what was praisable (not, I think, above its deserts), and complaining that there was no repose in the story, but always a stream of adventures, or an exhibition of costume. He told me the cause of this, which was, that Colburn keeps a reader and corrector of his manuscripts, who strikes out everything that is not in some degree stimulant, and by this person all his digressions and historical parts, which had been intended as a relief, were expunged.

Horace Smith is a very clever writer in light verse. I do not think we have a better. Novels I never look into, unless there is some special reason for so doing. He has repented of some impertinences towards Wordsworth, and made the *amende honorable* for them, and is, I believe, in all respects a wiser man than he was in his youth. If my letters were a little too complimentary (of which, however, I am not conscious), I should hardly repent of it: an ill-natured review to which you allude may perhaps have caused a tendency that way. I am vexed with the reviewal, as very needlessly severe—vexed that Lockhart should have published it, coupled with so much praise of his father-in-law, which, to say the least, was indiscreet; and vexed that it should have been written by a young man of very extraordinary powers, Heraud by name. I think you have heard me speak of him.

I know nothing of your Quaker friends, except that what little of theirs has fallen in my way has pleased me. Dear friend, I am inclined to think that those who are most reserved when they feel no liking are attracted with most warmth when they attract themselves. Towards the greater number of persons who come in my way I am cold and courteous. Some there are who make me draw into myself, like a tortoise, or roll myself up in my prickles, like a hedgehog; and sometimes, but rarely, I bristle like a porcupine at an odious presence. The more liking and love, therefore, have I for those who deserve them. Miss Jewsbury I have never seen. Dora Wordsworth is very fond of her; but they have never brought her here, probably because of her impertinence towards me, for which I daresay she cannot forgive herself as easily as I forgive her. The Goth is said to have a very amiable wife. He himself, I suspect, is in no good humour with me, on the score of his *Souvenir*, having failed to bargain with me, when he might have had *Eleëmon*, before the Keepsakers came for it. The fault was his own, not mine. I respect his talents, pity his temper, and have not the slightest ill will towards him.

Try what you can remember about Fielding for me. The *Voyage to Lisbon* is the most remarkable example I ever met with of native cheerfulness triumphant over bodily suffering and surrounding circumstances of misery and discomfort.

Murray has managed very ill with me about his *Family Library*, using my name without my leave or knowledge, and then making a most inadequate offer—not, in fact, half of what Longman offered. By-and-bye, however, I will write for him, if he pay as he ought to do, two or three volumes of Lives of our Divines, leaving out those of whom Izaak Walton has written. Biography is easily written, and I like to write it.

God bless you, dear friend.

ROBERT SOUTHEY.

CVIII.

TO ROBERT SOUTHEY.

BUCKLAND, *February* 20*th*, 1830.

Your goodness about Horace Smith rebukes me, though you do not, for my spitefulness; but really I bore *Zillah* in silence, having my heart full of wrath against that hard measure in the *Quarterly Review*, and would not have breathed one word of my secret thoughts, though he had gone on cockneyfying all antiquity; but when he invaded mine own territory, mine own dear Forest, where he dared get up a lion hunt in one of its quiet glades, which never echoed to any sound more terrible than "Come home, Willy, poor Willy" (the beautiful deer call), I could bear it no longer, especially when triumphantly told by that awful man you wrote of, that his friend had been encouraged in his literary career by my friend Mr. Southey; then he flourished away about your letter. That said worthy once very seriously advised my Uncle Burrard, in my hearing, to stick up "some artifical palm trees" on the bare neck of shingle whereon stands Calshot Castle. "I am afraid, Mr. K.," said my Uncle, with the greatest gravity, "they would hardly stand our south-westers." "Oh, yes, Sir H.," rejoined the lover of the picturesque; "you might have them all backed with stout boards, and the branches strengthened with iron.

That plan answered admirably at my friend William Spencer's villa, where he gave a *fête champêtre* last year."

My hope of raking out something relating to Fielding hangs on a very slender thread—on the recovery of an aged friend of mine (a living chronicle of the days that are gone), who has just completed her ninetieth year, but is very ill at present. Her mind and memory are perfect as in her youth, and if she lives to gossip with me again I may pick up something: my own second-hand recollections are too shadowy. You would smile to overhear a gossip between me and this venerable friend of mine—the delight of both of us, I believe—for I am so perfect in the stories of her youth and my grandmother's, that after a very little while, when wearied with her subject, she forgets I am not my grandmother, and says, "You remember so-and-so, my dear," which I always make a point of remembering in the way she intends at the moment, and so the conversation never flags, till, after some short pause,' she recollects herself, and scolds me for letting her cheat herself so long, and forget I am not my grandmother.

God bless you, dear friend.

CAROLINE A. BOWLES.

CIX.

TO CAROLINE BOWLES.

KESWICK, *March* 13*th*, 1830.

The paper upon the Pauper Colonies refers in its table to I believe all the publications upon the subject. There is one I think by Jacob, who is a very able and judicious man, and on whom full reliance may be placed. There will be great difficulties to overcome in England, arising mainly from want of sufficient authority in those to whom the direction of such an attempt may be entrusted, and to the insubordinate habits of the persons who are to be managed. Before any attempt is made, some one who is to take a part in it should go to Holland, and make himself acquainted with what has been done there upon the spot. The natural disadvantages were far greater there; the civil ones not so many, nor so difficult to overcome as with us.

This morning I finished my work with Bunyan, except what is to be done in correcting a few more proofs. Major (the publisher) has had the rare grace for a bookseller, of perceiving that I had done for him as much again as he had expected and bargained for (more perhaps than he had wished), and he has sent me a hundred instead of fifty guineas. So he is very well pleased, and so am I, although this is very much below the market-price of my handy-work at this time. But I consented to do it for him, because I liked the task, and thought, moreover, the price he offered was as much as the speculation could afford, especially as he offered also twenty-five guineas upon every after edition, which, though a mere contingency, is yet worth something. He proposed about forty pages, and the amount will be nearer ninety. He has asked me now to introduce in like manner an ornamented edition of *Robinson Crusoe*.

I have seldom been more disgusted with anything than with the account of Moore's *Life of Byron* in *Blackwood*—I mean with the spirit and manner of the writer, whom I suppose to be Wilson. Have you observed in the *Keepsake* the letter about Lord Byron calling me out, and what was to be done if he should be the *survivor*? He knew very well that all his calling would not have made me " come and be killed," like the ducks in the song; and a wholesome apprehension of the sort of answer which I should have returned to a challenge made him wisely determine not to send one.

Tuesday 15.—There is a certain *Fraser's Magazine*, à-la-*Blackwood*, which has invoked me to send them verses occasionally, whereunto I consent upon terms of ten guineas per hundred lines. They have got my " Young Dragon " in their clutches, and I shall be glad when the money is mine. The Dragon will then have been worth fifty-five guineas, which is as much as a good horse, and I retain my right over him for after publication.

They want the Devil also, but the Devil is not to be let loose unless a large offer is made for him.

Dear Caroline, God bless you.

ROBERT SOUTHEY.

CX.

TO CAROLINE BOWLES.

KESWICK, *April* 14*th*, 1830.

Lady Byron sent me her letter. If she thought it necessary to vindicate her parents, she could not have done it better. Moore is unpardonable for having made her think it necessary, and as for Campbell, it would be difficult to express the thorough disgust with which I read his rant, and the contempt with which I could not but regard the writer. So heartless, so empty, so vapouring a composition, never came in my way before. It might have been written by an Irish fortune-hunter, impudent enough to have formed a scheme for marrying Lady Byron, and fool enough to think the best way of succeeding in it would be to get into a quarrel as her volunteer champion, and perhaps receive a challenge.

The *Memoirs* I have not seen, but Henry Taylor sent me some passages about myself. Most probably in the next volume I shall occupy a more conspicuous place; but Moore, I suppose, will be cautious for his own sake.

Fraser's Magazine will not be much in the way of the Monster's, for no one will think of dropping *Blackwood* for the sake of taking another just of the same kind which has its reputation to make. They have behaved impudently in making use of my name without my leave; not that I care for it, nor should have refused it if they had asked it as a favour. But I shall give them a pretty strong reprimand as soon as I receive payment, not thinking the matter of consequence enough to write expressly about it.

You will have the whole life of Nelson in the *Family Library,* and a good many insertions. That life will occasion me some little difficulty in the volume of *Naval Biography* which I have undertaken for the *Cabinet Cyclopædia.* My best way will be to say that no life of Nelson is included there, because it would only repeat what I had elsewhere said, and to treat the great actions in which he was engaged under other names. This I believe can be done in every instance except the battle of Copenhagen.

Whenever I go to London you may be assured that my first movement beyond it will be to Buckland; and if it be in a fit season, then for the Isle of Wight. Indeed it will be the most pleasurable object to which I can look forward, on leaving home, whenever that may be.

By an ornamented edition of *Robinson Crusoe* I simply mean "adorned with cuts," much I suppose, in the same manner as the *Pilgrim's Progress,* in which, to my surprise, Murray has thought it worth his while to embark with Major. I have only to supply something prefatory either as a Memoir of Defoe, or bibliographically, treating of such real adventurers as resemble Defoe's fiction, and of such fictions as have been produced in imitation of it.

I have begun the life of Sidney. My series for the *Family Library* will most likely begin with the Black Prince, because I must reserve for the *Book of the State* those persons whose lives are inseparably connected with the national history of England, such as Alfred, and Robert Earl of Gloucester. The Black Prince's exploits were in foreign wars which in the *Book of the State* I shall only refer to in noting their effects upon the state and progress of society at home. The list for my first volume therefore stands thus at present :—The Black Prince, Chaucer, Wolsey, Sir T. More, Surrey, Roger Ascham, Fox the Martyrologist, and Essex. Tell me if you can call to mind any who should have a place among them. There is nothing more to be said of Wicliffe than what I have already said in the *Book of the Church:* and to qualify myself for writing a life of Roger Bacon would require more than any price could pay for, and indeed than at my age I could afford to bestow upon such a subject. Many years ago I urged Davy to take that subject as one suited to his talents and worthy of them.

Dear friend, God bless you.

ROBERT SOUTHEY.

CXI.

TO ROBERT SOUTHEY.

BUCKLAND, *April* 27*th*, 1830.

You have long ceased to speak of moving southward, and as I was conscious you could not speak of it as a desirable prospect on your own account, I hardly allowed myself to wish you might do so. My disinterestedness was, however, the less meritorious, as I feel my hold of earth too slight to allow me to build castles on it, as I was once too prone to do, and perhaps waywardly mourn that I can do so no longer. I would not live my youth over again for all the world, but some of its illusions I would give worlds to renew. You are much younger in spirit than I am; but it took many, many years (from the age of scarce fifteen to twenty-six) to depress, and at last almost crush the elasticity of mine, and the looking back upon all the strange troubles I then had to steer through affects my mind far more painfully now than at the time of their actual existence. All through that interval I knew that, for the most part, precious time was slipping past me unimproved, wasted, worse than wasted; and yet I could not help myself. I had hardly leisure to deplore the irretrievable loss, or to look on from the perplexing present to the uncertain future. Is it not sad to look back on such a youth, and to think how late I began to live? The thought might well strike despair into my heart if life ended here: it does not, and all will be well, for which acknowledgment's sake forgive all that precedes it.

I am glad to find you and I are so entirely agreed on the

subject of Campbell's letters. Were I Lady Byron, he should never more enter my presence after what I should consider such an insult to my feelings and womanly dignity. She cannot have sanctioned it; but I think she should not have sent her letter to you, entirely unacquainted with you, as I believe she is, opposed as you have always been in a peculiar manner before the eye of the public to Lord Byron, and hostile as he was to you. Lady Byron's referring to you, as she has done, looks too like an endeavour to enlist a champion in her cause, which needs none, would she let it find its level quietly and gradually.

I am longing to see some of Blake's engravings from his own extraordinary designs, of which I first heard from yourself. Do you know whether they are scarce, or dear? They are certainly not generally known. Cunningham's life of him in the *Family Library* has strengthened the interest for Blake and his works with which your account first inspired me. Mad though he might be, he was gifted and good, and a most happy being. I should have delighted in him, and would fain know how it fares with the faithful, affectionate partner of his honourable life. I hope she is not in indigence. Have I ever told you that I have lost my kind and valuable neighbours the Dalrymples? Poor Sir John died about five months ago, after much protracted suffering, and his widow, partly from pecuniary reasons, partly from distaste to her home since his death, has sold her pretty little villa to some near relations of mine, who formerly lived in this neighbourhood, and are now returning to end their days here—a Mr. and Mrs. Roche. She lived much in my father's house before she married, has always been in kindness and affection a second mother to me, and the person of all others in my own family on whom I rely most in time of need. You will be glad to hear such a friend is settling near me; but as yet my satisfaction in visiting their new purchase (where I am superintending some necessary works previous to their coming to take possession) is mingled with painful recollections of the late owners of the place. It is with a sort of dream-like feeling I sometimes find myself standing in the same drawing-room, now unfurnished and desolate, where so short a time since I was sitting with those now in the grave, or gone from thence for ever; who little suspected then how soon their guest would be giving orders for others in their happy home. So dreaming, I forget my business with carpenters and painters till they wake me with their questions, and then I feel as if I were heartlessly intruding some usurped authority, and I give my orders in a low voice, and tread softly, as if the dead could hear, and might reproach me. How this dreamy temper grows upon one!—upon me at least, as I advance in life. It does not help to fit one for this world assuredly, but it is no hindrance in our way to the other; at least so I am fain to persuade myself, perhaps. The best home news I have to tell you is, that I have three nightingales in my little flower garden; that I not only hear, but see them sing, so fearlessly do they sit in the bough of an acacia over my head (one of them, at least, and his rivals hard by on neighbouring trees). Last winter, during that long sharp frost, one of my garden blackbirds got so desperate from starvation, that he actually hopped into Mufti's house in the yard, and disputed his bones with him. Hunger makes strange messmates, as well as Poverty "strange bedfellows." Mufti's astonishment overcame his indignation, and Blacky hopped off with such a bone as I could not have believed his beak could have lifted, if I had not witnessed the feat. I heard the cuckoo this morning for the first time, and, by-the-bye, it is Knap I think, the author of the *Journal of a Naturalist*, who says that towards autumn and the cessation of its song that bird breaks its note into fragments—that odd "cuck! cuck! cuck! cuckoo!" you first made me observe, and I have since so often observed. Here I have written you two acres of letter. What it is to encourage some people! If my last was a week on the road to you, your reply was nearly as long on its way here.

Fare you well, and God bless you, dear friend.

CAROLINE A. BOWLES.

CXII.

TO CAROLINE BOWLES.

Keswick, *May 8th*, 1830.

You judge rightly about Lady Byron, as you always do; but though I have never seen her, nor held any communication with her, she does not consider me altogether as a stranger; for she was very well acquainted with my brother Dr. Southey before her marriage, and, indeed, before her acquaintance with Lord Byron, and it was through him that her letter was sent. Certainly no such thought ever passed across her mind as that of wishing me to appear in her defence. She sent it to me as to one of whom she had been accustomed to think well before my name was ever connected with Lord Byron's.

My lease is renewed, and I am, as far as ordinary foresight goes, settled here for the remainder of my days. I have taken the house for five years, with the choice of quitting it at the end of that time, or retaining it for another like term. Necessary repairs are to be made, as for a new tenant, and in fact workmen are now in the house, which little by little has undergone great improvement. I have a melancholy feeling that it will one day be too large for my family; but a smaller would not contain us now, nor my books at any time, and books are all but everything to me. I live with them and by them, and might almost say for them and in them.

I have nothing of Blake's but his designs for Blair's *Grave*, which were published with the poem. His still stranger designs for his own compositions in verse were not ready for sale when I saw him, nor did I ever hear that they were so. Much as he is to be admired, he was at that time so evidently insane, that the predominant feeling in conversing with him, or even looking at him, could only be sorrow and compassion. His wife partook of his insanity in the same way (but more happily) as Taylor the pagan's wife caught her husband's paganism.

And there are always crazy people enough in the world to feed and foster such craziness as his. My old acquaintance William Owen, now Owen Pugh, who, for love of his native tongue, composed a most laborious Welsh Dictionary, without the slightest remuneration for his labour, when he was in straitened circumstances, and has, since he became rich, translated *Paradise Lost* into Welsh verse, found out Blake after the death of Joanna Southcote, one of whose four-and-twenty elders he was. Poor Owen found everything which he wished to find in the Bardic system, and there he found Blake's notions, and thus Blake and his wife were persuaded that his dreams were old patriarchal truths, long forgotten, and now re-revealed. They told me this, and I, who well knew the muddy nature of Owen's head, knew what his opinion upon such a subject was worth. I came away from the visit with so sad a feeling that I never repeated it.

The exhibition of his pictures, which I saw at his brother's house near Golden-square, produced a like melancholy impression. The colouring of all was as if it had consisted merely of black and red ink in all intermixture. Some of the designs were hideous, especially those which he considered as most supernatural in their conception and likenesses. In others you perceived that nothing but madness had prevented him from being the sublimest painter of this or any other country. You could not have delighted in him—his madness was too evident, too fearful. It gave his eyes an expression such as you would expect to see in one who was possessed.

Whoever has had what is sometimes called the vapours, and seen faces and figures pass before his closed eyes when he is lying sleepless in bed, can very well understand how Blake saw what he painted. I am sure I can, from this experience; and from like experience can tell how sounds are heard which have had no existence but in the brain that produced them.

God bless you, dear friend. I am making up a packet for London, and will rather inclose this than wait for a fit of leisure which might fill the sheet. Since I began it, there is a chance—a likelihood—that I may be in the south during the summer, or autumn, in which case I shall see you.

ROBERT SOUTHEY.

CXIII.

TO ROBERT SOUTHEY.

BUCKLAND, *May* 20*th*, 1830.

I have been disappointed in my hope of acquiring some information relating to Fielding for you. My old friend has revived again, and we have had another gossip of old times; but I had only the mortification of learning that a few years ago it would have been in her power not only to obtain for me many interesting particulars about Fielding, but probably much of his correspondence. When Mrs. Bromfield (my old friend) was a young woman, she was the intimate friend of a Miss Collier, who was a very intimate friend of Fielding's. Miss C. and her family lived at that time at Ryde, in the Isle of Wight, in the only house at that time standing of a better sort than the few mean cottages of which Ryde then consisted. The ship in which Fielding sailed to Lisbon lay for some weeks off Ryde, and he used to come ashore often to visit the Colliers, and ramble about the island; and one of the characters in his novels is sketched (Mrs. Bromfield says) from the scolding landlady of the little Ryde inn, or rather ale-house, who used to quarrel with him fiercely—*pour cause, vraisemblement.*

Fielding corresponded till the close of his life with Miss Collier, and she, till her own decease, with Mrs. Bromfield, often writing of Fielding—but what, alas! neither you nor I shall ever bring to light, for my dear old friend, thinking her account with time was on the eve of an immediate close, some two months ago, had the old cabinet, containing long-treasured correspondence and lots of other preciously antique papers, brought to her bedside, and the whole destroyed with ruthless unsparingness; and of all the Collier family she lost sight after her friend's death, previous to which they had quitted the Isle of Wight to reside in another part of England, which she does not recollect. There is a long story about nothing for you— or rather (which is more provoking), of what might have been attainable two months ago, for a sight of Miss Collier's correspondence with Mrs. Bromfield might have given a clue to trace the survivors of the Colliers, in whose possession Fielding's letters to their relation may still be.

I have been disappointed in a scheme of my own, moreover, which, however, afforded me some amusement in the concocting of it, and seemed to wile me from myself at a time when I was suffering more than usual (last year) in mind and body. So I do not repent my folly. I *got up* the story of my cat in sublime style—a feline epic—illustrated it with appropriate pen etchings, wrote a very solemn preface, and pleased myself all the while with the thought of the said epic's presenting itself at Keswick all unannounced, if I could get it published without betraying my own identity, or, rather, that it was from the pen of the authoress of ——. Then, I had been told that your great man, the Hybrid, was the most likely gudgeon in the world to bite at any hook baited with rank and fashion, and half my sport was the idea of getting him to bring out my nonsense. So, I took a foreign title, sealed with a foreign coat-of-arms, all coronet, and sent my MSS. in a dashing carriage, to match, through the hands of a fair friend who was charmed to manage the intrigue, and whose air of fashion must have its weight, I fancied. But she could not see Murray, and left the MSS. At the end of a fortnight he returned it to the address indicated, with a very civil note, evidencing that he was a little puzzled by the mock seriousness of mine, but begging to decline the honour of publishing. So I lost my joke, and found I was an awkward plotter. But still hankering to come upon you by surprise, I tried two other printers, with no better success than that. "Though the thing was very well done," said one of them, "he feared to risk the expense of the illustrations"; and so fallen to the ground is the most unique epic that, I will venture to say, ever was strung together by Muse ancient or modern; and (to be serious), on thinking the matter over, I suspect I may have reason to be thankful to my rejectors for saving me from ridicule, which perhaps I might have winced under a little, if I had been detected; though, at the time of concocting, I thought of nothing in the world but my own sport, and a laugh with you, in fancy at least.

Now, I am about to attack you in the tenderest point— your partiality to albums.

Lady Dalrymple and her sister have entreated me to entreat you to bestow on each of them a few autograph words—a very few will be contentedly and thankfully received, and you will have my thanks into the bargain, if that consideration may be any makeweight. So I have said what I promised to say, and on my own account will add no more now than

God bless you, dear friend.

CAROLINE A. BOWLES.

CXIV.

TO CAROLINE BOWLES.

KESWICK, *Whitsunday*, 1830.

Here are your autographs, composed as you will see for the nonce, and you have applied for them just in time: for at the end of the Introduction to poor John Jones's verses, I have given public notice against all applications for such things, requested newspapers and other journals to copy my notification, and expressed a hope that Sir James Graham would mention it in Parliament.

I cannot yet tell you whether it will be in autumn or in summer that I shall see you, but in one season or the other (God willing), certainly. Business, but of no unpleasant nature, requires me to be in London; the time depends upon the proceedings in Parliament; about the middle of June, if the poor king lingers on, and the Session should in consequence be continued so as to carry through all the business before it—not till August if a dissolution follow upon his death. You will wonder why my movements should be dependent upon such matters. No one indeed knows anything of my intent as yet, except Rickman, with whom I shall have my head-quarters, nor will any other person know my object when I am there, the hay-asthma being a sufficient pretext for my appearance. But I may tell you that I am going to mix in society with public men, attend some of the debates, look with my own eyes into the mechanism of parties for which I shall have the best opportunities, and collect such facts, substantiated by irrefragable authorities and statements, that I may hope by making proper use of them to waken the land-holders and fund-holders to some sense of their imminent danger—revolution and their utter ruin being inevitable, and near at hand, unless they can be roused by frightening them. I am not without good hope of effecting this, knowing what I know; at any rate it will be a great satisfaction to feel, if the worst comes, that I have done my duty—as I will do it—strenuously. Breathe not a word of this. I wish August may be the time, not only because I could in the interim get through a world of work, but because I should then probably, at the end of a short Session, go with Rickman to his house at Portsmouth, and from thence to you.

Fielding must have known the Colliers before his voyage to Lisbon; he was then dying, as they say, by inches, and survived it only a very few weeks, for which reason his account of that voyage is to me the most extraordinary, and perhaps the most interesting of all his works. Never did any man's natural hilarity support itself so marvellously under complicated diseases, and every imaginable kind of discomfort. Thank you for what you would have procured for me, as well as for what you have done. At present I am working like a dragon upon Sir Philip Sidney's life, and for the *Quarterly Review*, hoping to clear myself of all quarterly labours for full six months, before I start from home.

Your cat-book must have amused (and will amuse) me—but

of course I should at once have known from whom it came.* If your lady-agent had seen Murray he might have been dazzled, cautious as publishers are now become. The former class of persons who purchased books can no longer afford to do so; the booksellers therefore are turning almost their whole attention to publications for those who buy cheap works; for those persons they will provide plenty of trash, crude and unwholesome, undigested and indigestable, and sometimes (unconsciously on the publishers' parts) carrying poison with it, as in Milman's History of the Jews—where, not being an infidel, shallowness and coxcombry have made him like one.

Public affairs were never so fearful, to those who have eyes to see, and hearts to reason with. You probably know Prince Leopold's reason for resigning his fool's-crown: a Regency must be provided with the new civil list, in case of King William-Henry's death before the Princess is of age, and this provides also (most unlikely) in case of his half-craziness again becoming whole-craziness. The Whigs mean to set up Leopold as Regent, for which he is undoubtedly the most fit person. I always thought him destined for this: but then I thought him a person of some discretion; and who but a fool would have accepted, as he did, the Kingdom of Greece?

Another week will go far towards bringing this house in at the windows again, it having been turned out of them for more than a fortnight. Meantime I work on unmolested, and murmur only when I have to hunt about for books whose individual places I used to know before the shelves were taken down to make place for plasterers and painters. Up they will go again ere long, and then I shall sing "O be joyful."

Dear friend, God bless you.

ROBERT SOUTHEY.

* The Cat-book was published in 1831 by Blackwood: "The Cat's Tail, being the History of Childe Merlin. A Tale. By The Baroness de Katzleben." It has three etchings by Cruikshank, after drawings by Caroline Bowles.

CXV.

TO CAROLINE BOWLES.

KESWICK, *August 8th*, 1830.

I am troubled by the events in France. Forty years ago I could partake the hopes of those who expected that political revolutions were to bring about a political millennium; now I perceive in how many circumstances the present crisis resembles that, and find more cause in them for fear than there is for hope in the circumstances wherein they differ.

If the young Duke of Bordeaux were made king, and the Duke of Orleans Regent and Protector, I should then think that never had any people behaved more gloriously nor more wisely than the Parisians. There would then be no after-evils to apprehend; the government would have a moral strength in itself, and it would have the support of other Powers, so that the spirit of democracy would be kept down. But the Duke of Orleans has neither wisdom nor virtue to profit by the opportunity which he has of acquiring one of the best reputations in history; the Devil offers him a crown, and he will take it; that crown was the object of his flagitious father's ambition; he obtains it now *in consequence* (though not because) of his father's crimes. I believe it has long been the object of his own ambition, and that the factious opposition to the Bourbons which has constantly been kept up for no avowed reason that any Englishman could comprehend has this end in view. " It is not" therefore, " and it cannot come to good." The tricolor cockade was his father's colours, but it became the Robespierrean badge; *as such* the flag has already been displayed with black crape over it, and by-and-bye I fear it will be dyed as it used to be, in blood.

I used to think (and often expressed that thought) that the Revolution would not have fulfilled its course till the two houses of Bourbon and of Austria were exterminated, so much blood was upon them both. But no more of this subject, which is far more in my mind that I wish it to be.

Thursday next, if I live to see it, will complete my fifty-sixth year, and it will be my first birthday on which there will have been no bell-ringing, for it happened to be the late poor king's. There is something melancholy in having seen the end of the Georges, the Georgian age having been in part the happiest, in part the most splendid, and altogether the most momentous age of our history. We are entering upon a new one, and with no happy auspices; but the rougher the road may be, the more satisfaction is there in knowing that the end of the journey cannot be far off.

Dear friend, farewell, and God bless you.

ROBERT SOUTHEY.

CXVI.

TO ROBERT SOUTHEY.

BUCKLAND, *August* 23rd, 1830.

Interesting as your letters always are to me, the last could not but be peculiarly so—most of all in what related to yourself; and I need not tell you, your birthday did not pass away with me unnoted and unnoticed, as too many days of our brief allotment are allowed to pass. If I live till the 6th of next December, I shall complete either my forty-third or forty-fourth year (I am doubtful which); and at that age, with my constitution, I may account myself farther advanced than you on the downhill way, well content that it should be so; but when we look back from Eternity to this brief account of Time, how little will it import us which first paid the reckoning! For the present I feel enough interest in this life to make me more than willing to outlive autumn; but to be with me before the last leaf falls, you must be beforehand with October, dear friend, for already they are so thickly strewn that before the beginning of that month it is probable the trees will be leafless. I never recollect such a premature autumn. You and I have never met but in autumn or winter—in the autumn of the year, as in that of our lives.

The late events in France have affected me exactly as they have affected you.

We shall see whether the revolutionary spirit—yet so active —will rest content with the "Citizen King." Already the government is rather a crowned democracy than a limited monarchy, and I cannot believe the anarchists will long submit even to that semblance of a crown. At all events, the late explosion is surely but the first of many for which the trains are laid ready under other countries. Spain, Portugal and Italy cannot be long inactive in the day of regeneration, and these are times to make all sovereigns think, if they can. Our mob king has not had a leisure moment yet.

I am just returned from an evening ride on my fairy steed, and I believe I have met—whom do you think?—travelling along our Hampshire road, in a britzka and four, without a single attendant, or outrider—no less personages, I verily believe, have I so encountered than the ex-king of France and Madame la Duchesse d'Angoulême, on their road to Lulworth Castle, lent them by my neighbours and acquaintances the Welds, who have preceded the royal exiles to prepare for their reception. I suspect the rest of the party have proceeded by water, but am almost sure the king and duchess (whom I knew formerly) were those who passed me. What a dream of greatness! what an abrupt transition! The ladies of the party have been living at the Fountain Inn at Cowes, for many days, walking about on the pier there and at Ryde, and talking to everybody who seemed inclined to talk to them. It was signified to the king and dauphin, who also wished to land, that it might be unsafe, so great is the spirit of exasperation against them; so they remained on board, the king gazing at the crowds assembled by a regatta, and greatly increased by the curiosity to see him and his family. This place has been actually depopulated, such is the rush towards Cowes of every creature who could move—except me, who would fain have been farther than I am even here from a sight so painful.

God bless you, dear friend.

CAROLINE A. BOWLES.

CXVII.

TO CAROLINE BOWLES.

KESWICK, *September* 14*th*, 1830.

We have had all sorts of people here. Dr. Bell, the Baroness Grey de Ruthin (a fine, lively, good-natured, bold baroness), with her mother, Lady Grey, and that mother's husband, Mr. Eden, an honourable clergyman. They were an agreeable party, with whom I presently became familiar. Then came a lady who inclosed to me a note of introduction, and sealed her note with *Maria*. When I went to look for her, Maria proved to be a splendid person, tall enough for a grenadier's wife in old Frederick's body-guard, very handsome, and agreeable also, though as blue as if she had been dipt in an indigo lake. Nobody ever shook hands with me so often in so short a time. She is a Miss Ross, of Scotland, where her brother has just succeeded Hume as Member for Montrose. I saw her only during a half-hour's visit, for she was on the wing, and I was bound that same morning for the top of Cawsey Pike. But had there been another interview, I think she would have sworn eternal friendship.

There was a report that Prince Polignac and his wife had arrived in Keswick, and were lodging here. Certain it was that an old gentleman and a young lady were here, who looked like foreigners, and conversed in French. "There are the French people," Cuthbert said to me the other day, in a low voice, as we were about to pass them on our outward way, he on a pony, I as his attendant footman. "There they are again," said he, as we returned. They had then halted, as if to let us pass, when the old gentleman took off his hat, and crossed over to accost me. Off came my cap, and I was prepared to hear myself addressed as M. Souté, and to muster up my best French in reply, when acquaintance was claimed with me in very good English by Robert Adair, once a political notoriety, whom I met eighteen years ago at Woburn, where he is still, and has puzzled me a little by not introducing the lady, who is young and a foreigner. He has sent me up a batch of French newspapers this evening, from which I have made some notable extracts for use.

Professor Airy came to-day with his bride. He is the only calculating prodigy whose other intellectual powers have not been absorbed by that peculiar talent; on the contrary, he is a person of great ability in all things. I hope Edward, who is gone to Whitehaven for the pleasure of going down into a coal-pit under the sea, will return in time to see him.

Lockhart, who has no easy office at this time, is disposed in some measure to lean upon me, and wants me to write upon the affairs of Europe, and especially of the Netherlands. The latter subject I have promised to undertake for him, and shall be led much into the other whenever the remainder of Robespierre's (real or supposititious) Memoirs reach me. He tells me that Sir Walter has been reviewing my *Life of Bunyan*.

Wednesday, 15th.—How fortunate it is that my good procrastinating bookseller at Brussels did not detain my books till this time, in hopes of laying his hand upon those which were mislaid, and are now, it must be feared, lost to me for ever. I should have despaired of getting them now, for that these revolutions will bring on a war all circumstances lead me to conclude. The course of foreign affairs, I think, may be foreseen; not so that part of our own concerns which relates to the administration, who are to be in and who out. The Duke, I am told, always makes his overtures through a woman—a Wellesley-like way of proceeding, for which there is the oldest of all examples in the third chapter of Genesis.

Through such a channel he has offered Lord Melbourne seats in the Cabinet for himself, the two Grants, Lord Palmerston, and any fifth person whom they may name, except Huskisson. But Huskisson is the strength of that party. On the other hand, I hear of what seems to be an impossible approximation between Lord Grey, Brougham, and the Duke of Newcastle. It is a comfort to look at these things, and wait for the event, without caring a straw how it may turn out, in the sad conviction that weakness on one side is working for the same end as wickedness on the other; and the sure consolation that Providence will bring about its own purposes at last. What those may be, you and I shall know when we are in some blessed star. If I knew which, I would purchase the best telescope that this house could hold, and look at it whenever it was to be seen. And if you and I had such wings as we shall one day have, dear Caroline, we should be eager to begin our flight there.

God bless you.

ROBERT SOUTHEY.

CXVIII.

TO ROBERT SOUTHEY.

BUCKLAND, *October 1st*, 1830.

The ex-royal family have been associating a good deal with friends of mine since their residence at Lulworth. Lately the Duchess de Berri, her children and suite were taking luncheon at my friend's house, and on Polignac's name being mentioned, the Duchess exclaimed, *Ah le traître ! nous lui devons tous nos malheurs.* I hear the other Duchess—Madame—says, if she were to meet him with a dagger in her hand, she would strike it to his heart. The Duke d'Angoulême's hand is still bound up for the hurt he received in it on catching at the blade of Marmont's sword during their altercation at Rambouillet.

Princess Polignac was a playfellow of mine when we were both girls, a daughter of Lord Rancliffe's. Poor woman! I fear her weak and guilty husband and his colleagues will pay the extreme penalty. A French gentleman, who left Paris last week, told me they cannot escape the infuriated populace, and that any attempt on the part of the king or government to remit the punishment of death, or favour their escape, would be the signal of another Revolution.

I was exceedingly disappointed to find the name of your Brobdingnagian lady was Miss Ross, not Miss C—, as I hoped it was on reading your description of her before I came to the cognomen. A certain Miss C— is stalking about the land with a literary pass, shaking people's wrists out of joint and overwhelming them in blue vapour.

So the last leaves will have fallen before I see you; my first impulse was to be very much disappointed at the procrastination; my next—how contradictory—almost bordering on satisfaction that I should have the cordial of expectation to cheer me so much longer. But welcome you will be whenever you come to me. And so, dear friend, "good night." That word recalls to me an affecting circumstance relating to a little cousin of mine who died about a week ago, a beautiful child of nearly four years old. He had been long perishing, and lay for a week before his death perfectly insensible. Just before he breathed his last, the child unclosed his eyes, and looked round at his mother and his mother's sister, who were watching by him. He smiled in their faces, stretched out his arms and said, "Good night, mamma; good night, aunt Caroline; good night all; now I go to sleep"—and so blessedly expired. His sensations must have been those of sinking into sweet slumber. Happy child!

God bless you, dear friend.

CAROLINE A. BOWLES.

CXIX.

TO CAROLINE BOWLES.

LONDON, *November 3rd*, 1830.

Here I am, dear Caroline, three hundred miles nearer to Buckland than I was this day week. I arrived on Monday night, and yesterday for the first time heard a debate in the House of Commons. Here I shall stay, and work hard as long as Parliament continues sitting, and then make my way to you, with the intent of proceeding into Devonshire and returning home by way of Bristol.

I am too busy and too weary to say more at present, being just returned from a four-hours' round of calls. Only I must not omit saying that your story of the child's death is one of the most touching I ever met with; and that I have fallen in with a certain Miss K—, who is a namesake of yours and is called by her friends *the* Caroline. A most comical person she is. She had the greatest dislike to seeing me, but a strong wish withal to see my cats. But there was a peculiar expression about her mouth, which (though she is very ugly) reminded me strongly of another Caroline. So I took her into my graces at once, and she took me into hers; and then, having made her previous arrangements in fear of me not to stay more than one night at Keswick, she went away confessing that she had been very foolish and very piggish (they were her own words), and wishing she could have remained longer to become better acquainted with the cats and with me.

God bless you, dear friend.

ROBERT SOUTHEY.

CXX.

TO CAROLINE BOWLES.

NEW PALACE YARD, *November* 10*th*, 1830.

I do not wonder, dear friend, that the state of affairs should appear more formidable to you at a distance than it does to me upon the spot.* There has been just danger enough to excite a very wholesome and necessary fear. The remnant of Thistlewood's desperadoes are at work. I *believe* that the intention was to murder the king, as well as the Duke, and to set London on fire, and I *know* there was a plan for massacring the new policemen. The streets on Monday and Tuesday were crowded with a set of dirty, resolute-looking men, evidently collected for some purpose, a great part of them not being Londoners, but from Manchester and other such hotbeds of mischief. I should have been struck both by their appearances and their extraordinary numbers, even if I had not had to make my way among them with a cheque for £100 in my pocket into Coutts's bank, and to come out of it with the bills. However, I brought them safely home, and slept very soundly, though the last thing which I saw was a strong body of police drawn up under the front windows. The military preparations were most extensive, and, I am told, excellently arranged; but they were wisely kept out of sight, and the only display was of the civil force. There are 6000 of these policemen, and a more respectable or efficient set of men no one could desire to see. The night passed over without disturbance in this quarter; in others the police (for the first time) made their bludgeons felt. There was no call for the soldiers, and the liberty-boys to-day

---

* In a letter of November 8th, Miss Bowles wrote: "My dear friend, I am so panic-struck at the aspect of the times, that I feel as if I longed to draw everyone I love close round me, that the same fate at least may involve us; but perhaps those who listen in darkness and loneliness to the advancing tide may be apt to fancy it approaches more awfully and impetuously than it does in reality."

have in great part disappeared. The best news is, that the Government is supposed to have obtained a clue to the movers of the mischief, and there is no doubt that the incendiaries are sent out by this knot of traitors.

Some of the many warnings which the Duke received came from men so far in league with the Radicals as to know their worst designs, but who now begin to tremble for themselves, when open rebellion was to be commenced with a massacre and with firing London.

The Duke certainly goes out, and Earl Grey will be at the head of the new ministry. The chief places in the House of Commons will, it is supposed, be filled by Lord Palmerston, the Grants, Stanley, and Sir James Graham. Brougham will probably be Master of the Rolls. It would be equally difficult for any administration to stand against him or with him, so great is his power, and so little his discretion.

I had scrawled through this hasty budget of news *pour votre consolation*, as the landlord at Besançon said to me when he assured me we should probably be robbed or murdered in crossing the Jura the next day. This I could not do in time for the post, but have been writing since I dressed for dinner, and before going out to that said dinner, for which my stomach is crying out loudly, though it was propitiated three hours ago by the sacrifice of a dozen oysters. It is at Murray's that I am to appease my hunger. You see that I have neither lost my spirits, nor my appetite. No man sees the danger more clearly in its whole extent, and no one, I believe, fears it less. My trust is in God's mercy, and my stand upon the Rock of Ages.

Farewell, dear Caroline. I shall be glad to find myself on the road to Hampshire. Bertha is on her way hither, and will, I hope, arrive on Saturday evening.

ROBERT SOUTHEY.

CXXI.

TO CAROLINE BOWLES.

London, *November* 20*th*, 1830.

A wet afternoon has given me resting time enough for writing a few lines. I have had an hour's conversation with the Archbishop, whom I have known some ten years, and with whom Bertha (to her great dismay) and I are to dine on Wednesday next. He is less pleased with the entrance of the Whigs than I am, for I expect most fully that before twelve months have expired they will furnish materials for a book to be entitled "God's Revenge against Liberalism and Whiggery."

After this visit I went with Telford and Rickman to see the filter by which Thames water is purified for those who do not (like Rickman) prefer it in its unclean state. Odd as you may think it, there are many who do. It makes better tea and better beer because of its impurity. You and I should agree in disregarding this, and choosing the cleaner beverage; but, after all, water that requires no cleaning is best, such as I have at Keswick, and you at Buckland.

Half the magistrates ought to be hanged for cowardice. The farmers are either frightened, or in league with the labourers against the Church and the landlords: they will even effect the desirable object of bringing the Whigs to their senses, and curing those persons who have been long employed in abusing the Government that protected them.

It is growing too dark and too late for writing more. The first quiet I shall have will be when I reach Buckland. Alarming as it must seem to have such troops of beggars at your door, you, who have no farm, are safe, and effectual force *must* speedily be employed.

God bless you, dear Caroline.

Robert Southey.

CXXII.

TO ROBERT SOUTHEY.

BUCKLAND, *November 27th*, 1830.

If the present state of things goes on, dear friend, your intended visit to me must be relinquished, or you will pay it at some peril to yourself, for this county is even in a more serious state of disturbance than you read of in the papers; and it has reached us, though as yet our moles are only local ones, and though the most worthless and least distressed of the population are hitherto so obliging as to be content with having everything conceded to them before they have half spoken their demands. What I now see in this neighbourhood explains to me proceedings in other counties; and while I feel sure that the least show of determined resistance to intimidation would quell the first indications of riot, I see that all is lost and everything to be feared from the indiscretion and pusillanimity of those who should stand forward. However, when the men are all cowards it is high time the women should pluck up heart, so I have put by my cowardice till there are men in the land again. We have as yet had no fires nearer than Southampton. But many threatening letters are received—night watches, &c., are established, and a most extraordinary measure resorted to here— all the smugglers with their chief captain of this coast called in and organised to act in our defence with the Preventive Service men! If "Poverty makes a man acquainted with strange bedfellows," insurrection creates strange combinations. Then the male population is converted, as in other places, into special constables—two-thirds of them on condition that they shall not be obliged to act unless—what do you think?—unless they like it! and I have not the slightest doubt that six old women might rout the whole posse with their bodkins and knitting-needles. At a meeting of magistrates, gentlemen, and farmers, assembled the other day in the Town Hall, the sight of a pitiful village mob marching towards them frightened

them so heartily that some poked their heads out of window
to promise everything, before anything was asked, and one
magistrate, taking courage to address them from the doorway,
began in his trepidation—" Gentlemen ! " then he stopt, and
opened his speech rather more appropriately; but knowing him,
I only wonder he had not burst out in his agitation with
" Friends! Romans! countrymen, lend me," &c. It would
have answered very well I am sure, and have been quite as
beneficial to the community as what he did say. The ringleader
of that band of mobbers was so kind as to stop at my door on his
triumphant way back, and volunteer a detail of their successes,
not forgetting to dwell with great compassion on having
"frightened the poor gentlemen terribly." If these proceedings are samples of those in other places and counties, who can
be surprised that we are now under mob law ?—yet bad as this
is, I should not feel much apprehension were it not for the
travelling mob, of near 2000, perambulating the county, actually sacking and plundering houses, as well as people on the
high road. The carriers coming in here to-day through Fordingbridge describe that place as having the appearance of having
been sacked and pillaged—which in fact it has been in great degree. The Cootes of Westcourt, near Fordingbridge, defended
their house gallantly with only six men, drove off the rioters,
but poor young Coote is badly wounded. An express came in
here yesterday for help for Lord Cavan at Fawley, eleven miles
from hence. How he has fared I know not; but the vagrant
mob, as it may be called, really a fearful one, made up of all
sorts of vagabonds, was at Hythe yesterday near 2000 strong
—twelve miles from here—no agreeable neighbourhood; and I
beg you will be a little concerned for me, though I cannot
afford to be afraid myself. I had felt very safe from our mob,
from my insignificance, but it has oddly happened that I have
as yet been the only individual in this immediate neighbourhood
who has had cause for rather serious apprehension, the cause of
which is now happily removed, a threshing-machine in a barn
almost touching my premises, which the owners would not give
up and which the mob would have : and so for three or four days

I have been receiving warnings (quite full of good will to me) from various quarters, to get rid of my neighbours, or it would be made into a bonfire with the premises it stood in, and mine could not escape, and I believe verily the attack was delayed for my sake. But at last the notice was imperative, and the obstinate farmer gave up his machine, and it has been torn to pieces this morning—to my infinite joy; for I shall now go to sleep a little more peacefully than I have done for some nights, though my house has been watched by the night patrols. A charming state of things this for such a one as me!

It may be sport to you to think of that same book that is to be "God's Revenge against Liberalism and Whiggery," but who will be left to read it? Is it not wonderful that a stronger arm than the civil one (Heaven strengthen it) is not put out to our aid when it is so urgently needed? You must bear with this country gossip if you please as it may seem to you at a distance, for I scorn to talk of fear here; and as there is a good deal pent up in my heart, talking of it to you acts as a sort of safety-valve. One very odd thing I must tell you:—all the dogs are turned radicals, and ought to be reported to Government, Mufti not excepted. Every night and all night long now, every road and lane is perambulated by night watchers; they come into our premises, close to doors and windows, &c., &c., and not a dog, the most restless, vigilant, and noisy, ever lifts up his voice at the disturbance in the faintest yelp or bark. I remarked it with astonishment in my own dog, and on mentioning the circumstance several gentlemen, captains of the night patrols, told me the silence was general, and greatly puzzled and surprised them. God bless you, dear friend. Shall I see you here? What may not happen to prevent it! But I will hope the best. My kind love to Bertha. Did she enjoy her visit to the Archbishop's more when it took place than in anticipation?

CAROLINE A. BOWLES.

CXXIII.

TO CAROLINE BOWLES.

London, *December* 1*st*, 1830.

You have a good heart, dear Caroline, in every sense of the expression. I wish I could disengage myself from this odious town, put myself into the stage, and be with you without delay. Come, however, I will, as soon as possible, which may probably be about the 20th. You are safe now that the threshing-machine is no longer your neighbour; and very soon we shall all be the safer for these outrages, out of which good will come, and is indeed already coming. Men will feel the use of a strong Government, and that the way to possess their property (be it little or much) in peace is not by abusing that Government and attacking the institutions of their country. The Whigs are well frightened, and something will be done for bettering the condition of the labourers, and providing outlets for their increasing numbers.

I am going to the levee this morning. You would smile were you to see me as I shall be two hours hence, in my brother's court dress, which hangs about me like a "capital fit" from Monmouth-street, with a bag at my head and a sword at my side. Inglis takes me there; and time and case-hardening have at length so changed me, that I, who was once one of the most shame-faced of all God's creatures, feel myself sufficiently at ease anywhere, and shall go to St. James's as I would to a raree-show.

You are a very useful person to me, for when I want to make a lady a present of some books, I always order some of yours. I shall not be so fine myself in bag and sword as a set of them is here in green morocco. I am interrupted, so

God bless you, dear friend,

Robert Southey.

CXXIV.

TO ROBERT SOUTHEY.

BUCKLAND, *January* 18th, 1831.

I caught a franker flying this morning, and you have told me you "loved my letters," besides giving me your address at Bristol till Saturday. Three indifferent reasons thus put together must make one good one why I should waylay you once more before you reach the end of your pilgrimage.* Then I shall fall again into more discreet habits; but as yet, so easily do we accustom ourselves to what we like, I am not reconciled to see the place opposite to me vacant, and to feel only that you have been here. Writing to you steals me from myself a little while, and so makes you the means of keeping me out of ill company, which you ought to rejoice at out of pure philanthropy.

Yesterday the shroud of vapour which has enveloped us ever since your departure was drawn aside for a few hours, and I ventured out on Minikin, but quarrelled with him as well as with my own company; made him go at a rate he never went before, I believe; and, four miles from home, as I was returning over a *poachy* common, fell in with two cavaliers, Mr. West and Major Roberts, who were so condescending as to form my escort home, to the inexpressible pride of Minikin, who capered along between their great tall horses in a way that would have made you laugh; but I could willingly have dispensed with my guard of honour—for, first, it was a great trouble to talk to them, mounted on such eminences above me; next, I was in no humour for talking to anybody—within reach; and thirdly, the chargers on either side bespattered me with mud from head to foot; and so I rode home, moralising on the axiom, that for small people there is more to be risked than gained in approximation with great ones.

One of my esquires, the M.P., Mr. West, told me he did not doubt there would be a dissolution of Parliament, and the same

* Southey was on his way back to Keswick, after a visit to Buckland.

opinion has been expressed to me from various other quarters. In a letter I received yesterday from Miss Rose, she mentions a rumour which has got abroad in some quarters, that Talleyrand's money has furnished no small proportion of that mysterious fund which so surely exists for the worst purposes. Knowing him to be, as he is, the worthy son of the "father of all lies" and all mischief, I should give more credit to this, were it not matter of notoriety that the ex-Bishop's idol is gold; that he has no abstract political principle, even in favour of anarchy, and would not risk a rouleau to revolutionise England, without being sure of doubling it by the speculation; the very reverse of which must result from our national ruin if, as I believe, he has large sums in our funds. But I wish he was out of the country; no good influences can emanate from such a traitor.

I send the little poem I mentioned to you on wild-flowers, which was written about two years ago; and another, to show you that what little power I had then is gone from me. I told you that the anecdote of little Leonard's death struck me so forcibly that I had scarce heard before I tried to versify it. The impulsive feeling was almost as strong as any I remember, and strong feeling has always been my only inspiration; therefore I ought to have composed these verses as well as it would ever have been in my power to have done, and they are miserable, weak common-places, that frighten me (do not laugh), for failure of mind I cannot think of without shuddering—mistrustful coward that I am! If we could but love and trust God as we can love and trust our fellow-creatures, what peace, "passing understanding," would be ours even in this world! Such peace is yours, I believe; so be it with you to the end, and God grant it to me before the end comes. I have fallen into too serious a mood to change for lighter matters, and besides, you have had enough of my solitary meditations for one chapter. So good night, dear friend; God bless you, and bring you safe to the haven where you would be—your own happy home.

Caroline A. Bowles.

To-day you will be in your own native city. I hope it is not wrapt in the sea of dense vapour that still enshrouds us, but that the whole beautiful picture may be as clear as you approach it as it can appear through that "watery film" that came over your eyes at Burton, and will hardly fail to cloud them when you look on Bristol for the first time after a lapse of years—so large a portion of mortal life—such a speck in the account of immortality.

CXXV.

TO CAROLINE BOWLES.

KESWICK, *January 27th*, 1831.

Here then I am, dear Caroline, at my own desk, and by my own fireside, in the cheerfulest room certes that ever author had for his workshop. I arrived on Tuesday, and, except a few lines to Rickman, inclosing a letter from Kate to Bertha by yesterday's post, this is my first epistle from home. Yesterday was passed in putting some of my things to rights, and stowing away the books which had arrived during my absence; a lengthy and somewhat too-early-timed visit from Chauncy Townshend cut out a great slice from the morning, and left me too short an allowance for a walk, and no time whatever for writing.

My journey, saving that I lost my beautiful pencil, by lending it to a person with whom I breakfasted at Dorchester, the day after leaving you, was prosperous throughout. Tuesday, Wednesday, and Thursday were as busily and perhaps more excitedly employed in Bristol than any of the days in London. I went into my father's house, and was told there that strangers had more than once gone into the shop to inquire if it was my birthplace. I walked to Bedminster and got admittance into my grandmother's; everything has been changed there; only some trees, principally fruit trees of my grandfather's and uncle's planting, are remaining.

Friday, in the mail to Birmingham; a wet, warm night. Saturday, still in the rain, to Shrewsbury; Mr. Warter met me there; he is a country gentleman fond of fishing and shooting, more fond of natural history, and an active magistrate; his wife a very mild and pleasing person; both altogether such persons as it is fortunate to be so connected with as I am likely to be. At eight on Tuesday morning I was on the Keswick stage; and here I am, thankful for having safely performed a circuit of a thousand miles, and especially for finding all well after thirteen weeks' absence.

But oh! the loads of letters there are now to be answered! To this task I must now betake myself, and work at it tooth and nail.

Will you tell me the name of Levett's house, and learn for me, if you can, the reason why the salt trade has declined at Lymington. To-morrow I hope to begin my Introduction.* Very hard I must work, but not so closely and unremittingly as at Buckland. I could not have done what I did there if I had been alone; but it was a refreshment to talk with you, and an encouragement to show you piece by piece as it was in progress.

Cuthbert thanks you for the asbestos and the fern, of which he is very proud. And my Governess thanks you for taking such good care of me, and Edith and Kate desire to be most kindly remembered.

You are a most unreasonable person if you are not satisfied with 'Little Leonard's Good-night.' It is what no one but yourself could have written. I should like you to relate some incidents which suit the manner in your own sweet blank-verse, in simple narrative rather than in a lyrical, which is a more ornamented kind; it would be worth while to try this (which is the most beautiful incident I ever heard) in such a form. The Swedish Miner's Body is another story of which the most close and faithful picture would be the most impressive. But I must break off.

Dear friend, God bless you.

ROBERT SOUTHEY.

* To the New Colloquies.

CXXVI.

TO CAROLINE BOWLES.

Keswick, *March 8th*, 1831.

I have been reading for the first time Lord Chesterfield's *Letters*, with more disgust than pleasure, and more pity than disgust. Such letters must have defeated their own main purpose, and made the poor youth awkward, by impressing him with a continual dread of appearing so. But it is painful to see what the father himself was—not, as it appears, from any want of good qualities, but because there was one *grace* a thought of which never entered his mind. I have been reading also a book of very different character—"Sermons upon the Application of Scriptural Principles to Real Life," by Miller, who sent them to me last week. They are of the very best kind—plain, practical, full of divine philosophy, and in the most Christian spirit. It is for the sake of such principles and such men that this Church and this nation are to be saved, if saved they may be.

To-day's paper tells me that Wynn has resigned his office, to my great joy, though he has gone much too far with the vile party who are now in power. I can tell you that the ministers altered their plan of reform, so as to make it very much more radical than they had designed, only two or three days before they brought it forward. And it is believed that they did this because, foreseeing, from the fate of their budget, that they could not long continue in office, they chose to go out in a blaze—rather in a stink. A villainous motion, but perfectly worthy of that party and that cause; they wish to leave affairs in the worst possible state for those who are to succeed them, and to prepare for themselves active allies among the Radicals. It would not much surprise me if the Grants were to do as Wynn has done; for their own sake I might wish it. But a Conservative ministry will be better without them.

March 11th.—And without them it will be, for Robert Grant has spoken, and chosen the evil part.

If you write to your Marquis, will you ask him in what repute the St.-Simonists are, and whether their system has any perceptible effect upon their manners, or whether they are as profligate as the rest of the world in which they live? I am reading the Exposition of their doctrine, which is written with very great ability. As yet I have not been able to get any satisfactory history of St.-Simon himself. Now the life of the founder enters materially into the view of a new religion. What he was I have no means of judging, but his disciples seem to be deliberately endeavouring to establish a new social order upon the basis of a pretended revelation, so reasonable in all its parts as to preclude any pretence of delusion or enthusiasm in them.

These men seem to me, having no religion themselves, to perceive that some religion is necessary for society; to suppose that Christianity is worn out because the French have very generally thrown it off in the only form in which it was known to them; to be aware that Theophilanthropism, which was tried under the Directory, failed for want of a foundation; and to be trying certainly the boldest experiment that has been attempted since the time of Mahomet, or of Manes. Whereas, if they knew what the Gospel is, they might see that by it, and only by it, the good at which they aim is to be effected.

God bless you, dear friend. And observe, let not your next letter be wickedly short.

ROBERT SOUTHEY.

CXXVII.

TO CAROLINE BOWLES.

KESWICK, *March* 26*th*, 1831.

The next *Quarterly Review* will contain a history of Babœuf's conspiracy, on which I am now at work, and the St.-Simonists will come in the number after. No two subjects could be better timed; for you must know that this new sect is aiming, by means of their new revelation, to bring about what Babœuf was for getting by spoliation and massacre.

I do not know who wrote the paper on Reform. I am much obliged to Mr. Fripp for his expressions of civility. As for private attentions, I should only have had too many of them had my stay in Bristol been longer, or my being there more generally known. But for public marks of respect there was but one which could have been shown to me; and though it would have annoyed me very much at the time, this Reform Bill, oddly enough, makes me wish that it had been offered— you will guess that I mean the freedom of the city. If they had presented me with this the Reform Bill would have taken it away, and upon that ground I would have sent up a petition solitary against the Bill in divesting me of what had been thus conferred.

April 7th.—An American lady is lodging in Keswick, who introduced herself to me five or six years ago by two little volumes of poetry and by a most wild letter—certainly the strangest letter I ever received. She has now accompanied her brother to Europe, and while he is travelling about on his mercantile business, she thought Keswick would be a good place in which to await, and accordingly here she came, with a longish poem which she wants to publish, but for which she can find no publisher. Her name is Mrs. Brooks.* She was betrothed to an old man at the age of fourteen, and married him at sixteen! And now, when she does not appear to be more than two or three and thirty, she has one son in business in the Isle of Cuba, and another at a military academy in the United States. She is a very mild and pleasing woman, to our utter astonishment at finding her so, as it would be to yours had you seen her letter.

Her poem is very fanciful, and, on the whole, beautifully written. The subject is like the story of Tobias—the love of a fallen angel for a Jewish girl. I believe she means to leave it in my hands, in the hope of its getting into the press at some

---

* " Maria del Occidente," author of *Zophiel*.

time or other. But by what I have seen of it, it would in some places require cooling, and if it should be necessary for me to let her know this, you may suppose that I shall be in a state which novelists might call delicate embarrassment; yet you could not help liking her were you to see her—not for beauty, nor for any other attractiveness than what proceeds from a meek, gentle, unassuming, unaffected, kind nature, and from perfect simplicity of manners. But, in truth, the longer I live the less am I disposed to trust to appearances, whether in man, woman, or child, or to speak more truly (for the disposition is not easily got rid of), the more reason I find for not forming a hasty judgment of them. One of the most calm and rational and sober-mannered men whom I ever met with was under that exterior a most dangerous madman, and this was never suspected till it was brought to light by his papers after he had committed suicide. I think you have seen his two anonymous letters to me, asking me to take charge of those papers.

After all, I like those people best who seem to be what they are, and are what they seem; indeed, they are the only people whom I can love.

April 17*th*.—You may be easy about the Reform Bill—the delusion is falling as rapidly as it was raised. Its manifold absurdities, its Whiggish roguery, its abominable injustice, its contempt of all constitutional principles, are producing their proper effect. All my letters agree in this. Even those who a fortnight ago looked for nothing better than the fall in the breach are now ready to toss their caps in the air for joy. Out the Whigs will be driven, and with more ignominy than ever, for their rashness, their folly, and what I cannot but call their wickedness. They kindled a fire which might have set the kingdom in flames, but will now suffocate them with its smoke.

Here is a song which I made at my usual time of inspiration, while shaving, tempted by the hero's name even more than by its merits. I sent it in a blank cover, and in Edith's writing, to *John Bull*, but the newspapers are afraid of this man, and so it has not appeared.

Must the Gorman Great O
Out of Parliament go?
Bad luck to that ugly committee!
If out he should call,
And then shoot them all,
There's no one would say, "What a pity!"

My patriot, my Paddy,
My mighty big Raddy,
Och! why did you, why did you bribe?
In the county of Clare,
The grief that is there
I cannot, I cannot, describe.

Och! my honey, my honey,
It was not for money
That the lads of the Roman communion
To Parliament sent you,
But with the intent you
Should get a repeal of the Union.

All Clare gave its voice
To that beautiful choice
That the sons of the Saxons and Normans
For once might see there
What true Irishmen were;
So we sent them the greatest of Gormans.

He soon let them know,
Did the Gorman Great O,
That he was not a man to be mister'd,
And who gave him offence,
Upon any pretence,
That man's tongue might have better been blister'd.

Och, the figure he made,
And the shirt he display'd!
His meaning was clear as a crystal;
One speech (bless him for't!)
In the very report,
Sounded just like a duelling pistol.

You may call him, I say, Gog,
Or, if you like, Magog—
D'ye hear me, Sir James?—if you dare it;
But demagogue, no!
For the Gorman Great O
Has sworn by the powers he won't bear it.

>   Sir James and young Stanley,
>   You'll be playing the manly
>   When he stands no longer before ye!
>   For you know that our Dan
>   Must not fight, but *he* can,
>   So we'll soon send him back in his glory.
>
>   But this I'll allow,
>   You may spare him just now
>   For awhile, to his own quiet nation,
>   For by what I hear say
>   You are in a fair way,
>   Without him for enough agitation.

You ask me about Sotheby's "Homer." I have not seen it, nor do I wish to see it. It may be very good in its way, but that way is radically bad, and no one who has any real feeling of Homer can possibly read without disgust a translation of Iliad and Odyssey in couplets, especially in modern couplets.

Cowper's translation is, of all the English ones, that which least disfigures the original. Old Chapman's I should reckon next to it. Hobbes's is marvellously bare and bald; Macpherson's impudently Ossianized. Sotheby's I daresay will be less glaringly unlike than Pope's, for Pope's Homer has done more than any, or all other books, towards the corruption of our poetry.

Dear friend, God bless you.

ROBERT SOUTHEY.

CXXVIII.

TO CAROLINE BOWLES.

KESWICK, May 2nd, 1831.

We shall weather this storm, though it is the fiercest that has ever yet assailed the country. But by God's providence the devices of the weak and the wicked are counteracted in a great degree by the growing prosperity of our manufactures, which extends of course to the agriculturists, and will continue till the Continent recovers from its revolutions. Fear not, I am in good heart. Wordsworth, who was here yesterday, said it was a comfort to see my cheerful face. God has not abandoned us, and will not while there are those who trust in him, and act in that path strenuously. There are many such. I am assured that the tide has turned among the youth at both Universities; they were taking the wrong course two or three years ago; they are now taking the right one. Many indeed of the rising generation have received their bias in some degree from Wordsworth's writings and from mine.

When I visit you next you shall have a large portion of my time, and I will not bring a task with me which shall keep me tongue- and table-tied like the last. But I will give myself a good resolute spell at poetry there. This may be sooner than I like to think of at present.

Here is a circumstance which would do well for poetry in your hands. At Roeskilde, the oldest cathedral in Denmark, Warter observed a fresh garland on a grave, and inquiring for whom it was placed, was told that every Sunday morning a daughter had placed one there on her mother's grave, for thirty years; verily, as Warter added when he wrote home the anecdote, "love is stronger than death."

Now have I three things more to say; first, that if your Merlin had but a white neck his portrait would just do for our Knurry-murry-purry-hurry-skurry, of whom a mouse might truly say—
"It is a green-eyed monster that doth mock
The food it feeds on";

but who is, nevertheless, the gentlest and most ladylike of cats.

Secondly, which you will be interested in hearing, if you do not know it already, that your friends the Howitts have taken Mrs. Wordsworth into their house in a most helpless state, when she was completely laid up with an attack of sciatica at an inn. They had no personal acquaintance with the Wordsworths before, and there she is now, and her daughter with her.

Thirdly, which of all things in this letter most concerns me, there is a certain portrait at Buckland, and a promise concerning it which I pray you not to forget.

Mrs. Brooks* sailed from Liverpool ten days ago. The history of her mind I can very well understand. She was married when almost a child to an elderly, if not an old man, who had no mental accomplishments in any degree to make amends for the disparity of years. She was passionately fond of poetry, and had a heart full of it; he thought of nothing but his affairs. And I dare say she has always been dreaming what a happy creature she might have been if she had been united to one who would have loved her as she could have loved him, and would have sympathized with her in her intellectual enjoyments. I am not without some suspicion that there may be a little flightiness about her; her eyes had an expression which looked that way, and I think the letter of which you heard would not have been written had she been mistress of herself at that time. The more we saw her, the better we liked her, and her brother seemed to be a thoroughly good sort of man, a Quebec merchant well informed for his station, and right-minded upon all subjects. You *would* have liked her, and could not have helped liking her.

Dear friend, God bless you.

ROBERT SOUTHEY.

CXXIX.

TO ROBERT SOUTHEY.

BUCKLAND, *July 8th*, 1831.

You are at home long before this I hope, dear friend, because it is "the haven where you would be"—and, though out of my turn, I am fain to write to you, because I am heavy-hearted, for

* " Maria del Occidente."

which writing to you is always my second best medicine; and now in particular, as I am sad at thought of parting with dear friends (the Levitts) whose final departure from Hampshire draws very near, I turn impulsively to one whose correspondence only I would not exchange for personal intercourse with any other human being, and who has led me by his hopeful spirit to look forward with more confidence and comfort than my weaker mind might have dared encourage to the renewal and perfecting in a better life of friendships contracted here in holiness of heart, and so faithfully enduring to the end. How should I bless you, if it were only for strengthening me in this blessed hope! I cling to it, as a shipwrecked creature to the life-boat.

I have been furnished with another pretence for writing to you by a request which has been addressed to me to be passed to you, but one so absurd, in my opinion, that I have made no promise of gravely preferring it, or any hope of a favourable hearing. It is the petition of the Miss Roses (Sir George's daughters) that I would contribute to a miscellaneous volume about to be compiled and published for the benefit of the starving Irish, and that I would use all my influence and interest with Mr. Southey to prevail on him to do the same. So I have said all I engaged to say, which is the utmost stretch of my complaisance, for I cannot afford a line of rhyme or prose to this very well intended but very ridiculous joint-stock affair—a book now to be got together, printed and published, for so urgent and immediate a purpose as that assigned! You are much better natured than I am—will you give something?

I think your friend the venerable Dr. Bell is no better than an impostor, drags you out of your den, at great inconvenience to yourself, to confer with him (I thought on his death-bed) about testamentary dispositions, &c., &c., and then, what do I hear, but that the dying man starts off with a Cheltenham party (a picnic I suppose), to show you to the Cheltenhamites, and to you ostensibly the source of the Thames? And at the Doctor's you fell in with my lively and clever acquaintance, Miss Alicia Allen, whose father's house is the great lion trap of Cheltenham—and there were such designs against you! You would have been obliged had they caught you to shake your mane and your tail far more meekly for the benefit of the company than you did here, on the only occasion I ever proved treacherous, and let in the Philistines upon you. Miss Alicia Allen says you frightened her about the state of the country. Now, you being the only person from whom I have heard a cheerful word on the subject for the last six months, if you begin to despair, I shall look for the worst.

The Levitts desire to be very kindly remembered to you; they have let their delightful house for five years, not having succeeded in finding a purchaser, and depart from it the last week in this month; I wish they were gone, just as one would wish hanging over. I will not suffer myself to be betrayed into any more intimacies. It is only storing up pain and disappointment. I used to comfort myself with the belief, that as I declined in years, I should become (as is fitting) less morbidly sensitive to those trials of the affections that break young hearts, but I find to my sorrow it is quite the contrary with me—that a young heart broken is not irreparable, but that an old one early bruised and ill repaired, and nobody's care but the owner's, is easily set aching by an ungentle touch, and shrinks to the very core at a rude one. Such is not healthy feeling, only pitiable, but God cares for and pities all His creatures, the wisest and the weakest.

God bless you, dear friend.

CAROLINE A. BOWLES.

CXXX.

TO CAROLINE BOWLES.

KESWICK, *July* 11*th*, 1831.

My visit to Cheltenham was as useless as I had anticipated, and as melancholy in all respects as it could be; but I was not exhibited there, and you may be sure that I did not exhibit myself. I went, by my own desire, to see the Springs, and two of the Allen family went with us; your friend was not one, but she called on the following day with her father, and they both seemed likeable persons. As to alarming them: I thought it quite fitting, in political cases (whatever it may be in medical ones), that people should be made to understand the nature and extent of their danger: and so far, it may be very likely that I alarmed some of the few persons with whom I had any conversation at Cheltenham; but, to them, as to you, I spoke with a confidence that Providence will bring us through these dangers, if we do not basely betray ourselves.

It was impossible for me to accept the trusteeship. Poor Doctor Bell's first concern is how to dispose of all his money in promoting his own system of education; and his second, that as much of it may go to Scotland for this purpose as can be disposed of there. After giving away £120,000, Three per cents. in trust, he had yet to direct the disposal of it; and on my arrival I found that he had resolved upon dividing it into twelve shares, six of which were appropriated to St. Andrew's, and four more for schools at Edinburgh, Glasgow, Aberdeen, and Inverness, which four may be considered as so much money thrown away. I was consulted about the other two: after observing that as this money had been derived wholly from the Church of England, some portion of it ought to return thither, I proposed that one twelfth should go to the augmentation of poor livings, and the other (which I knew was the only means of obtaining any favour for such advice) to founding one of his own schools in every parish so augmented. By vesting this sum in the hands of trustees, it might have been so managed that every £200 would have called forth as much more from Queen Anne's Bounty, so that forty poor livings might have been benefited to the extent of £400 each, that is, from £12 to £20 a-year, according as the money could be with more or less advantage invested. Well, he was delighted with this; and came into it with so much earnestness that I was quite affected at the thought of having been almost the accidental means of bringing about so much good. But the next day he changed his mind—schools, schools must have all. The newspaper brought an account that there was to be a new Royal Naval Asylum; he puts this paper into my hand at our first meeting in the morning, and writes on his slate "this is a God-send." Accordingly one twelfth went there, and there remains one more, and the eventual residue of his property, which, I suppose, is still considerable, to be disposed of. I mentioned the Clergy Orphans' Fund, the Society for propagating the Gospel, Bishop Middleton's College at Calcutta, or a like institution to be commenced at Madras; but all must be confined to schools, and the schools, if possible, to Scotland.

I mentioned his relations. He gives his only sister £400 a-year for her life, and nothing but the most trifling legacies to any other of his blood. They were not near to him, he said (on his slate, observe, for he has totally lost his speech), they had no claim on him. No claim, I admitted, but a reasonable hope, a reasonable expectation, where there were none nearer, where there was so much to bestow, and where the law would give it if he died intestate. He wrote "My discovery is my child." "Yes, sir," I replied, "it is your child, and you have taken very good care of it; but it is not all your kith and kin." This availed nothing, and when I expressed a wish that something more than £100 should be left to the person who had been most useful to him in his own way—Mr. Johnson, the master of the Central School—a shake of the head was the reply; all, all was to be devoted to his discovery; he would be (on the slate) " consistent and consecutive to the last." A stranger or more melancholy example of some ruling passion, good in itself, becoming evil in its excess, and stifling all other good and generous feelings, can hardly be imagined. The sister, I have no doubt, will endeavour to set the will aside. I endeavoured to turn this to some use, and advised him, instead of leaving her an annuity, to make her residuary legatee, and give her something of which she might dispose to her relations after her death; she would then be satisfied, and thus litigation would be prevented. But to this he would not listen; very, indeed, very indignant at her attempting to set up a plea of insanity against him. I represented to him that groundless as this is (and indeed nothing can be more so) and perfectly untenable, yet something must be allowed to her surprise and disappointment. He had made what all persons must consider a most extraordinary disposal of his property; many would think it unwise, and it was easy for those whose expectations were cut off by it to fancy that *insane* which they believed to be unreasonable. All that I said was taken in good part, and all to no purpose. But I suppose that my journey will not be altogether as unproductive of evil as it has been of good; it will, in all likelihood, take me before some Ecclesiastical Court to be examined as a witness when the will is disputed. Nor will it surprise me if the bequest intended for me, as joint editor of his works, should be expunged in the last edition of his will. Be that as it may, I shall always retain a lively and affectionate remembrance of him, such as he was when I knew him first, and for many years afterwards—a lover of children, if ever man was, from pure benevolence and kind feeling towards them ; and set beyond all men in the pursuit of one great object, and devoting his whole thoughts, his whole life, his whole fortune, to it.

Poor Bowles! I have seen only the first volume of his Life of Bishop Ken, and sorry I was that I could not review it without mortifying him, however carefully I might have abstained from noticing the faults of the book. But to have written Ken's life as it ought to be written would, in its effect, have been the most unkind thing I could have done, if done in the form of a review. This withholds me from a very tempting subject, the more tempting because I claim kin with Bishop Ken.

You ask about the Howitts. The Wordsworths left them full of gratitude for their kindness, and full of liking for Mary. But her husband, whom they might otherwise have liked much, though never quite so well, had the Reform fever upon him so strongly as to put the cloven foot of Quakerism offensively forward; not when Mr. Wordsworth was there, for all these people would as soon take a bull by the horns as to show theirs either to Mr. Wordsworth or to me, but to poor Dora, who left the room one day when he had been exulting on the near downfall of the Church, and asserting that any person who was a clergyman of the Establishment must be either a fool or a hypocrite: this to her, when her brother and uncle are clergymen! He apologised to her afterwards, and did not repeat the offence, having been well reproved for it by his wife; but the circumstance shows what these sectarians are when the latent spirit is brought out.

I have been working hard since my return, both at the *Colloquies* and at the *Peninsular War*, making hay while the sun shines—in other words, making good use of the interval between reviewing times. At this season I have seldom less than two hours' walk (including a delicious bath in the Greta) every day; for if I were disposed to stay within, Cuthbert comes up with an asking countenance, and I do not like to disappoint him. Bertha is come home with a sad debility about her; her ankles swell and disable her for the exercise which she requires. If they had not the happy spirits of youth, these daughters of mine would all be miserable invalids: and of course I cannot but think of the time when that season will be over, and they may, too probably, have less cheerful circumstances about them. Their mother is better than she has been for many years, and for that I am most truly thankful.

There is a story of a Spaniard who was fond of cherries, and whenever he ate them put on spectacles to make them look larger and finer. I do this with all my enjoyments of every kind: make little pleasures into great ones, and put on diminishing glasses when I look at inconveniences. Our dangers are to be looked at in their own just magnitude; there is no trifling with them; but this way of mine adds largely to the comforts, and diminishes in the same degree the annoyances of life. This my children seem to have inherited or learned; and with this true worldly wisdom, and that better wisdom which, prepared as they are, time will surely bring with it, of looking to the next state of existence with a constant and cheerful hope, they will so far be well fitted for whatever may befall them when I am gone. Anastasius Hope has left a posthumous book with his notion of heaven in it—the most preposterous heaven that ever was conceived. We are all, all of us, men, women, and children, good and bad, of all sorts, tempers, characters, and complexions, *all* to make up one great human being, this being the ultimate perfection of the human race! Why I would rather drink ale in Valhalla out of the skull of the Lord Advocate Jeffrey (he being mine enemy), or out of Thomas Babington Macaulay's, if his be the larger cranium and the ale be good. No, Caroline, you and I will not be mixed up with Anastasius Hope, and Solomon and all his wives and concubines, and the whole courts of Louis XIV. and Charles II., and all the monks and nuns that ever lived, and all the radicals, and all the Turks, Jews, Infidels—nay, not even with all deans and chapters (if there were nobody else), and all dissenting ministers, and all bazaar ladies. No, no, no; it would be no heaven for you and I to be mixed up in such a compound, and made bone of their bone, and flesh of their flesh. We shall keep our identities there, and all our good feelings, and all our recollections, that either are or can be made instrumental to our happiness, and we shall lose nothing but what it will be ease to part with— sorrows, and frailties, and infirmities. We shall not lose our own very selves, nor each other!

God bless you, dear friend, and bring us both (He will bring us) into that blessed state in his own good time, and fit us for it more and more till that time comes.—*July* 12*th*.

ROBERT SOUTHEY.

CXXXI.

TO CAROLINE BOWLES.

KESWICK, *November* 4*th*, 1831.

Your fit, dear friend, can have been nothing more than what they tell you it was. The strong are far more in danger of paralysis than the weak, and if his most senseless Majesty,

King William IV., should receive what, so far as he and his Ministers are concerned, would be the proper reward of his folly and their wickedness, you may live to see a Restoration.

Your former letter did not reach me till I was leaving Shrewsbury for Manchester, on Monday, the 10th, last. I had been four days at Cruck Meole, and left Edith there as happy as I could wish her. Mrs. Warter is a very amiable woman, and loving her eldest son dearly, was perfectly prepared to love her intended daughter; and as both have no greater pleasure than in talking of that son, they are the best possible company for each other. Mr. Warter was as kind to her as man could be. Dr. Butler told me that, of the many young men who had been under his care, there was not one of whom he had a higher opinion in all respects than John Warter. Perhaps you may not know that no school has for many years been in higher repute than his. At home he is just as much beloved for his disposition and his moral qualities, so that so far all is as well as could be wished. The family is also precisely in that station into which I could have chosen to place her, had the choice been in my power; for, thank God, I never desired riches either for myself or my children. Yet you may well suppose that this visit was not likely to exhilarate me while it lasted, and I did not leave Edith there without feeling that she seemed already to belong more to that family than to me.

I could not open my letters till I was seated in the stage for Manchester, luckily without a companion. With yours there came one proposing to me to become candidate for a Professorship at Glasgow, with all but a certainty of success. At the same time I had the news of the decision in the House of Lords—enough to think upon while I was travelling alone.

James White met me when the stage arrived. Tuesday I stayed with him, about a mile from the town, and went that day to see the railway and the Collegiate Church, which is a very fine one. Wednesday was the day of the meeting; and James White being frightened by his clerk with the apprehension of a riot, and taking it into his head that I might be as popular in

Manchester as Sir Charles Wetherall at Bristol, would not let me dine, as we were engaged to do, in the town, and set off from thence at six o'clock in the stage, but carried me off with his brother Charles, who was likewise bound for Keswick, by a circuit round the town to Bolton, where the stage took us up. This I call my *Hegirah* from Manchester; but, in truth, I had no apprehensions myself, and there would have been no danger.

I will make your verses for your poor musician when I can ; but verily I could plan such a poem as Thalaba more readily than those stanzas for music.

It is likely that the first volume of the new *Colloquies* may be published first, and at Christmas. This is desired, that the question of Reform may be brought forward there in time, some great change being now unavoidable. My aim is to make it as little dangerous as we can, aud I see no way by which this can be effected but by giving a vote to all who pay direct taxes, as householders, and rendering that concession safe by allowing them only to elect the ultimate electors from persons of a certain qualification.

God bless you, dear Caroline.

ROBERT SOUTHEY.

CXXXII.

TO ROBERT SOUTHEY.

BUCKLAND, *December* 2nd, 1831.

An officer with whom I conversed yesterday told me he had just read the copy of a military statement by which it appears that there is good reason for supposing the Bristol affair was but part of an extended plan of simultaneous rising between Birmingham, Manchester, and other cities, together with the Merthyr Tydvil people; that communication has been ascertained to have been carried on by means of carrier pigeons, and that the quick march of troops upon Bristol, and some towards Merthyr Tydvil, alone stopped the advance of an immense body of the latter people to join the coalition. These last were so determined, that they removed all the boats and vessels, to prevent the crossing of the king's troops, and endeavoured to disable a steamer, in which the military did eventually pass. If this statement is true, there has been a *coup manqué.* The Merthyr Tydvil men would be fearful auxiliaries.

I have read Moore's *Life of Lord Edward Fitzgerald,* with how much pleasure and disapprobation you must understand, even before I read your review of it, which did but coincide with all my feelings. Was ever such a lovable creature—such a beautiful character in private life? But from the first what the French call a *tête exaltée*—morbid craving for excitement. His marriage with Pamela certainly sealed his ruin; for, however tenderly all that concerns her is glossed over by the Leinster family and the biographer, all the Leinsters were obliged to give her up at last, so discreditable was her conduct; and the woman whose common coiffure after the murder of Louis XVI. and his family was a crimson handkerchief, then the reigning Paris mode, *censé* to have been dipped in the martyr's blood, was not likely to have acted the part of a restraining angel to her unfortunate, misguided husband. I was charmed with the tenderness with which you spoke of Lord Edward whenever you conscientiously could.

God bless you, dear friend.
CAROLINE A. BOWLES.

CXXXIII.

TO CAROLINE BOWLES.

KESWICK, *December* 11*th*, 1831.

My brother tells me, what I felt assured of before, that no house could be better situated than this in case of pestilence.

No doubt the cholera will make its way over the island, and nothing can be done but to await it, and trust in God's mercy for our own protection. We might consider ourselves in as little danger here as in any place, if it were possible to exclude vagrants from the town, the common carriers of all infectious diseases. I am one of the Board of Health, and at my suggestion all that we can do is doing to prevent these miserable pests of society from being harboured here, as they have hitherto been. Government recommends three precautionary measures, all of which are impossible—to keep the poor clean, to feed them well, and to lodge them in spacious and airy habitations! The sordid squalid wretchedness and the brutal depravity in which we have suffered the populace to remain, without the slightest attempt to correct either, threatens now to bring upon the nation their proper consequences. Yet my ever hopeful temper rests in the hope that Providence will manifest the whole danger to us as a warning, and then avert it.

I once sat in the next box to Pamela, in the Bath Theatre, and next to her, on the second row of the one box, while she was in the front seat of the other. There could not be a better situation for seeing her; and so beautiful she was that I think I can remember her face, though I have not the slightest recollection of Madame Genlis', who was much more an object of curiosity to me at that time. Pamela's history I heard at Christ Church; a clergyman, Jones by name, was the person who negotiated the business with her mother. The circumstances were well remembered at that place.

Lockhart struck out from that reviewal something of my own, and more of the extracts from Lord Edward's letters, which delighted me as much as they have done you, and he did not send me the concluding proofs, to which I meant to have added something. *He* added Lord Byron's sonnet, which is anything but *graceful*, and to which I should have objected on other accounts.

Has the useful pamphlet of Gibbon Wakefield fallen in your way? Nothing could be better timed than its exposure of the character, and disposition, and strength of the populace. I have no doubt that what you have heard respecting the intended insurrection in other cities, as well as in Bristol, is true, and it is no new design. Some ten years since, at the time of Hunt's progresses and what is called the Manchester massacre, the news of an insurrection there was to have been the sequel for a similar rising at Carlisle, and in expectation of it crowds were waiting for the arrival of the mail. This I was informed of at the time; and in this danger we shall always be till a radical reform be effected, and some order superinduced upon our most imperfect system of policy. The ministers themselves are heartily frightened. On the other hand, better men are recovering their spirits, whether it be that things really are more hopeful, or that they have become accustomed to the prospect of unavoidable evils, which, as long as they are not immediate, we contrive generally to consider as being uncertain. Both causes probably exist; but the letters which I receive are less gloomy than they were some little time ago.

I dare say the business at Lyons was directed by some of Buonarroti's disciples. We have just such a set of desperadoes at home, who cover themselves at present under the name of Owenites, but whose intentions are sufficiently disclosed in their journals. The St.-Simonites had their missionaries at Lyons, and they on such occasions are like the Quaker on board the merchant ship, who, expressing his horror at the intention which the master expressed of running down a small privateer, concluded his speech by saying: "If thou wilt do such a wicked thing, *starboard a little.*" Just so would these men direct a mischief which they had not directly conspired to bring about.

God bless you, dear friend.

ROBERT SOUTHEY.

CXXXIV.

TO CAROLINE BOWLES.

KESWICK, *January* 19*th*, 1832.

Thank you for your inclosures, which arrived this morning. The Whigs would smile at the one and tremble at the other. Irreligion cannot go farther than most of that party (and this I say advisedly) would very willingly go with it, but they are desperately afraid of radicalism, and indeed, at this time, very much in such a predicament with it as the young man who raised the Devil by reading in Cornelius Agrippa's book.

I do not know the book of Lord Clarendon concerning which you inquire, but there can be no difficulty in getting it from a London catalogue. Send to the library (if you have not read them) for D'Israeli's *Commentaries on the Life and Reign of Charles I.* Rogers said of him to me "There's a man with only half an intellect who writes books that must live." The origin of the book nobody knows but myself. I knew that Dr. Wordsworth, in consequence of his inquiries concerning the *Icon Basilike*, was collecting materials and preparing notes for an elaborate history of that reign; and knowing this, I invited some fit person (in the *Quarterly Review*) to undertake such a work, intending this as a call to him. D'Israeli supposed himself to be the person intended; told me so, and went to work. He has in consequence brought out a very entertaining and very useful book, which will not stand in the way of another, but rather assist in preparing the way for it.

Irving, beyond all doubt, is insane. Do you know that the St.-Simonists are sending a mission to England, and that the Minister of War in France has sent a circular to all the general officers directing them to warn the soldiers against listening to their doctrine, and requiring them to report such officers and men as may be made proselytes?

God bless you, dear friend.

ROBERT SOUTHEY.

CXXXV.

TO CAROLINE BOWLES.

KESWICK, *February* 21*st*, 1832.

I am indeed sorry for the death of your Minikin, whose like I shall not look upon again, and whose loss to you is not to be replaced. Poor fellow, he would probably have lived longer if he had more work and scantier food, for too much prosperity agrees neither with man nor beast.

Many pleasant hours have I passed in poor Dr. Bell's company; it was delightful to see him in company with children, for then he gave himself up wholly to enjoyment: never man, I verily believe, loved children more thoroughly. But when he was alone, or could get any person alone with him from whom he had no reserves, then his discovery possessed him like an evil spirit. Two thoughts may be said to have devoured all others in his mind—how to extend that system of instruction, and how to keep his own merits as the discoverer of it constantly before the public. He is now at rest from it. I did all that man could do to bring him into a healthier and happier state of mind as long as there was any hope of influencing him, and I believe that for many years there has been no person for whom he entertained a more sincere regard; for he could not but approve of the advice which he never followed.

The St.-Simonist missionaries in England have written to me, complaining that I have not done them justice, offering me their books for my further information, hoping I will visit them in London, and saying that if they come this way they will knock at my door. I have returned a courteous reply, letting them withal clearly understand that they would find in me a determined opponent if it were needful. But this it will not be, for they are not likely to make proselytes in England. I very much regret the loss of your friend M. de Custine's letter concerning them and their founder.

Rejoice with me that I am far advanced in the last chapter of the *War*. Next week, if I continue well, will assuredly bring me to the end of it; and then to other work.

The bill will be compromised in the House of Lords. Short-sighted men think it better to pass it with certain alterations than expose the Constitution to that certain overthrow which the creation of a regiment of peers would produce. They are grievously mistaken. Violence of that kind, if it were committed (and it is by no means certain that ministers would dare commit it), would at least leave the old peerage without dishonour; but when they lose honour, and give up the ground of principle to take their stand upon the shifting sands of expediency, they deserve the fate which shall overtake them. For myself, I do the best I can while I see the worst, and I keep a good heart and am cheerful.

God bless you, dear friend.

ROBERT SOUTHEY.

CXXXVI.

TO CAROLINE BOWLES.

KESWICK, *March* 19*th*, 1832.

Your long silence made me apprehend that you were ill, and I should long ago have written had I not been urgently employed upon the ever lengthening task of finishing the *Peninsular War*. You will not wonder that it is not yet finished when you hear that it has overrun my estimate by a full hundred pages, which is to me, as far as profit is concerned, pure loss of time; to the bookseller no gain; but the book will be much the better for it, and therefore I grumble not, but work on in good humour with myself and my employment. Very near the end, however, it is; in fact it only remains to relate the overthrow of the Constitution by Ferdinand, whom I have brought to Zaragosa on his way, and then to wind up.

The seeds will grow anywhere; there is not a hardier flower in this country; it grows and flourishes close under our kitchen window, where the flagstones leave just room for it between themselves and the wall. So abundantly does it flower, and so easily spread itself, that you may soon stock Hampshire with yellow poppies.

Charles Duveyrier, or —rice (for I know not which), and Gustave d'Eichthal are the two *Missionaires Saint-Simoniens en Angleterre*, who addressed a joint epistle to me. They have since sent me a small parcel of pamphlets to my brother's house, but no letter accompanied it: my answer had, no doubt, damped any hopes they might have entertained of converting me. I have not had a minute yet to look into their pamphlets, but I see by the *Times* that there are schisms among them, and that one party declares against marriage and all family ties.

You will see that I broke no rule in noticing Mrs. Bray's book, for there is no review of poetry. I have only told what surely is a touching story, and answered some of your objections to the encouragement of such persons.* You should be loath, you say, to have a servant so qualified; perhaps so; but, Caroline, if you had hired one not knowing that she was so qualified, and had afterwards discovered her qualifications, how should you have felt then? I will tell you: she would very soon have had a place in your esteem and in your affections; without ceasing to be your servant, she would have become your friend. I should be right glad to have a man-servant in whom I could find such a companion as you would have found in her. Nothing, I believe, gives a foreigner a more unfavourable notion of the English character than the relation in which servants stand to their employers so generally, and without any kindly feeling on either side.

But when you ask what chance there is for Mary Colling making a happy marriage in her own station, then indeed I candidly reply, that in that station it is better for anyone (in our disordered society) to be content with "single blessedness,"

---

* *i.e.* as Mary Colling, the poetical servant of Mrs. Bray.

and more especially for one of such quick and imaginative sensibilities as she evidently possesses; for though she has no power of expressing them in the language of verse, it is very evident that she possesses [them] in a· high, and perhaps a dangerous, degree. Perhaps her gentle blood shows itself in her, and perhaps it will keep her from any such marriage as you allude to. But the possibilily of another and worse danger has sometimes crossed my mind when speaking of her, lest some one with as much romance in his heart and head as there was in mine when I began life as a poet should fall in love with that sweet countenance of hers, and this should end in a marriage—not so unfitting indeed as that of her mysterious grandmother, but likely to be quite as disastrous in the consequences.

At present, however, no creature can be happier; and her master is almost as happy—a strange, eccentric, thoroughly good man, who, when the publication was determined upon, took upon him the whole cost of it, so that she receives not the profits but the whole produce. The Duke of Bedford sent £10 for his copy. Mary is now collecting all the traditions of the neighbourhood for Mrs. Bray, whom I have set upon writing all about Tavistock. A very entertaining book she is likely to make of it, and a good deal of it is likely to be Mary's work.

But I must break off, though I have much more to say.

Dear friend, God bless you.

ROBERT SOUTHEY.

CXXXVII.

TO ROBERT SOUTHEY.

BUCKLAND, *April* 12*th*, 1832.

When next you write to me, dear friend, do tell me what you know of one of your frankers, Mr. Hyde Villiers. I know he is son of the great government defaulter, nephew to Lord Clarendon, sprung from a race of courtiers, and himself a placeman; but it is rather puzzling to find a person so qualified brought down among us (a perfect stranger) by a little knot of fierce radicals, who have set the place in a flame, to canvass at this time for votes against the next election after the passing of the Reform Bill. I should have liked to hear his private and confidential account of the dinners with which he was treated by his reforming friends. His host, a half-pay captain, who turned patriot on losing all hopes of promotion in the army, from his mutinous conduct in India; this worthy's brother, our spiritual pastor (Heaven help us), who broke open the church in the morning to set the bells ringing, in spite of the church-wardens; two dissenting ministers, flaming orators; an infidel tallow-chandler; and a serious tailor, of which tailor more anon. But do tell me what you know of Mr. Hyde Villiers.

Before this reaches you the fate of this country will be in some sort decided by the decision in the Lords on the second reading of the bill. It is an awful crisis, and so Lord Grey must feel it, and he must shrink from exercising the power of creating peers, committed to him by the infatuated king. But the race he runs is neck or nothing, and he cannot draw back if he would. The rupture with Lord Durham must plunge him deeper in perplexity; and who is there to help us? Only the All-powerful and Wise; but in His hands is safety for those who trust.

Now for the tailor. Tailor Dixon "hight"—a long, lean, lank-limbed, lank-visaged, lank-haired anatomy, proprietor of a dissenting chapel, and preacher at the same (he whose name I made free with in a hoax on Mr. Levitt, of which I told you), a conchologist, a mineralogist, a reformer, and a lecturer at a Mechanics' Institute, and altogether a wonder of knowledge; but, as implied by his title, he condescends to make and mend male raiment, and waited on a friend of mine the other day in his professional capacity. My friend, a very delightful and well-informed Swiss lady, had to order some liveries for her men-servants. Tailor Dixon being deaf, she wrote her directions with a pencil, and among other articles, specified in her odd English "one groom coat." The tailor shook his head, and smiled compassionately, accepted the order, but begged leave, before he put it in his pocket-book, to point out a grammatical fault in the wording. "Madam!" quoth he, "you should have added an *s* to groom; the case is nominative." Talk of the march of intellect—why, it goes full gallop.

God bless you, dear friend.

CAROLINE A. BOWLES.

CXXXVIII.

TO ROBERT SOUTHEY.

BUCKLAND, *March 26th*, 1832.

I hope you have not seen the paragraph which heads my paper,* for I aspire at giving you the earliest notice of the honourable classification of "great men," in which you figure cheek by jowl with that congenial spirit, the Agitator! I congratulate you. And in good earnest, I thank you, dear friend, for your kind remembrance of my request anent the yellow poppy seed. This will be precious seed, for the sake of the gatherers and of the sender, and very much prized also as a beautiful addition to my flower collection, if it will be but good-natured enough to grow and blow for me—a doubtful case, I promise you, easy of culture as you think it, for I am told it is a capricious beauty; will flourish (as you say) anywhere when it sows itself, but oftenest baffles the hand of art. I have a sort of fellow-feeling with the creature, so perhaps it will oblige me. Mary Colling and I entirely sympathise in the feeling of companionship with flowers. I remember composing verses to mine when I stood between my father's knees, and he wrote for me. But you and I do not agree—that ever I

* *Great men that were indifferent to music.* Wyndham said that four of the greatest men he knew had no relish for music—Edmund Burke, Charles Fox, Dr. Johnson, and Pitt. To these we may add Pope, and in our own time Southey and O'Connell."—*Town.*

should say so! No; we are not yet agreed on the subject of poetical maid-servants; and, truth to say, it seems to me that in what you write to me (for I have not yet got sight of the *Quarterly Review*), you argue rather with the heart than the head—and yet Jesuitically too, for you adduce as a main point one which, so far from controverting, I agree in with you, heart and soul—the crying sin we are guilty of in converting servants from humble friends into mercenary dependents—the unavoidable effect of our detestable, cold-hearted, un-Christian system. I am thankful to my half Norman blood and parentage for having kept me clear of that sin at least. The dear old nurse who died in my arms after sixty years' service in my family would have rated you in her broken English if you had ventured to doubt that her master's grand-daughter could be less than her child in duty and affection.

You say, "that though I would not hire a poetical maid-servant, if I had hired one so qualified, and afterwards discovered her qualification, she would very soon have had a place in my esteem and affection." Secretly she might; but my endeavour would be, not to favour or distinguish her above her fellow-servants, unless she deserved it by more diligent performance of the duties of her station; other conduct on my part I should consider injudicious kindness to herself and injustice to others, and therefore, as I should certainly long to do just as Mrs. Bray has done, I would rather not have such a temptation thrown in my way as mistress of a family. It is scarcely in nature that other maid-servants should live in peace, and charity, and familiarity, with an equal so distinguished; and the friends and patrons to be acquired in a higher class can never make amends for the loss of those in the same station and circumstances as ourselves. Even Mary Colling writes and speaks with the warmth of wounded feeling, and some bitterness, of the envy and spite shown towards her. The time may come when she is no longer supported by the buoyant spirit of youth, and the generous sympathy of Mrs. Bray and her kind master, and those who now surround her with a sort of artificial atmosphere, and then, though she may not be in poverty, she will feel the want of human sympathy—that want that withers life, and dries up the heart-springs, and makes the mind shrink inward, and prey upon itself. For you know you have very coolly sentenced the poor thing to "single blessedness"; and single she had better be truly to the end of her days, lonely, deserted, starving, anything rather than mated to a coarse-minded clodpole. That other danger you admit is one I should less apprehend in our anti-romantic days than the liability you cannot but be aware of—that so engaging a creature, with so sweet a face, should become the victim of seduction. I should, in Mr. Bray's place, consider that I had taken upon myself a most serious responsibility—an engagement to watch over the principles, as well as fortunes, of the being who, through my instrumentality, would be in a manner isolated in the midst of society. You will think all my reasoning very weak, very fallacious probably, evidencing a narrow mind and most erring judgment. May be so; you may think what you will of the head (would you could mend it), provided you do not call me cold-hearted; and something assures me *that* you will not do. If you did but know how, from the very day-spring of life, my mind and heart have been driven in upon themselves, by what miserable circumstances, you would wonder I had a generous or kindly feeling left. Thank God! they did not perish under the ice, and I have a pleasure in feeling that, as I draw near the close of life, all the better feelings of my very early youth, and even childhood, are resuming more and more influence over me. This is surely right. If we bring into the world with us, as some have fancied, a lingering of heavenly light, it is no greater stretch of imagination to suppose that, as we approach the source, a few precursive rays may lighten the shadows of the dark valley. Dear friend, forgive my egotism. I meant to speak of Mary Colling only.

Peace and health be with you. I can wish you no richer earthly blessing, and so God bless you.

CAROLINE A. BOWLES.

I long to hear you have wound up the *War*. Not one word

of intelligence about the *Colloquies* have you vouchsafed me. Why, wait a little longer, and the book will be a voice of the past—obsolete under a new era, political and social. And what think you of the Irving sect? Half my family are bitten, seeing visions, having revelations, talking blasphemy; in short, as mad as Sister Nativity.*

CXXXIX.

TO CAROLINE BOWLES.

Hyde Villiers is a very intimate friend of Henry Taylor's, at whose lodgings I generally meet him, at breakfast, once during my visits to town.

Through Henry Taylor it is that he is one of my frankers. I believe his opinions upon most subjects are as far wrong as they can be; and the liking which he has both for my prose and verse is not connected with any sympathy in the more important points on which they touch. His manners are mild and courteous; and if he had not some very good qualities, Henry Taylor (who found him in the Colonial Office) would not have become so much attached to him as he is. I look at him with some wonder as the descendant of Buckingham and Clarendon, and think more of his genealogy than he does himself. He takes pains to acquire knowledge upon political subjects, and has acquired some reputation accordingly by speaking in Parliament. His father was one of the Evangelicals (I met him once at Mr. Wilberforce's), and this perhaps may in part account for the son's aberration in a different direction.

May 8th.—I cannot tell how long it is since this answer to your inquiry was written. Time seems to pass with me like a spendthrift's fortune—it goes as fast, and sometimes I am almost afraid to think that I could render as poor an account of it.

* Elsewhere Miss Bowles compares Irving in appearance to Fuseli's Lucifer.

My brother the Doctor, thank God, seems now to be recovered, though the use of one ear is, I believe, entirely lost; this however is a light misfortune. His death would have brought on me a world of cares; and those from another quarter, which we now divide, would then have come wholly upon me with a weight which it would have been impossible for me to support. Dear friend, my pillow will never be without thorns, but I did not gather them for myself. Public events I cease to think of when the newspaper is laid down ; when the pen is out of my hand I go to my books; I take exercise dutifully; make the most of little pleasures; find interest in little things if they interest others; keep a quiet mind when external circumstances will let me, a patient one at all times; and then plod on my pilgrimage with a firm step and cheerful countenance, though there is no station in the road at which I can ever hope, like Christian, to be relieved from the burthen on my back.

Write soon, for your letter makes me uneasy concerning you.* They who bear up with most fortitude in the midst of affliction suffer sometimes most in their health when it is over. Violent grief seems to spend itself in tears. I dare say your widow† who planted her husband's grave might have watered it with hers daily the first week.

God bless you, dear Caroline.

ROBERT SOUTHEY.

CXL.

TO ROBERT SOUTHEY.

BUCKLAND, *June 9th*, 1832.

I believe every Bowles has more or less of what the Scots call "a bee in the bonnet." I am sometimes sensible of the

---

* A letter written after the death of a cousin.
† See *Chapters on Churchyards*, chap. i.

humming of mine, and I am sure our poor friend of Bremhill* is haunted by a very tormenting familiar. Have you seen his late publication, *St. John at Patmos*? If you have, I am sure you have felt compassion for, rather than anger towards, him for the effusion of pique and disappointment directed towards yourself in the preface. You will not think me wanting in regard for you, or in a keen sense of feeling for all that concerns you, though I tell you I read that sentence with eyes filling with tears at thought of the bitterness of spirit the poor writer must have smarted under when he committed it to paper; and for *you* I am no way concerned, believing you would feel as I did. It is evident that he has from year to year cherished hopes of being noticed by your pen, a few words of commendation from which would, I believe, have consoled him for the heartless neglect and cutting scorn of a world which cares less than nothing for one who has nearly outlived the generation as well as the age that hailed his youthful Muse with lavish favour. He sent me his poem; I alluded to his preface, hoping however "it would be taken in good part." I tried to soothe him in my answer, and to persuade him of what I have heard from yourself—that his poetry ranked high in your estimation (his *early* poetry was in my mind), and that I was sure it would pain you to suppose he felt himself slighted or neglected by you (did I take too much upon me in speaking so after my own heart?); which brought me another letter from him by return of post, so characteristic of his infirmity of temper, and simplicity and real goodness of heart, that I must let you see it. His new poem is an epitome of his mental state, full of flashes of poetic beauty, holiness of heart, and profound feeling, but I think faulty in the choice of subject, desultory and confused in the arrangement, and wanting altogether what painters term "keeping," and "an eye to the picture."

The first part is little other than a paraphase of the Apocalypse. *St. John in Patmos* is of itself a fine and appropriate subject for the Muse of an old divine, but the mysterious Book

---

* W. Lisle Bowles.

is too awful to be woven into the work of an uninspired writer. I have been very tedious in this chapter about my sensitive namesake, but I really love and pity him, and respect him also as he deserves to be respected; and if I had power given me but for half-an-hour over your head and heart and hand, I would cause you to indite some kind, soothing, commendatory, little sentence, such as you know very well how to slip into your *Quarterly Review* and other articles, which should fall like balm on the old man's head, and fill his eyes, I answer for it, with tears of gratitude.

Farewell, dear friend, and God bless you.

CAROLINE A. BOWLES.

CXLI.

TO CAROLINE BOWLES.

KESWICK, *July 4th*, 1832.

You are perfectly right, dear Caroline, in supposing that I should feel anything rather than anger at poor Bowles's effusion of spleen. It is only from your letter that I have heard of it. I forgive him everything except his giving a proud and contemptuous nickname to one whose family history and whose character ought to have touched him, whatever he might think of her rhymes. I am sure that if he ever sees her portrait he will be pitiably ashamed of this.

He cannot suppose that I do not understand the difference between what is poetry and what is not as well as he does himself, and he ought to have seen in my reviewal of Mrs. Bray's book,* that my object was to interest people with the story, and in fact to apologise for the verses, without letting ordinary readers perceive that I thought any apology necessary for them. But you would see this, and so would any judicious reader.

* The Poems of Mary Colling.

The first time I ever saw Bowles was in 1802, and I took a dislike to him which did not wear off till I learnt from Sir George Beaumont what was his real character, many years afterwards; but the cause was just such an effusion of spleen against the Welsh bard Edward Williams, to whom he denied anything like genius because he wrote commonplace English verses, unmindful that the Welshman was writing in a foreign tongue.

More than once I have taken an opportunity of complimenting him, as he well deserves, when he came in my way, though I believe Gifford sometimes intercepted such compliments. And now, for your sake, if he does not come in my way, I will, on the first occasion, go out of mine to bring him in neck and shoulders.

I wished very much to have reviewed his *Life of Bishop Ken*, who was a kinsman of my mother's family. It is only the first volume that I have seen; but that is so bad that I was really deterred from my wish by the certainty of mortifying him, even if I totally abstained from noticing any of the faults in it, and only arranged his materials as he ought to have arranged them, and thrown his rubbish overboard. But I love dearly what is to be loved in his poetry, and you will believe me when I say that I shall have quite as much pleasure in taking the first opportunity of praising him as he can possibly have in being praised.

Summer is come in earnest, and with it a touch of my summer cold and the commencement of my summer interruptions. Last week I was most delightfully surprised by the apparition of Landor from Italy, whom I had not seen since I was at Como in 1817. He remained two days here, and holds out a hope of coming again to England three years hence, which to him seems not so long a time to look forward to as it does to me, for he has had no home-proofs of the uncertainty of human life.

Poor Sir Walter is in so pitiable and hopeless a state that his release is wished for by those who love him best. The attack had been preceded by great irritability, wholly the effect of disease, and by a failure of mental power. He wrote a great deal in Italy and sent it home for publication, but it was found to bear such marks of decay that this was impossible. It would have been a great shock to him had he known this.

God bless you, dear friend.
ROBERT SOUTHEY.

CXLII.

TO ROBERT SOUTHEY.

BUCKLAND, *July* 18*th*, 1832.

Yes; I was sure the poor poet of Bremhill's splenetic effusion could only affect you as it has done, with compassion for the infirmity of mind which can so pitiably pervert the feelings of a really kind, warm heart. A more cunning man would not have vented his spleen so palpably. I think I told you that I accompanied my cousin George Bowles to Salisbury last summer, on purpose to gratify the musical canon and poet by being present at his Cathedral during the performance of some hymns, of which the music and words were composed by himself for the benefit of a school charity; and we heard him preach also, in the same strange, desultory style (with poetic bursts interspersed) which characterises his *Life of Ken*. I never saw a man so delighted and overpowered as he was at what he called my great kindness in coming; the tears actually stood in his eyes when he thanked me, as if such trifling tokens even of regard and respect were rare to him now, who was once so used to them. After service he took possession of me, to show me, as he said, every nook and corner of his beloved Cathedral, the library, &c.; to tell me the stories of those who slept beneath the most remarkable tombs, and well and enthusiastically he began the task he had undertaken; but it so happened that as we were returning to the Cathedral, after taking some refreshment at his residence just opposite, we spied and heard two gentlemen calling for some person to liberate them from within the grated doors of the building, which they had been locked into by accident when we came out. They seemed very impatient of confinement, and I observed to my companion, who had stopt short to look down the avenue towards the prisoners, "I should be well content to be shut up for many hours in such a cage, and should have no objection to pass a moonlight night there quite alone." "God forbid, God forbid!" he muttered to himself in great agitation, dropping my arm; and then turning and looking strangely in my face he added, with a fearful emphasis, "Do you know where I should be the next day if I was shut up alone in that place one hour? In Finche's mad-house." Then he caught up my arm and rather dragged than led me on. The gentlemen were liberated, and came out laughing as we entered, but Mr. Bowles shuddered as he passed them, and I am sure put great force upon himself, in consideration of his promise to me, in entering at all. He hurried me over the library, the rest of the party following; then down to the body of the Cathedral, from tomb to tomb, from shrine to shrine, scarcely able to utter two connected sentences, and turning his head to look back towards the entrance every moment. At last he caught my hand, and whispered "Good God! if we should be shut in," and his distress was so painful to me that I feigned having seen enough. I drew him away, nothing loath, but too much agitated to be himself again while we stayed. After witnessing that scene, nothing he could say or do would affect me angrily.

Poor human nature! I suppose it is from sympathy that I feel so much for poor Bowles; and how he would resent such sympathy!

The *Life of Bishop Ken* might as well be the life of the man in the moon; but surely some of the irrelevant parts (how few are relevant) are beautiful in themselves as to poetic feeling; one might make a pretty little book of such episodes.

God bless you, dear friend. I was delighted to hear of the unexpected pleasure you had had in the visit of Mr. Landor, of whom I well remember you told me there was no person living you would go so far to see and converse with.

CAROLINE A. BOWLES.

CXLIII.

TO CAROLINE BOWLES.

KESWICK, *July* 31*st*, 1832.

Poor Bowles's poem came to me yesterday, with a note, two months old, from himself, saying that he was especially induced to send it because he had mentioned me in the preface, and professing all the personal good-will for which I always gave him credit. As you may suppose, I immediately read through the poem, and then wrote to thank him for it. I told him for what reasons I never reviewed the works of a living poet, and also for what reasons I had told Mary Colling's story in the Quarterly Review. It will not be my fault if the letter does not put him in good-humour both with himself and me.

His preface has served as a text in Fraser's Magazine for a discourse in which the Quarterly Review is charged with patronising humble poets for the pleasure of patronage, and abstaining from praising great ones for equally worthy motives. This introduces a criticism upon Mr. Pennie, the poet whom Bowles praises; but in the specimens which are given I see much more effort than power, and much less feeling than either. The truth is, that genius is common enough (I had almost said too common), but that nothing is so uncommon as the good sense which gives it its right direction. Fielding employed great part of his life in writing execrable comedies before he found where his talent lay; and I believe something of the same kind occurred to a very inferior writer—Marmontel.

Do you ever see *Fraser's Magazine?* It is just as disgusting as the Monster's, and just as clever; but it has the advantage of giving excellent portraits, with about the same inclination to caricature in them that a certain very dear friend of mine is conscious of in herself. In the reviewal of Mr. Pennie they say, very truly, that the merit of my prose consists in no artifice of composition, but in letting the language suit itself to the subject, and rise and fall with it.

And now, dear friend, farewell.

ROBERT SOUTHEY.

CXLIV.

TO ROBERT SOUTHEY.

BUCKLAND, *August 20th*, 1832.

Some days earlier you would have heard from me, dear friend, had not a long and severe attack of sickness still hung about me too oppressively to allow me to write with any degree of comfort. This is the first evening, almost the first hour, that I feel really revived, and able to breathe without pain. Only those who are familiar with sickness and suffering can appreciate the blessing of ease, mere bodily ease—not the less delightful for being accompanied, as is the case with me at this moment, by a degree of languor which seems to calm and compose, but not depress, the mind. After the fever of mind and body which has lately worn me to a shadow, it would be luxury to me this evening merely to lie still and think; but I am greedy of enjoyment after such long starvation; I must, therefore, think on paper—to you.

Thank you for your letter of the 4th. What you say of poor Lisle Bowles accounts to me for a report lately made to me by a friend, of his being in particular good spirits and good-humour, and talking of coming to see me. No doubt your kind note to him smoothed down all his bristles, and I should not wonder if he half repented of calling poor Mary Colling names. I hope if that interesting girl ever loses her kind master, he will either leave her sufficiently provided for, or that Mrs. Bray will take her into her family. It is not only provision, but protection, that poor Mary will want, for she must be isolated among persons of her own class in life. Did it ever strike you that the Devonshire cast of countenance, especially of beauty, is very peculiar to that province? We have had several Devonshire girls in the service of different persons of my family—two in our own house—all good-looking, and one beautiful, and all (the last especially) so much like the picture of Mary Colling, that it might have answered for both—the compressed lips and receding mouth, all marking provincial features, and a certain shrewdness, as well as sweetness of expression.

I am not sure that you will ever speak to me again when you know what atrocities (as you will call them) have been perpetrated, if not by my own hand, with my sanction after the fact. Whisper it not in the ears of Rumpelstilzchen, or the hearing of Pussy Bell, or in the groves of Cats' Eden, that within the short space of three weeks nine cats have been murdered on these premises by the hand of Dick, my servitor— caught by the necks and tails in wires set for the purpose round my pigeon-house, which had been pillaged unmercifully for the last twelve months by those abominable vermin, who swarm in this garden from all parts of the neighbourhood. Woe to the great Rumpel himself if he were to set foot here.

Spite of cats, however, a family of nightingales has been reared this summer, almost under my windows, by the parent birds, who took up their abode in the little front garden close to the house immediately on their arrival in April. The first notice I had of my welcome guests was the song of the male as he hovered in a seeming rapture over a rose-bush covered with early flowers close to the window—the eastern fable illustrated to the life. The pair brought up four young ones, and trained them mostly, when they first left the nest, on a pink thorn under my bedroom window, where I was many a half-hour longer in dressing than usual, but not engrossed by my looking-glass; and one morning when I came down to breakfast, one of the bold little creatures that had found its way into the house flew out over my shoulder, but nothing daunted, nor farther than to his family on the thorn close by. My pretty visitors are now of course departed, but I hope they will return next spring to the same quarters; next spring! well, if I am not here to welcome them, I shall be better off elsewhere, wherever that may be.

I have never seen, I think, more than three or four numbers of *Fraser's Magazine* since its commencement, and the two last that fell in my way I thought dull and heavy—proof of dulness in myself, I fear, since your opinion is so different—but I saw no sketches of character such as you mention. "Hast thou found me, O! mine enemy?" If I dare not disavow that besetting sin you hint at, be sure I do not love myself the better for it, and I should think it was the Evil One himself who put comical fancies into my head sometimes, if they were ever fashioned in malice, which I swear they are not, that I never could, would, or did caricature, with pen or pencil, man, woman, or child towards whom I was conscious of an unkind or angry thought, least of all, any who had ever injured or offended me. But I know there are laughing devils as well as others.

Pray, tell me, did you give it under your hand and seal to Satan Montgomery, that you considerd one of his poems (I forget which) equal in merit to *Paradise Lost*, and himself (said Satan) not second even to John Milton? Satan averred to a relation of mine, that he had this opinion in good black and white characters of your writing; but till I see them, no, till you certify the same to me, I must believe Satan lies—no great scandal.

God bless you and those you love, dear friend.

CAROLINE A. BOWLES.

CXLV.
TO CAROLINE BOWLES.

KESWICK, *August 26th*, 1832.

Robert Montgomery (wicked Caroline to call him Satan), I will venture to say, never told so absurd a lie as your informant has put into his mouth. He is a fine young man, who has been wickedly puffed and wickedly abused, and who is in no little danger of being spoiled by forcing. In thanking him for his books when he sent them to me, I neither made a fool of myself nor of him by any preposterous praise. The course he has taken has been the best possible for immediate success (and this his poverty rendered needful), but in other respects he could not have taken a worse. He has rushed in where angels should fear to tread. He has attempted subjects which ought never to be attempted, and in which it is impossible not to fail; yet these very subjects have obtained for him popularity, and the profit without which he could not have obtained the education of which he was worthy, as well as ambitious. When he lowers his flight, I wish he may not find that he has weakened his wings by straining them.

You deserve to be haunted by the ghost of Merlin for those repeated acts of felicide which you seem to feel no remorse for. If I had committed one such act, I could never again look a cat in the face. No such deeds are committed in Cats' Eden. We have had a sad tragedy here, in the fate of two owls, both taken from one nest, both bought from some boys for the sake of emancipating them as soon as they should be able to provide for themselves; and just as that had been accomplished and each was living about the premises upon the wing and at large, both, one after the other, drowned in the same water-cask, and both now buried in the orchard. Each was named Solon; and the death of the first, who was tame enough to answer from the trees to his name, and come at a call, vexed us all more than such things ought to disturb one.

God bless you, dear friend.

ROBERT SOUTHEY.

CXLVI.

TO CAROLINE BOWLES.

KESWICK, *September* 17*th*, 1832.

.I can but too well understand the situation of the young ladies concerning whom you speak. Every publisher is beset by persons seeking for this sort of employment, miserably as it is paid, and uncertain as it is. Few books are now translated, except such as from some immediate interest in the subject are sure of a present sale; and then, lest another publisher should get the start, the poor translator is unmercifully hurried in his task. So little is to be done in this way at any time, that at this time I see no hope of doing anything. There are but two courses open to women thus unhappily circumstanced—that of setting up a school, or of seeking a livelihood in the manner you mention. But both these require active friends, and such are rarely to be found.

Ah, dear Caroline, this is a hard-hearted, I had almost said a merciless, society in which we are living. It seems as if no sympathy could be excited for any but great criminals. They who deserve most compassion meet with least; and bounty seldom descends upon those on whom it would be best bestowed.

I never said anything like what you repeat about Robert Montgomery: when I have spoken of him to Sharon Turner (who must be the common friend alluded to), it has been to the same effect as I have expressed myself to you; encouraging him against his malevolent enemies, and giving him credit for good powers, which have been overtasked, and injudiciously both excited and extolled. Favourably no doubt I wrote, and kindly, but certainly neither flatteringly, nor falsely, nor like a fool. My sins of this kind never go beyond promising myself pleasure from the perusal of a book, when perhaps a glance may already have shown me that the way not to be disappointed in such a promise is to leave the unhappy book unread.

Friend Amelia might class this with the sorrow which is expressed in declining a disagreeable invitation, and sins of the same diminutiveness. But you know me well enough not to need any assurance that I flatter people in private as little as in public.

There can be no truth in any reports about Sir Walter's late papers. What he sent home from the Continent for publication was found by his friends wholly unfit for the press, so far had his faculties at that time failed him. I heard from Abbotsford on Sunday last; mortification had then existed for eight days; it was extending widely and deeply, and every night had been expected to be the last, yet still he lingered on. But this must soon close, and probably has closed ere this. It has been a pitiable case—the mind going slowly to ruins first, and the strong body maintaining so long and slow a struggle afterwards. The cholera is a merciful dispensation when compared with this. Yet I can believe a state of mind very possible in which the more or less of affliction in this world would appear all but infinitely insignificant to the sufferers themselves. There are few who attain it; and I wish I could feel that I were nearer to it for entirely believing it to be attainable.

You would be greatly pleased with Lord Ashley's letters to me, were you to see them. They express a warmth of attachment which is very unusual to meet with from anyone, and especially from one in his rank of life. He has sent Cuthbert his own Greek Testament, and promised him (God willing) the best piece of preferment that may ever be at his disposal. You need not be told that this was wholly unsolicited; even if I were in the habit of asking favours, or fishing for them, so remote a possibility would never have entered into my thoughts. But this will show you something of his character: my writings seem to have taken hold both of his heart and understanding. That they will bring forth good fruit in time I have never doubted.

Lady Malet is here, and is making a portrait of me which goes much nearer to satisfy everybody than any former attempt. She has made a very good one of Edith, which is going to

Copenhagen.* Do not forget yours when your hand is disposed to exercise its cunning. I am expecting a franker every minute, and if he comes in time shall take him to Watenlath and Borrodale before dinner.

Dear friend, God bless, and preserve you! Night and morning when I pray for protection, you are always in my thoughts.

ROBERT SOUTHEY.

CXLVII.

TO ROBERT SOUTHEY.

BUCKLAND, *October 15th*, 1832.

Have I ever spoken to you of "Sir Edward Seward's Narrative," edited by Miss Porter? Many persons persist in the belief that it is a true story. I cannot be so persuaded, but I do think the author, whoever he or she may be, deserves to rank with De Foe in the extraordinary art, evinced in this narrative, of giving the tone of verisimilitude to a story in all its details, and of individuality to the personages represented in it. I should imagine that the fiction is founded on some slender foundation of reality. Be it what it may, the book charmed me, and I devoured it with all the youthful appetite which gave such a relish to "Robinson Crusoe" some five or six-and-thirty years ago. How pleasant it is when such a gush of youthful feeling breaks up the cold surface that crusts over one's heart in middle age! But then the revulsion is too painful, and one had better keep under the crust. Of course you think so, or you would not renounce poor Poetry as you do. I have a huge mind to write a letter to Murray too, and call you a "Renegade." Will you never, never, never refresh my heart and mind with verse of yours again? They say "the devil

---

* To Mr. Warter.

quotes Scripture for his purpose." I saw your "Holly Tree" the other day in Lord Brougham's Magazine.

No increase of cholera at Southampton. None here, thank God, and may He be gracious to you.

CAROLINE A. BOWLES.

CXLVIII.

TO CAROLINE BOWLES.

KESWICK, *October 21st*, 1832.

I have been writing upon the last French revolution, taking for my text a pamphlet of poor Prince Polignac's, sent me from Brussels by Sir Robert Adair. My reply, saying that I would take up the subject in the *Quarterly Review,* was sent by Adair to his poor friend in person, and this has brought me a long letter from Polignac himself, containing much interesting matter, and concluding with assurance "de haute considera-tion." I could not but smile through sadness at the phrase. The poor princess too sends me her most grateful thanks for so poor a service as that of simply speaking the honest truth in vindication of a most unfortunate, but upright, man. Under present circumstances, however, no service could afford them so much gratification.

I have not made up my mind whether or not to bray Lord Nugent in a mortar. As regards myself, his letter is utterly unworthy of notice; and if I answered it, it would be as the reviewer, not in my own name, passing over his personali-ties with stinging contempt. The question is, is it worth while to notice the falsehood of his defence, and repeat in the strongest terms the charges of dishonesty which were advanced as courteously as they could be, and far more so than they ought to have been, in the *Quarterly Review?* That I can do this triumphantly is a temptation for doing it; whereas, on the other hand, I may be more profitably and pleasantly employed;

for to do it well I must make myself angry, and anger is not a wholesome feeling. If I see Wordsworth I may probably be guided by his opinion. In such matters I am easily persuaded.

Your clergyman's poems came yesterday, and I have read about half the volume. See the use of recommending such a book! I copied your recommendation of it to Wynn, who was then in the Isle of Wight, and he bought the only remaining copy at Newport, and was as much pleased with them as you are. I admire them greatly, and will notice them when reviewing "Neff's Life," a book written by Gilly (the Vaudois' friend). Neff was a Protestant clergyman in the French Alps, an imitation of Oberlin, without his amusing eccentricities, and in a more unfavourable situation, but an admirable man.

Mr. Sewell's poems are not always sufficiently intelligible. The fault they have is common with Keble's. I wish they could write as lucidly as you; and still more that you, whose poems have all the charm of theirs, and always the grace which they frequently want, would write more, and more, and more. As for me, it is not that the spring of poetry in me is dry, or frozen, but that I want time for it. Letters from all sorts of people, and upon all sorts of subjects, make longer drafts upon my time than anyone would suppose. By the time Cuthbert's lessons are over, and I have read the newspaper (which must be read), and answered my letters, so much of the morning is gone, that no more remains than is required for my daily walk; and I am glad to get that opportunity for miscellaneous reading. In the way of direct business, a little before breakfast, and the hours between tea and supper, are all that I can commonly make sure of.

God bless you, dear friend.
ROBERT SOUTHEY.

CXLIX.

TO ROBERT SOUTHEY.

BUCKLAND, *February 2nd*, 1833.

Dear friend, will you be at the trouble of looking over the accompanying verses? I have been reading accounts of the factory atrocities, and proofs of them in minutes of evidence taken before the House of Commons, that worked me up to a fever of indignation, which vented itself in verse—the little poem I inclose, and another of about the same length, this being, I think, the best of the two. And I have a half-formed plan of publishing them, with some notes annexed from the minutes of evidence. But I should be glad of encouragement from you, if you can give it me, or thankful for discouragement if my attempt deserves no better. I fancied if published soon the trifle might be successful. This will reach you, I hope, before you may be writing to me, for I should be sorry to draw twice upon your time, occupied as it now is.

God bless you, dear friend.

CAROLINE A. BOWLES.

CL.

TO CAROLINE BOWLES.

KESWICK, *February 6th*, 1833.

Your poem, dear friend, reached me this morning, and I would have written to you by this day's post if there had not at the same time arrived another letter upon the same subject, which required an immediate reply, because it consulted me upon the steps to be taken in Parliament against this most hellish of all slaveries. Print your poems by all means. This is a most painful and most true one, and cannot but be felt at this time, when it is of the greatest importance that the nation should be made to feel. You have written like yourself. I could not find any words that would express higher praise.

No task was ever taken up in Parliament under a deeper sense of duty than this will be. The delegates from the manufacturing districts have requested one, whose name I must not mention, but whom you will be at no loss to know, to take Sadler's position and urge on his Bill. He says to me, " I shrink from the task in perfect dismay, but still I think that you would advise me to undertake it. I have implored them to try others; they have done so; some fear, some refuse, some are unable by their position as members of manufacturing districts; yet it is a duty towards God and man." He refers to my *Essays*, which have taken deep hold on his mind, and he concludes with "God help me." How you would love him if you saw his letters to me!

I have read of the Slave Trade and of the Inquisition, but nothing ever thrilled my heart like the Evidences which you have been reading. It disturbed my sleep, and I laid the book aside in horror.

It is by this system that the ———— s have obtained their enormous wealth and purchased the ———— estates here as an appanage for the second son, that John —— who is to second the address, who in Leeds was returned instead of Sadler, and who, when I advised him to plant alders about the marshy borders of the lake, replied that "alders were worth only fourpence a foot." I wish you could have seen Bertha's countenance when he made that reply.

After such an experience I wonder (as far as I can wonder at anything in these times) that none of those cotton and worsted and flax kings have yet hanged themselves; that none of them have been pulled to pieces; that none of their factories have been destroyed; that the very pavement of the streets has not risen and stoned them.

I am glad to see that Sir H. Neale's treatment is stated in the *John Bull*. There is no baseness of which the present Ministers are not capable, and they have just such a king to deal with as they could desire, who thinks himself completely discharged of all moral responsibility, and is verily persuaded that while he does what his Ministers bid him, and they do what the mob bid them, the king can do no wrong!

No possible change can be foreseen that would deliver us from these profligate men. They have brought the country to such a state that no other party could carry on the government for a week; they themselves can only carry it on during the pleasure of the political unions, unless it be by the support of those whom they hate, and who most righteously execrate them. The Conservatives mean, I know (at least the better part), to stand by them mercifully against the Radicals, but to avoid all coalition with or approximation towards them as they would plague or infamy. This is my feeling.

God bless you.

ROBERT SOUTHEY.

CLI.

TO ROBERT SOUTHEY.

BUCKLAND, *February 21st*, 1833.

Two long letters I have cost you lately, dear friend! They have not been wasted on me, but I would fain have spared you the second. But I become more and more cowardly, and could not resolve to print my little stories without some encouragement from you; that received, I set to work briskly, added a third to the two I had ready, picked and stole certain notes from your *Essays* and *Colloquies*, added some of the minutes of Evidence which had so disturbed and excited me, and sent off my MS. last week, as Blackwood wrote to say he should be very glad to have it and print it immediately. He requested also to be allowed to publish the tales in his Magazine separately—a plan I do not much like, neither do I care greatly about it, so I did not forbid him, and he will do as he pleases.

I hope I have not done an absurd or over-bold thing in inscribing this little pamphlet, trifling as it is, to Mr. Sadler. He was the champion who first stood forward in behalf of those poor children; and all those who execrate that horrid system he has nobly dared to expose, and strives to put an end to, must love and respect him for his humanity and courage; for it is no small proof of moral courage in him, connected as I believe he is with the manufacturing interests, to stand forward as he has done. "God help" Lord Ashley, I say with all my heart, in his own words. I had seen a newspaper announcement that he was to bring forward Sadler's Bill, on the 5th of March it was said. How eagerly I shall look for his speech, and how my heart will go with him!

I am tired to death of scribbling Lords and Ladies, such as Lord Nugent, Lord Mulgrave, Lady Emmeline Stuart Wortley, and Lady C. Burney; and I suppose Blackwood will set me down for a Republican, for I told him I was sick of his Helicon bag of fashion, and did not care to keep such company. Those people have no feeling for truth and nature—how should they in their artificial atmosphere? And yet they pretend to "babble about green fields!" It makes me mad to hear them, as was Hotspur with him of the pouncet-box. I like lords and ladies in drawing-rooms very much, in their own element; but let them keep to it, and not prate about what they cannot comprehend—poor souls. Their attempts at rural simplicity always remind me of the young Cockney lady who, being for the first time in a country farm-yard, asked what those creatures were—meaning the cocks and hens; and on being told they were fowls, exclaimed: "La! where are their livers and gizzards?" Your Lord Ashley seems made of better stuff, however. Some plants, bury them how you will in rubbish and darkness, will force their way into light and life.

I feel no good-will to those who have set you such a task as you have undertaken for next summer—*The Life of Dr.*

Bell. You will never satisfy the worthy Davies*—that seems certain.

Have I ever told you that since my irreparable loss of those kind friends I have made a very agreeable, intimate acquaintance, who, as far as tastes go, suits me entirely?—further, I have not quite read her yet—a widow lady, about fifty, having lost her only son, and living much such a life as I do, among books, and flowers, and recollections. She is by birth half Swiss, half Dutch (a good compound), married at sixteen to an Englishman, having lived in half the courts of Germany, but retaining all her Swiss mountain tastes in their first freshness. I know you would like her hugely, and be amused at her originality and broken English—Madame Dayrolles by name, a person of good fortune, and doing much good with it, never visiting any more than myself, and living within ten minutes' walk from this house. This is a valuable acquisition to me—is it not?

I have a large glass of sweet violets at this moment before me, perfuming the room. There is no checking the thoughts that dim my eyes as I look at them. Are they the last I shall pick from my own garden? † Dear friend, if I go hence, as I believe I shall, my sorrow will be all of the heart. As for privations, I never think of them as regards myself. But spirits inhabit here with me, who will not accompany me hence.

It is strange that one should be no less attached to place by the past sorrows we have suffered in it—nay, more—than by the remembrance of happy and prosperous days. But God is everywhere, and where He is we must be well. May He be about your path, and about your bed, and keep you in all your ways.

And so farewell, dear friend.

CAROLINE A. BOWLES.

* Dr. Bell's secretary.
† In consequence of the apprehended loss of her annuity from Mr. Bruce, and the departure from her house which such loss would entail.

CLII.

TO CAROLINE BOWLES.

KESWICK, *March* 11*th*, 1833.

Murray's sin is great enough, God knows, in publishing those books of Lord Byron's, which very many persons would have been ashamed to have seen in their possession, before they appeared in this edition. As to what regards myself, he is altogether blameless. I dare say he would have destroyed that dedication if he could; but Byron took care that nothing of this kind should be lost, and his friends have been equally careful. You see it was not possible to keep the libel upon Rogers secret, though it shows the writer to have been the most treacherous of mankind. The very persons who cry out against Lady Blessington for bringing this to light are most likely the same who had the dedication of *Don Juan* printed upon a broadside, for popular sale in the streets. If Murray had omitted it in this edition, when some of the journals called for its insertion, he would have exposed himself to attacks that would have annoyed him; and he knew very well that the publication could neither annoy nor injure me.

I have not yet seen how my first volume looks when put together; it may perhaps be here on Thursday next, for I am patient enough to let it travel by wagon. My greatest pleasure in a book of my own is in cutting open the leaves as soon as it comes.

You ought not to have felt any misgivings about your *Tales of the Factories*. The question *cui bono* is very easily answered there. It is doing great good to impress, as you will do, upon all those into whose hands your verses will come, a deep sense of their abominable inhumanity—the great national sin—for it is such, more truly a national sin than ever the Slave Trade has been. Lord Ashley's Bill came to me by the morning's post. No doubt it is exactly what Sadler would have brought in, for Sadler is in town to advise him; and though it asks for too little—far, far too little—this has been a matter of prudence.

March 18.—Yesterday brought us what is one of the rarest of rare animals in this place at this season, and what, though common enough in Keswick during the laking months, is even then a rarity within these doors—a franker, to wit. A warm contest is going on for West Cumberland, and this has brought down the existing Member to support and propose one of the candidates. The said franker is a new Member and "full of Parliament," as poor Green the Ambleside artist tells us, he was "of dinner" one day when he began to ascend a mountain. Green, however, would be the better for his dinner, though a mountain climb was not likely to assist his stomach in digesting it. But to be full of Parliament is not much better than to be full of flatulence. He told me more than I had before learned of the blackguard insolence which the mob-members seek every opportunity of displaying, and which is likely to have some good effect, by disgusting those who have any sense of good manners, and any respect for the old decencies and civilities of society. Our trust at this time must be wholly in Providence—there are now no secondary helps to look to. The Conservatives are without a leader, and not likely to find one. Peel wants confidence in the strength which he really possesses, and in that of his cause; he wants warmth and heart also; it seems as if he did not feel what he believes : and that his principles, having their root in his understanding, had struck no deeper. The Ministers trust to this party for support against the Destructives, and to the Destructives for support against them. The measures with regard to the English Church are concerted with such secrecy that the bishops know nothing about them. Lockhart writes me that we are on the eve of some collision with the House of Lords: "the Lords," he says, "may not die in the right ditch, but die they must." I think another collision is nearer, and one that with God's help may save us. O'Connell will go all lengths in Ireland. When he heard the substance of Lord Grey's speech, which was reported to him in one of the passages between the Houses of Lords and Commons, he took off his hat (a new one), put it on the ground and stamped the crown of it out, saying there was another crown which he should dispose of in the same way. Mr. Stanley tells me there were many witnesses of this. So soon as he gives the word for open rebellion in Ireland, his allies here, the Political Unions, will show themselves in support of the Murder Unions. We may look for insurrection; and they will be put down; and such a turn will then take place in public opinion, that we shall then effect the now necessary Reform in Parliament. With this Parliament, or such a Parliament as this, no government can be carried on. We must have a Reform which will exclude the blackguards; and luckily there are gentlemen enough in the House at present to outnumber them.

I am looking daily and wishfully for your little book.

God bless you, dear friend.

ROBERT SOUTHEY.

CLIII.

TO CAROLINE BOWLES.

KESWICK, *April* 14*th*, 1833.

Many years it cannot be, in the course of nature, before we shall meet in a better world, even were we both to live out the full term of ordinary life. You have seen Quarles' Hieroglyphics of the life of man—a candle graduated from the age of ten, by tens, to four-score. Mine has just burnt down to three-score, and if I live till the 12th of August next I shall enter upon my sixtieth year. Sixteen years we have known each other, and nothing can be more unlikely than that our earthly intercourse should be prolonged to as many years more. Whichever goes first will be spared a poignant feeling here, and have the joy of bidding the other welcome to our new country. Meanwhile, every day brings us nearer to it, and whatever we do to render ourselves useful here by our writings will be rendering ourselves fitter for the change.

Your picture will be prized as a treasure, and you may be assured that it shall have a place of honour. A treasure it will be now, and a great one hereafter, to those who can attach no such feeling to it as I shall do.

As for my letter,* the whole business about it has been managed and mismanaged between Murray and Lockhart, without any communication to me: they agreed to put it in the *Review* without my having dreamt of such a destination for it: of course I was very much pleased with the arrangement; and then they determined with just as little ceremony to leave it out, and with this of course I am not pleased. But the first thing I did, upon hearing it was to appear as a pamphlet after all, was to desire that Henry Taylor would obtain an official frank for conveying one to you. I have not taken any notice of the matter yet, either to Lockhart or Murray. You know it is my way to take all things easily that can be taken so; and by the time I may find it necessary to write, my displeasure will have passed away. It takes a great deal to make me angry, yet you will see by the epistle that upon a proper occasion I can show a proper resentment of ill usage.

The *Naval History* occupies my evenings, and I must go over to Lowther on account of it as soon as the clergyman there (an old acquaintance) can receive me, which he will be glad to do. The family are not at the Castle, so that I cannot take up my quarters there, as I otherwise should. My motive for going is that there is a set of Rymer's *Fœdera* there. The republication of that work by the Record Commission carried me through my first volume, but there it ended; and I expect to find much matter which has escaped my predecessors, from the reign of Richard II. to that of Henry VIII. Two or three mornings doggedly devoted to this in the library will probably suffice.

Adam Clarke's *Life* is lying for me in London. I passed

---

* To Lord Nugent.

an evening in his company as far back as the year 1800, and have had three or four letters from him in later years. He was the most learned man the Methodists have ever had among them. I wish the book had reached me, for I expect to find in it much that is interesting. Another of my Methodist acquaintances (for you know I have acquaintances of all sorts) has spoilt what, if he had given in the genuine book, would have been one of the greatest curiosities in literature—" The Village Blacksmith, or the Life of Samuel Hick." I intend to review it when I can; but in this way it is not likely that I can do much this year, as the only time which can be given to it must be in the morning, between the hours of eleven and two, after Cuthbert's lessons are done, and before I take my daily walk; and in those hours it is that I must write my letters also, which, as you may suppose, very often occupy them entirely.

The Factory Bill will be carried in spite of the Commission. This is one of the occasions on which the Conservatives as a party have manifested an equal want of sense and principle. If they had not been both headless and heartless, they would have eagerly occupied a popular ground, which was open for them here.

Dear Caroline, God bless you.

ROBERT SOUTHEY.

CLIV.

TO CAROLINE BOWLES.

KESWICK, *July 1st*, 1833.

We had a most remarkable preacher from Ireland here—Archdeacon Trench, brother to the Archbishop of Tuam. His sermon was extempore and evangelical, but good of its kind, and as methodical as if it had been composed and written. Never did I see so much gesticulation in the pulpit; never, indeed, more upon the stage. If his head had not been well hung, off it must have come. This, however, was not mere acting, for in conversation his head and features are in the same earnest exercise, and his arms in as much motion as he can safely indulge in. On the whole, a very remarkable person, and never to be forgotten by those who have heard and seen him.

Mrs. Austin has sent me her *Characteristics of Goethe*. I had seen her as a child, and though she is connected with everything that is Liberal and Radical, some of that circle have a degree of tolerance towards me, of which this presentation is an instance. The book was brought here by Henry Robinson, a great friend of Wordsworth's, and something more than an acquaintance of mine. If you read the book you will see some communication in it from him, signed "H. C. R.," for he has been much in Germany.

There is perhaps no other writer with whom I find myself so often both in sympathy and in dyspathy as with Goethe. Our understandings often come to the same result, our feelings often coincide, our fancies sometimes meet; and yet the antipathies are not less frequent, and are, on the whole, the stronger. I can like persons who are very different from myself in all things; but it seems to me that, though Goethe was very far from an unamiable man, I never could have liked him, and that no intellectual sympathy could ever have overcome this dislike. His political opinions and feelings were as conservative as mine; but his infidelity has given a pernicious tendency to many of his writings, and made him thus a promoter of that revolutionary spirit which was what he most detested.

His notions of immortality were almost as wild as poor Mr. Hope's, and not a whit more consolatory, or good for anything.

You will read the book, and will be offended with many ugly Germanisms in the language, or rather, words taken from the German. But there is much that will interest you. It is a fact which ought to be brought out in the strongest light, that a petty German sovereign, whose dominions do not exceed or equal the estates of some of our great nobles, and whose revenues fall very far short of many a merchant's and manufacturer's income, has done more for the literature of his country (that is for Germany) than any king or emperor ever did for the literature of any country, or any age.

Did I tell you that Rumpelstilzchen died in peace about six weeks ago, and was deposited in the orchard, where some catmint will be planted, to mark the spot and gratify his ghost, if it should walk? Poor Rumpel, for two or three months he showed such marks of decay that we wished for his decease, and yet it saddened us all when it took place, and we heard that he had been lying dead under a hedge in the adjoining field. Cats' Eden is in possession of his posterity, and happy man would be my dole if I could make others as happy as my family of cats are made. They have everything that a cat's heart can desire. I am to them what the Duke of Saxe-Weimar was to Goethe and the other men of letters; and they seem to know and acknowledge. Knurry has a kitten just coming to perfection; its name is

Tuh-peaou-chung-keun-foo-tseang,

and its title

The Wae-wei.

God bless you, dear friend.

ROBERT SOUTHEY.

CLV.

TO ROBERT SOUTHEY.

BUCKLAND, *July* 19*th*, 1833.

I shall get Mrs. Austin's book certainly. I can perfectly comprehend your sentiments in regard to Goethe. It is your heart and your nobler nature and nobler aspirations which revolt against the earthly and sensual character of his. Goethe may have been an inspired writer, but his inspiration was not from above; and who has ever risen the purer, the better, or the happier from the purest and best of his writings? Admiration, disappointment, and disgust has been, I think, the sequence of feeling with which I have read them.

Do you not think Schiller, as a tragic writer, far superior to Goethe, and Körner in some of his lyrical pieces? Pray tell me if your Dutch friend Bilderdijk still lives.

I was not a little amused in reading Goethe's memoirs, when they came out some years ago, to find almost a *facsimile* of one of the freaks of my solitary childhood among the reminiscences of his. Do you remember where he describes his fanciful consecration of a sort of altar (I forget where) on which he was for some time in the habit of offering daily oblations of fruit and flowers? When I was about seven or eight years old, I built up a little altar of turf in the most private nook of our garden, and every morning for, I believe, a whole summer brought to it an offering of flowers, placing them on the green mound with feelings of reverential awe. That I well remember, and also my confused sense of something wrong in the act, which made me keep it a profound secret from my father and mother, and in the end troubled my mind so much that I demolished and destroyed all traces of my dear little altar, though with many tears and remorseful hesitation. But *my* offering was made to the one true God, in the fervour of a heart and mind full of the poetic beauty of Eve's morning sacrifices described in *The Death of Abel;* Goethe's were to the heathen deities.*

Surely you will immortalize Rumpel in immortal verse. I must go to Pekin to learn to pronounce his descendant's name, which will effectually prevent the possibility of its being pitched into rhyme. I like his title extremely.

I have had to undergo a real, sharp heart-twinge this week, in pronouncing sentence on my dear old pony, my faithful servant, and no small favourite of fifteen years' standing. I had been offered a run for life for him by two kind friends here and at Lyndhurst, but the poor old animal being diseased as well as old, I thought it would be no mercy to him to close with the

---

* This was not so; see *Dichtung und Wahrheit*, B. I.

proposal. I have not often felt a more painful contraction of the heart than when I patted his sleek coat for the last time, and he looked round at me with "eyes of human meaning." Women are not often so situated as to be compelled to pronounce words so painful. It is no enviable privilege of independence, and unhappily I do not find I become "used to it," as the eels do to skinning.

God bless you, dear friend.

CAROLINE A. BOWLES.

Your friend Satan Montgomery has not improved upon his former publications in that he has just given to the world. Kind as his intentions towards us are, I must say I never read a more dull and heavy poem, one more ill-arranged and devoid of interest than " Woman the Angel of Life." I owe him a grudge for tacking that syllable " Mont " on to his real patronymic " Gomery," and so cheating people " who swear by a name" into the belief that he is *the* Montgomery. I do beg and entreat you will undertake the task of making mince-meat (such as you can make) of my very dear friend and admirer, Simon Pure, viz., William Howitt. He has shown the cloven foot with a vengeance, and horns and tail beside.

CLVI.

TO CAROLINE BOWLES.

KESWICK, *August* 4*th*, 1833.

Next week, if I live so long, I enter upon my sixtieth year. Sixteen have elapsed since we became known to each other. Before another such term has run out, we may meet in eternity; in the ordinary course of nature my departure is not likely to be deferred so long. It is but a little way to look on; and I look to it as I used to do in my youth to the end of a long day's walk —not with the feeling of one who is weary of his labours, but with a willingness to be at rest; and the satisfaction of knowing assuredly that there will be that rest for me. Certainly if I had been an old Roman I should not have waited for the slow process of nature, but would have quitted my tenement before it fell to ruins.

The portrait has not yet arrived. From a fortnight to three weeks is the usual time upon the road; so it may be looked for every carrier's day till it arrives, and we have four in the week. I am looking by the same channel for a parcel of catalogue-books, among which is the old French romance of Astrea which I have wished for years to possess. Nearly thirty years ago I read it in the very vilest of all vile translations, but the original has such a charm of natural style that Fontaine made it his study. You may marvel, perhaps, that I, who take so little delight in modern romances that I scarcely cut their leaves when they are sent me, should continue to peruse old ones whenever they come in my way with as much delight as I did forty years ago. But so it is, and it would not be difficult to explain why it is so, and why it ought to be so.

I hope the Monster has sent you Captain Hamilton's *Men and Manners in America*. The author has sent it me. He lives at Rydal, and is in appearance what Don Quixote would have been if his countenance had not been rueful. The book will amuse you, but it will leave a very painful feeling concerning the Americans. The other day we had a New Englander here, from whom I gathered that what may be called the gentry in America live in the fear of the multitude; that they dread the progress of democracy, yet are afraid to utter a thought in opposition to it; and that no man, however rich, dares maintain an establishment the cost of which would exceed £2000 a year. The best private library in the United States is said to be that of Professor Ticknor, a correspondent of mine, and a very interesting person; it is not so large a library as my own!

He tells me that, in proportion to the population, madness is more frequent in America than in England, and that the most frequent cause is political excitement—ambition among a people where every man thinks every office to be within his reach, and where some kind of election is always going on. This is a sad picture; yet, in America, the better minds look with alarm upon the course which we are taking in England. Ticknor in his last letter hints at the possibility that the changes and chances of this world may bring me and mine to Boston. I think this country, whatever be the evils that await it, has less to go through than the United States. We shall save more from the wreck than they can hope during many generations to build up.

Monday, 5th.—The portrait has just arrived safely. It is a delightful picture as well as a very good likeness. Thank you, dear Caroline, thank you, thank you! The place for which I intended it will prove, I fear, too high for my sight, which has so far decayed that objects at a distance are indistinct, though for reading and writing it serves as well as ever. I fear another situation must be looked for. I meant it to have crowned one of the bookcases, as Kirke White does.

God bless you, dear friend. Let me hear of you, not that I may think the less, but the less anxiously.

ROBERT SOUTHEY.

CLVII.

TO CAROLINE BOWLES.

KESWICK, *August* 26*th*, 1833.

You may suppose how earnestly I have been engaged, and how unmercifully interrupted, to have let your last letter remain till now unanswered, when I would fain have replied to it instantly. Take the history of Saturday last as a sample. Mr. Phillips, a Melksham clothier and his wife, introduced by my aunt Hill's relations, the Awdrys, breakfasted here; good-natured, pleasant, sensible people, though the husband is a little be-whigged. When they were gone I sat down to make up my despatches with some proof-sheets for the post. Before this could be completed I was called down to Mr. J. Thornton (Reginald Heber's fellow-traveller), his son and two of his daughters. He opened upon me such a torrent of words that in the course of at least an hour and half's visit, during which it ceased only for half-minutes, I wished myself repeatedly in the bed of Lodore or under Scale Force for comparative repose. Toward the end of this awful visitation in came our curate, Mr. Whiteside, just returned from Ireland with his brother-in-law, full of remembrances and messages to me, none of which he could deliver while the Thornton cataract was in force. Of course he outstayed this dreadful linguist, that he might say his say, which I was willing enough to hear, though more willing at last to get up to my unfinished packet. Well, I had got to the inclosure when the bell rang again, and I am introduced to Mr. and Mrs. Mocatta by a note from Henry Coleridge; he, the son of a rich English Jew, but himself withheld from becoming openly a member of the Church of England by due respect to the invincible feelings of an aged father; she, the daughter of English parents but born at Santa Cruz. Caraccas is their home, and they have both travelled much in North America. As they were to depart the next morning, we had them that evening to tea. A very agreeable evening it was; but except in making up my covers for the proof-sheets, and writing a note with them to Dr. Lardner, not a line could I write that day, and the last callers deprived me of my usual walk.

You told me truly when you said that Adam Clarke's *Life* would delight me. It reached me last week, and very long it is since I have read so delightful a book. Charles Fox who is spoken of there is the person mentioned in *Espriella*, who when his house was on fire, and it was evident that nothing could be saved, retired to a convenient distance, and made a drawing of the scene. I knew him well, and met Adam Clarke at his house. I have profiles of him, his wife, and the parrot which used to take its place upon the tea board, make free with the sugar, and call him father. I mentioned this in a letter to good old Adam, and his son lately applied to me for copies of the profiles, which of course I had great pleasure in sending him.

Could anything be so brutal as that poor man's treatment at Kingswood school? The Simpson, husband to the she-devil who pickled poor Adam, I remember well, having heard him preach in my early boyhood. There is a portrait of Adam Clarke in one of the early volumes of the "Arminian Magazine," looking very much as he must have looked when he was in pickle, and with some such words as "A Babe of Grace" under it. Some thirty years later another portrait appeared in the "Methodist Magazine" (which is a continuation of the Arminian under a more *profitable* title), and there he looks like a respectable, and even dignified clergyman and scholar. I should like to get both these to insert in his *Life*.

Your picture could not be placed where I had intended; the position was too high. I have hoisted an oil portrait of myself there, and placed you in the vacancy thus made, which is in the parlour opposite my place at tea, and in the precious hour after supper when I have always one of my great old books, for a composing draught. Mufti's languish is most excellent. I would send my best compliments and respects to him, if he could understand the message.

Dear friend, God bless you.

ROBERT SOUTHEY.

CLVIII.

TO ROBERT SOUTHEY.

BUCKLAND, *September* 18*th*, 1833.

Dear friend, I possess so scanty a stock of that commodity in which you abound—patience, that it fretted me to read the history of your day as an epitome of what you are subjected to during the touring season. If time so precious were but spent on people who could appreciate the sacrifice and him who makes it, it would be something; but to think that half your gazers at least are animal machines on whom a donkey stuffed into the lion's skin would at any time pass for the lion himself—*that* makes me savage, and your patience provokes me into more spitefulness. What a dragon I should prove if I had to guard the entrance of your den! I have the reputation of being rather dangerous if disturbed in my own, by people who neither care for me, nor I for them.

I have had little time for reading of late, and have read little. *The Characteristics of Goethe* I have, however, looked over rather than read, with more interest than I should otherwise have felt, from what you had written me concerning the book. It is a strangely put together work: *mal cousu* the French would call it; some portions very interesting, and those relating to the Grand Duke and Duchess eminently so. My Swiss friend, Mrs. Dayrolles, has lived much at Weimar in the familiar society of that admirable woman the Grand Duchess Luise. She speaks of her with enthusiasm.

I knew you must delight in Adam Clarke. Poor dear Adam! his patience in pickle can only be equalled by yours with the tourists.

God's blessing be with you, dear friend.

CAROLINE A. BOWLES.

CLIX.

TO CAROLINE BOWLES.

KESWICK, *October 12th*, 1833.

I have seldom sate down to write to you with more satisfaction than at this time, having, after working at it most doggedly for the last nine days, sent off the conclusion of my second volume to Dionysius the cabinet-maker this morning.* When I tell you that for the last three days I have not written less than

* The second volume of the *Naval History;* Dionysius, *i.e.*, Dionysius Lardner, Editor of the *Cabinet Cyclopædia*.

nine of the printed pages per day, you will perceive that I must have been at it tooth and nail. The truth is that, owing to interruptions in the last three months which you can very well understand, and to the sinful propensity for "doing something else" (which you can also comprehend) in the three preceding ones, I was run hard, even to the very last day. My brother came here on Sunday the 29th, and remained till the Thursday following; of course my mornings were given to him, and most of my evenings also; but since his departure I laid aside letter-writing (except for one morning which letters of business demanded) and everything else, and stuck to this: though I did not omit my daily walk, nor give up my after-dinner sleep. Both these I deemed necessary. Dr. Bell's two hours were borrowed for the occasion. When the concluding sentence had been written this morning I danced about the room for joy; and you have here the first offering of my leisure. The volume itself you will receive from the Longmans as soon as it is published.

Last week I ascended Scawfell with my brother. Eight-and-twenty years ago we put off the ascent till a more convenient season, and we agreed now that it was not prudent to postpone it farther. So we went on wheels the nine miles to Seathwaite and were afterwards seven hours in going up and down. Cuthbert, Warter, and Errol Hill were of the party.

To-day brought me a letter from, apparently, a young American, who, because the *Colloquies* have won his heart, inclosed me an autograph letter of Washington's. Just as this American feels towards me, I always feel towards those of other ages by whose works or whose lives I have been interested; and often think what a pleasure it will be to see them face to face in another world, and claim acquaintance with them upon that score. Think of paying my dutiful respects to Laud and Cranmer, shaking hands with Spenser, and getting Sir Philip Sidney to present me to Queen Elizabeth! Think of seeing Wesley again, actually conversing with Sir Thomas More, and claiming connexion with Izaak Walton as a kinsman of Kenna his wife! There is an article in the Creed that warrants these expectations; and what a poor thing were life if it did not give us these inheritances from the past and this reversion for the future!

You will not be sorry to hear that I am treating with Moxon concerning a series of "Lives of the English Divines," to accompany a series of selections from their works, under some such title as "Christian Philosophy; exemplified in,"&c. My plan is not to insert whole sermons, but their pithiest parts, which many will read when thus presented to them, and which will induce some to drink their fill at the original sources. The Lives should be upon the scale of Johnson's "Lives of the Poets," and form a constituent and essential part of our literary history, and there should be an introduction containing a review of that part of theological literature relating to religious instruction, down to the time of Elizabeth, when the lives and selections would begin. If we come to an agreement (which is likely), this is a task upon which I shall enter with great good will.

Have you read *Zophiel?* probably not; or you would have mentioned it. It is not always perspicuous; though I do not know any poet whose diction is naturally so good as Mrs. Brooks's—*naturally*, I say, because it is not in her the effect of study, and of art. I have never seen a more passionate work, rarely one so imaginative and original. There is a song* in the last canto which in its kind is as good as Sappho's famous ode has been thought to be. You would like the poem better if you had seen the authoress; how gentle and how feminine she is, how sensible of any little kindness, and how full of feeling. I had no wish to see her, and was almost as much vexed as surprised when she let me know that she was in Keswick. I went to call upon her unwillingly; but my visit was an hour long, and during the few weeks that she continued here she won the liking of all this household in a very great degree.

And now, dear friend, God bless you. If you can tell me that you are at ease in body and in mind, it will be the best tidings

* " Day in melting purple dying," &c.

that I can hope to hear. As for public affairs, one revolutionary symptom follows another, and, looking to human causes, the only consolatory consideration is that as everything is likely to be overthrown without a struggle, so there is a possibility that when the mischief is done and the necessity of repairing all that can be repaired is felt, there may be as little resistance made to the work of restoration.—*Sunday* 13*th*.

Once more God bless you.

ROBERT SOUTHEY.

CLX.

TO ROBERT SOUTHEY.

BUCKLAND, *October* 21*st*, 1833.

Dear friend, if anything could have made *me* dance for joy it would have been the sight of your handwriting, for I had been sorely troubled by your long silence, though always endeavouring to reason myself into a belief of the true cause. But you know it is said of women that we reason more with our hearts than our heads, and the former organ is a bad casuist, and I (at my best of times not among the wisest of women) have of late years fallen into the bad and sinful habit of expecting evil. It was not my early nature to do so, but painful experience has engrafted it on natural weakness. This I must add, however, with vehement sincerity, that I would rather endure a week's anxiety than rob you of an hour's, nay half an hour's exercise; I do not say of five minutes; time enough *par parenthèse* to say "I am well," and fold up the missive. Will you behave better for the future? I mean to yourself and Providence, which has so far, thank God for it, kept you in health and safety, spite of your own endeavours to bring on some horrid seizure, or organic disease of the head (as poor Sir Walter did) by over-writing, over-tension of those precious faculties so dependent in this our imperfect state on the organs of sense.

But I am wasting my excellent logic all this while, and I suppose you do not pay more attention to Dr. Southey's arguments on the subject—for he must use such—than to mine. When I read of your "nine printed pages a-day" I shuddered; but here I hold your written resolution of reform, and moderation, and so on for the time to come. Keep it better than the Whigs have done their pledges or—I will call you a Whig, and if that does not touch you to the quick, nothing will.

How am I to get *Zophiel*? I have not seen it anywhere advertised, and it is probably published in America. But I shall try to get it. You spoke to me, I think when you were here, of this same Mrs. Brooks, and you have since named her in your letters. It will be a treat to see something really "imaginative and original and passionate," without being absurd or affected, blasphemous or disgusting. I begin to detest Annuals as well as albums. Such a flood of very pretty poetry have they let in upon us. Seldom do I now venture upon a page wherein I see the lines arranged in the suspicious form of metre. I am sick to death of the sweet Swans my sisters (all save one or two), and think to myself "I would rather be a kitten, and cry mew than one of those same ballad metre-mongers"; and yet—*moi aussi, j'ai vécu en Arcadie!* Think of my Monster very seriously requesting he might be permitted to affix my name at full length to whatever I sent him in future because—the Hon. Mrs. N. and Lady E. S. W., &c., &c., put theirs! Whereupon I made answer that if ever I saw my poor innocent name gibbetted in his Helicon bag of fashion, it would be the last autograph of mine found its way to Princes Street.

Yes, dear friend, but for memory and hope this would be a poor life truly. If you please, you shall introduce me to Sir Philip Sidney and his sister, "Pembroke's mother": as for Queen Elizabeth, to confess the truth, I should be as little ambitious of her acquaintance and patronage in another world (where the climate of her court may be too warm for comfort), as I should have been of a place in her household here. I would rather request of old Ascham to present me to his sweet, serious pupil Jane Gray.

The 23rd of this month will complete the year long before the close of which I thought to be an exile from this my home. Here, by God's blessing, I am still, and grateful, very grateful, for the temporary reprieve; but I cannot but consider the far more serious cause of anxiety* which has since been awarded me, as in some sort a punishment, and a just one, for the unwillingness with which I resigned myself to the sacrifice then required of me. Therefore, I do my best to be more cheerful now as well as equally submissive.

God bless you, dear friend.

CAROLINE A. BOWLES.

I was greatly concerned at reading in yesterday's paper that Mr. Wordsworth's sight is considered in danger. Tell me, if possible, the report is an exaggerated one.

CLXI.

TO CAROLINE BOWLES.

KESWICK, *November 3rd*, 1833.

I was fearful that the account of your amendment came in too remote and roundabout a way, willing as I was, and am, to believe what I hope. But I cannot bear to hear you accuse yourself of impatience—you of all persons whom I have ever known are least to be accused on that score. The feelings to which you allude can no more be imputed as a sin, than the sense of bodily suffering can be, because they belong essentially to our nature. Our Saviour himself prayed that the cup might pass away, and that prayer itself may have been partly intended for our consolation; may have been designed to convince us that what we call repining (repining such as yours!) that a natural, but subdued, weakness, that a resignation which though reluctant is resignation still, will not be deemed sinful. We never think so unworthily of our heavenly Father as when we limit His mercy or doubt of his indulgence.

* Anxiety caused by ill health.

Do not be apprehensive that I shall ever over-task myself. It was but for three or four days that I sate so closely at my work, and even on those days I never omitted my daily exercise; nor should I have been run so hard had it not been for some previous idleness, most part of which was employed in walking; and had not the publication been periodical, and so fixed to a day. I am in no danger of being over-wrought, though it is very likely that in a frame so highly sensitive as I know mine to be, the seat of sensation is the part which is most liable to give way. My occupations are too various for them ever to be injurious. The injury is where one subject takes possession either of head or heart: in the first case it strains and injures the faculties, in the latter it eats up the affections. Poor Scott employed himself always in one strain of invention, and that of a nature to excite him. But I have no doubt his embarrassments affected him much more than all his literary exertions.

I have agreed with Moxon, and in the way that you think best. Nothing will be published till I am ready to bring out the *Lives* each in its place; and the Introduction (which will cost most pains) first. The publication, therefore, cannot begin till this time twelvemonths at the soonest; probably not till the January after. Meantime, he will get forward with the portraits and vignette views of churches and parsonages; and by that time I shall be ready with the Introduction, and five or six lives. I begin immediately to look over my old stores, and select from them such notes as may be brought into use for this service; they are neither few in number nor unimportant in substance, and you may suppose what a satisfaction it is when materials patiently collected from time to time through a long course of years are turned to good account at last.

The account of Wordsworth's eyes was true; they have been saved for the present. But for many years he has been subject to frequent and severe inflammation of the lids, and when this extends to the eye the sight is seriously endangered; and there is always danger of new attacks, where an inflammatory habit has once been formed. Any emotion immediately affects the

U

diseased part; the excitement of conversation is sufficient for the evil: and by composing two sonnets during the last attack he had nearly brought on a relapse. This I hear from Hamilton (the author of "Men and Manners"), who breakfasted with me this morning (Monday).

Zophiel is printed in London, and you have only to write for it as you do for other books. You have received, I trust, ere this my second volume, of which the main merit is that I have done in it what nobody before ever thought worth doing—brought together the whole of our early naval history, and taken in no more of other transactions than were necessary for forming a connected and readable narrative. The time might have been better employed; and yet it was not a wearisome task.

God bless you, dear friend. I shall look anxiously to hear from you.

ROBERT SOUTHEY.

CLXII.

TO CAROLINE BOWLES.

KESWICK, *November 23rd*, 1833.

At present I am very busy in reviewing. The *Corn Law Rhymes* supply the text, and a very good one it is for reading my old correspondent Ebenezer Elliott a wholesome lecture upon the ferocious radicalism to which he has given vent. This I shall do in a way which he will not expect, and which very possibly may have some effect upon him. I shall also, if possible, get a life of Samuel Hick the Methodist blacksmith ready for the same number. It must go hereafter with my lives of Oberlin and Neff, neither as comparison or contrast exactly, but as relating to the same subject. The said Sammy, whom his biographer has canonized as far as his power and authority extend, was born without the sense of shame; certainly the most impudent man one has ever heard of, who was not at the same time a thorough rogue or thorough villain. Sammy, in spite of his impudence, was a worthy man at heart, and in spite of his ignorance and his fanaticism was, I dare say, very useful in his sphere. The book would amuse you and provoke you at the same time. If you are disposed to send for it upon this character, its title is *The Village Blacksmith; or, Memoir of S. Hick*, by James Everett.

Henry Taylor arrived yesterday. The first thing which struck him was your picture, in which he remarked a likeness to me in the forehead and eyes, such as might have been remarked had we been brother and sister. He very much admired the picture, and I assure you Mufti's languishing look was not lost upon him.

I knew you would like my project with Moxon, and have good hope that if I live to execute it, and you to see the execution, you will be pleased with it. The Introduction will cost me much time in research, and I shall want more books for it than I know where to find or to look for; but by good fortune there are some in my possession which it would not be easy to meet with elsewhere, and which will supply me with much curious matter. I have received one dissuasive letter, founded upon a doubt whether I am sufficiently versed in theology or have read enough in this line to undertake such a task, and also upon a fear that I may draw upon myself acrimonious censure if I should be found wanting in these points. But if the old friend* who writes thus had seen what my reading has been and continually is, or had he indeed called to mind the indication which some of my writings bear of it, he would not have entertained any such apprehensions. The more I contemplate the undertaking the better I like it, and feel more and more hopeful that in pursuing it I may be doing good both to myself and others.

God bless you, dear friend, and restore and support you. Bless you I know He will.

ROBERT SOUTHEY.

* This was Charles Wynn—he mentioned the subject to me. (*Note by Mr. Warter.*)

CLXIII.
TO ROBERT SOUTHEY.

BUCKLAND, *December 14th*, 1833.

Your letters, dear friend, do me more good than all my physicians, my other physicians, prescribe for me; they talk of hope, but your letters breathe hope, hope and encouragement even as to the things of this world, so connected with higher hopes and more blessed assurances, that while the effect of such mental communion with you lasts I am almost all I ought to be—not cast down by temporal suffering, and resting in perfect peace on the promises that cannot fail. But the bow-string will flag, as you well can understand, though the bow is not broken. Nothing seems to diminish my strength as to the power of walking, &c. This stubborn little frame of mine takes a great deal of pulling to pieces after all, like some scrubby skeleton of a tree or crazy old cottage that weathers out many a blast when one would think the first would lay it low. Perhaps we shall publish our book some day—what do you say to that?—if I outlive all your task-work. Never, never one line of verse from you now; I am obliged to go back perpetually to the sixteen volumes you have given me, to keep alive the assurance that you are a Poet.

I am charmed with Mr. Taylor's favourable opinion of my picture, because I now feel better satisfied than I did, that the indifferent drawing is not a disfiguring blot on your walls. I should like to believe there was the same likeness between the original and yourself that has struck him in the picture, and it is singular enough that two persons, John Kingston and (I think) Lady Malet made a similar observation to me once respecting the upper part of our two faces.

All the Whigs of my acquaintance and half the Tories are high in praise of Bulwer's late publication, *England and the English*. He is shrewd and clever, and speaks civilly of you, and writes some truths—biting ones; but for all that I should call his book a flashy, trashy work, full of fallacies, and on the whole insidious and mischievous.

We are approaching a new year, dear friend. May it bring with it blessings to you and yours—blessings in God's own way, of His good choosing! Neither you nor I, were the choice left to us, would dare make it for ourselves. Farewell for this year. It will be three years this Christmas since we last saw each other face to face, but I take delight in the assurance that our friendship is not of that nature which depends on, or even needs, the refreshing of personal intercourse; the enjoyment of it, however, would be such happiness that, to say the truth, I am most resigned to the deprivation when not permitting myself to dwell upon it.

Once more farewell, dear friend, and God bless you.

CAROLINE A. BOWLES.

CLXIV.

TO ROBERT SOUTHEY.

BUCKLAND, *February 14th*, 1834.

Have I then really and truly a fair hope of seeing you here again, and before this year hastens to a close? For a lohg season all anticipation of earthly events has been to me so joyless, to say the least, that a gleam of sunshine dazzles me, and I cannot look steadily forward; but it shines through the closed lids; and I am glad,˙ though I dare not be sanguine, for alas! it is now possible I might have to say "Do not come." I should do so for your sake, if I was suffering so much as I have suffered, for you read my silence right. I should have been eager to tell you I was better, and I can now gratefully say that I am so.

At last I obtained *Zophiel*. Do you ask me how I like it? I will tell you how I read it. The box of books was dropped by the evening coach, just as I was seating myself to write letters of some consequence; but I looked over the books, caught up *Zophiel*, and opened the volume just to glance over it, or at it rather, before I began my letter. Neither letter, nor business, nor time, nor any sublunary thing did I think of again that evening, till startled by the cramp from the uneasy posture in which I had begun reading, and puzzled by the half-darkness in which I was left by the red globular flame of the unsnuffed candles; and no letters were written that evening. Is not that evidence of the strongest of—what?—of my liking the poem? No; but of the extraordinary powers evinced in it, of its originality, of its exuberant fancy, its richness of diction, unperspicuous as it is. What a sensation such a poem as this would have made some twenty years ago, and now nobody has heard of it; no notice is taken of it. And this surprises me even in this cold, calculating age; because, though poetry no longer touches hearts, passion excites the organs that are called hearts by courtesy, and Byron and Moore have their full share of worshippers, neither of whom, I should say, have written anything so impassioned as *Zophiel*, or, I could almost add, more licentious. My dear friend, you told me of the lady when you were last here, and wrote of her and her poems from Keswick afterwards, and you then said it was to be left in your hands for publication, and you might be placed in a situation of "delicate embarrassment," by having to hint to the authoress the necessity of "cooling it in some parts." Now, if you have effected this refrigerating process, for Heaven's sake at what degree of temperature did it stand previously? How could a woman, and such a one as you describe, select such a subject (for her work is a paraphrase of the Book of Tobit), and how could she treat it as she has done with such unwomanly license? You say I should like the poem—her poem—the better if I had seen her. If I knew and loved her I should be grieved she had written it, splendid as it is. You do not think me prudish I am sure; but what woman, pure-minded as woman should be, could read that poem aloud with an unembarrassed voice? And can it become a woman to write anything that may not be brought fearlessly to this test?

God bless you, dear friend.

CAROLINE A. BOWLES.

CLXV.

TO CAROLINE BOWLES.

Your opinion of *Zophiel* is what I expected, and it accords altogether with my own. But the licentiousness is in the subject, and is, as it were, so rarefied and sublimed (not to say spiritualised) by the imaginative manner in which the whole story is treated, that it is quite harmless. I have seen as little of *Don Juan* as you have done. Byron and Moore and such men address themselves directly to the vicious part of human nature. This is never done in *Zophiel*.

Yet I dare say the poem had its origin in the circumstances of the authoress's life. So much was she possessed with this poem while composing it, that she is as well persuaded of the truth of the machinery as a Roman Catholic is when he introduces saints and devils into an epic poem.

March 9th.—I have been too closely employed to go on with this since the day that your letter, to which it replies, arrived. Meantime I have been round the world with Sir Francis Drake, and have put the last hand on the proofs to a wofully long and laborious paper upon the Corn Laws. It has cost me more time than I like to bestow upon such subjects, but not more than it will have been worth, if, as Lockhart expects, it should produce some effect. As for the Admirals, I am so much out of my element at sea, that I should wish them at the bottom of it, if I were not better paid for attending upon them than for anything else.

You may imagine how I shall miss Cuthbert. The course of life, indeed, is tending to make me more wholly intent upon my own pursuits than in any former part of my life. I shall have no companion in my walks when he is gone, and this will be a great loss, as it will withhold me from extending them to any distance such as ten or twelve miles. But you must know that our establishment (if you have not already been informed of so great an event) has been increased by a present from

Sir Thomas Ackland of an Exmoor pony, Pixey by name. The said Pixey has hitherto been intended only for riding, and has accordingly been provided with two saddles, male and female, and last summer Cuthbert was in his glory, when thus mounted, on a pony which he could look upon as his own. Next week Pixey is to come home, having been turned out all the winter; he is then to be tried in harness, and if we can get him to draw (which, as he is quite young, there seems no cause to doubt), then a little open carriage is to be procured, and Bertha undertakes to drive it. In this way I hope to get the girls, and sometimes their mother, out for a morning's length, and to accompany them as an old squire, on foot, condescending sometimes to take a seat.

A bookseller's parcel is on the way to me, containing naval stores. But it contains also a packet of letters from Mr. Newton, Cowper's friend, to Mr. Thornton, of which you shall hear more when I have seen their contents. Henry Taylor has procured them for me, through Stephen (Wilberforce's nephew), one of the best men living, in the best sense of the words. Through that same channel I have been made acquainted with something regarding Cowper much more remarkable than anything that is publicly known concerning him, or indeed than could possibly be imagined. One reason why I can only raise your curiosity without putting you at once in possession of the truth is, that I know not yet whether it can be told. All I can say is, that it renders him far more an object of extraordinary compassion than he already appears to be.

I shall begin upon his life as soon as the third volume of the Admirals is off my hands, which I trust it will be in the course of five weeks.

God bless you, dear friend. It is time for my walk, and I shall be disappointed if my parcel does not arrive before my return.

R. Southey.

March 13*th*.

CXLVI.

TO ROBERT SOUTHEY.

BUCKLAND, *March 27th*, 1834.

From the 27th of January to the 16th of March and not a word from Keswick! and my mind full of uneasy conjectures, and still I held back the hand which was every morning stretched out (when the post brought no letter) to invade your peace. But for that noble exercise of patience and self-restraint you are no ways indebted to *me*, dear friend, but to one far my superior in sense and patience, though my junior by many years—my good and dear cousin Laura Burrard, who, with her equally dear sister Frances, has been staying some weeks with me. "No letter again! I will write to-day," said I many a morning of disappointed expectation; "I am sure something is the matter." "No, no," would Laura reply, answering my self-addressed determination, "No, no! wait till to-morrow; think how much Mr. Southey has to do and you will regret having written, if you find his silence was occasioned by press of business." So I was tractable at least, and waited, and found, as I had often done before, that my gentle Laura's judgment was better than that of her old cousin. This evil habit of impatience has come upon me of late years; in some sort it is perhaps more deserving of compassion than reproof, for bitter experience of the insecurity of all earthly good has impressed me with a perpetual dread of impending evil; a most pitiable infirmity, too surely proving the "little faith" which cannot cast out fear.

I have been both pleased and pained lately at receiving a book and a letter from a person whom I believed to have dropt (and judiciously) all epistolary communications with me—Mary Howitt, the only one of all the literary persons of that class who have honoured me with their notice, to whom I ever replied willingly, with a feeling of frank kindliness and confidence. There was a simplicity and kindness in her style that thawed all the ice of my ungraciousness in a moment, and I really "took to her," as we say in Hampshire, and in a less degree to him also, for he too was my correspondent, and felt I should be glad to become personally acquainted with them. You gave the first shock to my confidence in the man by relating to me his insulting speech to Miss Wordsworth about clergymen, and when I read in some periodical extracts from his atrocious book, *The History of Priestcraft*, I shrank with horror at the thought of being the correspondent of the writer or his wife. That was, however, a first impulse and an unjust feeling; she was not in fairness to be considered responsible for her husband's violence, however she might partake of his opinions. But, all things considered, I thought and wished that she might not write to me again, and though I often thought of her, and regretted the loss of her correspondence, I was content that it should be so, and the more so when I saw her book announced, "The Seven Temptations of Man," and read a severe censure of the poem and its principles. But one day arrived the very book, with a letter from the authoress: such a charming, gentle, almost deprecating letter, giving me fully to understand that she was aware of what my sentiments towards her husband must be—towards them both perhaps; for which reason she had long forborne writing. She spoke of expecting the Wordsworths to stay with them on their way to London, and expressed her hope and belief that I as well as the Wordsworths might still meet her and her husband on that neutral ground free only to subjects unconnected with politics and party spirit. I could not turn coldly from advances made in so kind a spirit, but I replied in a manner that will not please *him* I suspect, for I should have accounted it heresy not to avow the horror I had conceived of his principles, religious and political. He threatened me with a visit too this year; the more reason why I should let him know my whole mind. But as for her book, it has been cruelly, unjustly censured. I do not like the plan; I do not like the style of writing (for a woman) requisite to illustrate it, nor do I approve of inserting in a work of this nature verses verbatim from the New Testament; but with these exceptions I do delight in great part of the poem or poems. I am curious to know what you think of it. The first, "The Poor Scholar," is charming, though many will call it an imitation of Goethe.

You have set my curiosity all on tenter-hooks about Cowper, but it is a painful curiosity. I cannot bear to think of him otherwise than as an object of respect and love joined to the tenderest pity. You never told me you were about to write his life, the very work I should have wished to be undertaken by you.

I too have had a pony sent me, by Mr. Levett, but the kind giver was deceived in him. I hope Pixie is more tractable than Oberon, my coal-black steed, who, for mischief, is a very fiend of a fay. The Levetts will be at Worthing this summer, and then I hope to become acquainted with Mr. and Mrs. Warter.

God bless you, dear friend.

CAROLINE A. BOWLES.

CLXVII.

TO CAROLINE BOWLES.

[KESWICK, *April*, 1834.]

Your good cousins were very kind in accounting for my sin of omission, for none but they who are in the house with me, and see how every hour brings its business with it, and how many a one its interruption also, can tell how little time remains at my own free and willing disposal. Often, very often, am I doing what poor Elmsley used to call "something else," something which is not exactly the thing on which I ought just then to be employed, but for which, for some reason or other, I am better inclined; but from six in the morning till eleven at night there is no interval of disoccupation, except it be when I am walking, or enjoying that sleep after dinner which is the soundest and most refreshing of my slumbers.

I thought I had told you of Baldwin and Cradock's proposal that I should edit a complete edition of Cowper in monthly volumes, and write his Life; and that I had consented for the love of Cowper. Some of Mr. Newton's correspondence with Mr. Thornton is in my hands at present, and I am to have the rest. In these letters the mystery is revealed, and my mind is made up, after consulting with Wordsworth, that if it ever be made public, it shall not be by me. It had better be discovered hereafter by some hunter after extraordinary facts, than embodied in the Life of so truly amiable and interesting a poet; for if it were there it would mingle distressingly with all one's thoughts and feelings concerning him. Moreover, positive as the testimony is, there is against it so strong an improbability, that I know not which is the weightier. At this moment, while writing thus mysteriously, it occurs to me that the most probable solution is to suppose it a mere conception of madness, not the real and primary cause of his insanity, but a hypochondriacal and imaginary effect of it.

Mary Howitt sent me her *Temptations* through Dora Wordsworth, with a message requesting me to divest myself of all prejudices, religious or political, in reading the book, and to give it a good word if I could; evidently implying a wish that I would review it. I cannot review it, and have not found time as yet to read it; inclination, in truth, having been wanting when I had so little time for reading books which are to instruct me. She complains to Dora of having lost one friend in consequence of political feelings. It will be long indeed before the animosities which have now been so fiercely rekindled will subside. I am glad that she has written to you. As for her husband, he is in the very gall of bitterness, and the savour will abide upon him as long as he lives.

All that I wrote upon Ebenezer Elliott, as an introduction to the Corn Law paper, has been cut off for the sake of shortening it. Whether it will be printed as a separate paper I know not; if it be, I must put a conclusion to it after extending it some little.

April 8th.—Yesterday being a beautiful day, I went up

Cawsey Pike, being my first mountain walk this year. Davies went with me and heartily enjoyed the ascent. Cuthbert was of the party, but rode to the foot of the hill for Pixey's sake. We have ordered a pony-carriage; it is to be a light two-wheeled affair of the plainest kind, to carry two persons; Bertha can drive. This will draw them in fine weather, whether they like it or not, to exercise the pony, and I count upon it as one means of improving my wife's health, and, therewith, her spirits.

The conclusion of the Corn Law paper, that is, all that purports to have been written after the debate in the House of Commons, is not mine : you would probably discover this, for it bears marks of a parliamentary tactician, and indeed I suppose it to be Croker's, wholly or in part, for he has often a hand there when the paper comes from another person. Lord Mahon was so ill pleased with the temper of some interpolations introduced into a paper of his that, to justify himself, he printed the paper as he had written it.

Dear friend, God bless you.

ROBERT SOUTHEY.

CLXVIII.

TO ROBERT SOUTHEY.

BUCKLAND, *May 3rd*, 1834—

And as lovely a May day as ever Poet sung—the earth teeming with beauty and fruitfulness; the air balmy and fragrant with the breath of honeysuckles—at least about my windows, where they are in luxuriant blossom; two nightingales trying to outsing each other in the garden beside the house; the cuckoo's voice uttering its first call (that I have heard this year); the pigeons feeding round me as I sit at the open window; not a cloud in the sky, but a few small fleeces that look like wafted blossoms from below.

On the subject of Sunday schools, and indeed national schools, to the extent they have been carried of late years, I have always felt persuaded, though with misgivings of my own judgment, that they were bad substitutes for home teaching, for parental instruction; and that the technical familiarity with Scripture (if I so express myself) acquired by poor children in the routine of school teaching ill supplies the place of that homely instruction which infuses practical piety rather than abstract ideas, and strengthens the holy ties of natural affection while inculcating our blessed faith in that simple form which is its glory, knowledge sufficient to salvation. But thinking thus as I do, and have always done, I see that the day is gone past when every poor cottage might have been, as was once the case in Scotland, a temple, where the "priest-like father read the sacred page" to the assembled family. Throughout all classes of the lower orders there is a frightful change in the domestic relations, not only in manufacturing but in agricultural districts; it manifests itself to me in almost every cottage I enter by tokens that make the heart sick : little ones, lisping infants, to be "got out of the way" (of the mother's way!) to Infant and other schools—and then the mother goes out charing, and the husband gets his meal at the beershop. The children get prizes for quick answers and clever distinctions between Melchizedek and Methusalem, while neither girl nor boy learns a single household duty—least of all the first and greatest, filial affection and respect; and the moment the young brood can fly, they do so, without a lingering look of love, or the old birds beat them off if they are slow at taking wing. What is to be the end of all this? This moral deterioration of the lower orders is the terrific feature of the times; and lo! the Trades Unions—the march of mind, the diffusion of knowledge (such knowledge) is powerfully illustrated there.

Your decision about the mystery connected with Cowper is just what I supposed it would be, if the circumstances made known to you were such as could not be made public without casting a shadow over the beautiful and lovable character of that "stricken deer," for such he surely was; and if there is anything criminating in the fact you are possessed of, I should feel as sure almost as of Cowper's existence, that it is to be laid to the score of insanity. One thing you may tell me : is Newton the relator of that fact? If he is, what dependence can be placed on the authority of the author of such autobiography as his, full of insane and disgusting fanaticism?

Pray tell me, when you have read it, how you like Mary Howitt's book. I hope you will like much of it. I fear I may be the friend the loss of whom she spoke of to Miss Wordsworth. I could not disguise or soften my opinion of her husband's sayings and doings when I replied to her letter—her charming deprecating letter. My heart smote me a little for the savage return I made to it; but my great reason for speaking very plain was, that she spoke of her husband's intention to visit me in the autumn. Shall I ask him to meet you?

I ride my pony in spite of his tricks. He, King Oberon, sends greeting to Pixie, one of his vassals of a certie. I wish the king was as well-behaved.

God bless you, dear friend.

CAROLINE A. BOWLES.

CLXIX.

TO CAROLINE BOWLES.

KESWICK, *May* 21*st*, 1834.

Summer is now bringing with it its train of interruptions. Bertha and Kate look to them with pleasure, and I expect them with my wonted patience, but their mother is in so miserable a state of spirits, that whether she sees some of the persons who may come, or keeps away from them all, I know not how to advise, because I know not which would have the most injurious effect. I am almost hopeless of any relief from medicines, because the hope which should assist in producing it is wanting.

However, Dr. Kidd of Oxford, my old schoolfellow, is coming early in July; and perhaps she may be induced to place some faith in him.

I shall probably take Kate into Sussex. Edith very much wishes to have her, being very much alone. My daughters have little chance of ever finding another home so cheerful as their father's *has been*. If one could choose one's lot, it would be to have the morning cloudy and the evening fine, that is, supposing we were sure of the whole day.

May 28*th*, 1834.—Mr. Swain is with me for a week—a Manchester poet who has made his way into daylight chiefly by the kind notice of James White, and the means of the *Literary Gazette*. You would like his poems, and you would like him. After many difficulties and misfortunes his prospects are now fair, and he wants nothing to render him as happy as he deserves to be, except, alas! a stronger constitution. But that received a shock some few years ago, and his countenance (a very fine one) has a dark and unhealthy hue, which shows that there is something amiss within. Just now, however, he is in a state of great enjoyment. Cats' Eden is a Paradise to him, which well it may be to one who lives at Manchester and never was at the Lakes before, nor ever before set foot upon a mountain. We soon made him feel that there was no one to be afraid of here; and his visit will not only furnish him with a stock of recollections on which he will love to dwell, but will be of some use to him in his own circle, by showing that he is thought something of beyond it.

Yesterday I went up Skiddaw with him and Davies, to the great delight of both. But Swain would hardly have accomplished the ascent if I had not administered three table spoonfuls of whiskey and water, as often as required. He is a very temperate man, and therefore felt the whole benefit of such a medicine, and to-day he is all the better, as well as the happier, for having performed so great a feat. It was a charming day, with air enough and not too much, and nothing could be more delightful than to be on the summit. I was not in the slightest degree fatigued : you may conclude therefore that I am in good condition at present; though the summer here for the last week or ten days threatened me with symptoms of my old catarrh.

Swain made very particular inquiries concerning my "dear friend, and sister poetess," for whose writings he has a true feeling.

Alas, I, too, am against the grain moving in political affairs! I have two petitions about the Universities, and the Dissenters on the circuit for subscriptions, and my assistance has just been asked for a third respecting the Poor Bill. Moreover, I suspect that a fourth is brooding against the beer-shops, in which also I shall be expected to become act and part. So you see that if the business of the nation should not go on as it ought to do, it will be no fault of the inhabitants of the town of Keswick and parish of Crosthwaite!

Dear friend, God bless you.

ROBERT SOUTHEY.

CLXX.

TO ROBERT SOUTHEY.

BUCKLAND, *July* 23rd, 1834.

Since I wrote to you I have made a voyage! a sea voyage! Not quite to either India, nor even across the Channel, but still a sea voyage in our Solent, to visit my cousin Tom Roche on board his ship the Victory, now Sir Thomas Williams's flag-ship at Portsmouth. I spent three hours on board, part of them you may be sure full of thoughtful interest, having your book all the while in my head and heart; most of all when I stood on that little spot, now distinguished by a brass plate, where Nelson fell, and afterwards in the small cabin partitioned off from the cockpit, where he breathed his last.

I have been holding silent converse lately with another friend of yours, that unhappy man Sir Egerton Brydges. Poesy never had a warmer, a more earnest and sincere votary;

and if I may judge from some of the sonnets in his Autobiography, he deserves to be classed in no mean rank of poets. What an indefatigable spirit! What varied powers and aims, and all how comparatively misapplied and ill-directed, or at least frittered away under the influences of an unhappy temper, and an ill-regulated mind, wanting the control and stay of religious principle. But considerate gentleness and kindness, such as he has met with from you, might have done much with the irritable and galled spirit; and I can well suppose how little sympathy and allowance he met with from the family and neighbours, to whom truly his pride and eccentricities must have made him anythng but an agreeable companion and acquaintance. Very beautifully he sometimes writes. Some parts of his *Imaginative Biography* put me in mind of Landor.

The Howitts will not take affront from me. She has sent me another charming little book she has just published for children, and he writes me a letter such as one can hardly fancy from the pen of the fierce Nottingham Demagogue. Shall I invite friend William to meet you here? He is galled, I see, at having his "offences," as he expresses it, "visited on his innocent wife."

I have been lately in company with Charlotte Smith's sister "The Peacock at Home," commonly called Mrs. Dorset. Retaining all her faculties—and shrewd ones they are—with the exception of hearing in full perfection at the age of eighty-four. She draws very beautifully; and her enthusiasm for the art is so unabated, that while staying in this neighbourhood with her niece Charlotte Smith she got a young friend of mine to give her some lessons in a new style of body-colour, and actually hurried off home (so her niece told me), that she might set to and practise her new acquirement without let or hindrance. She spoke with great admiration of some *Poems* of Hartley Coleridge published last year. What do you say of them?

I have made up all my differences with Oberon; and if not so perfect as Pixie, he will serve my turn as well I hope as Pixie does yours. My other pony, on which the servant used to follow to take care of me, fell sick; so being thrown on my own valour and made desperate, I got the better of my refractory steed and my own fears, and now ride all over the country, "sans peur et sans reproche" I hope, though such lady errantry rather outsteps the bounds of decorum; for these matters I choose to class myself with the privileged "better sort."

I like your project for next summer, for your own sake and Mr. Taylor's. I do not quite like Lockhart's review of *Philip Van Artevelde*. A rare game of puss in the corner the Cabinet have been playing! Lord Althorpe has, as the French say, "covered himself with glory." Beckford's book greatly offends me in all that relates to Holland and Germany, often offends me even in Italy, but for the most part delights me in Portugal and Spain. The vile, sneering, morbid tone that more or less pervades the first volume is detestable to me.

God bless you, dear friend.

CAROLINE A. BOWLES.

CLXXI.

TO CAROLINE BOWLES.

KESWICK, *August* 20*th*, 1834.

I returned yesterday from Lowther, whither I was invited to meet Rogers, now (in all human probability) on his last visit to this country. It may, almost as probably, be my last visit to that castle. Lord Lonsdale is seventy-six years of age; healthy and active as he is, his life hangs as by a thread; the first influenza that affects him may be expected to prove fatal, and after his death Lowther is not likely to be what it now is. His heir is not fond of the place, and it is supposed that he will live there as little as he can.

The Dowager Duchess of Richmond was there—a person who will be remembered in history for the ball that she gave at Brussels, from whence so many officers set out for the field in which they fell.

I walked home, starting at half-past six. The distance by the shortest line, which I succeeded in finding by paths some of which are seldom trodden, is nineteen miles; and when you hear that I was not fatigued, you will conclude that I am in good bodily health.

The time of our departure for the south cannot be fixed till we know whether Mr. and Mrs. Rickman come here to join their daughters and take them home. With all my dislike to moving, when it is once determined that the move must be made, I wish to be as soon as possible in motion, especially when so long a journey lies before me that it must carry me far into the winter. Most likely I shall take Kate with me as far as London, and send her from thence by the Worthing coach to her sisters. This seems to be settled, as far as I can see, but her mother is in miserable health and more miserable spirits; the disease in fact being there; and this evil is sure to be aggravated by parting with three at once, and two of them for a long time. Cuthbert's indeed will be a serious departure: this home will never again be his home except during vacation. At his age these things are not seen and understood and felt as they are at mine, and well it is that they are not—that the business and evils of life open upon us gradually.

You ask if I should like to see William Howitt. There is one reason why I should not, and that is that very possibly I may have occasion to answer his attack upon the Church; and as in that case I should most certainly deal with him as he deserves upon that score, it is much better that there should be no personal acquaintance between us. His wife, I am very sure, I should like; and very probably there is much in him that is to be liked also; but it is as an author that he is likely to come in my way, and only as an author do I wish to know him. There will then be nothing to withhold me from expressing myself fully and severely.

Henry Taylor's play has been remarkably successful. Rogers tells me they are reprinting it in America, and translating it (which was to be expected) at Brussels, but into French instead of Dutch. If Bilderdijk and his wife had been living he would, I think, have not wanted a competent Dutch translator. They knew him and liked him.

I have not seen Beckford's book, but should expect it to be as you describe it. No talents can compensate for that want of moral feeling which is likely to appear in anything he may write. His house near Cintra was only not the most beautiful place I ever saw, because there was one within two or three miles which was in some respects better. His was called Monserrat, because of the supposed resemblance between the mountains of Cintra and the Catalan mountain. The finer situation you may have heard your uncle speak of by the name of Penha Verde, the seat of the old Portuguese hero Don Joam de Castro. If I could make any spot in the world my own by a wish, it would be that, provided Portugal by the same wish could be made as peaceful as it was four-and-thirty years ago.

You have received, I hope, my third volume—of which all I have to say is, that the first Life in it would more properly have appeared in the fourth. How it came to be thus misplaced is not worth explaining. As soon as that was finished, I wrote a paper upon Dr. Watts—prefatory to a volume of his poems in the "Sacred Classics." In this I have done what his other biographers have left undone—looked into his opinions. And if I had had about as much space again allowed me, and if, moreover, it had not been necessary to abstain from any remarks which would have offended the dissenters, I could have made a much better and more useful essay. Now I go to the Life of Cowper as my chief occupation, creeping on at intervals with the Admirals. When I shall write anything for the *Quarterly Review* —or, if ever again—is altogether doubtful; meantime I have enough to do.

God bless you, dear friend.

ROBERT SOUTHEY.

CLXXII.

TO ROBERT SOUTHEY.

BUCKLAND, *September* 16*th*, 1834.

Already the periodical press is teeming with sayings and doings and letters of poor Coleridge; and I saw a sort of advertisement purporting "that the afflicted widow of a lately deceased poet earnestly requested all persons having letters or papers of his to place them in her hands," &c. This appeared within a fortnight of Coleridge's death. Was the nameless advertiser his widow?

I wish, as you yourself desire it, that you may be at liberty to set off this month on your southern pilgrimage; but even more heartily do I wish you could commence it under more cheerful auspices than are to be expected from what you tell me of Mrs. Southey's dejection of mind. Your last account disappointed me, a former letter having made cheerful report of her amendment. It is a heavy infliction to the poor sufferer, and those who witness a misery they cannot alleviate. "God help you" is all I can say on such a subject.

I anticipate your promised visit with less of gladness than on any former occasion, because I am sensible that more than one cause will sadden you on leaving home; but then, as you draw near Edith, your heart must be gladdened, and I dwell on that thought with more than pleasure.

I am in sorrowful, really sorrowful, expectation of hearing very shortly of poor Blackwood's death. My poor Monster! Always a kind Monster to me he has been, and must have had (though how acquired I can hardly tell) some regard for me; for I received last week a very affecting letter from his son, informing me of his father's almost hopeless state, after having languished on a bed of sickness and pain since March last, in the course of which melancholy interval he had often spoken of me; and the poor son added from himself that a letter from me would, he knew, afford great gratification to his father. You may guess how promptly I wrote, and with what feelings; but never, I think, a letter that cost me such thought and pain in the framing, for I was cautioned not to let him suspect his son's communication to me, for fear of awakening him to a sense of his imminent danger, which, his surgeons said, was to be carefully avoided.

My Monster was worth ten of yours, autocrat of fashion as he has been in his line. What trashy mischief the press now teems with! and to what depths of degeneracy will that public taste decline which admits and admires Bulwer, and such as Bulwer, as dictators in taste, literature, politics, and morals?

Lord Brougham should espouse Miss Martineau *à la main gauche*, though Lord Althorp, and the Bishop of London, and other champions and enactors of the Poor Law Bill might dispute the honour of her hand with him.

I am writing under the stupefying influence of a blinding cold—an excellent excuse for a stupid letter.

God bless you, dear friend.

CAROLINE A. BOWLES.

CLXXIII.

TO ROBERT SOUTHEY.

BUCKLAND, *Sunday Evening, October* 29*th*, 1834.

I am so glad to hear you do not part with Cuthbert this winter, for all your sakes, and he will be no loser by the delay. He will learn his first great lesson in human sorrow and human sympathy in the sanctuary of his home, where it will sink into his young heart with no rude or unsalutary pressure, where he will have the example of your faith and patience before him—a living lesson, better worth than Divines could teach, and the best stimulus to industry and exertion in the desire of proving his filial affection at a time when that of your children must be your chief earthly comfort. Thank God! precious as is that stay, it is not your only, or your chief, support.

Nothing can be more striking than the passage you transcribe, written on the very brink of your appointed trial.* Dear friend, God sees fit to prove you, even more sharply than the keenest and closest self-scrutiny could have effected; but He will bring you out of this ordeal also, as He did before, when your lovely and beloved were taken from you. Often have I so questioned with my own heart as to the nature of its resignation, and of late years I have humbly ventured to rest upon a very simple conclusion, that however imperfect my submission may and must be, it is still such resignation as will be accepted for Christ's sake, because I feel, and am sure, not only that God chasteneth me in mercy, but that I love Him the better for His fatherly correction. You know I am unskilled in any but the heart's logic, and that is often fallible. I hope not in my case in this matter. How much I should like to see your letter to Mrs. Hughes; but as you had forgotten it, I fear you have no copy.

I had something to tell you, in reserve for our meeting too; that I had heard lately of a very interesting miniature picture of Cowper, done when he was a child, about the age he describes in his affecting poem to his mother's picture. I had asked for and obtained the address of the person (in Ireland) who possesses this picture, thinking it might be desirable to procure an engraving from it for your projected Life. There is also a letter of Newton's to Hannah More (in Roberts's lately published work) that might be worth referring to. He pressed too hard, in his injudicious zeal, on poor Cowper's sick and tender spirit.

God bless you, comfort you, keep you now and ever, dear friend.

CAROLINE BOWLES.

---

* A passage on resignation in "The Doctor," written just before the true state of Mrs. Southey's mind declared itself.

CLXXIV.

TO CAROLINE BOWLES.

KESWICK, *November 2nd*, 1834.

Last night was the first good night's rest which I have had for many weeks; I did not awake till the clock struck seven; and to-day my nervous feeling has given way to a drowsy one, as if nature were taking its own course for bringing me into my usual state of health.

Thank you for your intimation concerning Cowper's portrait. I shall be very glad if it can be obtained. "Hannah More's Life" I will look for in due time. Newton unquestionably did some injury to Cowper by over-working him in religious exercises. All his (Newton's) letters to Mr. Thornton are now in my possession; the far greater part of their contents is perfectly worthless—that sort of religious writing which disgusts one as much with the *profession* of piety as a water-gruel diet would disgust one with food. Yet Newton was a man of extraordinary powers of mind, of ardent feeling, and perfect sincerity and great strength of heart. Thornton, who was his benefactor, required such letters from him once a fortnight, and poor Newton seems to have sat down to them as a schoolboy to his theme, or a sorry spin-text to his sermon at the latter end of the week. They cease upon his removal from Olney to London. Though they do not contain much about Cowper in proportion to their number, yet they tell me more than I could have gathered from any printed documents, or think it right to make public.

Have you seen "Bishop Jebb's Correspondence with Alexander Knox"? If you have not, send for it in your next parcel from the circulating library. I am sorry that I never saw Mr. Knox. He was little heard of out of his own circle; but in that circle he exercised a great influence which has been widely felt, in one instance (the Catholic question) for evil, in others for good, and the good effect is likely to continue and to extend. His other correspondence will be published by Mr. Hornby, the Rector of Winwick.

God bless you, dear friend. I boasted too soon yesterday of returning rest, and must try to-day what a longer walk will do for me by producing bodily weariness.—*Nov.* 3.

ROBERT SOUTHEY.

CLXXV.

TO ROBERT SOUTHEY.

BUCKLAND, *November* 18*th*, 1834.

Among my store of gossip for you when you came to me was a confession little creditable to me, that I had a very discreditable visitor—that meek man, William Howitt; yes, and liked him too! could not help it for my life, though I made it a point to keep all his sins on the first leaf of my remembrance, and to let him know that I did. He was touring through the New Forest, picking up materials for another "Book of the Seasons," or something of that sort. Well for him and his poor wife if he had kept to such blameless lucubrations. He was going from hence coast-wise into Cornwall, ten to one with some more mischievous purpose in view than his ostensible one; for the men of the extreme west are just the sort of people, and in that fermenting state, that would work well in his hands. And yet that man, as he showed himself to me, seems made up of all good and kindly elements, with a degree of plain-speaking frankness that pleased me, as he took special care not to call the clergy "knaves and fools" to me.

Well, the vermin have been smoked out with a vengeance! Can you guess of whom the new Cabinet will be composed? Can you even venture to wish among those who are most likely to be leaders? Whoever is in, the Pulchinello Chancellor will tumble in among them by some hocus-pocus manœuvre. How rarely he and Lord Durham have been performing Punch and Judy for the edification of the nation!

The miniature of Cowper in childhood is in the possession of James Cochrane, Esq., Sligo, Ireland. Mr. Cochrane is one of the principal merchants of Sligo. His picture was a copy (the only one) from the original, of which he gave a history to my friend Captain Felix, but the latter had forgotten it, and all I could extract from him was the address as above, and his assurance (which I could depend on) that the picture was most interesting.

May God be "about your bed and about your path," and keep you in all your ways, dear friend.

CAROLINE A. BOWLES.

CLXXVI.

TO CAROLINE BOWLES.

KESWICK, *December 7th,* 1834.

I wish you could have given a more favourable account of your own bodily afflictions. Your state of mind could not be better, and in this you set me an example. Yet a few years and we shall look back upon these trials as we now do upon the troubles of our childhood; but there is this difference between them, that it must be our own fault if we are not the better for the discipline which we now undergo.

So you were pleased with the revolutionary Quaker. I should like to know how far he is really a Quaker. If he is one to the full extent of Quakerism, he believes in as gross a delusion as ever was inculcated under any system of priestcraft. And if he stops short of that full belief, I should then like to know how far he is from infidelity, to which the liberalism of the Quakers closely approximates. In either predicament he may nevertheless have many estimable and amiable qualities; and if he has a kind heart and a feeling one, time is likely enough to teach him more wisdom, and, at least, to keep him from going farther wrong, even though it should not bring him into the right way. I dare say that if he and I were accidentally to meet, we should part in good will, each wondering that the other could be so grievously mistaken upon opinions of the greatest moment.

Time was when a political crisis like the present would have excited in me the liveliest interest. It is no good symptom as relating to myself that I now think of it only while the newspaper is in my hand; this, however, is not entirely because I am absorbed in my own concerns, but in great degree because, not knowing what to wish in the perplexed state of public affairs, I content myself with the quiet belief that whatever instruments may be employed, the designs of Providence will be brought about.

Dear friend, God bless you.

ROBERT SOUTHEY.

CLXXVII.

TO ROBERT SOUTHEY.

BUCKLAND, *December 21st*, 1834.

I have to thank you for recommending to me a book that has (the greater part of it) deeply interested me—"Jebb's Correspondence with Knox." In consequence of my own ignorance and incapacity, probably, I do not clearly comprehend what were the peculiar religious views of those two good men; for that they were peculiar Knox especially gives us often to understand.

In reading Roberts's four thick, heavy volumes of Hannah More's Life and Correspondence (an ill got-up work), I was not a little surprised never to find your name on a single page, I think not once; and yet her dear friend Wilberforce knew and loved you well. But I suppose you were not sufficiently orthodox (query, heterodox) to satisfy the "holy Hannah," whose great abilities, and excellent intentions, and wonderful exertions I admire and reverence heartily; but I never should have loved her. She was born with a birch rod in her hand, and worst of all was a shameless flatterer and insatiable of flattery; this I know from persons long and well acquainted with her, and in all other respects her warm admirers. Her acceptance of a pension in compensation for a husband is a vile blot, never to be expunged, in her character; and there is something wholly inexplicable to me in her living separate, as she did, from her widowed mother, and indeed in the apparent coolness of her filial affection. I am talking to you probably of a work you have not read and may little care to read, but my gossiping is easily laid aside, at least, if it is impertinent.

I continued this year to make a festival of a day that has long ceased to be one to me—of my birthday, the 6th of this month. Once more I assembled my little household at night to close the day with me, as we were wont till I became afflicted with that disease in my mouth two years ago. I felt less desolate that night when I went to rest than I had done for many years on the same anniversary, and the fruit of feelings was the little poem I inclose. That day would be to me a festival indeed which should bring me tidings of good hope and brightening prospects with you.

God bless you, dear friend.

CAROLINE A. BOWLES.

CLXXVIII.

TO CAROLINE BOWLES.

KESWICK, *December* 28*th*, 1834.

You will, no doubt, read both *Bishop Jebb's Life* and *Alexander Knox's Remains*, as I shall do as soon as they are published. Their system I take to be no other than the genuine Church of England doctrine, which, resting upon the old standard of Catholicism, allows none of that latitude that makes everyone his own interpreter of the Scriptures. This I

take to be their corner-stone. They held also (which is also the
Church doctrine) a real presence in the bread and wine, altogether unconnected with transubstantiation, and not attempting
to explain one of the mysteries of our faith. Knox published a
little treatise upon this, which I have, and which Mr. Hornby
will probably include among his *Remains*. Their other opinions
are all referable to a belief in the providential course of history
and all things.

I very much wish I had seen Mr. Knox. Wordsworth saw,
and was very much interested with him. Accidentally I saw a
number of the "Christian Observer" the other day, in which
this correspondence is attacked in the bitter spirit of what I call
the *Dys*angelical party—a proper name, because what they
preach would, if true, be *tidings of great woe*. Knox took up
his notion of my disbelief of the Devil from my speaking in the
"Life of Wesley" of the "personified principle of evil." That
there are evil spirits, as well as wicked men, no one who
believes in anything spiritual can reasonably doubt. My speculations upon subjects on which we may innocently speculate,
and where nothing beyond speculation is possible, you will one
day see, and in the most serious of them I am very sure that
you will cordially concur.

God bless you, dear Caroline.

ROBERT SOUTHEY.

CLXXIX.

TO CAROLINE BOWLES.

KESWICK, *February 8th*, 1835.

Mr. Knox's own principle, that extremes are permitted because they serve to counteract extremes, and thus ultimately to
bring about what, in the phrase of the day, must be called the
juste milieu, is exemplified in himself whenever he approximates
to the Dysangelical school (that name ought to be fixed upon

them, for they preach dismal tidings, evil tidings, the very opposite to those which were announced as "glory to God and good will towards men"). I have not seen his *Remains*, because in this uncertainty of my own movements I have not ordered any books from London. Hannah More's Life has been lent us, and I have had some extracts made from it, as notes for the *Life of Cowper* and for Dr. Bell's. The book itself comes from very incompetent hands. Whoever Mr. Roberts may be, he seems to have had no other qualification than that he was a "professor," as persons of that description call themselves. I am uncharitable enough to think that the proper Hebrew translation of the word would be Pharisee. Never was there a life written which told you so little of the history of the individual: everything that could have illustrated it is either hurried over or slurred over. The non-appearance of my name is, as you observe, remarkable enough; the more so, because in 1795 I dined with her at Cowslip Green, and called upon her at Bath in the winter of the same year. And when at Bristol, in 1830, I left a card at her door, upon an assurance from some of her friends that it would gratify her much to see me.

But you may observe that Wordsworth also is never named, nor any author indeed, Sir Walter excepted, out of the professional pale. Is this because she spoke with so little charity of all who were not within the line, that the Editor thought it prudent to suppress her opinions, or because she spoke with so much, that he deemed the suppression a duty, lest her approbation should afford a sanction to anything that came from that great division of the human race, described by him, and such as him, under the similitude of goats? That my name must often have occurred in her correspondence no one can doubt.

I liked her when I saw her much better than Mrs. Barbauld, or Miss Seward, who, however, with all her affectation, had a very likeable warmth and sincerity about her. Mrs. Barbauld was cold as her creed: her niece, Miss Lucy Aikin, when I saw her (which was before she commenced historian!), pert as a pear-monger.

God bless you, dear friend. You shall hear of my movements as soon as I can determine on them, and of everything that concerns me. Once more farewell.

ROBERT SOUTHEY.

CLXXX.

TO ROBERT SOUTHEY.

BUCKLAND, February 28th, 1835.

Are you, as the periodicals announce, about to edit the correspondence of Charles Lamb, and to write his life? They are mangling that, and his memory already, I see, according to the taste of the times. I would as lief have your "Mister Joseph" by my death-bed, if I was a great literary character, as one of those jackals of the Press, and the Evan—"Dis-evangelicals" as you well call them—are full as revolting in their way. Witness the short-hand collectors of last dying words that surrounded Hannah More and her poor sisters in their last moments; in her case treasuring up and revealing all that should have been most sacredly veiled, as indications of a decaying and weakened mind. Her Editor has done her memory more dishonour than the most slanderous of her accusers. Now what say you? I hear much talk and eulogy of Hannah More's fine and tender feelings. I think she was little troubled with the infirmity of a tender nature. What! she who could make one among the spectators in the Abbey when her best friend was laid in his grave! who could look into that grave, before the crowd, and come home and write about it! No— I never could have loved H. More; and then she talks of her own sensibility, and "cannot bear" forsooth "to think of her poor solitary widowed mother." Why did she leave her so? I love and respect sister Patty better a thousand times. My old venerable friend William Gilpin was very much displeased with Hannah for her "presumption," as he termed it, of publishing the letters on "The Education of a young Princess." "She might have left it to the Bishop her preceptor," said the old man; but Hannah was born like Minerva, ready armed, only with a birch rod—witness her appropriation, when a little child, of the coveted quire of writing paper; she scribbled it all over with letters of advice and rebuke, &c.

I must tell you an electioneering anecdote told to me by the brother-in-law of the gentleman (Sir John Rae Reed) in the course of whose canvass for Dover it occurred—" No," said the radical farmer, the honour of whose support Sir John was soliciting—" No, I'll never support no man what votes against animal Parliaments and universal suffering."

What a miserable business we have made of it with the Chinese; but I was delighted with their manifesto. What right have we Barbarians to force the trade?

And now farewell, and God bless you, dear friend.

CAROLINE A. BOWLES.

CLXXXI.

TO CAROLINE BOWLES.

KESWICK, May 10th, 1835.

We have now been nearly six weeks at home, and on the whole the amendment has been such, that though I dare not hope for complete recovery, it seems highly probable we may all migrate together to Sussex in the autumn. This is the only wish which my poor Edith will acknowledge, and this she certainly has at heart. She is perfectly contented, even when least herself; and this alone would make me rejoice in having brought her home; I need not say how much better it is for us to be with her than to have our thoughts continually dwelling upon her at a distance. Should our present plans take effect Cuthbert will come to us at the beginning of August, and we shall return with him in the latter end of September. In that case you will probably see me before the close of the year.

I have not yet thanked you for those lines of Cowper's; the invective parts have not been printed, but methinks there can be no objection to printing them now. Every day I have deferred writing to Mrs. Anne Bagot, because every day has brought with it more to do than it allowed time for doing. I should certainly be very glad to have Mr. Bagot's collection of letters entrusted to me, as I have Lady Hesketh's, and Mr. Unwin's (which are much more numerous than what you saw). These I am going over as an after-supper amusement, marking what has been omitted in the printed copies (which is often of as much value as the selected parts), and correcting the faults which the printers have introduced, and the editor overlooked, to the great injury of Cowper's own pure and easy style. Mrs. Unwin's grandson has sent this collection to the publisher for my use, and with it the manuscript of *John Gilpin* has come. One wonders that such a curiosity should have been thus hazarded, when there could be no use in sending it.

Some letters to a Mr. Clotworthy Rowley have been sent from Ireland; they are not many, but I collect some interesting facts from them. One is of earlier date than any that has been published, and it shows how Cowper regarded the prospect of his worldly affairs, the year before his malady broke out.

Alexander Knox wrote me a very long letter to show that Wesley was at no time actuated by ambitious feelings, but that whatever I had ascribed to such a motive in his conduct was nothing more than the inevitable effect of circumstances, his object being always the love of God and the good of his fellow creatures. The letter convinced me when I received it that he was right and that I had been mistaken, and I had his permission to print it whenever my "Life of Wesley" should be reprinted. If I ever reprint it (which I much wish to do), I should introduce it with an epistle dedicatory to Lord John Russell, who, as you have probably seen, attempted the other day to sneak into favour with the Methodists by saying that when he spoke ill of them it was because he had been deceived by my misrepresentations. He scruples at no subterfuge and no falsehood that will serve his purpose for a time.

The O'Connell tribe have probably learnt that ——————— has once been disordered in his intellect; how it manifested itself I never heard, but the father was said to have removed from London in order to withdraw him for a time from scenes of excitement. Overweening vanity, with nothing to ballast it, was probably the cause that overset him. His books represent him very faithfully; they are all (at least all that I have seen) clever, audacious and disagreeable. I wish he was more likeable, or more tolerable, for his father's sake, who is a thoroughly good-natured man.

My spirits, thank God, are quite equal to the demand upon them. Indeed now that the shock is over and that I see the worst, there is less to try them than there was while the disease was coming on, and its nature was utterly unsuspected; and this was for some years.

In the course of next month you shall have a certain third volume*—you will find yourself mentioned: and if the spirit moves you to write a story which it is there said that you could relate as it ought to be related, and that I will not relate because it is too mournful a task, do so, and it shall have its place in the next volume.

Dear friend, God bless you.

ROBERT SOUTHEY.

* Of *The Doctor:* see Chapter CV. "Caroline Bowles, whom no authoress or author has ever surpassed in truth, and tenderness, and sanctity of feeling, could relate such a story as it ought to be related,—if stories which in themselves are purely painful ought ever to be told."

CLXXXII.

TO ROBERT SOUTHEY.

BUCKLAND, *June 2nd*, 1835.

"Aballiboozobanganorribo!" what the deuce is the meaning of it? Such was my rather inelegant ejaculation, after cogitating for ten minutes over that awful word in a certain chapter of a certain book, my curiosity being of course whetted by prohibition. What a book! what a book! what a delectable book that is! How I congratulate myself upon having abstained from reading it till I had a head again—which did not come to pass for more than three weeks after you left me.

Why there is the concentrated essence of a life's reading in those two volumes, and better, of a life's feeling, and best of all to me, I found you in every chapter. I am sure I should have unriddled the riddle in the first ten minutes' reading had I read the book when you so demurely recommended it to me. Write, write, write on—next to talking with you and reading your letters, I shall enjoy this delightful gossip, that makes one laugh and cry, pleased and provoked, and out of all patience, all in a breath. *Mais tout en badinant* slip in words of wisdom that better the heart, and fill the mind with wholesome and serious thoughtfulness. So you have worked *me* in, with other odds and ends, in the third volume. Be sure I shall look for that page first. But how do you answer it to your conscience to tempt me to do that which you have not the heart to venture on yourself (mine is made of flint you suppose), and somewhere in these very volumes you condemn? I cannot make out the Bhow Begum? Is it Miss Hutchinson? I looked at my own black bag, and laughed. How Bowles of Bremhill would, I think, enjoy *The Doctor*.

I was painfully startled the other day by a newspaper announcement of the death of Mrs. Hemans. She was one of the very few female writers of our time with whom I had felt a wish to be acquainted. Her beautiful verses and my poor ones have often succeeded each other on the same pages in *Blackwood*, and I had acquired a habit of looking there for her, as for some familiar intelligence. I wish you would read her last lyric in *Blackwood's* May number. Though I know you did not rate her poems so highly as myself, I think you must award a meed of cordial praise to these; and dying as she was, and aware of her state, they are affectingly full of deep and solemn interest.

God bless you, dear friend.

CAROLINE A. BOWLES.

CLXXXIII.

TO CAROLINE BOWLES.

KESWICK, *June 22nd*, 1835.

The great word has no meaning whatever, but is of great use, which you will see explained and exemplified in the fourth volume, and for which use I composed it myself seven- or eight-and-thirty years ago. It then became a household word, but all those who used it with me have departed, or are now far away. On the day when the book arrived, when I went down to supper, Cuthbert was so full of that chapter that he rose from his seat before supper was ended to show me the long word, and he read the whole chapter to me that I might see what a queer book it was—the queerest he had ever seen! Twenty years before, that very chapter had taken the fancy of his brother, to whom I read the beginning when he came to his lessons the morning after it had been written, and he too entered fully into the humour of it. The book brings to me as many recollections of *this* kind as the sight of wild flowers in spring, and the singing of birds—sights and sounds that always carry us back to the past.

Miss Barker, who then lived in the next house, was the Bhow Begum: that whole chapter is from the life, and the book grew out of that night's conversation, exactly as is there related. But to go further back with its history, there is a story of Dr. D. D. of D. and his horse Nobs, which have, I believe, been made into a hawker's book. Coleridge used to tell it, and the humour lay in making it as long-winded as possible; it suited, however, my long-windedness better than his, and I was frequently called upon for it by those who enjoyed it, and sometimes I volunteered it when Mrs. Coleridge protested against its being told. As you may suppose, it was never told twice alike, except as to names and the leading features.

When I began the book, my view did not extend beyond two volumes. In the course of twenty years, however, enough in quantity (though not in sequence) for three was written, and a superabundance of materials collected for more. Miss Hutchinson then persuaded me to begin to print, Miss H. saying that if it was delayed longer, few of those who were in the secret and would enjoy it most would be living to enjoy it. The greater part of it she transcribed for the press—this having been her amusement for many years whenever she visited us.

Of the volume, which you will receive perhaps as soon as this letter, nearly four-fifths have been written since the two former were published, and about a fourth part while it was in the press. Enough, certainly, for three more is written, and how much there may be to interweave in these, who can tell? The bookseller's report of a prodigious sale is a bookseller's useful puff. One thousand copies were printed, and the *Quarterly Review* and the talk carried off little more than half that number by midsummer last. If another hundred has since dropt off I should be much surprised; but the new volume may put the remaining copies in motion.

Intending little more at first than to play the fool in a way that might amuse the wise, and becoming "a sadder and a wiser man" as I proceeded, I perceived that there was no way in which I could so conveniently dispose of some of my multifarious collections, nor so well send into the world some wholesome but unpalatable truths, nor advance speculations upon dark subjects, without giving offence or exciting animadversion. With something therefore of Tristram Shandy in its character, something of Rabelais, more of Montaigne, and a little of old Burton, the predominant character is still my own.

It was not till the book went to press that I thought of putting headings to the chapters, and finding mottos for each.

God bless you.

ROBERT SOUTHEY.

CLXXXIV.

TO ROBERT SOUTHEY.

BUCKLAND, *August 25th*, 1835.

I repented, for the thousandth time, of my impatience when your first letter of the 4th arrived, almost immediately after my persecuting one was despatched; and yet I will make no further excuse than to plead the infirmity of my nature and the intensity of my anxious feelings for you and yours under your present circumstances.

I bless God that you are supported, as you are assuredly, by Himself. What arm but His could bear you up under the crushing weight you are appointed to bear! But for His sake do not think of sending from you your dear filial comforters. You say you sometimes think you should be as well without them; I cannot believe it for a moment. It would be a tempting of Providence to isolate yourself so unnaturally.

It did me good to hear of your eighteen miles' walk, and eight hours' absence from home. As Pixie seems in favour, I conclude he has discontinued his obstreperous conduct. I wish my griffin of a steed would take example and reform, but he is bent on flinging me over his head, and it is a wonder he has not yet accomplished the feat. But desperation has made me so valiant that I am actually become a tolerable horsewoman, for which I take no small credit to myself, seeing that I never took to the exercise until an age when staid respectable persons begin to leave it off. If I live to fourscore, I may figure at a fox chase. Of late, however, I have had neither time, nor health, nor spirits for riding, or any idle pursuit. I think it is my fate to be a sort of solitary Beguine, always in requisition in some house of sorrow, sickness, or death; and indeed, lightly as I speak, I feel that God is very good to me in appointing me my work, and always giving me strength in time of need. For the last six weeks I have been leading a strange life—going backwards and forwards between my own house, where I had guests, and that of my relation Mr. Roche, whose eldest son has been in a dying state, and is still in a most precarious one. I have been ill, too, all the time, but never quite laid up, and I think I am now gaining a little ground. The worst to me is, that when I am leading this sort of restless, unsettled life, I cannot make the most (as I see others do) of the spare half hours, or hours even, that I may call my own; once out of the railroad of my own silent solitary life, I am absolutely good for nothing but mere mechanical exertion—and no matter, if the end be but peace.

Is the comet's tail whisking up all moisture from our sphere? and has it *par hazard* had anything to do with the late glorious deed at the commemoration of the three glorious days? A friend of mine, married to a Frenchman, told me the other day an anecdote delightfully characteristic of French sensibility. You read, no doubt, the account of the funeral ceremonies of the fourteen victims of the infernal machine; but it is not generally known that there ought to have been fifteen to complete the *coup d'œil* on the catafalque, and that the show was after all incomplete. Another person was mortally wounded, and his death hourly expected and waited for (and prayed for, no doubt) till the other bodies could wait no longer. Every day the moribund's door was besieged by crowds of anxious inquirers. Everywhere the question was asked—" *Est-il prêt ?* "

"*Pas encore,*" the mortifying reply; and actually the man was so perverse as first to outlive the day when his public appearance *en corps mort* would have added so greatly to the gratification of his affectionate fellow-citizens; and to sneak off in single blessedness, when not a soul cared sixpence about his exit! This is a real fact. What pretty playful tiger-cats those French are—not royal tigers.

I fear I must not entertain any hope of seeing you again this autumn. In truth, I had scarcely dared to encourage so cheering an expectation. If the cause of prevention were a happy one for yourself, my regret, being wholly selfish, would be far other than it is now. I think that my solitary, isolated life has disposed and led me to identify my feelings with those of absent friends—be they joyous or sorrowful—more than a continued course of social intercourse could have done. I know not whether this is a common characteristic, but in my case it is often a happy one, for good tidings of dear friends almost always charm away my melancholy moods. To be sure, there is the reverse, as I prove to you sometimes when anxious thoughts impel me to break wise resolves and write, when I had better wait patiently. Now, farewell, dear friend, and God bless you.

Caroline A. Bowles.

CLXXXV.

TO ROBERT SOUTHEY.

Buckland, *October 15th*, 1835.

How altered the circumstances of the two families of Greta Hall and Rydal since I passed those two happy months at Keswick.* May the cloud yet be withdrawn from above you

---

* Written shortly after the death of Wordsworth's sister-in-law, Miss Hutchinson.

even in this world, and, at all events, as you say, "but a little while, a very little." Those are the very words I oftenest murmur to myself when my heart is sad, and "the spirit vexed within me," and when a more bitter and less excusable fancy thrills, as it sometimes does, through this very weak heart of mine—a sudden passionate sense of deprivation and abandonment; if I do but whisper those other scriptural words "Something better, something better," they act upon my disturbance like oil on the troubled waves, or rather, like the Voice that said to them, "Peace, be still."

Do you know there is just one sentence I would fain expunge from the first volume of that delectable book you wot of. Many years ago you wrote it. Some years ago perhaps I should have read it without the sensation that makes me pause upon it now, as if I were treading irreverently on holy ground. You will understand, if you do not feel with me, when I point out the passage in the sixteenth page—"Ladies! the same stone," &c.* You see my informant was right; the first edition has gone off quicker than you anticipated.

As for the comet, it is quite a take-in—a lack-lustre creature, with a thin, draggled tail, like a sick turkey. Do not send my scientific observations to the newspapers; they have enough communications on the subject. I think Halley's comet must "keep a poet," as well as Mister Warren.

God bless you, dear friend.

CAROLINE A. BOWLES.

---

* "So ladies," said I, "the stone which the builders rejected," and then, looking at my wife's youngest sister, "Oh, it will be such a book!"

CLXXXVI.

TO CAROLINE BOWLES.

KESWICK, *November 8th*, 1835.

Henry Taylor has been in Keswick for the last twelve days. He took up his quarters at the Queen's Head, walked with me every day, and came up every evening to tea. After church this morning he departed, and we are left to ourselves for the winter. He is writing (for anonymous publication) a masterly treatise on the business of a statesman, and is meditating a tragedy, of which Becket is to be the chief personage.

You have, I trust, received the first volume of Cowper; you will have to wait a little for the second; eleven evenings given to Henry Taylor have been just so much stoppage of my work. However, it is not unfitting that there should thus be some such interruptions. But after the second the ensuing volumes will reach you monthly as they are published; and except the Homer, you will find some of my handiwork in all.

A letter of Mrs. Unwin's has reached me too late for use in its proper place; but it is a very important one, as confirming my opinion of the extreme want of judgment on the part of Cowper's religious friends, as they are called. It was written to Mrs. Newton while Cowper was on his long tarriance in the vicarage, and during an absence of Mr. and Mrs. Newton; and it appears that both they and Mrs. Unwin, though they thought *means* lawful and expedient in other cases, considered his a particular and exempt one, and were persuaded that "the Lord Jehovah would alone be exalted when the day of his deliverance came." This shows why so many months elapsed before any application was made to Dr. Cotton. Some letters of Lady Hesketh's have also been sent me, relating to her removal into Norfolk. They disclose things upon which Hayley did not like to touch, and of which Grimshawe knows nothing. Indeed, that man's ignorance respecting Cowper's real circumstances is marvellous. He is, without exception, the most grossly incompetent editor in every respect that ever ventured to appear in that capacity.

You object to an allusion which I see no irreverence in using, because, of all allusions, those to scriptural expressions and scriptural history occur most readily to my mind; partly, I suppose, because my mind is thoroughly imbued with that history, and partly perhaps because, of all others, one may presume that they are most generally and readily understood. (Yet will you believe that when I wrote "The breath of God goes forth, the dry bones shake," Croker said that, coming from me, he supposed it must be a scriptural allusion, and did not recognise it?) The Portuguese and Spaniards, in their religious poems, sport and even jest with subjects which they yet regard with such intense belief that they would put anyone to death for intentionally profaning them. I do not say this to excuse myself, but as a proof that light allusions may be a characteristic of serious belief, as puritanical ones are of phariseeism and hypocrisy.

God bless you.
ROBERT SOUTHEY.

CLXXXVII.

TO ROBERT SOUTHEY.

BUCKLAND, November 15th, 1835.

I know well enough that scriptural allusions may spring from anything but irreverence, for they suggest themselves to me so familiarly and appositely on all subjects on which I happen to be writing, that if I were not a little on my guard I should make a most puritanical patchwork on serious subjects, or interweave with light ones what on reflection would distress me. I have such a sin of this sort on my conscience! If I were to tell it you, you would admire the assurance with which I have dared to comment upon your application of those words. Perhaps my accusing conscience makes me more scrupulous than if I had never offended. Among the passages which I have returned to again and again in a certain work, is one which comes particularly home to my feelings. It is that which relates to the disuse of our Christian name, to which we become gradually sadly accustomed as we advance iu life. I did not think anyone could have felt that consequence of time as I have felt it. But I was mistaken; for reading that passage, it was as if my own heart spoke. When you first called me by my Christian name, the tears rushed into my eyes and I blessed you in my heart, for I felt at the moment as if the grave had restored to me a friend; a better feeling succeeded; I thanked God for having raised up one to me on whom I might rely even more surely than on those of my early unreflecting youth; God has been very good to me.

Just as I received your Cowper, a friend sent me the whole of Grimshawe's edition that I might look over the engravings, and I have thus had an opportunity of comparing the two most interesting with the same subjects in your first volume—Cowper and his mother's. Of the poet's portraits one must be no likeness, I should think, the features are so utterly dissimilar; the expression is also strikingly at variance in the two, but so it might have been in the original, according to his varying mood. Of the two, Grimshawe's strikes me as the most pleasing because the happiest expression, but it is less intellectual than the other, and that other is stamped with a peculiarity that would go far to prove it must be the better likeness—there is a character of insanity in it. It is, I think, by far the most spirited engraving, and the little vignette of Berkhampstead is a very pretty thing.*

* In a later letter Caroline Bowles writes of the *Life of Cowper* as follows :—

" Eke it out as I would, your second volume of Cowper came at last, like all created things, to the last page, and left me fretting for the rest. You have made me like Mrs. Unwin much better than I did, and she must have been loveable, from Lady Hesketh's account. But there is nothing loveable in that face of hers as represented in the engraving: hard, sharp, for-

I am no longer solitary in my walks nor by my fireside. I have a beautiful small spaniel "the prettiest of his race and high in pedigree," and as he already sets himself in a posture of defence if anybody pretends to strike or affront me, I give him credit for a character quite as intellectual as Beau's. I wonder you have never set up a dog, if only for a walking companion; and you had a tender regard for a certain Phillis.

God bless you, dear friend.

CAROLINE A. BOWLES.

CLXXXVIII.

TO CAROLINE BOWLES.

KESWICK, *February* 21*st*, 1836.

Though I keep no account of days, and have long since learnt that it is better, as much as possible, to put all private anniversaries out of mind, yet I happen to recollect that on this day twelvemonth Cuthbert and I arrived in London. The journey will form an epoch in his life, and it was one which I am not likely to forget while I remember anything. When I may be able to leave home again, God only knows. My presence

mal, and most puritanical-looking. I guessed at C—— L—— in that passage you allude to, and too well knew from what other source you had drawn sad experience. I see you have inserted the poem to Lord Thurlow as Mrs. Levett sent it to you, and there can be no reason at this day for your not doing so. I do think Cowper acted with something like caprice to Lady Austen, and she was too exacting. He should not have accustomed her to those daily periodical visits; or at least when he found it expedient to discontinue them, he should have given her the true reason honestly, and then if she had six grains of good sense and consideration she would not have felt neglected or given any querulous expression to her feelings. But having taken to her so warmly, friend Cowper does seem to me to whistle her down the wind very coolly. Lady Hesketh was worth a thousand Lady Austens, though the latter was a little spoiled by French sentimentality."

is necessary here, and there is no likelihood of any improvement that might render it prudent for me to be absent. We are thankful when the days pass quietly; and in taking no thought for the morrow, on this score I often feel that sufficient for the day is the evil thereof. God be thanked, sufficient is the good also!

The friend whom I have mentioned as resembling Cowper in the peculiar character of his madness is poor C—— L——; but the remark concerning the dreaminess of this state is confirmed by what I now continually observe. You will understand me if (as I conclude) you have by this time received my second volume. You will not be surprised to hear that the Evangelical party have declared war against me, even before this volume was published. Neville White tells me this; he says that in a "Church of England Magazine" belonging to that party they have put forth their candid regret that I should have taken up such a subject; and he says moreover, that in his part of the country (Norfolk) most amusing efforts have been made to advance the sale of Grimshawe's edition and impede mine; women are the most zealous parties in this affair, and seem, he says, to have taken it up as a holy cause—a sort of crusade. I wish Baldwin and Cradock may not feel the effect; but from what takes place in this parish I can see that this party are ready to "go the whole hog" in anything.

By way of making myself better acquainted with the middle of the last century, that is to say, with the state of the country, its manners, &c., during that time, I have been reading all the correspondence on which I could lay hands. Two volumes of Shenstone's and his friends published by Hull the actor, Lady Luxborough's Letters to Shenstone, Lady Hervey's, Mrs. Montague's, four volumes, but which stop at the year 1760. A brilliant creature she must have been in her bloom, yet methinks, notwithstanding her genius and her beauty I should not have been in love with her. Mrs. Carter and her friend Miss Talbot are both more to my liking, and Beattie is a man very much after my own heart. I wish his Memoirs had contained more of his letters. There is no entering upon any one line of reading without being led on, and feeling at every step how much more you ought to read in order to obtain anything like a satisfactory knowledge of it.

I have a drawer full of manuscript letters to go through, which I got possession of a few days ago. They are all that remain of Mr. Powley's papers; he married Miss Unwin; his widow died about eight months ago, and the papers, upon an intervening death, came to a Mr. Powley, who, having been a linen-draper in Bond-street, has retired to his native place near Penrith, and from him I have obtained them. The girls have sorted them for me; but as yet I have only been able to go through some from Mr. Haweis and from Lady Huntingdon—for they are all in the Evangelical line, and will be of much more use in the "Life of Wesley" than of Cowper. Haweis is pretty well known for a rogue. In a letter of 1768 he says, "Dear Newton and Mr. Cowper have been here, precious men, whose company is ever a blessing." This I believe is the earliest mention of Cowper that I have found anywhere, except the acknowledgment (without his name) of his papers in the "Connoisseur." As for Lady Huntingdon, she writes like a Head of her own Church, a She Bishop or Pope Selina. I expect to meet with a great deal of curious and applicable information in this correspondence.

There are many of Newton's letters, and these no doubt will help me in his *Life*. I am not without hope that I may find materials here for a sketch of the rise and progress of the Evangelical clergy to be introduced in the *Life of Wesley*.

In a fortnight or three weeks at farthest I hope to finish the *Life of Cowper*. There will still be enough to do in the way of notes and biographical sketches, besides the lives of Mr. Newton and Madame Guyon, but the brunt of the business will be over, and I shall forthwith resume the fourth volume of the *Admirals*, for which I am better paid than for anything which I ever wrote before. This volume will contain Essex, Raleigh, Sir William Monson, Blake and Monk; and then I mean to drop the biographical form, and with one volume of naval history from the Revolution to the close of the last war, or perhaps the battle of

Algiers, conclude the work. This is an alteration which *may* be made, because from that time there is less of personal adventure; personal character becomes less conspicuous, and the events belong more directly to the general history of the country; and it *must* be made, because it is very practicable to wind up in one volume upon this plan, whereas to proceed biographically might require three or four. Moreover, I escape all difficulty about Nelson.

Dear friend, God bless you.

ROBERT SOUTHEY.

CLXXXIX.

TO CAROLINE BOWLES.

KESWICK, *Easter Monday, April 4th*, 1836.

This has been a day taken up in advance from summer, and it drew me out for a walk round the lower part of Leatheswater, and over the three bridges at its division, a round of fourteen miles. Now that the pressure of business is over, I mean to allow myself a whole morning's walk once a-week. Davies will be here to-morrow or next day to accompany me, for a long walk usually leads me into unfrequented ways, and therefore it is better not to be alone. See how prudent I am in thus bearing always in mind the possibility of some accident!

The last proof of the third volume* was returned to-day, unless they should think it necessary to send me the Contents. At any rate you will receive it in the course of next week, and in the remaining portion of the Life you will find more that will be new to you than in the former volumes. I have done my best to relieve a melancholy tale; and I am sure you will think I have done right in making no flourish at the end, but

* Of Cowper.

concluding simply with the epitaphs. What more there may be to say of Cowper's status in literature, and his effect upon his successors, will come better among the supplementary works of supererogation.

I have found out that Mr. Unwin was not thought evangelical enough by his brother-in-law Powley, Mr. Newton, and that party. Indeed I have been employed before breakfast upon Powley's papers for the last four or five weeks, and have extracted from them a good deal which will be useful in various ways; but the most remarkable [incident?] which has come to my knowledge is the story of John Cowper and the fortune-teller, mentioned in vol. i., p. 219. The only person *probably* now living who knew all the circumstances, and *certainly* the only one who could have authenticated them, has sent me a full and most remarkable account of them. It is one of those relations which it is impossible *not* to believe, and equally impossible to account for in any satisfactory manner. I shall insert the letter among the Biographical Sketches at the end of the Correspondence.

You told me the author of *The Doctor* was a Scotchman.* But some friends of H. Taylor say that he is Dr. Bowring, a retired practitioner at Doncaster, which has a very likely sound with it. These persons know all about him. What will Blackwood say to this?

God bless you, dear Caroline.

ROBERT SOUTHEY.

* In a letter of October 15th, Caroline Bowles had written:—"I had almost forgotten, owing to my long illness, a curious observation that was made to me some time previous, at a dinner party. A strange gentleman who sat by me descanted much on the merits and demerits of 'The Doctor.' He was cautious of declaring his own opinion, and rather puzzled, I believe, as to forming any; but, after fishing in vain for mine (I soon found he was not worth talking to), he assumed a more oracular tone, and informed me that he was certain of two points on the best authority—that the author was a Scotchman, and a decided enemy to the Church! I received the intimation with the most deferential meekness, and without moving a muscle; after that, may I not boast of command of countenance *à toute épreuve?*"

CLXC.

TO CAROLINE BOWLES.

Keswick, *May* 29*th*, 1836.

You are right in supposing that it was a wholesome employment for me to write the Life of Cowper; no other, I verily believe, could have been more so. It is not the least remarkable part of his case, that when he became decidedly insane on one point, he recovered the right use of his intellectual powers upon all others; for certainly there is reason to believe that if he had continued in what both he and Mr. Newton considered his state of grace, he would never have written a verse above the pitch of the *Olney Hymns*, nor a letter which breathed any other feeling than that of the narrow sectarian circle within which he was, as it were, spell-bound. He would have been lost for ever to his relations and to the world.

I wonder what sort of a reception Henry Taylor's "Statesman" will meet with. Considered in itself, it is a very able and judicious treatise; but though nothing can be written more inoffensively, nor in a calmer philosophic spirit, it will be wormwood to some of those persons who are most likely to read it. Little interested as you may be in the subject, it is very well worth your reading, even if you were not curious enough to desire to see it for the writer's sake. Have you read the "Life of Sir Thomas Munro"? If not, you will do well to send for it.

The Levetts are expected on the 9th. I wish you knew Mr. B——, who engaged their quarters for them. You would delight to see and hear him in the pulpit, and you would marvel at the simplicity of his character, which is such that Parson Adams was a man of the world in comparison. His wife is a great invalid, and being a real sufferer imputes much of her suffering to the spot where she happens to be fixed; so that they have led a sort of migratory life for several years, Buttermere being the place which she has tried oftenest, and on the whole liked best. But owing to his utter deafness, and her state of health, the children have grown up like young colts; and the "incoherent transactions" of the whole family would fill a volume. The eldest daughter is a nice girl, about seventeen, who smiles up to her eyes with good-nature; and fears neither wind nor weather, man nor beast, when she is mounted on her pony. Her sister, about a year younger, is such a girl that when we had a huge caravan of wild beasts here last week (fourteen carriages), somebody said she would be in her place if she were attached to them. Poor girls! it is very unfortunate for them that we cannot have them sometimes, where they might have learned a little needful restraint, a little needful prudence, and some of the ways of that class in society to which they belong.

They are living now at Leatheswater, six miles from hence. As Mr. B—— drives backward and forward, he takes up any-one whom he finds on the road, without distinction of persons, clean or unclean matters not to him.

One of the Bagots, who was with him here as a pupil, was the only person who could keep the younger children in any order; the mother letting them make what uproar they will, and the father being so deaf that he could not hear the Last Trumpet unless his own should happen to be at hand. But with all his eccentricities you would be charmed with him : his whole heart is in his duty: he is overflowing with kindness, and you never saw a more cheerful and benevolent countenance.

God bless you, dear friend.

ROBERT SOUTHEY.

CXCI.

TO CAROLINE BOWLES.

KESWICK, *June* 12*th*, 1836.

I am looking every day for your little book,* and should be glad to hear that there is more in it than the single poem, if I

* " *The Birthday, &c.*" " From this date Miss C. Bowles's letters [with one exception] are unhappily lost. They were all tied up together,

were not sorry that you had curtailed that poem, of which all that I saw was very sweet. The Levetts arrived on Thursday, and seem disposed to like everything. They have not been here yet; indeed there has been no time, for I went to look for them on the Friday (doubting whether they would have come through the unceasing rain of the preceding day), and yesterday evening took Bertha to call on them. Kate is from home just now. She went on Tuesday last to Rydal, much to dear Dora's comfort; and if a situation on the coast can be found to which it is possible for Dora to be removed, Kate will go with her. Fond as my daughters (I must cease to call them girls) always were of Dora and her mother, Miss Hutchinson's death seems to have drawn those cords of affection closer—for in *her* I hardly know which family lost most. Wordsworth is in London, and talks of going to France. He is better anywhere than at home, where his extreme anxiety for Dora worries her. God knows there is but too much cause for him to be anxious! But if he can be less uneasy at a distance, it is better on everybody's account that he should be away.

There is so much that you will delight in, in Sir Thomas Browne's works, that if you are not already acquainted with them I think you will thank me for advising you to send for the new edition in four volumes, published by Pickering. He is one of my worthies. I am sure you will agree with me that it would have been a sin in the Editor if he had withheld his wife's letters, or any of the postscripts relating to little Tommy. But Sir Thomas was a wise and good man, a true philosopher in the best sense of the word; and if his wife is not to be classed as a writer with Mrs. Hutchinson, or the wife of Sir William Temple, or that Duchess of Newcastle who seems rather a creature of romance than of real life, yet, I dare say Sir Thomas found her a good helpmate. When the book comes to you, turn to page 108 in the fourth volume, and see how admirably he describes the feelings of threescore.

and collected according to the year, when I was last at Buckland. My idea is that they were burnt (by mistake) with other papers."—(*Note by Mr. Warter*).

I have outgrown all wish for making any new acquaintances in this world; but I have a deep desire to become acquainted in the next with all those whom I regard as I do Sir Thomas Browne. I shall know him by his likeness to Charles the First.

I have put Levett in possession of the Ark, and supplied the ladies with books. There is something very delightful in that familiarity which springs up at once from school-acquaintance, after so long an interval, and when you find that the old man is what, from your knowledge of the boy, you had supposed him to be.

God bless you, dear friend.

ROBERT SOUTHEY.

CXCII.

TO CAROLINE BOWLES.

KESWICK, *September* 10*th*, 1836.

My poems are to be got into ten volumes, by close packing; each of the long poems will be comprised in one volume, and the others compressed in the same proportion. My brother's advice was to begin with *Joan of Arc*, which has been some years out of print, and so let the three-deckers force a passage for the small craft. Wordsworth is inclined to agree with him, and in things of no greater moment than this I am always willing to follow the opinion of others.*

---

* In a letter of August 10th, 1836, Southey speaks of this preparation for a collective edition of his poems as "a step towards setting my house in order." "On Friday," he says, "I enter upon my sixty-third year, which used to be deemed the most critical according to a philosophy about numbers, which, in the revolution of opinion, is coming into vogue again; seven and nine are the critical numbers in the human constitution, and they meet in sixty-three; but it has been very truly said that the age of nine times nine is even more critical still. *That*, I trust, I shall not be called upon to experience.

The Levetts leave Keswick on the 27th; they have taken very bad weather with very good humour. Miss Hussey has taken to Bertha and Kate, and they cannot help liking her quiet, modest, *creep-mouse* manner. She is learning to bind books in their fashion, and is a very promising apprentice, being remarkably clever with her hands, which is the most serviceable kind of cleverness. It is to be hoped she may find some one who will know how to appreciate her gentle, confiding, affectionate disposition.

I think of cutting out some work, or rather of setting some aside, to be done in Buckland, as in 1831, so I shall just show Cuthbert to you, send him on to Tarring, and follow him after a few days.

It is now settled that I may extend my *Naval Biography* to six volumes, and this pleases me well, though I should rather be employed upon the *History of Portugal.* A fifth volume will contain all the remaining lives down to the Revolution. I may then more conveniently drop the biography, and resume the form of continuous history, because after that time individual character becomes less conspicuous, and naval actions are more connected with general politics. There is an end indeed of personal interest, and the interest of adventure also, for which I must endeavour to find compensation in clear general views. Concluding with the Battle of Algiers, the book will have by good fortune the termination possible; because in the next war steam must be brought into action; the character of naval warfare must undergo a change, with which a new epoch will commence. It is not unlikely that this work may be worth correcting and improving from materials which I did not possess, or was not acquainted with during its progress.

Dear Caroline, God bless you.

ROBERT SOUTHEY.

CXCIII.

TO CAROLINE BOWLES.

BEDMINSTER, *November 6th*, 1836.

Here I am, dear Caroline, on the way to the Land's End. Monday we made for Birmingham, and thence, six miles, to an old and large house called Pipe Hayes, where Mr. Egerton Bagot (a clergyman and a widower), the son of Cowper's correspondent, is living like a hermit alone. We dined with him that day, and remained till four o'clock on the Wednesday, during which time I read over all his father's correspondence, and found enough to repay me for the days so spent. But we saw no other person while we were there, such is the solitary life that he appears to lead. Thursday we went from Birmingham to Bristol, and here we are in the house of my old friend and early publisher Joseph Cottle, the simplest and kindest-hearted of men.

Alas! I have work to do which I could not get through at home.

This morning I am going to the church which I used to frequent with my grandmother, and have never entered since the year 1782.

The seat into which the sextoness introduced me (for the Cottles are dissenters) was exactly opposite the spot on which my grandmother's pew had stood. *That* I perfectly remembered, and recollected an old monument above it; but the whole inside of the church has been fitted up some ten or twenty years ago. Still it was the same church, externally unchanged, and the same hills were seen through the same windows; and perhaps—nay, probably even—of all the persons who had been present in that church when I was last in it, fifty-four years ago, I may have been the only survivor.

There have been times, and are, dear friend, when I feel like Eleëmon, as if the fountain of tears were dry; as if my eyes had been seared, and my heart had been so often and so long upon the anvil that it had been rendered insensible. But to-day it was with great difficulty that I could so far command myself as not to let my emotions be seen.

After church we walked to Bristol, where I left a card with your kinsman of unhappy name. He was not returned from church. I shall accept no invitation, except to breakfast, during my stay here, because we are a mile and a half from the town, and because my evenings will be required for work. Cuthbert is very much pleased with Bristol, which Landor (who is here) agrees with me in thinking beyond all comparison the most interesting and beautiful city in England. I have shown him a great deal already, and shall show him to-morrow my grandmother's house and the garden—which was my Garden of Eden—where some of the fruit-trees which my grandfather had planted were standing when I was there in 1831. Tuesday, if weather be favourable, I shall take him to look at my old school at Corston.

We go on Saturday next to visit Bowles, then to Taunton, where my good aunt is ready and waiting for her release, at a great age. The hope of seeing her once more in this world has been one of the inducements to this journey, for she was as fond of Cuthbert when he was two years old as she had been of me when I was of the same age. We then go down the north coast to Derwent Coleridge, at the Land's End, and up the south, making sundry halts upon the way. Christmas I expect to pass with my old friend Lightfoot, near Crediton, and New Year's Day most probably with you. The resolution with which I left home was not to hurry myself upon this circuit, but to see as much as we could upon the way, and not to regard a week or two of time, or a little additional expense, upon a journey which (in its full extent) I am never likely to repeat, and which Cuthbert will always remember.

My accounts from home could not be more favourable. My first letter produced an expression of some interest in its contents; my absence occasions no uneasiness, and my return will, I dare say, be looked for with as much pleasure as my poor Edith is now capable of finding in anything. For myself, I shall be the better for this journey, shall lay up much for remembrance and for use, and be heartily glad to find myself once more at rest in my appointed course of duty.

God bless you, dear, dear friend.

ROBERT SOUTHEY.

CXCIV.

TO CAROLINE BOWLES.

KESWICK, *February* 23rd, 1837.

On Tuesday I sent off a short preface to Cowper's Homer, reserving my remarks upon that translation for the Cowperiana, of which there are to be two volumes: one relating to him, his family, and his literary friends, the other containing the lives of Mr. Newton and Madam Guyon. Your communications from Mr. F. Ross were of signal use. I obtained from Inglis a sight of the sealed letter. How little are men's memories to be trusted upon points of which they have no cause to take particular notice at the time! The letter was not from Newton to Mr. Thornton, but from Thornton to him; and the facts of the disappearance, the tracing of the lost person to France, and the supposed cause of his thus absconding, relate to the *other* William Cowper, as clearly ascertained by the date. What then becomes of all the collateral traditional evidence respecting *my* Cowper's real or supposed malformation? Have the two namesakes been confounded, like the two Dromios and their two masters in the *Comedy of Errors?* Or did *my* Cowper apply to himself what was reported of his kinsman, and engraft this miserable imagination upon his other delusions?

All that I have done since my return has been to write letters, and I am still far from seeing the end of this occupation, so many which reached me during my travels, or awaited me here, remain yet unanswered. Except this, I have merely begun to revise *Joan of Arc*, correcting the diction wherever it can be done without more cost of time than it is worth. Longman wishes to get three or four volumes through the press before the monthly publication commences, which will be a month after that of Cowper is completed; if, as I suppose, there should be a (supplementary) 15th volume of *Cowper*, containing the yet remaining letters and the translation of the *Henriade*, we shall begin with the month of August.

Friday, 24th.—To-day I have seen the sun for the first time since my return. The weather continues piercingly cold; but I made the most of the sunshine, and took a dutiful walk to the Druidical Arch. You have received, I hope, the fourth volume of Admirals (which has marvellously little to do with sea service), and the tenth of Cowper. I delight in the prospect of supplying you with a monthly volume for many months to come; and every little improvement that I make in the process of revision gives me the more pleasure, because I know that in some instances you will observe it, and that in others it removes something which you would, might, or ought to have felt amiss.

And now, dear friend, God bless you. Let me hear that you are are gaining strength. I would send Dash a most friendly greeting if he could understand it.* Once more, farewell.

ROBERT SOUTHEY.

---

* Miss Bowles had written after Southey's departure from Buckland: "Sorely and sadly I have missed you, and shall miss you until that feeling of deprivation softens into one of grateful and pleasant retrospection, such as I have learnt to live upon and be thankful. I will not agree with you that it may be better never to meet than only meet to part. The next pleasure I shall have will be to hear you are in haven again, and that your return home and the welcome of your dear daughters has been as little saddened as possible under the cloud with which it pleases God still to overshadow you. I must tell you that Dashie has felt your departure very sensibly: I found him the next day scratching at your bedroom door; and when my solitary dinner was brought up to me on the tray, he rushed down again and bounced open the bedroom door, barking with all his might to call you to partake."

CXCV.

TO CAROLINE BOWLES.

KESWICK, *Easter Monday*, 1837.

I sent a dose of cooling admonition to the poor girl* whose flighty letter reached me at Buckland. It was well taken, and she thanked me for it. It seems she is the eldest daughter of a clergyman, has been expensively educated, and is laudably employed as a governess in some private family. About the same time that she wrote to me, her brother wrote to Wordsworth, who was disgusted with the letter, for it contained gross flattery to him, and plenty of abuse of other poets, including me. I think well of the sister from her second letter, and probably she will think kindly of me as long as she lives.

The revision of *Joan of Arc* is finished, and were you to see the corrected copy you would certainly admire my resolution, and, perhaps, my workmanship also. I have made some progress in the general preface, and have another to write for this poem. Except in prefatory matter to the long poems, there will be little other trouble with the rest of the volumes than that of correcting the proof sheets, the alterations being merely verbal or metrical improvements, many, indeed most of them, made long ago. But among the minor poems you will find many which have not before been collected.

Your Irvingite pamphlets have told me a great deal which I had never heard of before, and which is well worth knowing. Shall we ever see any great effect produced by delusion and imposture of this kind, as in former times? It would be rash to say *no* too positively, and I shall note it down as a question to be discussed in colloquy. The failure of the St.-Simonians does not prove it to be impossible; they were much too reasonable in some of their political views, and much too profligate in their conduct. Strict morals and extravagant doctrines would have

---

* Charlotte Brontë.

succeeded better. It is neither by one nor the other that our dissenters increase wherever they are increasing; their persuasion is their party, and worldly convenience is in every sect the bond of union.

God bless you, dear friend.
ROBERT SOUTHEY.

CXCVI.

TO CAROLINE BOWLES.

KESWICK, June 26th, 1837.

I have learned to look, if not with complacency, at least with great composure, upon the progress of political events—not as being indifferent to the course which they may take, but in a quiet confidence that all things will be better ordered for us than we could order them for ourselves. The young Queen's behaviour at her Proclamation was so natural, and so much what one would have wished it to be, that I shall endeavour to make some use of it, as soon as I can determine in what form to embody what I have to say. At present I incline to prefer that kind of lyric unrhymed verse in which most of my *ex-officio* odes have been written. The strain will be hopeful and consolatory, showing her that her task is not difficult, that her paths may well be those of pleasantness and peace, and introducing some wholesome hints respecting the Poor Laws and the factory-children, to tell her what the reforms are of which the nation stands in need, and cheer her with an assurance that the heart of England will be with her, and the Lord the strength of her salvation.

What you lose in all translations of Homer is the beauty of the style, which, with the simplicity of the old ballad, has the advantage of the most harmonious language in the world, and the finest metre—a strain of verse which always satisfies and delights the ear. No translation can either represent this or afford any compensation for it. The Greek tragedies are not in the same manner injured by translation, because neither their tragic metre nor their lyrical verse is better than our own.

Homer is still a mystery. I am inclined to agree with those critics who suppose that the Iliad is a Macphersonized collection of genuine Ossianic poems, not the work of one man; that the form in which we have it was given it in the time of Pisistratus, and that the language, like that of all poems which have been orally transmitted, had undergone a gradual modernisation, so as to be that of the age in which the fragments were thus embodied. The people to whom the poem relates seem to have been as nearly as possible in the same stage of barbarism or civilization (call it which you will) as the South Sea Islanders when the missionaries became acquainted with them. I like such people as little as you do; but magnanimity and matured affections are found in all stages of society, except where men are thoroughly corrupted in the rottenness of civilization, or where they are embruted by living on the limits of the living world, and so case-hardened by what they are exposed to as to be deprived of half their feelings. I am sure that there are passages in Homer which have brought tears into your eyes. What can be more truly heroic than Hector? What more touching than Andromache and old Priam?—and how generous is their treatment of Helen! A volume of letters will follow the Odyssey, and complete the works. The Cowperiana must be at my convenience; but the first volume of my poems will be ready for you the month after Cowper is completed.

Bertha has counted the books lately—they amount to more than 12,500. Storage could not be found for more than another 500, so you see there must soon of necessity be a stop put to their increase. The review of Mrs. Bray's book has been a mill-stone about my neck, and I am not yet rid of it, but expect to be so soon. What I have made most way with has been Bell's Life.

June 28th.—I must now make up the *haughtygraffs* which I have just written, and, as I now perceive, mis-dated. Ask me without scruple whenever you wish for another such packet. A wholesome text is the most useful thing I can write on such occasions, and it is always at hand, and in this shape they go conveniently in a letter. Cuthbert and his sister desire their kindest regards. I shall be with you once a-month in print for the next twelve months, and perhaps in person again before the end of that time.

Dear friend, God bless you.

ROBERT SOUTHEY.

CXCVII.

TO CAROLINE BOWLES.

KESWICK, *July* 23rd, 1837.

That you should like Cottle's book, dear Caroline, is as impossible as it would be for you to dislike Cottle himself, if you knew him as I know him; but unless you knew him thus thoroughly, you could not believe that such simple-heartedness and such inordinate vanity were to be found in the same person. One thing he has made me fully sensible of, and that is, how liable the most cautious biographer is to be misled by what should seem to be the most trustworthy documents. Such a confusion of times and circumstances as he has made in his *Recollections* I never met with in any other book; and for this reason, no doubt, that my own knowledge could never in any other instance enable me to detect it.

Wordsworth and I have always dreaded the indiscretion of Coleridge's admirers, and the exposure of his character which was certain to ensue. Cottle has withheld a good deal, upon his own sense of propriety, little scrupulous as he may seem to have been; and he has struck out more at my desire; and yet the impression which his book leaves is just what you describe upon all those who feel that intellectual strength affords no excuse for the disregard of moral obligation.

Charles Lamb's letters have just reached me. If the whole story could have been told, this would have been one of the most painfully interesting books that ever came from the press. When

I saw Talfourd in January last, he seemed fully aware how much better it would have been to have delayed the publication for some years. But in this age, when a person of any notoriety dies, they lose as little time in making a book of him as they used to do in making a mummy. To be sure, there are some reputations which will not *keep*, and must therefore be brought to market while they are fresh. But poor Lamb's is not of that kind. His memory will retain its fragrance as long as the best spice that ever was expended upon one of the Pharaohs.

You may well suppose that all these recent publications, in which there is so much concerning myself, bring with them to me anything but what is cheering.

August 12.—To-day I send off the advertisement, &c., to the concluding volume of Cowper's works. The edition is now complete. But to complete my purpose there must be two volumes of Cowperiana, which you will have in due time. It is a great thing to have this off my hands.

Dear friend, God bless you.

Robert Southey.

CXCVIII.

TO CAROLINE BOWLES.

Keswick, *November 29th*, 1837.

Winter has begun with us unusually early, and it is as cold now as in the ordinary course of the seasons it is at Christmas. This, however, is better than the heavy storms of wind and rain which preceded this frost, and rendered it impossible for Bertha and Kate to get out of doors. Yesterday was the first day that they could walk out. Their health, thank God, has not suffered, and at their time of life their spirits, in the wise order of nature, have a tendency to recover their healthy tone.* For myself,

---

* Mrs. Southey died on November 16th, 1837.

truly and deeply thankful as I ought to be and am, for a deliverance which has long been to be desired, I continually feel the separation. I never felt wholly like myself anywhere but at home, and the change is so great that I now no longer feel like myself there. This, however, will be the best place for me for some time to come, so that if it were convenient for me in other respects to move, I should deem it advisable to let some months elapse before I commenced a journey,

December, 1.—By this time you will have received my second volume. The building in the frontispiece is the same as in the vignette title-page—another view of the school. I took Cuthbert there last year; the day unluckily proved wet, so that we could not walk over the precincts as I had intended, but we obtained admission into the house, now in a wofully dilapidated state, being half inhabited as a farm-house.

Your Bristol kinsman has written to me about a monument to Chatterton, and an inscription for it. I have not replied to his letter: indeed it came at a time when it could not be replied to. But my intention is neither to subscribe to a monument, nor write an inscription for it. Poets require no monuments to keep their memory alive—if it deserves to live. And I will not undertake as a school-task, or rather imposition, what never could be done well unless it were done from the spontaneous and warm impulse of good will. I did my part for Chatterton when I made the first collection of his works, and published them for the benefit of his sister.

The preface to *Joan of Arc* has brought me a very pleasing letter from one who says it was his " allotted task at the age of fifteen, and even then a very little boy, to set up, in the new great primer type, had expressely for the purpose, the first page of the first edition of *Joan of Arc*. But what prompts the pride (he says) with which I have ever cherished the remembrance of this event is the vivid recollection that I did it in your immediate presence. The entire scene is fresh before my mind's eye at this moment—my priggish, powdered master, Mr. Rosses, standing with your juvenile self near the stove in the centre of the large office, and I, blushing under the honours of my appointed task, and strongly do I retain the remembrance of the feeling nearly allied to envy with which I eyed the slender youth who stood near me, the author of a quarto volume of poetry." The whole letter may very fitly be made use of in the posthumous edition of my works. In the present both prudence and propriety require that I should say no more of myself than belongs to the design of the prefaces. But garnish of this kind will be very serviceable hereafter.

The writer of this letter is now rector of Athelington and vicar of Cretingham, Suffolk. His name is Richard Brudenell Exton. He has sent me some local and political satire in Spenserian verse, with a good deal of cleverness, and "A Discourse delivered at the 16th Anniversary of the Framlingham District Committee of the Society for Promoting Christian Knowledge, in the Parish Church of Framlingham, September 17, 1832." I have transcribed the whole title for you because this sermon is actually in blank verse. Rub your eyes if you will, as well you may. In blank verse he composed this sermon, and in blank verse he preached it, and I wish you and I had been there to hear it. I am sorry to say the verse is very bad; indeed he does not seem to know what blank verse is, though some of his Spenserian stanzas show both ability and skill.

Tell me how you bear these frequent changes of weather. I have increased my daily dose of exercise, and am looking in hope to the lengthening of the days, when daylight will allow me to rise earlier.

God bless you, dear friend.

ROBERT SOUTHEY.

CXCIX.

TO CAROLINE BOWLES.

KESWICK, *January* 21*st*, 1838.

I got Warner's *Recollections* for a few shillings from a catalogue lately; you know I looked at it at Buckland. How much better it is in every respect than any other of his books that have fallen in my way. But it is hardly possible that anyone should not write agreeably when relating his own recollections of early life. Even with all allowances for vanity and self-deceit, the truest of all history is what we thus draw from ourselves.

Many of the persons whom Warner mentions I knew something of, both of his Christ Church acquaintances and his Bath ones. What a tremendous change has taken place in the general character of society within his memory and mine, though I suppose him to be nearly ten years my senior. And as if the old mail coach rate of eight miles an hour was not fast enough for the march of civilization, the devil has been raised in the shape of steam to impel us at his own pace. You remember the proverb "Needs must go when *he* drives." One of the worst things attending this revolution in public travelling is, it leaves you no choice. At this time there is only one coach, which runs from Manchester to London. The Birmingham Railway has already produced this effect, and an utter recklessness to the convenience and safety of the passengers is one consequence of the monopoly which has thus been gained. The confusion when the luggage of a whole train is thrown down at the end of its course is said to exceed anything one has ever seen of this kind. As to personal safety, there must be less danger than in an overloaded coach, and there is also less fatigue in the motion itself, to say nothing of the great saving in that respect by going twenty miles an hour, instead of eight. But, after all, slow and sure would be more to my liking. My pleasantest, or I might better say happiest, travels have been either at a mule's foot-pace, or with a knapsack on my own shoulders.

The Longmans' account of the poems to my brother is, that they are selling "very fairly." The impression of 1500, they say, will just about cover the expenses, leaving profit to be derived from the future use of the stereotypes and engravings. The profit upon any additional 500 would be considerable; but I suppose that not many sets will be called for after the monthly publication is completed; there will be more demand for single volumes, or portions. What an abomination is the engraving of Keswick in the third volume! I never saw anything worse.

God bless you, dear friend.

ROBERT SOUTHEY.

APPENDIX.

I.—CORRESPONDENCE WITH SHELLEY.*

I.

SHELLEY TO SOUTHEY.

MESSRS. LONGDILL & Co., 5, GRAY'S INN SQUARE,
March 7th, 1816.

MY DEAR SIR,

I cannot refrain from presenting you with a little poem,† the product of a few serene hours of the last beautiful autumn. I shall never forget the pleasure which I derived from your conversation, or the kindness with which I was received in your hospitable circle during the short period of my stay in Cumberland some years ago. The disappointment of some youthful hopes, and subsequent misfortunes of a heavier nature, are all that I can plead as my excuse for neglecting to write to you, as I had promised, from Ireland. The true weight of this apology you cannot know. Let it be sufficient that, regarding you with admiration as a poet, and with respect as a man, I send you, as an intimation of those sentiments, my first serious attempt to interest the best feelings of the human heart, believing that you have so much general charity as to forget, like me, how widely in moral and political opinions we disagree, and to attribute that difference to better motives than the multitude are disposed to allege as the cause of dissent from their institutions.

Very sincerely yours,
PERCY B. SHELLEY.

* See Introduction, and p. 76 of Correspondence. † i.e. *Alastor.*

APPENDIX.

II.

SHELLEY TO SOUTHEY.

PISA, *June 26th*, 1820.

DEAR SIR,

Some friends of mine persist in affirming that you are the author of a criticism which appeared some time since in the *Quarterly Review* on the "Revolt of Islam."

I know nothing that would give me more sincere pleasure than to be able to affirm from your own assurance that you were not guilty of that writing. I confess I see such strong internal evidence against the charge, without reference to what I think I know of the generous sensibility of your character, that had my own conviction only been concerned, I should never have troubled you to deny what I firmly believe you would have spurned to do.

Our short personal intercourse has always been remembered by me with pleasure; and when I recalled the enthusiasm with which I then considered your writings, with gratitude for your notice, we parted, I think, with feelings of mutual kindness. The article in question, except in reference to the possibility of its having been written by you, is not worth a moment's attention.

That an unprincipled hireling, in default of what to answer in a published composition, should, without provocation, insult over the domestic calamities of a writer of the adverse party—to which perhaps their victim dares scarcely advert in thought—that he should make those calamities the theme of the foulest and the falsest slander—that all this should be done by a calumniator without a name—with the cowardice, no less than the malignity, of an assassin—is too common a piece of charity among Christians (Christ would have taught them better), too common a violation of what is due from man to man among the pretended friends of social order, to have drawn one remark from me, but that I would have you observe the arts practised by that party for which you have abandoned the cause to which your early writings were devoted. I had intended to have called on you, for the purpose of saying what I now write, on my return to England; but the wretched state of my health detains me here, and I fear leaves my enemy, were he such as I could deign to contend with, an easy, but a base victory, for I do not profess paper warfare. But there is a time for all things.

I regret to say that I shall consider your neglecting to answer this letter a substantiation of the fact which it is intended to settle—and *therefore* I shall assuredly hear from you.

     Dear sir, accept the best wishes of
           Yours truly.
            P. B. SHELLEY.

III.

SOUTHEY TO SHELLEY.

SIR,
 You have done me justice in believing that I am not the author of the criticism in the *Quarterly Review* upon the "Revolt of Islam." I have never in any of my writings mentioned your name, or alluded to you even in the remotest hint, either as a man, or as an author. Except the "Alastor" which you sent me, I have never read or seen any of your publications since you were at Keswick. The specimens which I happen to have seen in Reviews and Newspapers have confirmed my opinion that your powers for poetry are of a high order, but the manner in which those powers have been employed is such as to prevent me from feeling any desire to see more of productions so monstrous in their kind, and so pernicious in their tendency. You perceive, sir, that I speak as I think, and therefore you will not ascribe my ready and direct denial of the criticism to the sort of menace which your note conveys, nor understand it as acknowledging in any man a right to call upon me for such a denial, upon no better grounds than a mere suspicion which he or his friends may choose to entertain. Those friends of yours who have persisted in affirming that I am the author can have had no other ground. They have committed the gross impropriety of affirming positively what they could not possibly know to be true, and what happens to be absolutely false.

 I reply to you, sir, because I cannot think of you without the deepest compassion. Eight years ago you were somewhat displeased when I declined disputing with you upon points which are beyond the reach of the human intellect—telling you that the great difference between us was, that you were then nineteen and I was eight-

and-thirty. Would that the difference were no greater now! You wrote to me when you sent me your "Alastor," that as you tolerated my opinions, you supposed I should tolerate yours. Few persons are less intolerant than myself, by disposition as well as by principle, but I cannot admit that any such reciprocity is justly to be claimed. Opinions are to be judged by their effects—and what has been the fruit of yours? Do they enable you to look backward with complacency or forward with hope? Have you found in them a rule of life conducive either to your own happiness, or to that of those who were most nearly and dearly connected with you? Or rather, have they not brought immediate misery upon others, and guilt, which is all but irremediable, on yourself?

The tone of your letter gives me a right to address you thus; and there is one passage in it which induces a hope that I may not be addressing you in vain, for it appears that deadly as your principles have proved, they have not yet wholly hardened your heart. Attend, I beseech you, to its warnings. Do not let any feeling of pride withhold you from acknowledging to yourself how grievously and fatally you have erred. You rejected Christianity before you knew—before you could possibly have known—upon what evidence it rests. How utterly unlike in this, and in every other respect to the superstitions and fables of men's devices, with which you in your presumptuousness have classed it. Look to that evidence while you are yet existing in Time, and you may yet live to bless God for any visitation of sickness and suffering which, by bringing you to a sense of your miserable condition, may enable you to hope for forgiveness, and teach you where to look for it. God in his infinite mercy bring you to this better mind!

This is not the language of party animosity, nor of personal ill-will. Of the latter you will at once acquit me; and if you do not acquit me as readily of the former, it is because you do not know me enough, and are too much under its influence yourself.

I can think of you only as of an individual whom I have known, and of whom I had once entertained high hopes—admiring his talents —giving him credit for good feelings and virtuous desires—and whom I now regard not more with condemnation than with pity.

Believe me, therefore, to be your sincere well-wisher,

ROBERT SOUTHEY.

IV.

SHELLEY TO SOUTHEY.

Pisa, *August* 17*th*, 1820.

Dear Sir,

Allow me to acknowledge the sincere pleasure which I received from the first paragraph of your letter. The disavowal it contained was just such as I firmly anticipated.

Allow me also to assure you, that no menace implied in my letter could have the remotest application to yourself. I am not indeed aware that it contained any menace. I recollect expressing what contempt I felt, in the hope that you might meet the wretched hireling who has so closely imitated your style as to deceive all but those who knew you into a belief that he was you, at Murray's, or somewhere, and that you would inflict my letter on him, as a recompense for sowing ill-will between those who wish each other all good, as you and I do.

I confess your recommendation to adopt the system of ideas you call Christianity has little weight with me, whether you mean the popular superstition in all its articles, or some more refined theory with respect to those events and opinions which put an end to the graceful religion of the Greeks. To judge of the doctrines by their effects, one would think that this religion were called the religion of Christ and Charity, *ut lucus a non lucendo*, when I consider the manner in which they seem to have transformed the disposition and understanding of you and men of the most amiable manners and the highest accomplishments, so that even when recommending Christianity you cannot forbear breathing out defiance, against the express words of Christ. What would you have me think? You accuse me, on what evidence I cannot guess, of *guilt*—a bald word, sir, this, and one which would have required me to write to you in another tone, had you addressed it to any one except myself. Instead, therefore, of refraining from "judging that you be not judged," you not only judge but condemn, and that to a punishment which its victim must be either among the meanest or the loftiest not to regard as bitterer than death. But you are such a pure one as Jesus Christ found not in all Judea to throw the first stone against the woman taken in adultery!

With what care do the most tyrannical Courts of Judicature weigh evidence, and surround the accused with protecting forms; with what reluctance do they pronounce their cruel and presumptuous decisions compared with you! You select a single passage out of a life otherwise not only spotless but spent in an impassioned pursuit of virtue, which looks like a blot, merely because I regulated my domestic arrangements without deferring to the notions of the vulgar, although I might have done so quite as conveniently had I descended to their base thoughts—this you call *guilt*. I might answer you in another manner, but I take God to witness, if such a Being is now regarding both you and me, and I pledge myself if we meet, as perhaps you expect, before Him after death, to repeat the same in His presence—that you accuse me wrongfully. I am innocent of ill, either done or intended; the consequences you allude to flowed in no respect from me. If you were my friend, I could tell you a history that would make you open your eyes; but I shall certainly never make the public my familiar confidant.

You say you judge of opinions by the fruits; so do I, but by their remote and permanent fruits—such fruits of rash judgment as Christianity seems to have produced in you. The immediate fruits of all new opinions are indeed calamity to the promulgators and professors; but we see the end of nothing, and it is in acting well, in contempt of present advantage, that virtue consists.

I need not to be instructed that the opinion of the ruling party to which you have attached yourself always exacts, contumeliously receives, and never reciprocates, toleration. "But there is a tide in the affairs of men"—it is rising while we speak.

Another specimen of your Christianity is the judgment you form of the spirit of my verses, from the abuse of the Reviews. I have desired Mr. Ollier to send you those last published; they may amuse you, for one of them—indeed neither have anything to do with those speculations on which we differ.

I cannot hope that you will be candid enough to feel, or if you feel, to own, that you have done ill in accusing, even in your mind, an innocent and a persecuted man, whose only real offence is the holding opinions something similar to those which you once held respecting the existing state of society. Without this, further correspondence, the object for which I renewed it being once obtained, must, from the differences in our judgment, be irksome and useless. I hope some day to meet you in London, and ten minutes' conversation is worth ten folios of writing. Meanwhile assure yourself that,

among all your good wishers, you have none who wish you better than, dear sir,
Your very faithful and obedient Servant,

P. B. SHELLEY.

P. S.—I ought not to omit that I have had sickness enough, and that at this moment I have so severe a pain in the side that I can hardly write. All this is of no account in the favour of what you, or anyone else, calls Christianity; surely it would be better to wish me health and healthful sensations. *I hope the chickens will not come home to roost!**

V.

SOUTHEY TO SHELLEY.

Yesterday, sir, I received your present of the Cenci and the Prometheus. I thank you for these books, and little as the time is which I can allow for correspondence of any kind, I think it proper to [reply to?] your letter of August 29th,† which announced them.

You tell me that I have selected out of a life "otherwise not only spotless, but spent in the impassioned pursuit of virtue, a single passage which looks like a blot, merely because you regulated your domestic arrangements without reference to the notions of the vulgar," and you accuse me of passing a rash and unjust judgment. Let us look to the case—I will state it with no uncharitable spirit, and with no unfriendly purpose.

When you were a mere youth at College you took up atheistical opinions—you endeavoured to make proselytes to these opinions in a girls' boarding-school. One of the girls was expelled for the zeal with which she entered into your views, and you made her the most honourable amends in your power by marrying her. Shortly afterwards you came to Keswick. There was no appearance, when I saw you, that your principles had injured your heart. As yet you had had no proof of this tendency in yourself, but you had seen a memorable one

---

* In reference to the motto of "The Curse of Kehama"—"Curses are like young chickens, they always come home to roost."

† Probably an error in Caroline Bowles's transcript: query *August* 17*th*.

in the conduct of your first speculation (speculative?) and literary associate, who accompanied you to Scotland on your matrimonial expedition, and on your way back would have seduced your wife. This I had from your own lips: your feelings at that time were humane and generous, and your intentions good. I felt a greater interest in your welfare than I expressed to you, and took such indirect means as were in my power of assuring your father that, erroneous as your conduct was, it was still to be expected that your heart would bring you right, and that everything might be hoped from your genius and your virtues.

Such was my opinion of you when we parted. What I heard of your subsequent conduct tended always to lower it, except as regarded your talents. At length you forsook your wife, because you were tired of her, and had found another woman more suited to your taste. You could tell me a history, you say, which would make me open my eyes: perhaps they are already open. It is a matter of public notoriety that your wife destroyed herself. Knowing in what manner she bore your desertion, I never attributed this to her sensibility on that score. I have heard it otherwise explained: I have heard that she followed your example as faithfully as your lessons, and that the catastrophe was produced by shame. Be this as it may, ask your own heart, whether you have not been the whole, sole, and direct cause of her destruction. You corrupted her opinions; you robbed her of her moral and religious principles; you debauched her mind. But for you and your lessons she might have gone through the world innocently and happily.

I will do you justice, sir. While you were at Keswick you told your bride that you regarded marriage as a mere ceremony, and would live with her no longer than you liked her. I dare say you told her this before the ceremony, and that you persuaded her that there was nothing sacred in the tie. But that she should have considered this as the condition upon which she was married, or that you yourself at that time looked forward to a breach of the connexion, I do not believe. I think still too well of your original nature to believe it. She trusted to your heart, not your opinions. She relied upon your generosity, your affection, your tenderness, your first love. The wife of your youth might well rely upon these, and with the more confidence when she became the mother of your first children.

No, sir, you were not depraved enough to think you could ever desert her when you talked of it as a possible event; and if you had not tampered with your own heart with speculations upon such possibilities, and contemplating them as lawful and allowable, her confidence in you could not have been deceived. That sophistry which endeavours to confound the plain broad distinction between right and wrong can never be employed innocently or with impunity. Some men are wicked by disposition, others become so in their weakness, yielding to temptation; but you have corrupted in yourself an excellent nature. You have sought for temptation and courted it; and have reasoned yourself into a state of mind so pernicious that your character, with your domestic arrangements, as you term it, might furnish a subject for the drama more instructive, and scarcely less painful, than the detestable story of the Cenci, and this has proceeded directly from your principles.* It is the Atheist's Tragedy. You might have regulated your domestic arrangements, you say, quite as conveniently to yourself if you had descended to the base thoughts of the vulgar. I suppose this means that you might have annulled your marriage as having been contracted during your minority. You say that your only real crime is the holding opinions something similar to those which I once held respecting the existing state of society. That, sir, is not your crime, it would only be your error; your offence is moral as well as political, practical as well as speculative. Nor were my opinions ever similar to yours in any other point than that, desiring, as I still desire, a greater equality in the condition of men, I entertained erroneous notions concerning the nature of that improvement in society, and the means whereby it was to be promoted. Except in this light, light and darkness are not more opposite than my youthful opinions and yours. You would have found me as strongly opposed in my youth to Atheism and immorality of any kind as I am now, and to that abominable philosophy which teaches self-indulgence instead of self-control.

The Christianity which I recommended to your consideration is to be found in the Scriptures and in the Book of Common Prayer. I would fain have had you to believe that there is judgment after death, and to learn, and understand, and feel all sins may be forgiven through the merits and mediation of Jesus Christ. You mistake my meaning when you suppose that I wished you to be afflicted with bodily suffering: but I repeat, that any affliction which might bring you to a better mind would be a dispensation of mercy. And here, sir, our

---

* Two words in the attempted Greek characters of Caroline Bowles are here indecipherable.

correspondence must end. I never should have sought it; but having been led into it, it appeared to me a duty to take that opportunity of representing you to yourself as you appear to me, with little hope indeed of producing any good effect, and yet not altogether hopeless; for though you may go on with an unawakened mind, a seared conscience, and a hardened heart, there will be seasons of misgivings, when that most sacred faculty which you have laboured to destroy makes itself felt. At such times you may remember me as an earnest monitor whom you cannot suspect of ill-will, and whom it is not in your power to despise, however much you may wish to repel his admonitions with contempt.

Believe me, sir, your sincere well-wisher,

ROBERT SOUTHEY.

II.—SOUTHEY'S DREAMS.*

November 7th, 1804.—A certain king had a precious cup, giftee with some magical property, of such exceeding value that he suffered no person to see it, its loss would have been so great an evil. A model, however, was in his daughter's keeping, and by winning her love he who coveted the original obtained sight of this, which was doing much, for though the real cup could not be stolen nor won by any unworthy means (such was the spell), it was attainable by intensity of desire and fixedness of mind, as the Fakeers obtain beatitude, and Mainanduc pretended to heal diseases at a distance. Thus far had I got in the dream when the child awoke me. I was sensible that it was a fairy tale, and yet the story seemed to be acting before me.

About ten days ago a very valuable dream which I had has induced me to commence this record. I was haunted by evil spirits, of whose presence, though unseen, I was aware. There were also dead bodies near me, though I saw them not. Terrified as I was, far beyond any fear that I ever experienced in actual life, still I reasoned and insisted to myself that all was delirium and weakness of mind, and even sent away the person who I thought was present with me, that I might be left alone to exert myself. When alone the actual

* *See* p. 110 of this volume.

presence of the tormentors was more certain, and my horrors increased, till at length an arm appeared through the half-opened door, or rather a long hand. Determined to convince myself that all was unsubstantial and visionary, though I saw it most distinctly, I ran up and caught it. It was a hand, and a lifeless one. I pulled at it with desperate effort, dragged in a sort of shapeless body into the room, trampled upon it, crying out aloud the while for horror. The extreme efforts I made to call for help succeeded so far as to awake Edith, who immediately delivered me from the most violent fear that ever possessed me.

This is a valuable dream, for an old monk would have believed all to have been verily what it appeared, and I now perfectly understand by experience what their contests with the devil were.

November 8th.—I was in Bonaparte's palace, where some sort of contest was taking place between him and Sir Sidney Smith, who came to me for a knife to cut something which prevented him from drawing his sword. Bonaparte struck me; I had an axe in my hand; he saw that I was half inclined to cut him down, and attempted to kill me. I struck him with the axe, and brought him down, and dragged him out into a public hall, not being yet dead, and there beheaded him. This is the first time I ever killed him in self-defence, though I have more than once done it upon the pure principle of tyrannicide.

November 25th.—I saw my mother, and kissed her, and wept upon her. This often occurs in my dreams. I never see her without sorrow, the feeling which predominates whenever I think of her still remaining, even when death is forgotten, and her perfect image living before me. Once I remember the spirits of my mother and cousin entered my room in a dream; all who were present were terrified; but I went up firmly, with such feelings as the reality would have produced, and touched the apparition, and exclaimed "It is substantial."

December 7th.—I was sent to the Court of Haroun Alraschid, God knows on what political errand; but it was a very important one, and I carried with me a beautiful woman, related to me Heaven knows how, who travelled for security in boy's clothes, I also being dressed meanly, to escape danger. The Caliph was a very good-natured man, but his interpreters, two Spanish renegados, were exceedingly insolent, so that I beat them both before his face, not without a struggle, and insisted that some honester person should be called—not rascals who had renounced their religion, and who would falsify what I should say, for the sake of injuring me. This was of consequence, as I had to deliver my fair charge to the Commander of the Faithful, and convince him that I had faithfully acquitted myself of my trust.

Some time ago I saw Adam—an old man, half stupefied with age; he lived in a little lonely cottage, and complained to me that Eve was grown old, and did not use him kindly—she did not get his supper comfortably for him. He told me there were a great many of his descendants whom he had never seen, and particularly one William Taylor, of Norwich, who, he had heard, was a very clever fellow, and he wished to know if I knew him.

January 7th, 1805.—I was supping at Garrick's house, and seated at his left hand, at the top of the table; my memory had made up his face accurately; he got upon the table, and spoke an epilogue of his own writing in the character of a cook-maid, and promised, at Mrs. Garrick's desire, to recite a serious poem afterwards, that I might hear him.

Westminster often makes a part of my dreams, which are always uncomfortable. Either I have lost my books, or have Bible exercise to do, and feel that I have lost the knack, or am conscious that it is not befitting me to continue at school, and so determine to leave it by my own will. It is odd enough that school never appears to me as it was, with my contemporaries about me, but always as it would be if I were there now, among boys all strange to me. Of Oxford I never remember to have dreamt, so little has a college life entered into my being. Of Portugal very often. The language of my dreams is almost as often Portuguese as English.

One of the oddest dreams in my recollection befell me when a mere child, about six years old, but it is as fresh in my memory as if it were a last night's scene. It was that the devil came to pay Miss Palmer a morning visit in the dining-room in Galloway's Buildings, and I was the only person in the room with her. There I sat trembling upon one of the flat-bottomed mahogany chairs, while she was bustling about in all the hurry and delight of receiving unexpectedly a visit from a great person ' Be seated, dear Mr.

Devil." Her smile and his smirk, and the villainous nose and eyes of old Horny, and his diabolical tail, are before my eyes this moment.

January 12*th.*—Cæsar in Balliol I thought was uninhabited, and going to ruin, like Pompey. I went up with somebody to Lightfoot's rooms, and found two fellows at work with a crucible. I saw they were coining, and one of them ran at me to murder me. I ran downstairs, but found that at the bottom, instead of a door to get out at, there was the foot of another staircase, which would lead me up again, so that I made for a window, and got out; the fellow followed, but being fairly out, I contrived to place myself between him and his haunt, and give the alarm, so that in his turn he fled, and was taken.

February 5*th.*—Some little girl, a mere child, in her zeal against the Mass, was resolved to throw down the pix in the midst of the ceremony. I followed her to protect her; we went through a long, low cavern, or vaulted passage, from whence a flight of steps led up into the church, and she made for the altar, and took out the wafer, and threw it down. The church was very large, and the people but few, so that no tumult ensued; but the priest immediately seized her, and led her away. By good fortune this priest was Wingfield—*ipsissimus* Gubby—so I took him by the arm, and engaged him in conversation, pleading for the child, while she made her escape along the same vault whereby we had entered.

February 8*th.*—To my great surprise I discovered that Edith had a former husband living. He was either by birth or descent a Spaniard, but in the English army; he had been dotingly fond of her, and she of him, till in some action he received a musket ball in his leg, which as long as it remained there rendered him feeble, and he would not suffer it to be extracted, because some old woman had told him the operation would be fatal. Upon this he abandoned his wife. I now, however, understood that he was perfectly recovered. The way by which I first learnt all this was by seeing a Spanish grammar, so philosophically and ably arranged, as to make me inquire for the anonymous author, who proved to be this person. Upon questioning Edith, she said it was all true; that he was the handsomest man she ever saw, and had made her a very affectionate husband, but that he had behaved very ill in deserting her. I asked if I should write to him, or find him out. She said "no," because she felt still a regard for him which he did not deserve. I now found some Latin verses which he had written; they were upon the birds in their brooding season, and concluded with a reference to the happiness he had once enjoyed at Bristol, but which he had by his own folly forfeited. These I explained to Edith, saying that perhaps he was in want, and we ought to find him out and relieve him. But she still seemed unwilling to have any communication with him, and I could perceive that this was rather because she loved him too much than too little.

I have uniformly in my dreams fancied that whenever I attempted to read, the page was blank, or, to speak more accurately, that there were lines without letters, and the perplexity occasioned by being obliged to divine what words would fill up the due spaces, analogous to the feeling perpetually occurring in sleep of losing one's hat or shoes in the street—an uncomfortable and disquieting sense that something is wanting, you cannot tell why. This impossibility of reading is perfectly explicable; the mind cannot form its associations and embody or print them co-instantaneously. One operation must precede the other, and it is as impossible in dreams to read what is passing as it is to overtake your own shadow.

February 10*th*.—I discovered that King Fernando el Catholico was my father, to my inexpressible grief, and told my mother, that of all human beings there was scarcely one whom I regarded with more horror and hatred, and that I would submit to any torments which could purge his blood out of my veins.

February 18*th*.—There was some building to be entered, but it required faith, and fearlessness, and fortitude to enter it, for the ground before the entrance was fiery, and the nearer the door the more intense the burning, and they who were unworthy would be thrust back by some unseen power. What was within I knew not; but once in, and there was an end of all pain or calamity for ever. I took the child, and being barefooted and almost naked, went on, exclaiming from some inexplicable association: "Jesus and St. Ignatius Loyola!" There were two persons before me engaged in the same adventure, and, in spite of the burning ground, we all got in. Some dozen or score had succeeded before us, and as soon as I had entered they began to dance, and wanted me to join, as if triumphantly; but I, who had the sort of feeling as if death were over, and I was now in the world to come, turned away with anger at the proposal, and began to examine what place I was in. It was a huge church of white marble, Parian, without spot, or streak, or stain; and there were seats around it, rising one above another, as in a theatre, and the seats were of the same pure white marble as the building. I went through the building into a park, and here the connexion ceased, and the dream became vague and worthless.

Five nights ago, at Grasmere, I thought a fiend and a good spirit were shooting arrows at each other, many of which fell near me, and I gathered them, and endeavoured to shoot at the fiend also, who was very little, but never could fit them to the bow. The good spirit at last heaped coals and peat upon the head of his enemy, so as to bury him completely, till he, by the fieryness of his nature, kindled them, and they blazed and burnt, burning him, who yet could not be consumed.

February 27th.—I saw a man whose name was Apollonius, who for some grievous sin had received a grievous punishment. A worm like a viper, about three inches in length, and proportionately thin, was fastened upon one of the nerves of a decayed tooth, and I saw it hanging therefrom, though at times it lay coiled within the cavity. The poor wretch was relating his sufferings to me with so much contrition and resignation, that his repentance was accepted, and the worm fell off. It crawled into a fire, and here the dream adapted itself to old notions, for as the creature entered the flames it put out legs like a salamander, and lay parching in that shape till it was dried up and consumed.

Not unfrequently I have dreamt of being among old graves newly opened, or vaults, and the smell of the dead has been particularly offensive; the smell has always resembled the bitter pungency of cheese in its blackest state of putrefaction. This being uniform, must depend on some physical cause.

April 2nd.—I thought I was assisting at the removal of my grandfather's body, with so much recollection of place and persons that Ashton was the scene, and Lewis the clergyman who was to read the funeral service. The coffin was of an odd shape, bearing some resemblance to a body, and appeared to be of a thin and yellowish metal; some of the bystanders moved away from it, but I observed it could not occasion any offensive smell, as nothing but bones could possibly remain of a man who had been dead above forty years. But presently the coffin moved, and it was evident the body was alive; it was opened, and after some struggles the body threw off its outer coat of skin, and got up, to everybody's astonishment. I looked to my uncle to see if it was really his father, and finding this was the case, formed a theory that we had hitherto mistaken the nature of death, which did nothing more than bring man into a chrysalis state, in which he was to lie awhile, and then cast his slough, and come out fresh as a bird after moulting.

May 15*th*.—I was at some dramatic representation, which was enacted within a circumvallation of stones, like a Roman camp, on which I stood, not without wondering at the theatre; from thence I went to introduce myself to George Rose, who lived in a very fine house, and said how much he was obliged to me for the visit, and how he should have been mortified if I had gone on without calling on him. I was somewhat ashamed of my hat this while, and endeavoured to hide the ragged part of the lining. We talked of Christ Church and Burton, &c. Presently I was in my bedroom, as his guest, with a sense of danger. I thought that, having dressed under this apprehension, and left the room, I stept back into it, for something which I had forgotten, upon which a spell took effect, which would have been vain if I had not returned there, and I became the prisoner of Mrs. Rose, for she was a malignant enchantress. Some dim association about young Rose and Amadis must have produced this.

Afterwards I found myself with Edith sitting down to dinner with the prophet Mohammed in some far country, where we noticed with wonder that the furniture and food were both in the English fashion. Some alarm was given, I know not what, except that we all were in danger of being taken up. What became of the prophet? If he himself cannot tell, nobody else can; but I worked a miracle like a Domdanielite, pronouncing aloud I remember not what, with such faith, that Edith and I were taken up in the air, and conveyed away.

October 1*st*.—Here is a long gap. During the whole summer I have been so engaged with visitors and walking about the country, that having no Daniel to remember my dreams for me, they are irrecoverably gone.

Last night I had met a Mr. Trevilian, a Somersetshire man. I dreamt that I was visiting him in his own county, and this reminding me of Glastonbury, I thought that we went to see the ruins. But the ruins which I saw in my dream were far nobler than Glastonbury, or probably than any existing pile. I thought that, descending a long flight of steps, like those which lead from Redcliffe church door, or in the Deanery at Westminster, only that they were under the roof of the building, we entered a prodigious church, deserted and bearing marks of decay, though all its parts were still entire. I have the picture vividly before me, the arched windows, and meeting columns, the grass between the stones; the sound of my own footsteps is still fresh in my ears, and the feeling of delight and reverence which made me in the dream stand half-way down the steps and shed tears. Presently I was led to a part of the building which was called the Beatorio; the most extraordinary place I ever fancied. It was so called as being the burial-place of the monks, who were all presumed to be in bliss, and the whole floor was covered with statues, admirably executed in a fine white stone, of these men rising from the dead all in different attitudes, each as large as life, and each made to the living likeness of the man whom it represented. One side of this place was open to the cloisters, so that all was seen in a strong light. The other walls were in like manner covered with figures issuing out.

I now thought a sort of *Auto* of the Last Judgment was to be acted in the church. A number of the most ill-looking men had been got together to play the damned, and express as much damnation as possible in their looks and gestures when they were set aside after sentence. The dream now began to confound things: these persons seemed to be really the damned; and I, who did not quite like such company, as they were becoming obstreperous, rose to make my escape. Some fellow half-damned, half-devil, was placed in the gateway to prevent me from going out; I forced my way by, and creating wings with the effort, fled away. A long flight brought me to the mountains, and I awoke, just at the fit time, when the whole dream was fairly brought to a conclusion.

October 28*th*.—Looking at the mountains opposite, which appeared more rocky and precipitous, a huge mass of rock was thrown down by some sudden convulsion of nature, and I saw falling with it a woman of gigantic size, as if out of the heart of the cliffs, where she had occasioned the earthquake.

January 18*th,* 1806.—Elmsley was walking with me in Tindal's Park, such as it was twenty years ago. Over the stile (which I remember as the best I ever crost), and just by the pond a little hole had been freshly dug, from whence we saw that the head of a man had been taken out; the body having been buried upright, and presently the trunk rose slowly up in such a state as one sees the ribs of a horse left by the dogs and crows. My attention was taken from this ghastly sight by something more extraordinary : a figure rose from the earth precisely like Elmsley, even in dress; and in fact he proved to be the real Elmsley who touched the one at my side, and made him crumble away.

January 23*rd.*—I was in Germany, and because some German friend was going to poison himself, agreed to poison myself to keep him company. Accordingly, in a large party I first drank to him "to our next meeting," then let him put the poison into my next glass, unperceived by anyone. It was a brown powder which by no means improved the wine. Presently we were both seized with violent pains in the stomach, and both fell; I suppose by the pain which I actually felt that I must have been plagued with flatulence at the time. We were each laid on a bed to die there, and not one of the company, though they now knew what had happened, went for any assistance ; it seemed to be a matter of etiquette to let us die if we chose it. Now for my part, though I was perfectly well satisfied to go upon a voyage of discovery to the next world, yet it certainly would not have displeased me to have had the physician sent for. My pain, however, abated and got into the abdomen. I went to my friend and told him this, and that I suspected the dose would not do its work. He said he was in the last agonies, and so should I be presently; but, however, it all went off.

July 14*th.*—A Bible which had been Chatterton's was in the possession of some woman to whom I went in quest of it. She was as wicked a looking creature as can well be imagined, and her looks did not belie her. This Bible she had prepared for some magical purpose—I know not what—staining every leaf with the heart's blood of an infant. It was the Book of Life, she said, and every leaf was to have a life in it, and she had not spared lives to make it complete. As soon as this was known, a mob collected, and to my great satisfaction determined to set fire to her house, and burn her in it with all that it contained. At first I felt a revengeful and righteous pleasure at this, but the house stood in a narrow street, and therefore I and young Shepherd, who was with me, thought it best to call upon the commanding officer in the town and inform him of the danger. We forced our way with much difficulty through the crowd, and came into the room where he was drinking his wine: he heard our tale with the utmost coolness, smiled at the alarm we seemed to be in, and said he had heard it already and given orders accordingly. From hence we returned, but by a backway; and here, as it very often occurs in my dreams, it seemed as if I were crawling along a subterranean way where it was scarcely possible to form a passage. At the upper end of this long vault, which was under a street, and as rugged as possible, not being arched, we found a box and these words written on it: "Take good heed." I opened it and found some minerals and four volumes of alchemy: it was left there for some person who was attempting the grand secret: a man came for it, and I desired him, when he had succeeded and could make gold, to be so good as to remember me. This did not break the dream. When we came out the house was on fire, but I learnt that the woman was not in it. Once she had attempted to run out, but was forced back again by the mob, but a man-servant staid with her to the last, and the people were so struck by his fidelity, that they suffered them both to come out. The woman was scorched from head to foot, her legs being black as cinders, and in this state she was reserved for justice.

August 10*th.*—I and Mr. Bunbury were in my room at Clough's, which then belonged to him: there was in the room a large mahogany case like a shop counter, which he opened, and showed me under it a sort of arch-work of wood at both ends and stone in the middle, so secured, that like the patent coffins, it could neither be opened from within, nor from without. Some villain he said had murdered a man, and made this place to hide the body in, but he had arrived in time to inclose the murderer there with the dead body, and there, though this was long ago, he was alive still. I was for attempting to open it, and seeing the mystery.

November 19*th.*—Walking from my father's into High Street, I found the people shutting their shops because there was a great show coming, and I waited to see it. Presently the volunteers came one by one on horseback, each wielding his own particular weapon, which were swords of every possible shape, some even made expressly for back strokes. Everything was as cheerful as possible till, on a sudden, two women, half undrest, weeping, and with swollen eyes and cheeks, brought in an armed-chair, which they carried like a sedan, a dead man naked. A ghastlier sight I never called up in any hour of waking imagination, and shall not soon forget the shock it gave me. This, it seemed, was the corpse of Lord St. Vincent, who had just expired. Presently I found myself (the French phrase is philosophically applicable to the change of place in dreams) at my father's again, in the back parlour Lord St. Vincent with me; for though he was dead, the Devil was not yet come for him. We were looking out of the window upon some water-works which he had made in his lifetime. These were of a very extraordinary kind—a rough and roaring stream came rolling down to a dam formed by four sluices which reached completely across it. This stream was accustomed to carry down with it many things swept from its banks, which, of course, struck the dam; immediately, by some machinery, one of the four sluices opened below, swallowed up the thing which struck against it, and vomited it up on the other side with prodigious force. Some of these water-volcanoes opened on the tops of the houses, so that no place seemed safe from their fury. St. Vincent was about to open one just over my head, upon which I took the liberty of reminding him that as he was in momently expectation of the Devil's coming to fetch him, he might employ his time better. He said "yes," he felt something like brimstone tingling at his fingers' ends already, and would go and say his prayers; and thus my dream left him making the best use of his time.

I had been reading aloud overnight the opening of "Kehama," and St. Vincent may have been the shadow of Arvalan; the dam at the water-works was the mill-weir behind St. James's bath, which in my infancy I saw so often from John Ashbourne's, and remember so well, though I have never been since in that direction; and the housetops, on which the sluices vomited up, were those on the right hand of the Plume of Feathers over Ewbank's kitchen.

December 15*th*.—I was reading of a Doctor Bocardo, who had discovered a mode of curing fevers by putting the patient into what he called one of his Burning Hells, which was a place heated to the greatest degree that life could bear. The extreme heat decomposed the matter of the disease.

December 7th, 1807.—Alas! my dreams are as good as Nebuchadnezzar's, and I can remember them no better. Last night all that I can recall to mind is that an old man, I know not why or wherefore, was to leap from a precipice as high as the summit of Skiddaw. It was some religious act, or voluntary one, for everybody regarded him with reverence; I went to behold him, not without some struggle of feelings. The old man appeared upon the precipice, his stature seeming larger than life; he was in a full green habit, not unlike a friar's; he lifted up his right hand to heaven and said something which we could not hear, and then leaped off. I saw him descending in an upright posture; it was in a situation where I could not see him when he came to the ground, and I hastened away, deafening myself that I might not hear the fall. Altogether the effect was very awful, but I cannot call back the circumstances which sanctified it.

August 16*th*, 1808.—Last night I and the King of Denmark were taken prisoners by Charles XII. of Sweden, I having been grievously wounded in the thigh. He was determined to put us to death, and sent for us into his chamber to tell us so. How it happened I know not, but I and my brother of Denmark—for I was as good a king as himself—were not on good terms. However, I helped him to a chair, for he was desperately hurt, and seated myself. And then I gave Charles what I really believe was a very eloquent philippic: the murder of Patkul, I told him, was the crime which had damned him in this world and the next. I stung him to the very heart, and by way of generosity he told us he would put off our execution till one in the morning, and we might go to bed if we pleased. I made answer that with that wound in my thigh and a wife and children in England it was not very likely I should go to sleep, and that if I did, I should not like to get up at one in the morning to be put to death. So the sooner that business was performed the better.

July 13*th*, 1818.—I have spent an hour vexatiously in looking in vain for my dream-book, which I very foolishly have disused for many years. Last night I had so strange a one that it renewed in me the old desire of preserving such things.

I was with Landor. He and I an hundred years ago had stabbed a man, and that man, by some art magic, was laid in a stone coffin to sleep for a century, at the end of which time we, whether we liked it or not, were to read the characters upon the stone which covered him, and this would bring him to life. The operation of time had been suspended upon us during the hundred years; the time was now full; the inscription was nearly illegible; but I, though with some horror and much unwillingness, could not help making out the word Barabra; and Landor, with equal unwillingness, made out the rest, the stone rising as he read, and bringing up the coffin to a level with the ground. I looked under the lid as it lifted itself, and saw a pale-looking man, in a wig of Charles the Second's time: he had a wound in his side and was waking.

November 26th, 1818.—Every one knows the sense of flying in dreams; with me it requires a perpetual effort of self-propulsion, and is accompanied with a sort of apprehension, upon rising to any height above the ground, that I may not be able to sustain the effort, and may therefore fall. Last night this very common form of dream was curiously modified, for I thought I was sitting upon a low stool, and made it fly through the air by the application of a short stick to the ground, in the manner of *punting*. While thus employed I met an ugly spectacle—a living human head, which had been so born without any *body* belonging to it. Waking then, and dwelling upon this till I presently again fell dreaming, I thought I was in a castle where there were several such heads, well-born, and enjoying respect and all the comforts that could be given them. They were sustained by odours, and had all the pleasure of taste, but swallowed nothing; and they had power enough of motion to turn themselves as they liked.

December, 1818.—I thought I was at school with poor T. Lamb, and questioning myself whether it were a dream or not, seemed to satisfy myself that it was not. (I never remember any instance but this of such a conclusion.) Presently, however, I recollected having read of his death, and looking at him earnestly, I asked him if it were true. His countenance appeared mournful, and he said it was. I asked if it was well with him, and his reply was not satisfactory, and then I asked in much emotion if I could do anything which might avail him. I was very much affected, so that the strong feeling wakened me.

Some weeks ago I had just the same dream respecting poor Matthew Lewis, only that I was less agitated, as never having had any affection for the man.

Everyone knows the common feeling in dreams of an inability to get the limbs on when they are in haste. A similar defect of power to correspond with the will I often experience in my sleep, but which I do not remember to have seen described. In the midst of an impassioned conversation my voice appears to fail; the lips, and tongue, and larynx perform their part in endeavouring to articulate, but I am sensible that no sound is produced. It might seem from this, that at other times when I am holding forth in a dream (the only time in which I can play the orator) I talk in my sleep; but this is not the case. This is the solution. Both in the attempts to sing and to articulate the dream passes the ordinary limits of sleep, in which the body should be passive, and attempts to excite action, which the waking will alone can call forth.

July 17*th*, 1819.—I was in a church, or covered cemetery, where bodies were placed in recesses in the wall, the stone which closed the recess bearing the epitaph. Major Christian was there, employed in removing two of these stones, because the persons whose names were there inscribed were of disgraceful memory. Two old-fashioned coffins were thus left exposed. While I was blaming him in thought for making this exposure he opened another recess, in which the coffin was placed upright, and handling it clumsily, the coffin broke, and its tenant, a tall corpse, dressed in the fashion of cloak and doublet, trunk-hose, and large, hanging, short boots, came out, sword in hand, and fell into the body of the church, where it moved about on its legs, without sense or sight, with a drunken sort of motion. The dream now became more grotesque than frightful. I was a school-boy again. Wynn and Combe were with me, and our sport was to keep off this blind vampire, as he stalked, or reeled about, slashing with his sword.

July 27*th*, 1819.—The Princess of Brazil died, and her body having been embalmed, was brought in full dress, in a chair, to be deposited, sitting upon a scaffold, in some church, and the remains of an attendant with her, also in full dress, but differing in this respect, that only the skeleton remained—a ghastly figure it was in its silks, and gauzes, and lace! The more so to me when they said it was my old acquaintance Miss Palmer. Presently I found myself engaged in procuring an asylum for the child of the Princess—the last of the House of Braganza.

When I slept again I was at Swift's house at Dublin, where he was living with two sisters—the one very plain; the other very accomplished and beautiful, deeply in love with him, and breaking her heart, like Mrs. Johnson, because of his strange conduct. She sung to him a song of her own composing, alluding to her own condition.

July 7th, 1821.—Some person took me to call upon Mr. Spence, near Lewes, the humourist, who built Pigmy Hall. And there I saw three old ladies, whose ages were—one, one hundred and thirty-five; one, one hundred and twenty-five; and one, one hundred and two. The youngest was the only one whose faculties were unimpaired. But the odd part of the dream was, that all their chins had grown to a great length, being prolonged eight or ten inches in a curve, and covered with a thick, black, bushy beard. I thought that this curious growth was akin to the production of the ligneous fungus which grows upon old wood, as if Nature were thus whimsically disposing of materials for which it had no better use.

December 4th, 1821.—Palmerin of England gave me Arcalaus, the enchanter, in the shape of an egg, the enchanter having taken that form, and bade me deliver him to Urganda. Urganda took the egg, and said her husband should eat it for his supper.

Isabel had been reading Amadis and Palmerin, and talking to me a great deal about both; hence this jumbled dream.

January 4th, 1823.—St. Antonio was in Westminster Abbey, as his own monument, in perfect preservation, and so veritably sentient and alive that he answered me when I asked him, in Portuguese, if he were the identical St. Antonio of Lisbon and Padua with whom I was so well acquainted in history. The miracle staggered my Protestantism, and I requested Dr. Wordsworth, who was Dean of Westminster, to assist me in verifying the fact, and ascertaining that the body actually had been there so many centuries, for if this were indeed so, the saintship must be admitted, with all its consequences.

January 15*th.*—I was visiting an old man, who was an extraordinary mechanist, and when he was showing me some of his knick-knack performances with their secret springs his daughter observed, in a half whisper, that for some of his performances a greater power than that of mechanism was required. The old man, seeing that I did not readily believe in his magical power, followed me to the door, and asked if I chose that he should call a spirit, and make him take me up into the air, to convince me. I answered that I was willing, in God's name, to see the proof. It was night, and accordingly a spirit—whether good or bad was yet to be discovered—appeared in the form of a man, and desired me to get upon his back. I pronounced something between adjuration and prayer, mounted, and up we went; he had no wings, and I compared the motion to that which I was myself in the habit of performing in dreams; but then I was sure that I was not dreaming now. I continued, however, my ejaculations, and found presently that they made my bearer uneasy, and that he seemed very much disposed to throw me off; but I stuck close, and the most practised exorcist could not have attacked a foul fiend more successfully than I assailed mine till I brought him to the ground, and alighted safe and sound. My next business was to read a lecture to the old magician, who, bating that he dealt with the devil, was a good-hearted, meritorious person.

October 5*th*, 1823.—I thought I had been reading in Muratori that he buried Johns on a Monday, Williams on a Tuesday, and so had different days of the week appointed for interment, according to the Christian names of the dead. An odd custom, it struck me, unreasonable, and especially inconvenient in a climate like that of Italy. He commented also upon the unfitness of depositing persons of holy life in promiscuous cemeteries, owing to which, he said, the relics of sinners and criminals had sometimes been honoured as those of saints. There was, however, he said, this advantage, that the body of the true saint manifested itself in such a place by its incorruptibility. Presently I thought that I found myself naked, and laid at length in the niche of a catacomb, among the dust of the dead, which resembled damp snuff, or moistened bark, in colour and consistency. What was worse, I was clasped in the arms of a living skeleton, which endeavoured to break in my ribs by its grasp. Grief is as intense in dreams as in reality, but we can bear horrors in sleep which would certainly deprive us of our waking senses, if not of life. I struggled with the body of this Death, and at the same time called for help. The sexton heard my cries, for I heard him approaching to ascertain the cause. This made the skeleton renew his efforts to crush my bones, while I worked upon his with the same intent. My attempts to cry aloud disturbed Edith, and she awoke me from this singularly frightful dream, which left me with a sensation in both sides, as if they had been bruised.

October 14*th*, 1823.—I went to get some bread of P. Antonio Vieyra, who was thought to make better bread than any other person. He was drest as in his portrait, in the Jesuit habit, and so like that portrait, though somewhat older, that I knew him instantly. There was a perplexity in my mind about his being still alive, though he said he was more than a hundred years old. He told me he had a sad, profligate son, whose name was Daniel Vieyra, and I was reasonable enough to be surprised at his having given him a Jewish name. I complained of the injustice which his wretched biographer had done him in representing him as a mere Jesuit, and wholly overlooking his political character and his universal charity. Vieyra was very sensible of this, and I wanted him to write his own memoirs.

October 25*th*, 1826.—Yesterday I had read some of Hurdis's poems, and was writing concerning them for the *Quarterly Review*. This made me dream that I saw him and his sisters at their own house, when he showed me two volumes of his works in that edition which he had printed himself. The printing, to my surprise, was remarkably good, and there was a snowy whiteness in the paper which I never saw before. Upon my admiring it, he requested me to accept it, and upon hesitating because he had no other copy, he told me that the set was imperfect, being two volumes instead of three, and he begged I would take one as a pledge of friendship.

March 1*st*, 1830.—The night before last my dream was that I had climbed to the top of a tall tree without branches, and when at the top, could not come down by sliding as I had expected, for I seemed to gravitate upwards.

May 8*th*, 1830.—Yesterday I read in my brother's MS. Memoir poor dear Gooch's dream of his dead child. Though I had no recollection of it in my sleep, it undoubtedly contributed to what I dreamt last night.

I was at a table somewhere, surrounded with guests, and directly opposite was my old schoolfellow and friend, poor Bean. One who sat next me asked me if I knew who that singular-looking person was. I answered that I knew him very well and had a great regard for him, but was amazed at seeing him, because I heard (which was the fact), from what seemed undoubted authority, that being paymaster to a regiment in the East Indies, and taking money for the troops from one East Indian island to another, he had been murdered by the Malay boatmen and thrown overboard. Presently Bean came round and stood by me. I asked him then if he were dead or alive. "Dead," he said; but had come thus to convince me of the resurrection of the dead. I replied that I had not needed such proof, for I believed in Moses and the Prophets. And then I awoke with emotion, not of fear, but of grief, and with tears in my eyes.

July 6*th*, 1830.—I was in that most frequent of all dreamy states: self-suspended in the air, exercising that power of moving without wings which is always accompanied by a sense of insecurity, a constant tendency to rise, and as constant a danger of falling headlong. Perhaps in such dreams the stories of saints being elevated in their prayers may have originated; they have dreamed that they were so, and mistaken, or chosen to mistake the dream for reality.

Last night I was not only thus buoyant myself, but had before me a volume of the *Acta Sanctorum* buoyant in a like manner, open as on a desk. Alighting after this, I went into a church with an old man, who had witnessed the miracle; but I had some vague notion that I was about to be ordained there, but the miracle had rather disturbed me than inspired confidence. I knew that it had not depended in any degree on myself as relating to the book, and that it could not possibly give any additional authority to the book itself, and that I could not render the book buoyant, though I might raise myself into the same precarious situation.

May 10*th*, 1832.—Some whimsical person died, and it appeared by his will that he had left me an estate of ten thousand pounds a-year, on condition that I should never again wear breeches, pantaloons, trousers, or any other modification of that masculine garb. So I was deliberating whether to adopt a Moorish or a Highland dress, though I feared the former might not be allowed, or to wear coat and waistcoat with the philibeg.

NOTES.

(1). SOUTHEY AND SHELLEY.—Mr. Garnett has with much kindness contributed towards the completeness of the materials in this volume relating to Southey and Shelley by giving me a copy of Shelley's "satire upon satire"—a fragment—spoken of in a letter to Leigh Hunt, dated Pisa, Jan. 25, 1822: "I began once a satire upon satire, which I meant to be very severe; it was full of *small knives*, in the use of which practice would have soon made me very perfect" (Forman's edition of Shelley's Prose Works, vol. iv. pp. 255, 256). This fragment is now first published:—

> If gibbets, axes, confiscations, chains,
> And racks of subtle torture, if the pains
> Of shame, of fiery Hell's tempestuous wave,
> Seen through the caverns of the shadowy grave,
> Hurling the damned into the murky air
> While the meek blest sit smiling; if Despair
> And Hate, the rapid bloodhounds with which Terror
> Hunts through the world the homeless steps of Error,
> Are the true secrets of the commonweal
> To make men wise and just;
> And not the sophisms of revenge and fear,
> Bloodier than is revenge
> Then send the priests to every hearth and home
> To preach the burning wrath which is to come,
> In words like flakes of sulphur, such as thaw
> The frozen tears
> If Satire's scourge could wake the slumbering hounds
> Of Conscience, or erase the deeper wounds,
> The leprous scars of callous infamy;
> If it could make the present not to be,
> Or charm the dark past never to have been,
> Or turn regret to hope; who that has seen
> What Southey is and was, would not exclaim,
> Lash on!   be the keen verse dipped in flame;
> Follow his flight with winged words, and urge
> The strokes of the inexorable scourge
> Until the heart be naked, till his soul
> See the contagion's spots   foul;
> And from the mirror of Truth's sunlike shield,
> From which his Parthian arrow

NOTES.

Flash on his sight the spectres of the past,
Until his mind's eye paint thereon—
Let scorn like   yawn below,
And rain on him like flakes of fiery snow.
This cannot be, it ought not, evil still—
Suffering makes suffering, ill must follow ill.
Rough words beget sad thoughts,   and, beside,
Men take a sullen and a stupid pride
In being all they hate in others' shame,
By a perverse antipathy of fame.
'Tis not worth while to prove, as I could, how
From the sweet fountains of our Nature flow
These bitter waters; I will only say,
If any friend would take Southey some day,
And tell him, in a country walk alone,
Softening harsh words with friendship's gentle tone,
How incorrect his public conduct is,
And what men think of it, 'twere not amiss.
Far better than to make innocent ink ——

(2). Mr. Garnett suggests that the word *bald*, p. 361, ten lines from bottom; "*guilt*—a bald word, sir, this," should be *bold*. It is certainly *bald* in the transcript by Caroline Bowles.

(3). Mr. Garnett suggests that Shelley's letter accompanying the copy of *Alastor* may have remained unanswered, having reached Southey near the time of the death of his son Herbert.

(4). Mr. Garnett notes with reference to the dream (p. 371) of February 27th, 1805; "St. Apollonia is the saint invoked to cure the tooth-ache, which accounts for the name Apollonius."

(5). *Corrections.*—Page 32, twelve lines from bottom, for *paiera* read *paieras;* p. 171, eleven lines from bottom, for *lAonzo* read *Alonzo*; p. 176, l. 19, for *propably* read *probably*; p. 366, l. 15, for *giftee* read *gifted*.

INDEX.

"ACTA SANCTORUM," Stories from, 81, 82.
"Admirals," 336. 343.
Aiken, Lucy, 319.
Airey, Professor, 206.
"All for Love," 139.
Ambleside, 33.
"America, Men and Manners of," 279.
Annuals, 135. 137. 142.
"Astrea," 279.
Austen, Lady, 334.
Austin, Mrs., 275, 276.
Autographs, 197. 350.

Barbauld, Mrs., 319.
Barton, Bernard, 166.
Basil, St., Legend of, 139.
Bazaars, 146.
Beattie, 335.
Beaumont, Lady, 124. 125.
Beaumont, Sir George, 115.
Beckford, 307. 309.
Bell, Dr., 227. 229. 240. 268. 350.
Bilderdijk, Mr., 56. 84. 131.
Bilderdijk, Mrs., 84. 85. 88. 102.
Birthdays, 69. 204. 317.
Blackbirds, 163.
Blackwood, 187. 310.
Blake, 191. 193.
Books, 52. 87. 108. 122. 193. 199. 270. 350.
Books, Naming of, 95. 98. 99.
"Book of the Church," 25. 77. 80. 108. 129.
Bowles, Caroline. Sends to S. MS. of "Ellen Fitzarthur," 1. Thanks S. for advice, 8. Requests S. to suggest a subject for verse, 13. Sends "Ellen Fitzarthur" to S., 19. Offers a vol. to Longman, 23. Headaches, 29. Regrets at leaving Keswick, 33. Robbery at Buckland, 38. Fears with respect to "Robin Hood," 43. Receives from S. his collected works, 47. Sends first contribution to "Robin Hood," 57. Happiness in friendship with S., 67. 227. Recollections of her visit to Greta Hall, 68. Influence of early sorrow, 8. 79. On growing old, 138. Early recollections, 134. 153. Receives S.'s dedication of "All for Love," 155. Its effect on the public, 165. Suggests to S. a joint vol., 168. Longings for summer, 170. On late marriages, 179. Destruction of letters and MSS., 182. Retrospections, 190. Dreaminess, 192. Dissatisfaction with her own work, 216. Sensitiveness, 228. Serious illness, 256. Caricatures, 258. Urges S. to write verse, 262. Attachment to Buckland, 269. Childish religion, 277. Warns S. against overwork, 286. Heavenly acquaintances, 289. May at Buckland, 301. Visits the "Victory," 305. Delight in S.'s visits, 80. 106. 310. Her riding, 328. Power of sympathy, 329.
Bowles, W. Lisle, 26. 28. 93. 231. 250. 252. 253.
Bray, Mrs., 242. 246. 251. 350.
Bristol, 15. 22. 344.
Brontë, Charlotte, 348.
Brooks, Mrs., 110. 221. 226. 285. 287. 294. 295.
Brougham, Lord, 311.
Browne, Sir Thomas, 341.
Burrard, Paul, 50. 60. 91.
Burrard, Laura, 297.
Byron, Lady, 187. 188. 191. 193. 237. 270.
Byron, Lord, 26. 37. 71. 75. 76. 140.

Calshot, 134. 185.
Campbell, Letters of, 188. 191.
Canning, 86. 115. 119. 121.

Carter, Mrs., 335.
Catherine of Russia, 73.
Catarrh, Ode upon, 62.
Cats, 35. 225. 257. 276. 277.
Cats' Eden, 259. 276. 304.
Cats, Jacob, 88.
"Cat's Tail," 196. 199.
Chesterfield, Lord, Letters of, 219.
Church, Captain Benjamin, Portrait of, 66.
"Churchyards, Chapters on," 163.
Clarke, Adam, Life of, 273. 281. 292.
Cochrane, James, 315.
"Cock and Hen," 143.
Coleridge, John, 87. 93.
Coleridge, Sara, 56. 87. 175. 177.
Coleridge, S. T., 93. 310. 326.
Collier, Miss, 195. 198.
Colling, Mary, 242. 245. 257.
"Colloquies," 133. 151. 154.
Comet, 328. 630.
Co-operative Societies, 171, 172. 175. 176.
Corn Laws, Paper on the, 290. 295. 301.
Cottle, Joseph, 344. 351.
Country, State of, 209. 211. 234.
Croker, 301. 332.
Cunningham, Allan, 137. 143. 161.
Cowper, William, 296. 299. 302. 312. 315. 333. 335. 337. 339. 346.
Cowper's translation of Homer, 224.

Day-dreams, 36. 42. 44.
Davidson, Lucretia, 170.
Dayrolles, Mrs., 269. 283.
"Devil's Walk, The," 92, 93. 111. 188.
D'Israeli, 140. 239.
"Divines, Lives of," 185. 285. 289. 291.
Doctor, The, 323, 324. 326. 330. 338.
Doddridge, Philip, 182.
"Don Juan," 295.
Dorset, Mrs., 306.
"Dragon, The Young," 161. 187.
Dreams, Register of, 110.

"Eleëmon," 145. 184.
Elia, Letter of, 35.
Elliott, Ebenezer, 290. 301.
Evangelicals, 172. 335. 336.

Factories Bill, 266. 270. 274.
"Factories, Tales of the," 265. 267. 268.
Family Library, 185. 189. 191.
Fiction, 189. 262. 279.
Fielding, 184. 186. 195. 198.
Foreign Review, 136.
Fox, Charles, 281.
"Fraser's Magazine," 187, 188. 255, 256. 258.

"Gentleman's Magazine," 128.
Gifford, 71.
Gilpin, William, 320.
Goethe, 276, 277.
"Goethe, Characteristics of," 275. 283.
Gomer, Baron de, 32.
Grignan, Madame, 97.
Grimshawe, 331. 333.

Hallam, "Constitutional History," 128.
Haweis, 336.
Haydon, 23.
Hayley, 63. 64. 65. 331.
Hazlitt, 75.
Hemans, Mrs., 324.
Heraud, 116, 184.
Hesketh, Lady, 322. 331. 334.
Hick, Samuel, Life of, 274. 290.
Hobhouse, Pamphlet of, 76.
Holcroft, Translation of Hermann und Dorothea, 27.
Homer, 349.
Hope, Anastasius, 233.
Howitt, Mary and William, 166. 225. 231. 278. 297. 300. 303. 306. 308. 314. 315,
Hutchinson, Miss, 117. 131. 326. 329. 341.
Huntingdon, Lady, 336.

"Inscriptions," 50. 54. 60. 94.
Irish, Vol. of poems for the, 227.
Irving, 239. 248. 348.

Jacob, 186.
Jeffrey, 37. 223.
Jewsbury, Miss, 162. 164. 184.
Jews' Society, 102, 103.
"Joan of Arc," 101. 342. 346. 348.

"Keepsake," 137. 139. 147. 182. 187.
Ken, Bishop, 231. 252. 254.
"King of the Crocodiles," 85.
Knowles, Herbert, 18.
Knox, Alexander, 313. 316, 317, 318. 322.

Lady-missionaries, 103. 173.
Lamb, Charles, 37. 40. 45. 71. 320. 350.
Landor, 63. 71. 74. 252. 255.
Letters of Southey and C. Bowles, 180.
Letters, Lord Chesterfield's, 219.
Lightfoot, 27. 70. 87.
Liverpool, Lord, 115. 119.
Lockhart, 92. 98. 123. 161. 184. 207. 237. 273.
"London Magazine," 75.
Longman, 19. 180. 185.
Lowther, 109. 273. 307.
Lymington, 6.

INDEX. 387

Mahon, Lord, 301.
Major, publisher, 187.
"Maria del Occidente" (see Brooks, Mrs.)
Martineau, Miss, 311.
Marivaux, 148.
Medwin, Captain, 71. 75, 76.
Memoirs, Old French, 99, 100.
Methodists, 172. 175, 176.
Metre, 48. 51. 53. 56. 58. 107.
Milman, 118. 120.
Milner, 87, 102.
Montague, Mrs., 335.
Montgomery, 258, 259, 260. 278.
Moore, "Life of Byron," 140. 187, 188. 295.
Moore, "Life of Lord E. Fitzgerald," 236.
More, Sir Thomas, Portrait of, 151.
Mufti, 141. 148. 159. 192. 213. 282.
Murray, 13. 42. 73. 75. 87. 100. 123. 125. 156. 185. 273.

Names, Christian, 333.
"Naturalist's Journal, The," 161.
"Nelson, Life of," 189.
"New Monthly Magazine," 20.
Newton, 296. 300. 312, 313. 331. 338.
Nightingales, 192. 257.
Novels, 183. 279.
Nugent, Lord, 263. 273.
Nuthatch, 158. 160. 163.

O'Connell, Anecdote of, 271.
O'Gorman, Song to, 223.
"Oliver Newman," 68. 100.
O'Meara, "Voice from St. Helena," 31.
Opie, Mrs., 101. 105. 145. 173. 261.
Owen, William, 194.
Owls, 259.

Pamela, 236, 237.
"Paraguay, Tale of," 72. 77. 87. 89. 100.
Pauper colonies, Paper upon, 186.
"Peninsular War," 28. 72. 88. 96. 114. 118. 133. 241.
Pennie, Mr., 255.
Philip's War, 66.
"Philip Van Artevelde," 307, 308.
Pigeons, 166.
"Poet's Pilgrimage," 34.
Polignac, Letter from, 268.
Politics, 115. 199. 207. 209. 219. 222. 224. 241. 266. 271. 305. 314. 321. 349.
Politics, French, 200, 201. 204.
Ponies, 40. 215. 277. 296. 299. 303. 306. 327.
Pope, Letter of, 71. 75. 93.
Porson, 111, 112.

Powley, Mr., 336. 338.
"Priestcraft, History of," 278, 298.
Publishers, 199.

Quakers, 166. 231. 315.
"Quarterly Review," 87, 88. 92. 102. 118. 123. 137. 174. 181. 198. 263. 309.
"Queen Mary's Christening," 169.

Reform Bill, 221, 222. 241. 272.
Rickman, 198. 308.
"Robinson Crusoe," 187. 189.
Robinson, H. C., 275.
"Roderick," 56.
Rogers, 110. 307.
"Roprecht the Robber," 161.
Rowley, Mr. Clotworthy, 322.
Russell, Lord John, 322.

Sadler, 176. 268.
"Santarem, Legend of," 82. 143. 168.
Sewell, Mr., Poems of, 264.
Scott, Sir Walter, 75. 86. 138. 161. 252. 261.
Scotland, Tour in, 17.
"Sea of Life," 25.
"Selborne," White's, 161.
Sevigné, Madame de, 85. 96. 98.
"Seward, Sir Edward," 162.
Seward, Miss, 319.
Shelley, 27. 72. 76. 136.
Shenstone, Letters of, 335.
Shields, 54.
Shovel, Sir Cloudesley, 54.
"Sinner well saved," 150.
Sleep, 53. 313, 314.
Smith, Horace, 116. 183. 185.
Societies, Religious, 103. 116.
Sotheby, 224.
Southey, Cuthbert, 35. 37. 40. 71. 88. 261. 295. 308. 311. 321. 345.
Southey, Robert, Criticism of "Ellen Fitzarthur," 6. Offer of advice, 6. Advice on composition, 10. The New Forest as subject for a poem, 14. Criticises the "Widow's Tale," &c., 24. Interruptions to work, &c., 20. 71. 135. 148. 280. 303. Reasons for writing on pleasant subjects, 25. 164. 170. Friendships, 27. 342. Proposes a joint poem on "Robin Hood," 42. 45. Hay-fever, 28. 61. 117. Sends C. B. part of "Robin Hood," 55. Completes his fiftieth year, 66. Receives a sketch of herself from Caroline Bowles, 77. Sympathy with her loneliness, 77. 90. Celestial journeys, 89. 92. Natural frankness, 93. Despairs of growing rich, 94. Journey to Continent, 107. Receives gold

medal, 122. Returned M. P. for Downton, 108. Home delights, 109. 140. 217. Plans for Harrogate, 117. 121. May at Keswick, 139. Pic-nic at Leatheswater, 125, 126. Invites C. B. again to Keswick, 129. Silhouettes, 132. Proof-sheets, 133. Thoughts on the New Year, 150. Portraits, 151. 261. Commences the "Shipwreck," 171. Changes at Greta Hall, 177. Undertakes charge of C. B.'s letters and MSS. in case of death, 174. 249. 282. 299. 321. 337. S.'s daily life, 54. 148. 181. 249. 264. 282. 284. 299. 321. 337. Manner to strangers, 184. Pleasure in visits to Buckland, 189. Renews lease of Greta Hall, 193. Visit to London for political reasons, 198. Completes fifty-sixth year, 201. Arrives in London, 203. Visitors at Keswick, 206. Goes to Court, 214. Joy at return home, 53. 217. Capacity for content, 232. Cholera at Keswick, 236. Troubles gather, 249. Completes his fifty-ninth year, 272. 278. Receives portrait of Caroline Bowles, 280. On suicide, 279. Heavenly acquaintances, 284. 342. Patience, 288. Visit to the south, 344.

Southey, Thomas, "History of the West Indies," 63.
"Souvenir," 90, 91. 147. 184.
"Spectator," 165.
Spirits, 318.
St. Barbe, Mr., 71. 75.
St.-Simonists, 220. 238, 239. 242.
Sumner, Bird, 172.
Sunday schools, 302.
Swain, Mr., 304.

Talbot, Miss, 335.

Talleyrand, 216.
Taylor, Henry, 93. 110. 123. 177. 180. 248. 291. 296. 331. 339.
Thornton, Mr., 296. 300. 313. 346.
Ticknor, 279.
Trench, Archdeacon, 274.
"Triad, The," 152.
Turner, Sharon, 260.
Tyler, Miss, 75.

Unwin, Mr., 322. 331. 333.
Unwin, Mrs., 331. 333.

Vaudois, Article on, 88. 93. 95. 100.
Villiers, Hyde, 243. 248.
"Vindiciæ," 88. 90. 95, 96.

Wakefield Gibbon, his pamphlet, 237.
Warter, Mr., 217. 225. 234.
Watts, Alaric, 90. 129. 135. 137. 142.
Watts, Dr., 309.
Wellington, Duke of, 72, 73.
Werner, 136.
Wesley, 332, 336.
Whitbread, Mrs., 147.
White, Henry Kirke, 49.
White, Neville, 49. 335.
Wilberforce, 77. 80.
Williams, Sir Charles Hanbury, 72.
Wilson, Horace Hayman, 136.
Wilson, Sir Robert, 120.
Wolfe, General, 126, 127, 128. 131. 145.
Wollstonecraft, Mary, 51. 62.
Women as letter-writers, 10.
Wordsworth, Dora, 152. 184. 300. 303.
Wordsworth, William, 33. 80. 124, 125. 131. 151. 164. 184. 225. 231. 288, 289. 318. 341, 342, 348.

Yahoos, Country of the, 34.

"Zophiel," 285. 287. 290. 293. 295.

THE END.

DUBLIN UNIVERSITY PRESS SERIES.

THE Provost and Senior Fellows of Trinity College have undertaken the publication of a Series of Works, chiefly Educational, to be entitled the DUBLIN UNIVERSITY PRESS SERIES.

The following volumes of the Series are now ready, viz.:—

Six Lectures on Physical Geography. By the REV. S. HAUGHTON, M.D., Dubl., D.C.L., Oxon., F.R.S., *Fellow of Trinity College, and Professor of Geology in the University of Dublin.*

An Introduction to the Systematic Zoology and Morphology of Vertebrate Animals. By ALEXANDER MACALISTER, M.D., Dubl., *Professor of Comparative Anatomy in the University of Dublin.*

The Codex Rescriptus Dublinensis of St. Matthew's Gospel (Z). First Published by Dr. Barrett in 1801. A New Edition, Revised and Augmented. Also, Fragments of the Book of Isaiah, in the LXX. Version, from an Ancient Palimpsest, now first Published. Together with a newly discovered Fragment of the Codex Palatinus. By T. K. ABBOTT, B.D., *Fellow of Trinity College, and Professor of Biblical Greek in the University of Dublin.* With two Plates of Facsimiles.

The Parabola, Ellipse, and Hyperbola, treated Geometrically. By ROBERT WILLIAM GRIFFIN, A.M., LL.D., *Ex-Scholar, Trinity College, Dublin.*

An Introduction to Logic. By WILLIAM HENRY STANLEY MONCK, M.A. *Professor of Moral Philosophy in the University of Dublin.*

Essays in Political and Moral Philosophy. By T. E. CLIFFE LESLIE, Hon. LL.D., Dubl., *of Lincoln's Inn, Barrister-at-Law, late Examiner in Political Economy in the University of London, Professor of Jurisprudence and Political Economy in the Queen's University.*

The Correspondence of Cicero: a revised Text, with Notes and Prolegomena.—Vol. I., The Letters to the end of Cicero's Exile. By ROBERT Y. TYRRELL, M.A., *Fellow of Trinity College, and Professor of Latin in the University of Dublin.*

Faust from the German of Goethe. BY THOMAS E. WEBB, LL.D., Q.C., *Regius Professor of Laws, and Public Orator in the University of Dublin.*

[*Over.*

DUBLIN UNIVERSITY PRESS SERIES—*continued.*

The Correspondence of Robert Southey with Caroline Bowles: to which are added—Correspondence with Shelley, and Southey's Dreams. Edited, with an Introduction, by EDWARD DOWDEN, LL.D., *Professor of English Literature in the University of Dublin.*

The Mathematical and other Tracts of the late James M'Cullagh, F.T.C.D., *Professor of Natural Philosophy in the University of Dublin.* Now first collected, and edited by REV. J. H. JELLETT, B.D., and REV. SAMUEL HAUGHTON, M.D., *Fellows of Trinity College, Dublin.*

A Sequel to the First Six Books of the Elements of Euclid, containing an Easy Introduction to Modern Geometry. With numerous Examples. By JOHN CASEY, LL.D., F.R.S., *Vice-President, Royal Irish Academy; Member of the London Mathematical Society; and Professor of the Higher Mathematics and Mathematical Physics in the Catholic University of Ireland.*

Theory of Equations: with an Introduction to the Theory of Binary Algebraic Forms. By WILLIAM SNOW BURNSIDE, M.A., *Erasmus Smith's Professor of Mathematics in the University of Dublin:* and ARTHUR WILLIAM PANTON, M.A., *Fellow and Tutor, Trinity College, Dublin.*

In the Press:—

Evangelia Antehieronymiana ex Codice vetusto Dublinensi. Ed. T. K. ABBOTT, B.D.

The Veil of Isis; or, Idealism. By THOMAS E. WEBB, LL.D., Q.C., *Regius Professor of Laws, and Public Orator in the University of Dublin.*

DUBLIN: HODGES, FIGGIS, AND CO.

LONDON: LONGMANS, GREEN, AND CO.

39 Paternoster Row, E.C.
London, *April* 1881.

GENERAL LISTS OF WORKS
PUBLISHED BY
MESSRS. LONGMANS, GREEN & CO.

HISTORY, POLITICS, HISTORICAL MEMOIRS, &c.

History of England from the Conclusion of the Great War in 1815. By SPENCER WALPOLE. 8vo. VOLS. I. & II. 1815-1832 (Second Edition, revised) price 36s. VOL. III. 1832-1841, price 18s.

History of England in the 18th Century. By W. E. H. LECKY, M.A. VOLS. I. & II. 1700-1760. Second Edition. 2 vols. 8vo. 36s.

The History of England from the Accession of James II. By the Right Hon. Lord MACAULAY.
STUDENT'S EDITION, 2 vols. cr. 8vo. 12s.
PEOPLE'S EDITION, 4 vols. cr. 8vo. 16s.
CABINET EDITION, 8 vols. post 8vo. 48s.
LIBRARY EDITION, 5 vols. 8vo. £4.

Lord Macaulay's Works. Complete and uniform Library Edition. Edited by his Sister, Lady TREVELYAN. 8 vols. 8vo. with Portrait, £5. 5s.

Critical and Historical Essays contributed to the Edinburgh Review. By the Right Hon. Lord MACAULAY.
CHEAP EDITION, crown 8vo. 3s. 6d.
STUDENT'S EDITION, crown 8vo. 6s.
PEOPLE'S EDITION, 2 vols. crown 8vo. 8s.
CABINET EDITION, 4 vols. 24s.
LIBRARY EDITION, 3 vols. 8vo. 36s.

The History of England from the Fall of Wolsey to the Defeat of the Spanish Armada. By J. A. FROUDE, M.A.
POPULAR EDITION, 12 vols. crown, £2. 2s.
CABINET EDITION, 12 vols. crown, £3. 12s.

The English in Ireland in the Eighteenth Century. By J. A. FROUDE, M.A. 3 vols. crown 8vo. 18s.

Journal of the Reigns of King George IV. and King William IV. By the late C. C. F. GREVILLE, Esq. Edited by H. REEVE, Esq. Fifth Edition. 3 vols. 8vo. price 36s.

The Life of Napoleon III. derived from State Records, Unpublished Family Correspondence, and Personal Testimony. By BLANCHARD JERROLD. In Four Volumes, 8vo. with numerous Portraits and Facsimiles. VOLS. I. to III. price 18s. each.

Russia Before and After the War. By the Author of 'Society in St. Petersburg' &c. Translated from the German (with later Additions by the Author) by EDWARD FAIRFAX TAYLOR. Second Edition. 8vo. 14s.

Russia and England from 1876 to 1880; a Protest and an Appeal. By O. K. Author of 'Is Russia Wrong?' With a Preface by J. A. FROUDE, M.A. Portrait and Maps. 8vo. 14s.

The Early History of Charles James Fox. By GEORGE OTTO TREVELYAN, M.P. Third Edition. 8vo. 18s.

The Constitutional History of England since the Accession of George III. 1760-1870. By Sir THOMAS ERSKINE MAY, K.C.B. D.C.L. Sixth Edition. 3 vols. crown 8vo. 18s.

Democracy in Europe; a History. By Sir THOMAS ERSKINE MAY, K.C.B. D.C.L. 2 vols. 8vo. 32s.

Introductory Lectures on Modern History delivered in 1841 and 1842. By the late THOMAS ARNOLD, D.D. 8vo. 7s. 6d.

On Parliamentary Government in England. By ALPHEUS TODD. 2 vols. 8vo. 37s.

Parliamentary Government in the British Colonies. By ALPHEUS TODD. 8vo. 21s.

History of Civilisation in England and France, Spain and Scotland. By HENRY THOMAS BUCKLE. 3 vols. crown 8vo. 24s.

Lectures on the History of England from the Earliest Times to the Death of King Edward II. By W. LONGMAN, F.S.A. Maps and Illustrations. 8vo. 15s.

History of the Life & Times of Edward III. By W. LONGMAN, F.S.A. With 9 Maps, 8 Plates, and 16 Woodcuts. 2 vols. 8vo. 28s.

The Historical Geography of Europe. By EDWARD A. FREEMAN, D.C.L. LL.D. With 65 Maps. 2 vols. 8vo. 31s. 6d.

History of England under the Duke of Buckingham and Charles I. 1624-1628. By S. R. GARDINER. 2 vols. 8vo. Maps, 24s.

The Personal Government of Charles I. from the Death of Buckingham to the Declaration in favour of Ship Money, 1628-1637. By S. R. GARDINER. 2 vols. 8vo. 24s.

Memorials of the Civil War between King Charles I. and the Parliament of England as it affected Herefordshire and the Adjacent Counties. By the Rev. J. WEBB, M.A. Edited and completed by the Rev. T. W. WEBB, M.A. 2 vols. 8vo. Illustrations, 42s.

Popular History of France, from the Earliest Times to the Death of Louis XIV. By Miss SEWELL. Crown 8vo. Maps, 7s. 6d.

A Student's Manual of the History of India from the Earliest Period to the Present. By Col. MEADOWS TAYLOR, M.R.A.S. Third Thousand. Crown 8vo. Maps, 7s. 6d.

Lord Minto in India; Correspondence of the First Earl of Minto, while Governor-General of India, from 1807 to 1814. Edited by his Great-Niece, the COUNTESS of MINTO. Post 8vo. Maps, 12s.

Waterloo Lectures; a Study of the Campaign of 1815. By Col. C. C. CHESNEY, R.E. 8vo. 10s. 6d.

The Oxford Reformers— John Colet, Erasmus, and Thomas More; a History of their Fellow-Work. By F. SEEBOHM. 8vo. 14s.

History of the Romans under the Empire. By Dean MERIVALE, D.D. 8 vols. post 8vo. 48s.

General History of Rome from B.C. 753 to A.D. 476. By Dean MERIVALE, D.D. Crown 8vo. Maps, price 7s. 6d.

The Fall of the Roman Republic; a Short History of the Last Century of the Commonwealth. By Dean MERIVALE, D.D. 12mo. 7s. 6d.

The History of Rome. By WILHELM IHNE. VOLS. I. to III. 8vo. price 45s.

Carthage and the Carthaginians. By R. BOSWORTH SMITH, M.A. Second Edition. Maps, Plans, &c. Crown 8vo. 10s. 6d.

WORKS published by LONGMANS & CO.

History of Ancient Egypt. By G. RAWLINSON, M.A. With Map and numerous Illustrations. 2 vols. 8vo. price 63s.

The Seventh Great Oriental Monarchy; or, a History of the Sassanians. By G. RAWLINSON, M.A. With Map and 95 Illustrations. 8vo. 28s.

The History of European Morals from Augustus to Charlemagne. By W. E. H. LECKY, M.A. 2 vols. crown 8vo. 16s.

History of the Rise and Influence of the Spirit of Rationalism in Europe. By W. E. H. LECKY, M.A. 2 vols. crown 8vo. 16s.

The History of Philosophy, from Thales to Comte. By GEORGE HENRY LEWES. Fifth Edition. 2 vols. 8vo. 32s.

A History of Classical Greek Literature. By the Rev. J. P. P. MAHAFFY, M.A. Crown 8vo. VOL. I. Poets, 7s. 6d. VOL. II. Prose Writers, 7s. 6d.

Zeller's Stoics, Epicureans, and Sceptics. Translated by the Rev. O. J. REICHEL, M.A. New Edition revised. Crown 8vo. 15s.

Zeller's Socrates & the Socratic Schools. Translated by the Rev. O. J. REICHEL, M.A. Second Edition. Crown 8vo. 10s. 6d.

Zeller's Plato & the Older Academy. Translated by S. FRANCES ALLEYNE and ALFRED GOODWIN, B.A. Crown 8vo. 18s.

Zeller's Pre-Socratic Schools; a History of Greek Philosophy from the Earliest Period to the time of Socrates. Translated by SARAH F. ALLEYNE. 2 vols. crown 8vo. 30s.

Zeller's Aristotle and the Elder Peripatetics. Translated by B. F. C. COSTELLOE, Balliol College, Oxford. Crown 8vo. [In preparation.
*** The above volume will complete the Authorised English Translation of Dr. ZELLER'S Work on the Philosophy of the Greeks.

Epochs of Modern History. Edited by C. COLBECK, M.A.
Church's Beginning of the Middle Ages, 2s. 6d.
Cox's Crusades, 2s. 6d.
Creighton's Age of Elizabeth, 2s. 6d.
Gairdner's Houses of Lancaster and York, 2s. 6d.
Gardiner's Puritan Revolution, 2s. 6d.
―――― Thirty Years' War, 2s. 6d.
Hale's Fall of the Stuarts, 2s. 6d.
Johnson's Normans in Europe, 2s. 6d.
Longman's Frederic the Great and the Seven Years' War, 2s. 6d.
Ludlow's War of American Independence, 2s. 6d.
Morris's Age of Anne, 2s. 6d.
Seebohm's Protestant Revolution, 2s. 6d.
Stubbs's Early Plantagenets, 2s. 6d.
Warburton's Edward III. 2s. 6d.

Epochs of Ancient History. Edited by the Rev. Sir G. W. COX, Bart. M.A. & C. SANKEY, M.A.
Beesly's Gracchi, Marius & Sulla, 2s. 6d.
Capes's Age of the Antonines, 2s. 6d.
―――― Early Roman Empire, 2s. 6d.
Cox's Athenian Empire, 2s. 6d.
―――― Greeks & Persians, 2s. 6d.
Curteis's Macedonian Empire, 2s. 6d.
Ihne's Rome to its Capture by the Gauls, 2s. 6d.
Merivale's Roman Triumvirates, 2s. 6d.
Sankey's Spartan & Theban Supremacies, 2s. 6d.
Smith's Rome and Carthage, the Punic Wars, 2s. 6d.

Creighton's Shilling History of England, introductory to 'Epochs of English History.' Fcp. 1s.

Epochs of English History. Edited by the Rev. MANDELL CREIGHTON, M.A. Fcp. 8vo. 5s.
Browning's Modern England, 1820-1874, 9d.
Cordery's Struggle against Absolute Monarchy, 1603-1688, 9d.
Creighton's (Mrs.) England a Continental Power, 1066-1216, 9d.
Creighton's (Rev. M.) Tudors and the Reformation, 1485-1603, 9d.
Rowley's Rise of the People, 1215-1485, price 9d.
Rowley's Settlement of the Constitution, 1688-1778, 9d.
Tancock's England during the American & European Wars, 1778-1820, 9d.
York-Powell's Early England to the Conquest, 1s.

WORKS *published by* LONGMANS &- CO.

The Student's Manual of Ancient History; the Political History, Geography and Social State of the Principal Nations of Antiquity. By W. COOKE TAYLOR, LL.D. Cr. 8vo. 7s. 6d.

The Student's Manual of Modern History; the Rise and Progress of the Principal European Nations. By W. COOKE TAYLOR, LL.D. Crown 8vo. 7s. 6d.

BIOGRAPHICAL WORKS.

Reminiscences. By THOMAS CARLYLE. Edited by JAMES ANTHONY FROUDE, M.A. formerly Fellow of Exeter College, Oxford. 2 vols. crown 8vo. 18s.

Autobiography. By JOHN STUART MILL. 8vo. 7s. 6d.

Felix Mendelssohn's Letters, translated by Lady WALLACE. 2 vols. crown 8vo. 5s. each.

Memoirs of the Life of Anna Jameson, Author of 'Sacred and Legendary Art' &c. By her Niece, G. MACPHERSON. 8vo. Portrait, 12s. 6d.

The Life and Letters of Lord Macaulay. By his Nephew, G. OTTO TREVELYAN, M.P.
CABINET EDITION, 2 vols. crown 8vo. 12s.
LIBRARY EDITION, 2 vols. 8vo. 36s.

William Law, Nonjuror and Mystic, Author of 'A Serious Call to a Devout and Holy Life' &c. a Sketch of his Life, Character, and Opinions. By J. H. OVERTON, M.A. Vicar of Legbourne. 8vo. 15s.

The Missionary Secretariat of Henry Venn, B.D. Prebendary of St. Paul's, and Hon. Sec. of the Church Missionary Society. By the Rev. W. KNIGHT, M.A. With Additions by Mr. Venn's Two Sons, and a Portrait. 8vo. 18s.

A Dictionary of General Biography. By W. L. R. CATES. Third Edition, revised throughout and completed to the Present Time; with new matter equal to One Hundred pages, comprising nearly Four Hundred Memoirs and Notices of Persons recently deceased. 8vo. 28s.

Apologia pro Vitâ Suâ; Being a History of his Religious Opinions by JOHN HENRY NEWMAN, D.D. Crown 8vo. 6s.

Biographical Studies. By the late WALTER BAGEHOT, M.A. Fellow of University College, London. Uniform with 'Literary Studies' and 'Economic Studies' by the same Author. 8vo. 12s.

Leaders of Public Opinion in Ireland; Swift, Flood, Grattan, O'Connell. By W. E. H. LECKY, M.A. Crown 8vo. 7s. 6d.

Essays in Ecclesiastical Biography. By the Right Hon. Sir J. STEPHEN, LL.D. Crown 8vo. 7s. 6d.

Cæsar; a Sketch. By JAMES ANTHONY FROUDE, M.A. formerly Fellow of Exeter College, Oxford. With Portrait and Map. 8vo. 16s.

Life of the Duke of Wellington. By the Rev. G. R. GLEIG, M.A. Crown 8vo. Portrait, 6s.

Memoirs of Sir Henry Havelock, K.C.B. By JOHN CLARK MARSHMAN. Crown 8vo. 3s. 6d.

Vicissitudes of Families. By Sir BERNARD BURKE, C.B. Two vols. crown 8vo. 21s.

Maunder's Treasury of Biography, reconstructed and in great part re-written, with above 1,600 additional Memoirs by W. L. R. CATES. Fcp. 8vo. 6s.

MENTAL and POLITICAL PHILOSOPHY.

Comte's System of Positive Polity, or Treatise upon Sociology. By various Translators. 4 vols. 8vo. £4.

De Tocqueville's Democracy in America, translated by H. REEVE. 2 vols. crown 8vo. 16s.

Analysis of the Phenomena of the Human Mind. By JAMES MILL. With Notes, Illustrative and Critical. 2 vols. 8vo. 28s.

On Representative Government. By JOHN STUART MILL. Crown 8vo. 2s.

On Liberty. By JOHN STUART MILL. Post 8vo. 7s. 6d. crown 8vo. 1s. 4d.

Principles of Political Economy. By JOHN STUART MILL. 2 vols. 8vo. 30s. or 1 vol. crown 8vo. 5s.

Essays on some Unsettled Questions of Political Economy. By JOHN STUART MILL. 8vo. 6s. 6d.

Utilitarianism. By JOHN STUART MILL. 8vo. 5s.

The Subjection of Women. By JOHN STUART MILL. Fourth Edition. Crown 8vo. 6s.

Examination of Sir William Hamilton's Philosophy. By JOHN STUART MILL. 8vo. 16s.

A System of Logic, Ratiocinative and Inductive. By JOHN STUART MILL. 2 vols. 8vo. 25s.

Dissertations and Discussions. By JOHN STUART MILL. 4 vols. 8vo. £2. 7s.

The A B C of Philosophy; a Text-Book for Students. By the Rev. T. GRIFFITH, M.A. Prebendary of St. Paul's. Crown 8vo. 5s.

A Systematic View of the Science of Jurisprudence. By SHELDON AMOS, M.A. 8vo. 18s.

Path and Goal; a Discussion on the Elements of Civilisation and the Conditions of Happiness. By M. M. KALISCH, Ph.D. M.A. 8vo. price 12s. 6d.

The Law of Nations considered as Independent Political Communities. By Sir TRAVERS TWISS, D.C.L. 2 vols. 8vo. £1. 13s.

A Primer of the English Constitution and Government. By S. AMOS, M.A. Crown 8vo. 6s.

Fifty Years of the English Constitution, 1830-1880. By SHELDON AMOS, M.A. Crown 8vo. 10s. 6d.

Principles of Economical Philosophy. By H. D. MACLEOD, M.A. Second Edition, in 2 vols. VOL. I. 8vo. 15s. VOL. II. PART I. 12s.

Lord Bacon's Works, collected & edited by R. L. ELLIS, M.A. J. SPEDDING, M.A. and D. D. HEATH. 7 vols. 8vo. £3. 13s. 6d.

Letters and Life of Francis Bacon, including all his Occasional Works. Collected and edited, with a Commentary, by J. SPEDDING. 7 vols. 8vo. £4. 4s.

The Institutes of Justinian; with English Introduction, Translation, and Notes. By T. C. SANDARS, M.A. 8vo. 18s.

The Nicomachean Ethics of Aristotle, translated into English by R. WILLIAMS, B.A. Crown 8vo. price 7s. 6d.

Aristotle's Politics, Books I. III. IV. (VII.) Greek Text, with an English Translation by W. E. BOLLAND, M.A. and Short Essays by A. LANG, M.A. Crown 8vo. 7s. 6d.

The Politics of Aristotle; Greek Text, with English Notes. By RICHARD CONGREVE, M.A. 8vo. 18s.

The Ethics of Aristotle; with Essays and Notes. By Sir A. GRANT, Bart. LL.D. 2 vols. 8vo. 32s.

Bacon's Essays, with Annotations. By R. WHATELY, D.D. 8vo. 10s. 6d.

An Introduction to Logic. By WILLIAM H. STANLEY MONCK, M.A. Professor of Moral Philosophy in the University of Dublin. Crown 8vo. price 5s.

Picture Logic; an Attempt to Popularise the Science of Reasoning. By A. SWINBOURNE, B.A. Post 8vo. 5s.

Elements of Logic. By R. WHATELY, D.D. 8vo. 10s. 6d. Crown 8vo. 4s. 6d.

Elements of Rhetoric. By R. WHATELY, D.D. 8vo. 10s. 6d. Crown 8vo. 4s. 6d.

The Senses and the Intellect. By A. BAIN, LL.D. 8vo. 15s.

The Veil of Isis, or Idealism. By THOMAS E. WEBB, LL.D. Q.C. Regius Professor of Laws, and Public Orator in the University of Dublin. [*Nearly ready.*

On the Influence of Authority in Matters of Opinion. By the late Sir. G. C. LEWIS, Bart. 8vo. 14s.

The Emotions and the Will. By A. BAIN, LL.D. 8vo. 15s.

Mental and Moral Science; a Compendium of Psychology and Ethics. By A. BAIN, LL.D. Crown 8vo. 10s. 6d.

An Outline of the Necessary Laws of Thought; a Treatise on Pure and Applied Logic. By W. THOMSON, D.D. Crown 8vo. 6s.

Essays in Political and Moral Philosophy. By T. E. CLIFFE LESLIE, Hon. LL.D. Dubl. of Lincoln's Inn, Barrister-at-Law. 8vo. 10s. 6d.

Hume's Philosophical Works: Edited, with Notes, &c. by T. H. GREEN, M.A. and the Rev. T. H. GROSE, M.A. 4 vols. 8vo. 56s. Or separately, Essays, 2 vols. 28s. Treatise on Human Nature, 2 vols. 28s.

Six Lectures on the History of German Thought, from the Seven Years' War to Goethe's Death, delivered in 1879 at the Royal Institution of Great Britain. By KARL HILLEBRAND. Crown 8vo. 7s. 6d.

MISCELLANEOUS & CRITICAL WORKS.

Faiths and Fashions; Short Essays republished. By Lady VIOLET GREVILE. Crown 8vo. 7s. 6d.

Selected Essays, chiefly from Contributions to the Edinburgh and Quarterly Reviews. By A. HAYWARD, Q.C. 2 vols. crown 8vo. 12s.

Miscellaneous Writings of J. Conington, M.A. Edited by J. A. SYMONDS, M.A. 2 vols. 8vo. 28s.

Short Studies on Great Subjects. By J. A. FROUDE, M.A. 3 vols. crown 8vo. 18s.

Literary Studies. By the late WALTER BAGEHOT, M.A. Fellow of University College, London. Edited, with a Prefatory Memoir, by R. H. HUTTON. Second Edition. 2 vols. 8vo. with Portrait, 28s.

Manual of English Literature, Historical and Critical. By T. ARNOLD, M.A. Crown 8vo. 7s. 6d.

English Authors; Specimens of English Poetry and Prose from the earliest times to the present day; with references throughout to the 'Manual of English Literature.' Edited by T. ARNOLD, M.A. Crown 8vo. [*In the press.*

The Wit and Wisdom of
the Rev. Sydney Smith. Crown 8vo. 3s. 6d.

Lord Macaulay's Miscellaneous Writings :—
LIBRARY EDITION, 2 vols. 8vo. 21s.
PEOPLE'S EDITION, 1 vol. cr. 8vo. 4s. 6d.

Lord Macaulay's Miscellaneous Writings and Speeches.
Student's Edition. Crown 8vo. 6s.
Cabinet Edition, including Indian Penal Code, Lays of Ancient Rome, and other Poems. 4 vols. post 8vo. 24s.

Speeches of Lord Macaulay,
corrected by Himself. Crown 8vo. 3s. 6d.

Selections from the Writings of Lord Macaulay.
Edited, with Notes, by G. O. TREVELYAN, M.P. Crown. 8vo. 6s.

Miscellaneous Works of Thomas Arnold,
D.D. late Head Master of Rugby School. 8vo. 7s. 6d.

A Thousand Thoughts
from Various Authors. Selected and arranged by ARTHUR B. DAVISON. Crown 8vo. 7s. 6d.

A Cavalier's Note Book;
being Notes, Anecdotes, and Observations of W. BLUNDELL, of Crosby, Lancashire, Esq. Captain in the Royalist Army of 1642. Edited by the Rev. T. ELLISON GIBSON. Small 4to. with Facsimile, 14s.

German Home Life; a
Series of Essays on the Domestic Life of Germany. Crown 8vo. 6s.

Realities of Irish Life.
By W. STEUART TRENCH. Crown 8vo. 2s. 6d. boards, or 3s. 6d. cloth.

Apparitions; a Narrative
of Facts. By the Rev. B. W. SAVILE, M.A. Second Edition. Crown 8vo. price 5s.

Evenings with the Skeptics;
or, Free Discussion on Free Thinkers. By JOHN OWEN, Rector of East Anstey, Devon. 2 vols. 8vo. 32s.

Selected Essays on Language, Mythology, and Religion.
By F. MAX MÜLLER, K.M. Foreign Member of the French Institute. 2 vols. crown 8vo. 16s.

Lectures on the Science
of Language. By F. MAX MÜLLER, K.M. 2 vols. crown 8vo. 16s.

Chips from a German Workshop;
Essays on the Science of Religion, and on Mythology, Traditions & Customs. By F. MAX MÜLLER, K.M. 4 vols. 8vo. £1. 16s.

Language & Languages.
A Revised Edition of Chapters on Language and Families of Speech. By F. W. FARRAR, D.D. F.R.S. Crown 8vo. 6s.

The Essays and Contributions of A. K. H. B.
Uniform Cabinet Editions in crown 8vo.

Recreations of a Country Parson, Three Series, 3s. 6d. each.

Landscapes, Churches, and Moralities, price 3s. 6d.

Seaside Musings, 3s. 6d.

Changed Aspects of Unchanged Truths, 3s. 6d.

Counsel and Comfort from a City Pulpit, 3s. 6d.

Lessons of Middle Age, 3s. 6d.

Leisure Hours in Town, 3s. 6d.

Autumn Holidays of a Country Parson, price 3s. 6d.

Sunday Afternoons at the Parish Church of a University City, 3s. 6d.

The Commonplace Philosopher in Town and Country, 3s. 6d.

Present-Day Thoughts, 3s. 6d.

Critical Essays of a Country Parson, price 3s. 6d.

The Graver Thoughts of a Country Parson. Three Series, 3s. 6d. each.

DICTIONARIES and OTHER BOOKS of REFERENCE.

One-Volume Dictionary of the English Language. By R. G. LATHAM, M.A. M.D. Medium 8vo. 14s.

Larger Dictionary of the English Language. By R. G. LATHAM, M.A. M.D. Founded on Johnson's English Dictionary as edited by the Rev. H. J. TODD. 4 vols. 4to. £7.

Roget's Thesaurus of English Words and Phrases, classified and arranged so as to facilitate the expression of Ideas, and assist in Literary Composition. Revised and enlarged by the Author's Son, J. L. ROGET. Crown 8vo. 10s. 6d.

English Synonymes. By E. J. WHATELY. Edited by R. WHATELY, D.D. Fcp. 8vo. 3s.

Handbook of the English Language. By R. G. LATHAM, M.A. M.D. Crown 8vo. 6s.

Contanseau's Practical Dictionary of the French and English Languages. Post 8vo. price 7s. 6d.

Contanseau's Pocket Dictionary, French and English, abridged from the Practical Dictionary by the Author. Square 18mo. 3s. 6d.

A Practical Dictionary of the German and English Languages. By Rev. W. L. BLACKLEY, M.A. & Dr. C. M. FRIEDLÄNDER. Post 8vo. 7s. 6d.

A New Pocket Diction- ary of the German and English Languages. By F. W. LONGMAN, Ball. Coll. Oxford. Square 18mo. 5s.

Becker's Gallus ; Roman Scenes of the Time of Augustus. Translated by the Rev. F. METCALFE, M.A. Post 8vo. 7s. 6d.

Becker's Charicles; Illustrations of the Private Life of the Ancient Greeks. Translated by the Rev. F. METCALFE, M.A. Post 8vo. 7s. 6d.

A Dictionary of Roman and Greek Antiquities. With 2,000 Woodcuts illustrative of the Arts and Life of the Greeks and Romans. By A. RICH, B.A. Crown 8vo. 7s. 6d.

A Greek-English Lexi- con. By H. G. LIDDELL, D.D. Dean of Christchurch, and R. SCOTT, D.D. Dean of Rochester. Crown 4to. 36s.

Liddell & Scott's Lexi- con, Greek and English, abridged for Schools. Square 12mo. 7s. 6d.

An English-Greek Lexi- con, containing all the Greek Words used by Writers of good authority. By C. D. YONGE, M.A. 4to. 21s. School Abridgment, square 12mo. 8s. 6d.

A Latin-English Diction- ary. By JOHN T. WHITE, D.D. Oxon. and J. E. RIDDLE, M.A. Oxon. Sixth Edition, revised. Quarto 21s.

White's College Latin- English Dictionary, for the use of University Students. Royal 8vo. 12s.

M'Culloch's Dictionary of Commerce and Commercial Navigation. Re-edited, with a Supplement shewing the Progress of British Commercial Legislation to the Year 1880, by HUGH G. REID. With 11 Maps and 30 Charts. 8vo. 63s.

Keith Johnston's General Dictionary of Geography, Descriptive, Physical, Statistical, and Historical; a complete Gazetteer of the World. Medium 8vo. 42s.

The Public Schools Atlas of Ancient Geography, in 28 entirely new Coloured Maps. Edited by the Rev. G. BUTLER, M.A. Imperial 8vo. or imperial 4to. 7s. 6d.

The Public Schools Atlas of Modern Geography, in 31 entirely new Coloured Maps. Edited by the Rev. G. BUTLER, M.A. Uniform, 5s.

ASTRONOMY and METEOROLOGY.

Outlines of Astronomy. By Sir J. F. W. Herschel, Bart. M.A. Latest Edition, with Plates and Diagrams. Square crown 8vo. 12s.

Essays on Astronomy. A Series of Papers on Planets and Meteors, the Sun and Sun-surrounding Space, Stars and Star Cloudlets. By R. A. Proctor, B.A. With 10 Plates and 24 Woodcuts. 8vo. 12s.

The Moon; her Motions, Aspects, Scenery, and Physical Condition. By R. A. Proctor, B.A. With Plates, Charts, Woodcuts, and Lunar Photographs. Crown 8vo. 10s. 6d.

The Sun; Ruler, Light, Fire, and Life of the Planetary System. By R. A. Proctor, B.A. With Plates & Woodcuts. Crown 8vo. 14s.

The Orbs Around Us; a Series of Essays on the Moon & Planets, Meteors & Comets, the Sun & Coloured Pairs of Suns. By R. A. Proctor, B.A. With Chart and Diagrams. Crown 8vo. 7s. 6d.

The Universe of Stars; Presenting Researches into and New Views respecting the Constitution of the Heavens. By R. A. Proctor, B.A. Second Edition, with 22 Charts (4 Coloured) and 22 Diagrams. 8vo. price 10s. 6d.

Other Worlds than Ours; The Plurality of Worlds Studied under the Light of Recent Scientific Researches. By R. A. Proctor, B.A. With 14 Illustrations. Cr. 8vo. 10s. 6d.

Saturn and its System. By R. A. Proctor, B.A. 8vo. with 14 Plates, 14s.

The Moon, and the Condition and Configurations of its Surface. By E. Neison, F.R.A.S. With 26 Maps & 5 Plates. Medium 8vo. 31s. 6d.

Celestial Objects for Common Telescopes. By the Rev. T. W. Webb, M.A. Fourth Edition, revised and adapted to the Present State of Sidereal Science; Map, Plate, Woodcuts. Crown 8vo. 9s.

A New Star Atlas, for the Library, the School, and the Observatory, in 12 Circular Maps (with 2 Index Plates). By R. A. Proctor, B.A. Crown 8vo. 5s.

Larger Star Atlas, for the Library, in Twelve Circular Maps, with Introduction and 2 Index Plates. By R. A. Proctor, B.A. Folio, 15s. or Maps only, 12s. 6d.

Air and Rain; the Beginnings of a Chemical Climatology. By R. A. Smith, F.R.S. 8vo. 24s.

NATURAL HISTORY and PHYSICAL SCIENCE.

Elementary Treatise on Physics, Experimental and Applied, for the use of Colleges and Schools. Translated and edited from Ganot's Traité Élémentaire de Physique (with the Author's sanction) by Edmund Atkinson, Ph.D. F.C.S. Professor of Experimental Science, Staff College. Ninth Edition, revised and enlarged; with 4 Coloured Plates and 844 Woodcuts. Large crown 8vo. 15s.

Natural Philosophy for General Readers and Young Persons; a Course of Physics divested of Mathematical Formulæ and expressed in the language of daily life. Translated and edited from Ganot's Cours de Physique (with the Author's sanction) by Edmund Atkinson, Ph.D. F.C.S. Professor of Experimental Science, Staff College. Fourth Edition, revised; with 2 Plates and 471 Woodcuts. Crown 8vo. 7s. 6d.

Professor Helmholtz on the Sensations of Tone, as a Physiological Basis for the Theory of Music. Translated by A. J. ELLIS, F.R.S. 8vo. 36s.

Professor Helmholtz' Popular Lectures on Scientific Subjects. Translated and edited by EDMUND ATKINSON, Ph.D. F.C.S. Professor of Chemistry &c. Staff College, Sandhurst. FIRST SERIES, with a Preface by Professor TYNDALL, F.R.S. Second Edition, with 51 Woodcuts. Crown 8vo. 7s. 6d.

Professor Helmholtz' Popular Lectures on Scientific Subjects, SECOND SERIES, on the Origin and Signification of Geometrical Axioms, the relation of Form, Shade, Colour and Harmony of Colour to Painting, the Origin of the Planetary System, &c. Translated by EDMUND ATKINSON, Ph.D. F.C.S. Professor of Chemistry &c. Staff College, Sandhurst. With 17 Woodcuts. Crown 8vo. 7s. 6d.

Arnott's Elements of Physics or Natural Philosophy. Seventh Edition, edited by A. BAIN, LL.D. and A. S. TAYLOR, M.D. F.R.S. Crown 8vo. Woodcuts, 12s. 6d.

The Correlation of Physical Forces. By the Hon. Sir W. R. GROVE, F.R.S. &c. Sixth Edition, revised and augmented. 8vo. 15s.

A Treatise on Magnetism, General and Terrestrial. By H. LLOYD, D.D. D.C.L. &c. late Provost of Trinity College, Dublin. 8vo. 10s. 6d.

Elementary Treatise on the Wave-Theory of Light. By H. LLOYD, D.D. D.C.L. &c. late Provost of Trinity College, Dublin. 8vo. price 10s. 6d.

The Mathematical and other Tracts of the late James M'Cullagh, F.T.C.D. Professor of Natural Philosophy in the University of Dublin. Now first collected, and Edited by the Rev. J. H. JELLETT, B.D. and the Rev. S. HAUGHTON, M.D. Fellows of Trin. Coll. Dublin. 8vo. 15s.

A Text-Book of Systematic Mineralogy. By H. BAUERMAN, F.G.S. Associate of the Royal School of Mines. With numerous Woodcuts. Small 8vo. 6s.

A Text-Book of Descriptive Mineralogy. In the same Series of *Text-Books of Science*, and by the same Author. Small 8vo. Woodcuts. [*In preparation.*

Fragments of Science. By JOHN TYNDALL, F.R.S. Sixth Edition, revised and augmented. 2 vols. crown 8vo. 16s.

Heat a Mode of Motion. By JOHN TYNDALL, F.R.S. Sixth Edition (Thirteenth Thousand), thoroughly revised and enlarged. Crown 8vo. 12s.

Sound. By JOHN TYNDALL, F.R.S. Fourth Edition, including Recent Researches. [*Nearly ready.*

Contributions to Molecular Physics in the domain of Radiant Heat. By JOHN TYNDALL, F.R.S. Plates and Woodcuts. 8vo. 16s.

Professor Tyndall's Researches on Diamagnetism and Magne-Crystallic Action; including Diamagnetic Polarity. New Edition in preparation.

Professor Tyndall's Lectures on Light, delivered in America in 1872 and 1873. With Portrait, Plate & Diagrams. Crown 8vo. 7s. 6d.

Professor Tyndall's Lessons in Electricity at the Royal Institution, 1875-6. With 58 Woodcuts. Crown 8vo. 2s. 6d.

Professor Tyndall's Notes of a Course of Seven Lectures on Electrical Phenomena and Theories, delivered at the Royal Institution. Crown 8vo. 1s. sewed, 1s. 6d. cloth.

Professor Tyndall's Notes of a Course of Nine Lectures on Light, delivered at the Royal Institution. Crown 8vo. 1s. swd., 1s. 6d. cloth.

Text-Books of Science,
Mechanical and Physical, adapted for the use of Artisans and of Students in Public and Science Schools. Small 8vo. with Woodcuts, &c.

Abney's Photography, 3s. 6d.

Anderson's (Sir John) Strength of Materials, 3s. 6d.

Armstrong's Organic Chemistry, 3s. 6d.

Ball's Elements of Astronomy, 6s.

Barry's Railway Appliances, 3s. 6d.

Bauerman's Systematic Mineralogy, 6s.

Bloxam's Metals, 3s. 6d.

Goodeve's Mechanics, 3s. 6d.

Gore's Electro-Metallurgy, 6s.

Griffin's Algebra & Trigonometry, 3/6.

Jenkin's Electricity & Magnetism, 3/6.

Maxwell's Theory of Heat, 3s. 6d.

Merrifield's Technical Arithmetic, 3s. 6d.

Miller's Inorganic Chemistry, 3s. 6d.

Preece & Sivewright's Telegraphy, 3/6.

Rutley's Study of Rocks, 4s. 6d.

Shelley's Workshop Appliances, 3s. 6d.

Thomé's Structural and Physiological Botany, 6s.

Thorpe's Quantitative Analysis, 4s. 6d.

Thorpe & Muir's Qualitative Analysis, price 3s. 6d.

Tilden's Chemical Philosophy, 3s. 6d.

Unwin's Machine Design, 3s. 6d.

Watson's Plane & Solid Geometry, 3/6.

Six Lectures on Physical Geography,
delivered in 1876, with some Additions. By the Rev. SAMUEL HAUGHTON, F.R.S. M.D. D.C.L. With 23 Diagrams. 8vo. 15s.

An Introduction to the
Systematic Zoology and Morphology of Vertebrate Animals. By A. MACALISTER, M.D. With 28 Diagrams. 8vo. 10s. 6d.

The Comparative Anatomy
and Physiology of the Vertebrate Animals. By RICHARD OWEN, F.R.S. With 1,472 Woodcuts. 3 vols. 8vo. £3. 13s. 6d.

Homes without Hands;
a Description of the Habitations of Animals, classed according to their Principle of Construction. By the Rev. J. G. WOOD, M.A. With about 140 Vignettes on Wood. 8vo. 14s.

Wood's Strange Dwellings;
a Description of the Habitations of Animals, abridged from 'Homes without Hands.' With Frontispiece and 60 Woodcuts. Crown 8vo. 7s. 6d.

Wood's Insects at Home;
a Popular Account of British Insects, their Structure, Habits, and Transformations. 8vo. Woodcuts, 14s.

Wood's Insects Abroad;
a Popular Account of Foreign Insects, their Structure, Habits, and Transformations. 8vo. Woodcuts, 14s.

Wood's Out of Doors;
a Selection of Original Articles on Practical Natural History. With 6 Illustrations. Crown 8vo. 7s. 6d.

Wood's Bible Animals;
a description of every Living Creature mentioned in the Scriptures, from the Ape to the Coral. With 112 Vignettes. 8vo. 14s.

The Sea and its Living
Wonders. By Dr. G. HARTWIG. 8vo. with many Illustrations, 10s. 6d.

Hartwig's Tropical
World. With about 200 Illustrations. 8vo. 10s. 6d.

Hartwig's Polar World;
a Description of Man and Nature in the Arctic and Antarctic Regions of the Globe. Maps, Plates & Woodcuts. 8vo. 10s. 6d.

Hartwig's Subterranean
World. With Maps and Woodcuts. 8vo. 10s. 6d.

Hartwig's Aerial World;
a Popular Account of the Phenomena and Life of the Atmosphere. Map, Plates, Woodcuts. 8vo. 10s. 6d.

A Familiar History of
Birds. By E. STANLEY, D.D. New Edition, revised and enlarged, with 160 Woodcuts. Crown 8vo. 6s.

Rural Bird Life; Essays on Ornithology, with Instructions for Preserving Objects relating to that Science. By CHARLES DIXON. With Coloured Frontispiece and 44 Woodcuts by G. Pearson. Crown 8vo. 7s. 6d.

The Note-book of an Amateur Geologist. By JOHN EDWARD LEE, F.G.S. F.S.A. &c. With numerous Woodcuts and 200 Lithographic Plates of Sketches and Sections. 8vo. 21s.

Rocks Classified and Described. By BERNHARD VON COTTA. An English Translation, by P. H. LAWRENCE, with English, German, and French Synonymes. Post 8vo. 14s.

The Geology of England and Wales; a Concise Account of the Lithological Characters, Leading Fossils, and Economic Products of the Rocks. By H. B. WOODWARD, F.G.S. Crown 8vo. Map & Woodcuts, 14s.

Keller's Lake Dwellings of Switzerland, and other Parts of Europe. Translated by JOHN E. LEE, F.S.A. F.G.S. With 206 Illustrations. 2 vols. royal 8vo. 42s.

Heer's Primæval World of Switzerland. Edited by JAMES HEYWOOD, M.A. F.R.S. With Map, 19 Plates, & 372 Woodcuts. 2 vols. 8vo. 16s.

The Puzzle of Life and How it Has Been Put Together; a Short History of Praehistoric Vegetable and Animal Life on the Earth. By A. NICOLS, F.R.G.S. With 12 Illustrations. Crown 8vo. 3s. 6d.

The Origin of Civilisation, and the Primitive Condition of Man; Mental and Social Condition of Savages. By Sir J. LUBBOCK, Bart. M.P. F.R.S. 8vo. Woodcuts, 18s.

Light Science for Leisure Hours; Familiar Essays on Scientific Subjects, Natural Phenomena, &c. By R. A. PROCTOR, B.A. 2 vols. crown 8vo. 7s. 6d. each.

A Dictionary of Science, Literature, and Art. Re-edited by the Rev. Sir G. W. COX, Bart. M.A. 3 vols. medium 8vo. 63s.

Hullah's Course of Lectures on the History of Modern Music. 8vo. 8s. 6d.

Hullah's Second Course of Lectures on the Transition Period of Musical History. 8vo. 10s. 6d.

Loudon's Encyclopædia of Plants; the Specific Character, Description, Culture, History, &c. of all Plants found in Great Britain. With 12,000 Woodcuts. 8vo. 42s.

De Caisne & Le Maout's Descriptive and Analytical Botany. Translated by Mrs. HOOKER; edited and arranged by J. D. HOOKER, M.D. With 5,500 Woodcuts. Imperial 8vo. price 31s. 6d.

Rivers's Orchard-House; or, the Cultivation of Fruit Trees under Glass. Sixteenth Edition. Crown 8vo. with 25 Woodcuts, 5s.

The Rose Amateur's Guide. By THOMAS RIVERS. Latest Edition. Fcp. 8vo. 4s. 6d.

Town and Window Gardening, including the Structure, Habits and Uses of Plants. By Mrs. BUCKTON With 127 Woodcuts. Crown 8vo. 2s.

Loudon's Encyclopædia of Gardening; the Theory and Practice of Horticulture, Floriculture, Arboriculture & Landscape Gardening. With 1,000 Woodcuts. 8vo. 21s.

CHEMISTRY and PHYSIOLOGY.

Experimental Chemistry for Junior Students. By J. E. REYNOLDS, M.D. F.R.S. Professor of Chemistry, University of Dublin. Part I. Introductory. Fcp. 8vo. 1s. 6d.

Practical Chemistry; the Principles of Qualitative Analysis. By W. A. TILDEN, D.Sc. Lond. F.C S. Professor of Chemistry in Mason's College, Birmingham. Fcp. 8vo. 1s. 6d.

WORKS published by LONGMANS & CO. 13

Miller's Elements of Chemistry, Theoretical and Practical. Re-edited, with Additions, by H. MACLEOD, F.C.S. 3 vols. 8vo.
PART I. CHEMICAL PHYSICS. 16s.
PART II. INORGANIC CHEMISTRY, 24s.
PART III. ORGANIC CHEMISTRY, in Two Sections. SECTION I. 31s. 6d.

Annals of Chemical Medicine; including the Application of Chemistry to Physiology, Pathology, Therapeutics, Pharmacy, Toxicology, and Hygiene. Edited by J. L. W. THUDICHUM, M.D. VOL. I. 8vo. 14s.

Health in the House: Twenty-five Lectures on Elementary Physiology in its Application to the Daily Wants of Man and Animals. By Mrs. BUCKTON. Crown 8vo. Woodcuts, 2s.

A Dictionary of Chemistry and the Allied Branches of other Sciences. Edited by HENRY WATTS, F.C.S. 8 vols. medium 8vo. £12.12s.6d. Third Supplement, completing the Record of Chemical Discovery to the year 1877. PART II. completion, is now ready, price 50s.

Select Methods in Chemical Analysis, chiefly Inorganic. By W. CROOKES, F.R.S. With 22 Woodcuts. Crown 8vo. 12s. 6d.

The History, Products, and Processes of the Alkali Trade, including the most recent Improvements. By C. T. KINGZETT, F.C.S. With 32 Woodcuts. 8vo. 12s.

Animal Chemistry, or the Relations of Chemistry to Physiology and Pathology: a Manual for Medical Men and Scientific Chemists. By C. T. KINGZETT, F.C.S. 8vo. 18s.

The FINE ARTS and ILLUSTRATED EDITIONS.

Notes on Foreign Picture Galleries. By C. L. EASTLAKE. F.R.I.B.A. Keeper of the National Gallery, London. Crown 8vo. fully Illustrated. [*In preparation*.
Vol. I. The Brera Gallery, Milan.
„ II. The Louvre, Paris.
„ III. The Pinacothek, Munich.

In Fairyland; Pictures from the Elf-World. By RICHARD DOYLE. With 16 coloured Plates, containing 36 Designs. Folio, 15s.

Lord Macaulay's Lays of Ancient Rome, with Ivry and the Armada. With 41 Wood Engravings by G. Pearson from Original Drawings by J. R. Weguelin. Crown 8vo. 6s.

Lord Macaulay's Lays of Ancient Rome. With Ninety Illustrations engraved on Wood from Drawings by G. Scharf. Fcp. 4to. 21s. or imperial 16mo. 10s. 6d.

The Three Cathedrals dedicated to St. Paul in London. By W. LONGMAN, F.S.A. With Illustrations. Square crown 8vo. 21s.

Moore's Lalla Rookh. TENNIEL'S Edition, with 68 Woodcut Illustrations. Crown 8vo. 10s. 6d.

Moore's Irish Melodies, MACLISE'S Edition, with 161 Steel Plates. Super-royal 8vo. 21s.

Lectures on Harmony, delivered at the Royal Institution. By G. A. MACFARREN. 8vo. 12s.

Sacred and Legendary Art. By Mrs. JAMESON. 6 vols. square crown 8vo. £5. 15s. 6d.

Jameson's Legends of the Saints and Martyrs. With 19 Etchings and 187 Woodcuts. 2 vols. 31s. 6d.

Jameson's Legends of the Monastic Orders. With 11 Etchings and 88 Woodcuts. 1 vol. 21s.

Jameson's Legends of the Madonna. With 27 Etchings and 165 Woodcuts. 1 vol. 21s.

Jameson's History of the Saviour, His Types and Precursors. Completed by Lady EASTLAKE. With 13 Etchings and 281 Woodcuts. 2 vols. 42s.

The USEFUL ARTS, MANUFACTURES, &c.

The Elements of Mechanism. By T. M. GOODEVE, M.A. Barrister-at-Law. New Edition, re-written and enlarged, with 342 Woodcuts. Crown 8vo. 6s.

The Amateur Mechanics' Practical Handbook; describing the different Tools required in the Workshop. By A. H. G. HOBSON. With 33 Woodcuts. Crown 8vo. 2s. 6d.

The Engineer's Valuing Assistant. By H. D. HOSKOLD, Civil and Mining Engineer. 8vo. price 31s. 6d.

Industrial Chemistry; a Manual for Manufacturers and for Colleges or Technical Schools; a Translation (by Dr. T. H. BARRY) of Stohmann and Engler's German Edition of PAYEN's 'Précis de Chimie Industrielle;' with Chapters on the Chemistry of the Metals, &c. by B. H. PAUL, Ph.D. With 698 Woodcuts. Medium 8vo. 42s.

Gwilt's Encyclopædia of Architecture, with above 1,600 Woodcuts. Revised and extended by W. PAPWORTH. 8vo. 52s. 6d.

Lathes and Turning, Simple, Mechanical, and Ornamental. By W. H. NORTHCOTT. Second Edition, with 338 Illustrations. 8vo. 18s.

The Theory of Strains in Girders and similar Structures, with Observations on the application of Theory to Practice, and Tables of the Strength and other Properties of Materials. By B. B. STONEY, M.A. M. Inst. C.E. Royal 8vo. with 5 Plates and 123 Woodcuts, 36s.

Recent Naval Administration; Shipbuilding for the Purposes of War. By T. BRASSEY, M.P. 6 vols. 8vo. with Illustrations by the Chevalier E. de Martino. [*In the press.*

A Treatise on Mills and Millwork. By the late Sir W. FAIRBAIRN, Bart. C.E. Fourth Edition, with 18 Plates and 333 Woodcuts. 1 vol. 8vo. 25s.

Useful Information for Engineers. By the late Sir W. FAIRBAIRN, Bart. C.E. With many Plates and Woodcuts. 3 vols. crown 8vo. 31s. 6d.

The Application of Cast and Wrought Iron to Building Purposes. By the late Sir W. FAIRBAIRN, Bart. C.E. With 6 Plates and 118 Woodcuts. 8vo. 16s.

Hints on Household Taste in Furniture, Upholstery, and other Details. By C. L. EASTLAKE. Fourth Edition, with 100 Illustrations. Square crown 8vo. 14s.

Handbook of Practical Telegraphy. By R. S. CULLEY, Memb. Inst. C.E. Seventh Edition. Plates & Woodcuts. 8vo. 16s.

A Treatise on the Steam Engine, in its various applications to Mines, Mills, Steam Navigation, Railways and Agriculture. By J. BOURNE, C.E. With Portrait, 37 Plates, and 546 Woodcuts. 4to. 42s.

Catechism of the Steam Engine, in its various Applications. By JOHN BOURNE, C.E. Fcp. 8vo. Woodcuts, 6s.

Handbook of the Steam Engine, a Key to the Author's Catechism of the Steam Engine. By J. BOURNE, C.E. Fcp. 8vo. Woodcuts, 9s.

Recent Improvements in the Steam Engine. By J. BOURNE, C.E. Fcp. 8vo. Woodcuts, 6s.

Examples of Steam and Gas Engines of the most recent Approved Types as employed in Mines, Factories, Steam Navigation, Railways and Agriculture, practically described. By JOHN BOURNE, C.E. With 54 Plates and 356 Woodcuts. 4to. 70s.

Ure's Dictionary of Arts, Manufactures, and Mines. Seventh Edition, re-written and enlarged by R. HUNT, F.R.S. assisted by numerous Contributors. With 2,604 Woodcuts. 4 vols. medium 8vo. £7. 7s.

Cresy's Encyclopædia of
Civil Engineering, Historical, Theoretical, and Practical. With above 3,000 Woodcuts. 8vo. 25s.

Kerl's Practical Treatise on Metallurgy. Adapted from the last German Edition by W. CROOKES, F.R.S. &c. and E. RÖHRIG, Ph.D. 3 vols. 8vo. with 625 Woodcuts. £4. 19s.

Ville on Artificial Manures, their Chemical Selection and Scientific Application to Agriculture; a Series of Lectures given at the Experimental Farm at Vincennes. Translated and edited by W. CROOKES, F.R.S. With 31 Plates. 8vo. 21s.

Mitchell's Manual of Practical Assaying. Fourth Edition, revised, with the Recent Discoveries incorporated, by W. CROOKES, F.R.S. Crown 8vo. Woodcuts, 31s. 6d.

The Art of Perfumery, and the Methods of Obtaining the Odours of Plants; the Growth and general Flower Farm System of Raising Fragrant Herbs; with Instructions for the Manufacture of Perfumes for the Handkerchief, Scented Powders, Odorous Vinegars and Salts, Snuff, Dentifrices, Cosmetics, Perfumed Soap, &c. By G. W. S. PIESSE, Ph.D. F.C.S. Fourth Edition, with 96 Woodcuts. Square crown 8vo. 21s.

Loudon's Encyclopædia of Gardening; the Theory and Practice of Horticulture, Floriculture, Arboriculture & Landscape Gardening. With 1,000 Woodcuts. 8vo. 21s.

Loudon's Encyclopædia of Agriculture; the Laying-out, Improvement, and Management of Landed Property; the Cultivation and Economy of the Productions of Agriculture. With 1,100 Woodcuts. 8vo. 21s.

RELIGIOUS and MORAL WORKS.

A Handbook to the Bible, or, Guide to the Study of the Holy Scriptures derived from Ancient Monuments and Modern Exploration. By F. R. CONDER, and Lieut. C. R. CONDER, R.E. Second Edit. ; Maps, Plates of Coins, &c. Post 8vo. 7s. 6d.

A History of the Church of England; Pre-Reformation Period. By the Rev. T. P. BOULTBEE, LL.D. 8vo. 15s.

Sketch of the History of the Church of England to the Revolution of 1688. By T. V. SHORT, D.D. Crown 8vo. 7s. 6d.

The English Church in the Eighteenth Century. By CHARLES J. ABBEY, late Fellow of University College, Oxford; and JOHN H. OVERTON, late Scholar of Lincoln College, Oxford. 2 vols. 8vo. 36s.

An Exposition of the 39 Articles, Historical and Doctrinal. By E. H. BROWNE, D.D. Bishop of Winchester. Eleventh Edition. 8vo. 16s.

A Commentary on the 39 Articles, forming an Introduction to the Theology of the Church of England. By the Rev. T. P. BOULTBEE, LL.D. New Edition. Crown 8vo. 6s.

Sermons preached mostly in the Chapel of Rugby School by the late T. ARNOLD, D.D. Collective Edition, revised by the Author's Daughter, Mrs. W. E. FORSTER. 6 vols. crown 8vo. 30s. or separately, 5s. each.

Historical Lectures on the Life of Our Lord Jesus Christ. By C. J. ELLICOTT, D.D. 8vo. 12s.

The Eclipse of Faith ; or a Visit to a Religious Sceptic. By HENRY ROGERS. Fcp. 8vo. 5s.

Defence of the Eclipse of Faith. By H. ROGERS. Fcp. 8vo. 3s. 6d.

Nature, the Utility of Religion, and Theism. Three Essays by JOHN STUART MILL. 8vo. 10s. 6d.

A Critical and Grammatical Commentary on St. Paul's Epistles. By C. J. ELLICOTT, D.D. 8vo. Galatians, 8s. 6d. Ephesians, 8s. 6d. Pastoral Epistles, 10s. 6d. Philippians, Colossians, & Philemon, 10s. 6d. Thessalonians, 7s. 6d.

Conybeare & Howson's Life and Epistles of St. Paul. Three Editions, copiously illustrated.

Library Edition, with all the Original Illustrations, Maps, Landscapes on Steel, Woodcuts, &c. 2 vols. 4to. 42s.

Intermediate Edition, with a Selection of Maps, Plates, and Woodcuts. 2 vols. square crown 8vo. 21s.

Student's Edition, revised and condensed, with 46 Illustrations and Maps. 1 vol. crown 8vo. 7s. 6d.

Smith's Voyage & Shipwreck of St. Paul; with Dissertations on the Life and Writings of St. Luke, and the Ships and Navigation of the Ancients. Fourth Edition, revised by the Author's Son; with a Memoir of the Author, a Preface by the BISHOP OF CARLISLE, and all the Original Illustrations. Crown 8vo. 7s. 6d.

The Angel-Messiah of Buddhists, Essenes, and Christians. By ERNEST DE BUNSEN. 8vo. 10s. 6d.

Bible Studies. By M. M. KALISCH, Ph.D. PART I. *The Prophecies of Balaam.* 8vo. 10s. 6d. PART II. *The Book of Jonah.* 8vo. price 10s. 6d.

Historical and Critical Commentary on the Old Testament; with a New Translation. By M. M. KALISCH, Ph.D. Vol. I. Genesis, 8vo. 18s. or adapted for the General Reader, 12s. Vol. II. Exodus, 15s. or adapted for the General Reader, 12s. Vol. III. Leviticus, Part I. 15s. or adapted for the General Reader, 8s. Vol. IV. Leviticus, Part II. 15s. or adapted for the General Reader, 8s.

The Four Gospels in Greek, with Greek-English Lexicon. By JOHN T. WHITE, D.D. Oxon. Square 32mo. 5s.

Ewald's History of Israel. Translated from the German by J. E. CARPENTER, M.A. with Preface by R. MARTINEAU, M.A. 5 vols. 8vo. 63s.

Ewald's Antiquities of Israel. Translated from the German by H. S. SOLLY, M.A. 8vo. 12s. 6d.

The Types of Genesis, briefly considered as revealing the Development of Human Nature. By A. JUKES. Crown 8vo. 7s. 6d.

The Second Death and the Restitution of all Things; with some Preliminary Remarks on the Nature and Inspiration of Holy Scripture. By A. JUKES. Crown 8vo. 3s. 6d.

The Gospel for the Nineteenth Century. Fourth Edition. 8vo. price 10s. 6d.

Supernatural Religion; an Inquiry into the Reality of Divine Revelation. Complete Edition, thoroughly revised. 3 vols. 8vo. 36s.

Lectures on the Origin and Growth of Religion, as illustrated by the Religions of India; being the Hibbert Lectures, delivered at the Chapter House, Westminster Abbey, in 1878, by F. MAX MÜLLER, K.M. 8vo. 10s. 6d.

Introduction to the Science of Religion, Four Lectures delivered at the Royal Institution; with Essays on False Analogies and the Philosophy of Mythology. By F. MAX MÜLLER, K.M. Crown 8vo. 10s. 6d.

Passing Thoughts on Religion. By Miss SEWELL. Fcp. 8vo. price 3s. 6d.

Thoughts for the Age. By Miss SEWELL. Fcp. 8vo. 3s. 6d.

Preparation for the Holy Communion; the Devotions chiefly from the works of Jeremy Taylor. By Miss SEWELL. 32mo. 3s.

Private Devotions for Young Persons. Compiled by ELIZABETH M. SEWELL, Author of 'Amy Herbert' &c. 18mo. 2s.

WORKS *published by* LONGMANS & CO. 17

Bishop Jeremy Taylor's Entire Works; with Life by Bishop Heber. Revised and corrected by the Rev. C. P. EDEN. 10 vols. £5. 5s.

Hymns of Praise and Prayer. Corrected and edited by Rev. JOHN MARTINEAU, LL.D. Crown 8vo. 4s. 6d. 32mo. 1s. 6d.

Spiritual Songs for the Sundays and Holidays throughout the Year. By J. S. B. MONSELL, LL.D. Fcp. 8vo. 5s. 18mo. 2s.

Christ the Consoler; a Book of Comfort for the Sick. By ELLICE HOPKINS. Second Edition. Fcp. 8vo. 2s. 6d.

Lyra Germanica; Hymns translated from the German by Miss C. WINKWORTH. Fcp. 8vo. 5s.

Hours of Thought on Sacred Things; Two Volumes of Sermons. By JAMES MARTINEAU, D.D. LL.D. 2 vols. crown 8vo. 7s. 6d. each.

Endeavours after the Christian Life; Discourses. By JAMES MARTINEAU, D.D. LL.D. Fifth Edition. Crown 8vo. 7s. 6d.

The Pentateuch & Book of Joshua Critically Examined. By J. W. COLENSO, D.D. Bishop of Natal. Crown 8vo. 6s.

Lectures on the Pentateuch and the Moabite Stone; with Appendices. By J. W. COLENSO, D.D. Bishop of Natal. 8vo. 12s.

TRAVELS, VOYAGES, &c.

The Flight of the 'Lapwing'; a Naval Officer's Jottings in China, Formosa, and Japan. By the Hon. H. N. SHORE, R.N. With 2 Illustrations and 2 Maps. 8vo. 15s.

Turkish Armenia and Eastern Asia Minor. By the Rev. H. F. TOZER, M.A. F.R.G.S. With Map and 5 Illustrations. 8vo. 16s.

Sunshine and Storm in the East, or Cruises to Cyprus and Constantinople. By Mrs. BRASSEY. With 2 Maps and 114 Illustrations engraved on Wood by G. Pearson, chiefly from Drawings by the Hon. A. Y. Bingham; the Cover from an Original Design by Gustave Doré. 8vo. 21s.

A Voyage in the 'Sunbeam,' our Home on the Ocean for Eleven Months. By Mrs. BRASSEY. Cheaper Edition, with Map and 65 Wood Engravings. Crown 8vo. 7s. 6d.

Eight Years in Ceylon. By Sir SAMUEL W. BAKER, M.A. Crown 8vo. Woodcuts, 7s. 6d.

The Rifle and the Hound in Ceylon. By Sir SAMUEL W. BAKER, M.A. Crown 8vo. Woodcuts, 7s. 6d.

Sacred Palmlands; or, the Journal of a Spring Tour in Egypt and the Holy Land. By A. G. WELD. Crown 8vo. 7s. 6d.

One Thousand Miles up the Nile; a Journey through Egypt and Nubia to the Second Cataract. By Miss AMELIA B. EDWARDS. With Facsimiles, &c. and 80 Illustrations engraved on Wood from Drawings by the Author. Imperial 8vo. 42s.

Wintering in the Riviera; with Notes of Travel in Italy and France, and Practical Hints to Travellers. By WILLIAM MILLER, S.S.C. Edinburgh. With 12 Illustrations. Post 8vo. 7s. 6d.

San Remo and the Western Riviera, climatically and medically considered. By A. HILL HASSALL, M.D. Map and Woodcuts. Crown 8vo. 10s. 6d.

Himalayan and Sub-Himalayan Districts of British India, their Climate, Medical Topography, and Disease Distribution; with reasons for assigning a Malarious Origin to Goître and some other Diseases. By F. N. MACNAMARA, M.D. With Map and Fever Chart. 8vo. 21s.

C

WORKS published by LONGMANS & CO.

The Alpine Club Map of Switzerland, with parts of the Neighbouring Countries, on the scale of Four Miles to an Inch. Edited by R. C. NICHOLS, F.R.G.S. 4 Sheets in Portfolio, 42s. coloured, or 34s. uncoloured.

Dr. Rigby's Letters from France, &c. in 1789. Edited by his Daughter, Lady EASTLAKE. Crown 8vo. 10s. 6d.

The Alpine Guide. By JOHN BALL, M.R.I.A. Post 8vo. with Maps and other Illustrations :—

The Eastern Alps, 10s. 6d.

Central Alps, including all the Oberland District, 7s. 6d.

Western Alps, including Mont Blanc, Monte Rosa, Zermatt, &c. Price 6s. 6d.

On Alpine Travelling and the Geology of the Alps. Price 1s. Either of the Three Volumes or Parts of the 'Alpine Guide' may be had with this Introduction prefixed, 1s. extra.

WORKS of FICTION.

Novels and Tales. By the Right Hon. the EARL of BEACONSFIELD, K.G. The Cabinet Edition. Eleven Volumes, crown 8vo. 6s. each.

Endymion, 6s.	
Lothair, 6s.	Venetia, 6s.
Coningsby, 6s.	Alroy, Ixion, &c. 6s.
Sybil, 6s.	Young Duke &c. 6s.
Tancred, 6s.	Vivian Grey, 6s.
Henrietta Temple, 6s.	
Contarini Fleming, &c. 6s.	

Blues and Buffs; a Contested Election and its Results. By ARTHUR MILLS. Crown 8vo. 6s.

Yellow Cap, and other Fairy Stories for Children, viz. Rumpty-Dudget, Calladon, and Theeda. By JULIAN HAWTHORNE. Crown 8vo. 6s. cloth extra, gilt edges.

The Crookit Meg: a Scottish Story of the Year One. By JOHN SKELTON, LL.D. Advocate, Author of 'Essays in Romance and Studies from Life' (by 'SHIRLEY'). Crown 8vo. 6s.

Buried Alive; or, Ten Years of Penal Servitude in Siberia. By FEDOR DOSTOYEFFSKY. Translated from the German by MARIE VON THILO. Post 8vo. 10s. 6d.

'Apart from its interest as a picture of prison life, *Buried Alive* gives us several curious sketches of Russian life and character. Of course it is of the criminal side, but it seems to agree with what we learn from other sources of other classes.'
ST. JAMES'S GAZETTE.

Whispers from Fairyland. By the Right Hon. E. H. KNATCHBULL-HUGESSEN, M.P. With 9 Illustrations. Crown 8vo. 3s. 6d.

Higgledy-Piggledy; or, Stories for Everybody and Everybody's Children. By the Right Hon. E. H. KNATCHBULL-HUGESSEN, M.P. With 9 Illustrations. Cr. 8vo. 3s. 6d.

Stories and Tales. By ELIZABETH M. SEWELL. Cabinet Edition, in Ten Volumes, each containing a complete Tale or Story :—

Amy Herbert, 2s. 6d. Gertrude, 2s. 6d. The Earl's Daughter, 2s. 6d. The Experience of Life, 2s. 6d. Cleve Hall, 2s. 6d. Ivors, 2s. 6d. Katharine Ashton, 2s. 6d. Margaret Percival, 3s. 6d. Laneton Parsonage, 3s. 6d. Ursula, 3s. 6d.

The Modern Novelist's Library. Each work complete in itself, price 2s. boards, or 2s. 6d. cloth :—

By Lord BEACONSFIELD.

Lothair.	Henrietta Temple.
Coningsby.	Contarini Fleming.
Sybil.	Alroy, Ixion, &c.
Tancred.	The Young Duke, &c.
Venetia.	Vivian Grey.

By ANTHONY TROLLOPE.
Barchester Towers.
The Warden.

THE MODERN NOVELIST'S LIBRARY—*continued.*

By Major WHYTE-MELVILLE.
Digby Grand. | Good for Nothing.
General Bounce. | Holmby House.
Kate Coventry. | The Interpreter.
The Gladiators. | Queen's Maries.

By the Author of 'The Rose Garden.'
Unawares.

By the Author of 'Mlle. Mori.'
The Atelier du Lys.
Mademoiselle Mori.

By Various Writers.
Atherstone Priory.
The Burgomaster's Family.
Elsa and her Vulture.
The Six Sisters of the Valleys.']

Novels and Tales by the Right Honourable the Earl of Beaconsfield, K.G. Ten Volumes, crown 8vo. cloth extra, gilt edges, price 30s.

POETRY and THE DRAMA.

Poetical Works of Jean Ingelow. New Edition, reprinted, with Additional Matter, from the 23rd and 6th Editions of the two volumes respectively; with 2 Vignettes. 2 vols. fcp. 8vo. 12s.

Faust. From the German of GOETHE. By T. E. WEBB, LL.D. one of Her Majesty's Counsel in Ireland; sometime Fellow of Trinity College, now Regius Professor of Laws and Public Orator in the University of Dublin. 8vo. 12s. 6d.

Goethe's Faust. A New Translation, chiefly in Blank Verse; with a complete Introduction and copious Notes. By JAMES ADEY BIRDS, B.A. F.G.S. Large crown 8vo. 12s. 6d.

Goethe's Faust. The German Text, with an English Introduction and Notes for the use of Students. By ALBERT M. SELSS, M.A. Ph.D. &c. Professor of German in the University of Dublin. Crown 8vo. 5s.

Lays of Ancient Rome; with Ivry and the Armada. By LORD MACAULAY. 16mo. 3s. 6d.

The Poem of the Cid: a Translation from the Spanish, with Introduction and Notes. By JOHN ORMSBY. Crown 8vo. 5s.

Festus, a Poem. By PHILIP JAMES BAILEY. 10th Edition, enlarged & revised. Crown 8vo. 12s. 6d.

The Iliad of Homer, Homometrically translated by C. B. CAYLEY. 8vo. 12s. 6d.

The Æneid of Virgil. Translated into English Verse. By J. CONINGTON, M.A. Crown 8vo. 9s.

Bowdler's Family Shakspeare. Genuine Edition, in 1 vol. medium 8vo. large type, with 36 Woodcuts, 14s. or in 6 vols. fcp. 8vo. 21s.

Southey's Poetical Works, with the Author's last Corrections and Additions. Medium 8vo. with Portrait, 14s.

RURAL SPORTS, HORSE and CATTLE MANAGEMENT, &c.

Blaine's Encyclopædia of Rural Sports; Complete Accounts, Historical, Practical, and Descriptive, of Hunting, Shooting, Fishing, Racing, &c. With 600 Woodcuts. 8vo. 21s.

A Book on Angling; or, Treatise on the Art of Fishing in every branch; including full Illustrated Lists of Salmon Flies. By FRANCIS FRANCIS. Post 8vo. Portrait and Plates, 15s.

Wilcocks's Sea-Fisherman: comprising the Chief Methods of Hook and Line Fishing, a glance at Nets, and remarks on Boats and Boating. Post 8vo. Woodcuts, 12s. 6d.

The Fly-Fisher's Entomology. By ALFRED RONALDS. With 20 Coloured Plates. 8vo. 14s.

Horses and Roads; or, How to Keep a Horse Sound on his Legs. By FREE-LANCE. Second Edition. Crown 8vo. 6s.

Horses and Riding. By GEORGE NEVILE, M.A. With 31 Illustrations. Crown 8vo. 6s.

Youatt on the Horse. Revised and enlarged by W. WATSON, M.R.C.V.S. 8vo. Woodcuts, 7s. 6d.

Youatt's Work on the Dog. Revised and enlarged. 8vo. Woodcuts, 6s.

The Dog in Health and Disease. By STONEHENGE. Third Edition, with 78 Wood Engravings. Square crown 8vo. 7s. 6d.

The Greyhound. By STONEHENGE. Revised Edition, with 25 Portraits of Greyhounds, &c. Square crown 8vo. 15s.

Stables and Stable Fittings. By W. MILES. Imp. 8vo. with 13 Plates, 15s.

The Horse's Foot, and How to keep it Sound. By W. MILES. Imp. 8vo. Woodcuts, 12s. 6d.

A Plain Treatise on Horse-shoeing. By W. MILES. Post 8vo. Woodcuts, 2s. 6d.

Remarks on Horses' Teeth, addressed to Purchasers. By W. MILES. Post 8vo. 1s. 6d.

A Treatise on the Diseases of the Ox; being a Manual of Bovine Pathology specially adapted for the use of Veterinary Practitioners and Students. By J. H. STEEL, M.R.C.V.S. F.Z.S. With 2 Plates and 116 Woodcuts. 8vo. 15s.

WORKS of UTILITY and GENERAL INFORMATION.

Maunder's Biographical Treasury. Latest Edition, reconstructed and partly re-written, with above 1,600 additional Memoirs, by W. L. R. CATES. Fcp. 8vo. 6s.

Maunder's Treasury of Natural History; or, Popular Dictionary of Zoology. Revised and corrected Edition. Fcp. 8vo. with 900 Woodcuts, 6s.

Maunder's Treasury of Geography, Physical, Historical, Descriptive, and Political. Edited by W. HUGHES, F.R.G.S. With 7 Maps and 16 Plates. Fcp. 8vo. 6s.

Maunder's Historical Treasury; Introductory Outlines of Universal History, and Separate Histories of all Nations. Revised by the Rev. Sir G. W. COX, Bart. M.A. Fcp. 8vo. 6s.

Maunder's Treasury of Knowledge and Library of Reference; comprising an English Dictionary and Grammar, Universal Gazetteer, Classical Dictionary, Chronology, Law Dictionary, Synopsis of the Peerage, Useful Tables, &c. Fcp. 8vo. 6s.

Maunder's Scientific and Literary Treasury; a Popular Encyclopædia of Science, Literature, and Art. Latest Edition, partly re-written, with above 1,000 New Articles, by J. Y. JOHNSON. Fcp. 8vo. 6s.

The Treasury of Botany, or Popular Dictionary of the Vegetable Kingdom; with which is incorporated a Glossary of Botanical Terms. Edited by J. LINDLEY, F.R.S. and T. MOORE, F.L.S. With 274 Woodcuts and 20 Steel Plates. Two Parts, fcp. 8vo. 12s.

The Treasury of Bible Knowledge; being a Dictionary of the Books, Persons, Places, Events, and other Matters of which mention is made in Holy Scripture. By the Rev. J. AYRE, M.A. Maps, Plates & Woodcuts. Fcp. 8vo. 6s.

A Practical Treatise on Brewing; with Formulæ for Public Brewers & Instructions for Private Families. By W. BLACK. 8vo. 10s. 6d.

The Theory of the Modern Scientific Game of Whist. By W. POLE, F.R.S. Twelfth Edition. Fcp. 8vo. 2s. 6d.

The Correct Card; or, How to Play at Whist; a Whist Catechism. By Major A. CAMPBELL-WALKER, F.R.G.S. Latest Edition. Fcp. 8vo. 2s. 6d.

The Cabinet Lawyer; a Popular Digest of the Laws of England, Civil, Criminal, and Constitutional. Twenty-Fifth Edition, corrected and extended. Fcp. 8vo. 9s.

Chess Openings. By F.W. LONGMAN, Balliol College, Oxford. New Edition. Fcp. 8vo. 2s. 6d.

Pewtner's Comprehensive Specifier; a Guide to the Practical Specification of every kind of Building-Artificer's Work. Edited by W. YOUNG. Crown 8vo. 6s.

Modern Cookery for Private Families, reduced to a System of Easy Practice in a Series of carefully-tested Receipts. By ELIZA ACTON. With 8 Plates and 150 Woodcuts. Fcp. 8vo. 6s.

Food and Home Cookery. A Course of Instruction in Practical Cookery and Cleaning, for Children in Elementary Schools. By Mrs. BUCKTON. Woodcuts. Crown 8vo. 2s.

The Ventilation of Dwelling Houses and the Utilisation of Waste Heat from Open Fire-Places, &c. By F. EDWARDS, Jun. Second Edition. With numerous Lithographic Plates, comprising 106 Figures. Royal 8vo. 10s. 6d.

Hints to Mothers on the Management of their Health during the Period of Pregnancy and in the Lying-in Room. By THOMAS BULL, M.D. Fcp. 8vo. 2s. 6d.

The Maternal Management of Children in Health and Disease. By THOMAS BULL, M.D. Fcp. 8vo. 2s. 6d.

American Food and Farming. By FINLAY DUN, Special Correspondent for the 'Times.' 8vo. [*In the press.*

The Farm Valuer. By JOHN SCOTT, Land Valuer. Crown 8vo. 5s.

Rents and Purchases; or, the Valuation of Landed Property, Woods, Minerals, Buildings, &c. By JOHN SCOTT. Crown 8vo. 6s.

Economic Studies. By the late WALTER BAGEHOT, M.A. Fellow of University College, London. Edited by RICHARD HOLT HUTTON. 8vo. 10s. 6d.

Economics for Beginners By H. D. MACLEOD, M.A. Small crown 8vo. 2s. 6d.

The Elements of Banking. By H. D. MACLEOD, M.A. Fourth Edition. Crown 8vo. 5s.

The Theory and Practice of Banking. By H. D. MACLEOD, M.A. 2 vols. 8vo. 26s.

The Resources of Modern Countries; Essays towards an Estimate of the Economic Position of Nations and British Trade Prospects. By ALEX. WILSON. 2 vols. 8vo. 24s.

The Patentee's Manual; a Treatise on the Law and Practice of Letters Patent, for the use of Patentees and Inventors. By J. JOHNSON, Barrister-at-Law; and J. H. JOHNSON, Assoc. Inst. C.E. Solicitor and Patent Agent, Lincoln's Inn Fields and Glasgow. Fourth Edition, enlarged. 8vo. price 10s. 6d.

INDEX.

Abbey & Overton's English Church History 15
Abney's Photography 11
Acton's Modern Cookery 21
Alpine Club Map of Switzerland 18
——— Guide (The) 18
Amos's Jurisprudence 5
——— Primer of the Constitution............. 5
——— Fifty Years of the English Constitution 5
Anderson's Strength of Materials 11
Armstrong's Organic Chemistry 11
Arnold's (Dr.) Lectures on Modern History 2
——————— Miscellaneous Works 7
——————— Sermons 15
——————— (T.) English Literature 6
——————————— Authors 6
Arnott's Elements of Physics.................... 10
Atelier (The) du Lys 19
Atherstone Priory.................................... 19
Autumn Holidays of a Country Parson ... 7
Ayre's Treasury of Bible Knowledge 21
Bacon's Essays, by Whately 6
——— Life and Letters, by Spedding ... 5
——— Works 5
Bagehot's Biographical Studies 4
——— Economic Studies 21
——— Literary Studies 6
Bailey's Festus, a Poem 19
Bain's Mental and Moral Science........... 6
——— on the Senses and Intellect 6
——— Emotions and Will...................... 6
Baker's Two Works on Ceylon............... 17
Ball's Alpine Guides 18
——— Elements of Astronomy 11
Barry on Railway Appliances 11
Bauerman's Mineralogy 10
Beaconsfield's (Lord) Novels and Tales 18 & 19
Becker's Charicles and Gallus................. 8
Beesly's Gracchi, Marius, and Sulla 3
Black's Treatise on Brewing 21
Blackley's German-English Dictionary...... 8
Blaine's Rural Sports 19
Bloxam's Metals 11
Bolland and Lang's Aristotle's Politics...... 5
Boultbee on 39 Articles........................... 15
———'s History of the English Church... 15
Bourne's Works on the Steam Engine...... 14
Bowdler's Family Shakespeare 19
Bramley-Moore's Six Sisters of the Valleys . 19
Brande's Dictionary of Science, Literature, and Art 12
Brassey on Shipbuilding 14
Brassey's Sunshine and Storm in the East . 17
——— Voyage of the 'Sunbeam'......... 17
Browne's Exposition of the 39 Articles...... 15
Browning's Modern England 3
Buckle's History of Civilisation 2
Buckton's Food and Home Cookery......... 21
——— Health in the House 13
——— Town and Window Gardening... 12
Bull's Hints to Mothers 21
——— Maternal Management of Children. 21
Bunsen's Angel-Messiah 16
Burgomaster's Family (The) 19
Buried Alive 18
Burke's Vicissitudes of Families............... 4
Cabinet Lawyer...................................... 21

Capes's Age of the Antonines................... 3
——— Early Roman Empire 3
Carlyle's Reminiscences 4
Cates's Biographical Dictionary 4
Cayley's Iliad of Homer 19
Changed Aspects of Unchanged Truths ... 7
Chesney's Waterloo Campaign 2
Church's Beginning of the Middle Ages ... 3
Colenso on Moabite Stone &c. 17
———'s Pentateuch and Book of Joshua. 17
Commonplace Philosopher...................... 7
Comte's Positive Polity 5
Conder's Handbook to the Bible 15
Congreve's Politics of Aristotle 5
Conington's Translation of Virgil's Æneid 19
——————— Miscellaneous Writings...... 6
Contanseau's Two French Dictionaries ... 8
Conybeare and Howson's St. Paul 16
Cordery's Struggle against Absolute Monarchy 3
Cotta on Rocks, by Lawrence 12
Counsel and Comfort from a City Pulpit... 7
Cox's (G. W.) Athenian Empire 3
——— Crusades 3
——— Greeks and Persians................. 3
Creighton's Age of Elizabeth 3
——— England a Continental Power 3
——— Shilling History of England ... 3
——— Tudors and the Reformation 3
Cresy's Encyclopædia of Civil Engineering 15
Critical Essays of a Country Parson......... 7
Crookes's Chemical Analysis 13
Culley's Handbook of Telegraphy............ 14
Curteis's Macedonian Empire 3
Davison's Thousand Thoughts 7
De Caisne and Le Maout's Botany 12
De Tocqueville's Democracy in America... 2
Dixon's Rural Bird Life 12
Doyle's (J.) Fairyland............................. 13
Dun's American Food and Farming 21
Eastlake's Foreign Picture Galleries......... 13
——— Hints on Household Taste 14
Edwards on Ventilation &c. 21
Edwards's Nile.. 17
Ellicott's Scripture Commentaries 16
——— Lectures on Life of Christ 15
Elsa and her Vulture 19
Epochs of Ancient History...................... 3
——— English History 3
——— Modern History 3
Ewald's History of Israel 16
——— Antiquities of Israel................ 16
Fairbairn's Applications of Iron 14
——— Information for Engineers...... 14
——— Mills and Millwork 14
Farrar's Language and Languages 7
Francis's Fishing Book 19
Freeman's Historical Geography 2
Froude's Cæsar 4
——— English in Ireland 1
——— History of England 1
——— Short Studies......................... 6
Gairdner's Houses of Lancaster and York 3
Ganot's Elementary Physics 9
——— Natural Philosophy 9
Gardiner's Buckingham and Charles I. ... 2
——— Personal Government of Charles I. 2

WORKS published by LONGMANS & CO. 23

Title	Page
Gardiner's Puritan Resolution	3
——— Thirty Years' War	3
German Home Life	7
Gibson's Cavalier's Note Book	7
Goethe's Faust, by Birds	19
——— by Selss	19
——— by Webb	19
Goodeve's Mechanics	11
——— Mechanism	14
Gore's Electro-Metallurgy	11
Gospel (The) for the Nineteenth Century	16
Grant's Ethics of Aristotle	6
Graver Thoughts of a Country Parson	7
Greville's Faiths and Fancies	6
——— Journal	1
Griffin's Algebra and Trigonometry	11
Griffith's A B C of Philosophy	5
Grove on Correlation of Physical Forces	10
Gwilt's Encyclopædia of Architecture	14
Hale's Fall of the Stuarts	3
Hartwig's Works on Natural History and Popular Science	11
Hassall's Climate of San Remo	17
Haughton's Physical Geography	11
Hawthorne's Fairy Stories	18
Hayward's Selected Essays	6
Heer's Primeval World of Switzerland	12
Helmholtz on Tone	10
Helmholtz's Scientific Lectures	10
Herschel's Outlines of Astronomy	9
Hillebrand's Lectures on German Thought	6
Hobson's Amateur Mechanic	14
Hopkins's Christ the Consoler	17
Horses and Roads	20
Hoskold's Engineer's Valuing Assistant	14
Hullah's History of Modern Music	12
——— Transition Period	12
Hume's Essays	6
——— Treatise on Human Nature	6
Ihne's Rome to its Capture by the Gauls	3
——— History of Rome	2
Ingelow's Poems	19
Jameson's Sacred and Legendary Art	15
——— Memoirs by Macpherson	4
Jenkin's Electricity and Magnetism	11
Jerrold's Life of Napoleon	1
Johnson's Normans in Europe	3
——— Patentee's Manual	21
Johnston's Geographical Dictionary	8
Jukes's Types of Genesis	16
Jukes on Second Death	16
Kalisch's Bible Studies	16
——— Commentary on the Bible	16
——— Path and Goal	5
Keller's Lake Dwellings of Switzerland	12
Kerl's Metallurgy, by *Crookes* and *Röhrig*	15
Kingzett's Alkali Trade	13
——— Animal Chemistry	13
Knatchbull-Hugessen's Fairy-Land	18
——— Higgledy-Piggledy	18
Landscapes, Churches, &c.	7
Latham's English Dictionaries	8
——— Handbook of English Language	8
Lecky's History of England	1
——— European Morals	3
——— Rationalism	3
——— Leaders of Public Opinion	4
Lee's Geologist's Note Book	12
Leisure Hours in Town	7
Leslie's Essays in Political and Moral Philosophy	6
Lessons of Middle Age	7
Lewes's History of Philosophy	3
Lewis on Authority	6
Liddell and *Scott's* Greek-English Lexicons	8
Lindley and *Moore's* Treasury of Botany	20
Lloyd's Magnetism	10
——— Wave-Theory of Light	10
Longman's (F. W.) Chess Openings	21
——— Frederic the Great and the Seven Years' War	3
——— German Dictionary	8
——— (W.) Edward the Third	2
——— Lectures on History of England	2
——— Old and New St. Paul's	13
Loudon's Encyclopædia of Agriculture	15
——— Gardening	12
——— Plants	12
Lubbock's Origin of Civilisation	12
Ludlow's American War of Independence	3
Lyra Germanica	17
Macalister's Vertebrate Animals	11
Macaulay's (Lord) Essays	1
——— History of England	1
——— Lays, Illustrated Edits.	13
——— Cheap Edition	19
——— Life and Letters	4
——— Miscellaneous Writings	7
——— Speeches	7
——— Works	1
——— Writings, Selections from	7
MacCullagh's Tracts	10
McCulloch's Dictionary of Commerce	8
Macfarren on Musical Harmony	13
Macleod's Economical Philosophy	5
——— Economics for Beginners	21
——— Theory and Practice of Banking	21
——— Elements of Banking	21
Macnamara's Himalayan Districts of British India	17
Mademoiselle Mori	19
Mahaffy's Classical Greek Literature	3
Marshman's Life of Havelock	4
Martineau's Christian Life	17
——— Hours of Thought	17
——— Hymns	17
Maunder's Popular Treasuries	20
Maxwell's Theory of Heat	11
May's History of Democracy	2
——— History of England	2
Melville's (Whyte) Novels and Tales	19
Mendelssohn's Letters	4
Merivale's Fall of the Roman Republic	2
——— General History of Rome	2
——— Roman Triumvirates	3
——— Romans under the Empire	2
Merrifield's Arithmetic and Mensuration	11
Miles on Horse's Foot and Horse Shoeing	20
——— on Horse's Teeth and Stables	20
Mill (J.) on the Mind	5
Mill's (J. S.) Autobiography	4
——— Dissertations & Discussions	5
——— Essays on Religion	15
——— Hamilton's Philosophy	5
——— Liberty	5
——— Political Economy	5
——— Representative Government	5
——— Subjection of Women	5
——— System of Logic	5
——— Unsettled Questions	5
——— Utilitarianism	5
Miller's Elements of Chemistry	13

WORKS published by LONGMANS & CO.

Miller's Inorganic Chemistry	11
——— Wintering in the Riviera	17
Mills's Blues and Buffs	18
Minto (Lord) in India	2
Mitchell's Manual of Assaying	15
Modern Novelist's Library	18 & 19
Monck's Logic	6
Monsell's Spiritual Songs	17
Moore's Irish Melodies, Illustrated Edition	13
——— Lalla Rookh, Illustrated Edition	13
Morris's Age of Anne	3
Müller's Chips from a German Workshop	7
——— Hibbert Lectures on Religion	16
——— Science of Language	7
——— Science of Religion	16
——— Selected Essays	7
Neison on the Moon	9
Nevile's Horses and Riding	20
Newman's Apologia pro Vitâ Suâ	4
Nicols's Puzzle of Life	12
Northcott's Lathes & Turning	14
Ormsby's Poem of the Cid	19
Overton's Life, &c. of Law	4
Owen's Comparative Anatomy and Physiology of Vertebrate Animals	11
Owen's Evenings with the Skeptics	7
Payen's Industrial Chemistry	14
Pewtner's Comprehensive Specifier	21
Piesse's Art of Perfumery	15
Pole's Game of Whist	21
Powell's Early England	3
Preece & Sivewright's Telegraphy	11
Present-Day Thoughts	7
Proctor's Astronomical Works	9
——— Scientific Essays (Two Series)	12
Public Schools Atlases	8
Rawlinson's Ancient Egypt	3
——— Sassanians	3
Recreations of a Country Parson	7
Reynolds's Experimental Chemistry	12
Rich's Dictionary of Antiquities	8
Rigby's Letters from France, &c. in 1789	18
Rivers's Orchard House	12
——— Rose Amateur's Guide	12
Rogers's Eclipse of Faith	15
——— Defence of Eclipse of Faith	15
Roget's English Thesaurus	8
Ronalds' Fly-Fisher's Entomology	20
Rowley's Rise of the People	3
——— Settlement of the Constitution	3
Russia and England	1
——— Before and After the War	1
Rutley's Study of Rocks	11
Sandars's Justinian's Institutes	5
Sankey's Sparta and Thebes	3
Savile on Apparitions	17
Seaside Musings	7
Scott's Farm Valuer	21
——— Rents and Purchases	21
Seebohm's Oxford Reformers of 1498	2
——— Protestant Revolution	3
Sewell's History of France	2
——— Passing Thoughts on Religion	16
——— Preparation for Communion	16
——— Private Devotions	16
——— Stories and Tales	18
——— Thoughts for the Age	16
Shelley's Workshop Appliances	11
Shore's Flight of the 'Lapwing'	17
Short's Church History	15
Skelton's Crookit Meg	18
Smith's (Sydney) Wit and Wisdom	7
——— (Dr. R. A.) Air and Rain	9
——— (R. B.) Carthage & the Carthaginians	2
——— Rome and Carthage	3
——— (J.) Voyage and Shipwreck of St. Paul	16
Southey's Poetical Works	19
Stanley's Familiar History of Birds	11
Steel on Diseases of the Ox	29
Stephen's Ecclesiastical Biography	4
Stonehenge, Dog and Greyhound	20
Stoney on Strains	14
Stubbs's Early Plantagenets	3
Sunday Afternoons, by A. K. H. B.	7
Supernatural Religion	16
Swinbourne's Picture Logic	6
Taucock's England during the Wars, 1778-1820	3
Taylor's History of India	2
——— Ancient and Modern History	4
——— (Jeremy) Works, edited by Eden	17
Text-Books of Science	11
Thomé's Botany	11
Thomson's Laws of Thought	6
Thorpe's Quantitative Analysis	11
Thorpe and Muir's Qualitative Analysis	11
Thudichum's Annals of Chemical Medicine	13
Tilden's Chemical Philosophy	11
——— Practical Chemistry	12
Todd on Parliamentary Government	2
Tozer's Armenia and Asia Minor	17
Trench's Realities of Irish Life	17
Trevelyan's Life of Fox	2
Trollope's Warden and Barchester Towers	18
Twiss's Law of Nations	5
Tyndall's (Professor) Scientific Works	10
Unawares	19
Unwin's Machine Design	11
Ure's Arts, Manufactures, and Mines	14
Venn's Life, by Knight	4
Ville on Artificial Manures	15
Walker on Whist	21
Walpole's History of England	1
Warburton's Edward the Third	3
Watson's Geometry	11
Watts's Dictionary of Chemistry	13
Webb's Celestial Objects	9
——— Civil War in Herefordshire	2
——— Veil of Isis	6
Weld's Sacred Palmlands	17
Wellington's Life, by Gleig	4
Whately's English Synonymes	8
——— Logic	6
——— Rhetoric	6
White's Four Gospels in Greek	16
——— and Riddle's Latin Dictionaries	8
Wilcocks's Sea-Fisherman	20
Williams's Aristotle's Ethics	5
Wilson's Resources of Modern Countries	21
Wood's (J. G.) Popular Works on Natural History	11
Woodward's Geology	12
Yonge's English-Greek Lexicons	8
Youatt on the Dog and Horse	20
Zeller's Greek Philosophy	3

www.ingramcontent.com/pod-product-compliance
Lightning Source LLC
Chambersburg PA
CBHW022141300426
44115CB00006B/288